VILLAGE B

"One of France's most original historians, Alain Corbin has set himself the task of documenting the 'culture of the sense' in nineteenth-century France. *Village Bells* addresses the 'auditory landscape,' looking at the crucial place of sound as a means of communication in the lives of ordinary people: bells sounded alarms and celebrated joyous occasions, they spread news of individuals and men of state, announced arrivals and departures, summoned villagers to religious and civic ceremonies, and marked the passing of the hours of the day. The place of bells and the practice of bell-ringing could be a source of conflict and great political tension. Beautifully written, brilliantly interpreted, full of the stories that reveal the strange difference of the past, the book is at once a rich cultural history and a meditation – on the craft of the historian – a craft Corbin practices in startlingly imaginative and pleasing unconventional ways."

Joan W. Scott, Institute for Advanced Study

"Alain Corbin is in my opinion the most original and interesting historian now writing about modern France. After brilliantly tackling changing sensibilities to the senses of smell and sight in previous books, he now turns to hearing. His subject is the way in which people in nineteenth-century France listened to and understood the sounds of the ringing of village bells. He imaginatively places their cultural, social, and political significance in the context of the rhythms, spaces, language, structure of authority, and symbols of rural life. How ordinary people heard and understood the sounds of bells, and sometimes fought over them, makes for fascinating reading. After enjoying this tour de force, you will never listen to church bells or think of *l'esprit du clocher* in the same way again."

John Merriman, Charles Seymour Professor of History,
Yale University

ALAIN CORBIN is Professor of Contemporary History at the Sorbonne. He is the author of numerous books including *The Foul and the Fragrant; The Lure of the Sea; Village Cannibals: Rage And Murder in France, 1870;* and *Women for Hire: Prostitution and Sexuality in France after 1850.*

ALSO AVAILABLE IN PAPERMAC

The Foul and the Fragrant: Odor and the Social Imagination

VILLAGE BELLS

Sound and Meaning in the 19th-Century French Countryside

ALAIN CORBIN

TRANSLATED BY MARTIN THOM

PAPERMAC

First published 1998 by Columbia University Press

First published in Great Britain 1999 by Papermac
an imprint of Macmillan Publishers Ltd
25 Eccleston Place, London SW1W 9NF
Basingstoke and Oxford

Associated companies throughout the world

ISBN 0 333 75280 5

Translation copyright © 1998 Columbia University Press

Originally published in France by Albin Michel as *Les Cloches de la Terre*

Translated by Martin Thom

9 8 7 6 5 4 3 2 1

A CIP catalogue record for this book is available from
the British Library.

Printed and bound in Great Britain by
Mackays of Chatham plc, Chatham, Kent

CONTENTS

Foreword to the English Translation

*M*any will be astonished at the idea of treating bell ringing as a subject of historical investigation, and yet it offers us privileged access to the world we have lost. If one can agree that landscape is a way of analyzing space, of loading it with meanings and emotions, and of making it available for aesthetic appreciation, the landscape defined by various kinds of sound fits this definition particularly well. Since the Renaissance, France has been known as the country of "ringing towns." French landscape painting at the end of the nineteenth century grants a central place to the bell tower, around which the representation of village space is ordered. The Third Republic, regarding itself as a gathering of some thirty thousand communities whose territories were defined by the ringing of bells, granted great symbolic importance to this ostentatory architecture. It is claimed that in 1981, a surprisingly late date, President François Mitterand owed his election to a poster showing him standing at the foot of a village bell tower. For all the above reasons, a surprisingly large number of articles in the French press were devoted to *Village Bells* in 1994, the year in which the book was published.

The Romantics—Schiller, Chateaubriand, and Lamartine among them—had grasped the intense power of the bell to evoke, to impart a feeling of time passing, foster reminiscence, recover things forgotten, and to consolidate an individual's identification with a primordial auditory site. Nineteenth-century historians, beginning with Michelet, well understood that the ringing of bells could evoke temporal depths more effectively than any description of towns built in stone or wood, and could re-create in a reader's or a listener's mind the dynamic of times gone by.

The importance of this historical object, however, does not solely derive from the sphere of the emotions, from its capacity to restore a lost past and procure the sad pleasures to be had from uttering "nevermore." In nineteenth-century France a village community could not live without its bells, hence the eagerness with which municipalities set about reconstituting peals that had been destroyed during the Revolution. To judge by local budgets from the first half of the nineteenth century, it was deemed fitting to spend more on this object than on relieving poverty or promoting education. This abiding concern alone demonstrates the great significance of bells. It is, however, the sheer diversity of uses that accounts for a community's passionate commitment. It was through ringing that knowledge about others was transmitted, an indispensable function in a society defined in terms of mutual acquaintance. Bells provided a sort of auditory certification, transmitted information about the major events of private life, and solemnized rites of passage. When natural disaster threatened, when bandits or enemies loomed, when a fire took hold, only the tocsin could sound the alarm. Possessing a peal of bells was a prerequisite of modernity in a society increasingly subject to haste but as yet without any other means of transmitting information instantaneously.

The bell was also the voice of authority and the means by which public announcements were made. It prevailed over rumor because it alone could mark what was new in the sea of truth. Within aerial space, over which it still held a monopoly, this bronze voice, falling from above, hammered home the injunctions of authority; it called to mind the connivance established around a system of norms.

The bell called upon listeners to foregather. It summoned people to religious services and punctuated their most solemn moments. It called them to prayer, and sacralized its auditory territory. The theologians of the Catholic Reformation ascribed to it the power to open a path for the good angels from heaven and ward off the creatures of hell. It was the bell that announced festivals on the eve of their celebration, and that proclaimed collective rejoicing. It imparted a rhythm to the ordinary functioning of the community. As an auditory synchronizer, the bell told its listeners when the market had opened, when the tax collector had arrived, when a flock had set off for the mountains, when the wine harvest was declared, when the community's bell was present, or when work on the roads had recommenced. As a consequence, a subtle auditory rhetoric was developed. A bell had to have its own language, which varied from one commune to the next.

In order to write the history of the bell, one has constantly to shift levels of analysis. The emphasis is on the locality, but bells also serve to announce events of significance in the national sphere, be it military mobilization, the declaration of war, victory or defeat, the death of the sovereign, coronation, birth of the heir to the throne, or a visit of the president.

Where so much was at stake one can readily understand why conflicts over bell ringing were so bitter and prolonged. It is therefore fitting that this historical subject be taken seriously. The unfolding of campanarian disputes, the intensity of the passions they aroused, and the entrenched positions of the contending parties serve to show just how important the thousands of such quarrels over bells are for anyone wishing to follow the ways in which an apprenticeship in politics was realized. I know this from firsthand experience, from having been involved, in 1958, in a belated conflict built upon the model elaborated in the previous century.

This book is thus devoted to an element in the history of the auditory landscape. However this history constitutes a vast field of research, the surface of which has barely been scratched. The time has come to tackle it and thus to address a mass of primary materials that have scarcely been touched. These materials affect reality to a pronounced degree because they were very often constructed in haste, because they are instantaneous in their effects and because they reconstitute the flavor of territories. A history of representations of space and of the social imagination can no longer afford to neglect materials pertaining to auditory perception.

Americans wishing to understand what France essentially is cannot settle merely for visiting its capital. The history of village bells, as recounted here, may also be construed as an invitation to become a tourist of the emotions and be privy to an auditory patrimony that serves as an index of a deeper mode of existence. This book should lead to a sharpening of attention, and its readers should be less distracted by photography and less at risk of succumbing to the primacy of the visual. In order to celebrate the new millennium, the French government is thinking of casting a bell that would be the most powerful on the planet, and that could be heard within a radius of thirty kilometers. This proposal bears out the symbolic value of the bell, and the part it plays in the construction of national identity.

The territory of the United States, being infinitely more vast than that of France, is subject to overlapping auditory cultures—a fact that may well distort or complicate our analysis. It remains the case, however, that the Liberty Bell constitutes a powerful political symbol and, to a foreign visitor, the plethora of bells on university campuses is striking. Be this as it may, the evocation of the bells of yesteryear delineates a history within which that of the auditory landscape, the elaboration of collective and territorial identities, the emotion aroused by the environment and the modes of construction of the individual personality all intersect.

Alain Corbin

Preface: Exploring a Vanished World

On 4 Frimaire Year VIII (25 November 1799), the municipal authorities in the canton of Brienne (Aube) "sent in" its secretary to deal with a "scandal."[1] Notwithstanding the law, the bells of the commune had been rung "upon several occasions and for a long period of time." Three times in a row, the secretary had evicted the crowd, and shut the door of the bell tower:

Three times too it was broken down by a group of girls of various ages who indulged in "excesses" whose motive, or so we gather, was the commemoration of an *ancient custom* consecrated by fanaticism upon the so-called festival of Saint Catherine. The noise from the bells having continued at intervals until three in the evening, and having failed to curb it *through negotiation*, the municipal officer accompanied by his deputy, *both wearing their sash of authority*, having betaken themselves to the spot at which the citizens were gathered, and having climbed the tower in which the aforesaid bells were, the aforementioned agent demanded in the name of the law that the citizens and children who were present and ringing should immediately desist, under pain of prosecution.

That same day, the "repeated ringing of a bell" was heard "at a quarter to eight in the evening . . . *to the great astonishment* of the members of the undersigned authorities. . . . The authorities, being concerned to *verify the cause of the sound* and to stop it forthwith, made their way to the aforesaid tower, asked some children ringing the bells who had persuaded them to commit this extraordinary act." They claimed that they had done it to orient some soldiers from the Corrèze who had lost their way. "These citizens [the children] have admitted the wrong they have done, and have expressed the deepest regret at having yielded too readily to the promptings of their hearts."

On 14 Frimaire (5 December), in the aftermath of this scandal, the municipal officer and deputy "made their way, accompanied by the secretary [and] by a picket of the national guard preceded by its drum, to rue de l'Égalité and at intervals had read out" the decree, dated 8 Frimaire, reiterating the ban on the ringing of the bells, "which seemed to *surprise* and *provoke* those present."

The above texts, drawn from the minutes of the municipal council's sessions, bring out the essential feature of such episodes, namely, mutual incomprehension. The administrators denounce the persistence of the ancient custom and ascribe it to fanaticism. They voice their indignation at the resistance shown to the law, their astonishment at the inefficacy of republican ceremonial, and their exasperation at the utter failure of the municipal "representation" to curb such "excesses." Where the authorities, whether sincerely, insincerely, or melodramatically, admitted that they simply could not comprehend a phenomenon so "out of the ordinary," the young women and children adopted a fairly relaxed attitude. The other citizens evinced surprise at what had in fact been law for over four years.

Suppose we move forward to 1830, by which date the law had changed. Since the Year X it had been legal to ring the principal ceremonies of the religious year. Misunderstandings still arose. Thus on 6 December 1830, the Mayor of Brienne—once again known as Brienne-le-Château—wrote announcing his intention to honor the request of the subprefect of Bar-sur-Aube that the national guards of his arrondissement be equipped and armed. Nonetheless, the municipal magistrate refused to levy any extraordinary tax for that purpose, on the grounds that the majority of the 1,800 inhabitants of the commune were "smallholders with vineyards [who were] . . . none too well off,"[2] and that the harvest that year had been very bad. Brienne-le-Château had three bells in good condition. The fourth, the "great" bell, was cracked. The sale of this instrument, which had been "not in use for several years," and the value of which was estimated at four or five thousand francs, would fund the equipping and arming of the national guard, the building of a schoolhouse and the purchase of a "clock for the church." The municipal council resolved to put it up for auction, a decision that reflects the desire for modernity characteristic of provincial councillors at the dawn of the July Monarchy.[3]

The administrators of the commune would, however, soon discover that they had misjudged the reception that such a sale would have. In December 1832, on the day appointed for the auction, a "riot" broke out. If we go by the mayor's own account,[4] "fanatics" and "loudmouths" invaded the town hall chamber, there being, according to the subprefect, some eighty of them. This was the first civil unrest at Brienne-le-Château since the advent of the July Monarchy. Subsequently, a petition was circulated calling for the auction to be canceled.

According to the Bishop of Troyes,[5] the disturbances were the work of "honest people," who had been "much aggrieved" at the idea of their bell being sold, for it weighed two tons, had been the pride and joy of their fathers, and had celebrated their own births. The mayor, on the other hand, blamed the unrest on the "rabble . . . the lowest class of the people,"[6] as the subprefect put it—"all the *unruly* elements in the area." These people, "hideously rustic . . . have swarmed into the taverns." They rejected "the parliamentary forms" characteristic of the new regime. The troublemakers were in fact the henchmen of the "man all in black" (the parish priest) who had enrolled them in the Confraternity of Saint Vincent, recently founded by himself. These same "fanatics" were planning, on the day of the "abduction," to foment yet another "forum scene." They would stop at nothing to hold on to the fourth bell, which would serve "no other purpose save *to deafen.*"

The mayor was worried. He requested that on the day in question he be protected by the national guard, and that the subprefect support him by putting in an appearance. Here is the latter's account of this same episode:[7]

The whole day of 30 [January] was spent detaching and lowering the bell through a window in the tower. . . . In the evening, the moment the bell was brought down, the whole population was gathered around the church. . . . The moment the bell actually fell, the crowd surged forward. The men swore, and embraced it; the women called upon all the saints in Paradise to prevent its destruction and, weeping all the while, lavished the most tender expressions upon it, bringing their young children forward to kiss it. I confess that *I was far from having expected* this scene of fanaticism, which took me far indeed from the nineteenth century.

There was then a lull, and the strange events of that winter evening drew to a close. "Gradually the crowd dispersed, and all we could make out were the flickering brands of a handful of believers who, under cover of darkness, satisfied their pious curiosity."

The subprefect knew perfectly well that clerical influence could not by itself account for this display of collective emotion. "It was in this same commune," he added, "that in 1830 the same priest did not dare to leave his house, fearing the lengths to which the populace might go. . . . The selfsame men that today are at the head of the Confraternity of Saint Vincent were smashing crosses and desecrating churches in 1793!" The subprefect, in interpreting the event politically, was thus applying criteria in a mechanical fashion to a phenomenon that he did not really understand. The astonishment he professed was a response to the brutal display of loyalties to a system of evaluation that was wholly alien to him.

As an educated man, the subprefect could, however, have reacted differently. In Bourrienne's *Memoirs*, for example, these same sonorities from the tower at Brienne seem to embody the attraction, so exalted by the Romantics, of village bells. Likewise, when Napoleon was out walking in the park at Rueil, and heard a peal of bells, it was once again Brienne he thought he could hear.[8*] In this regard, the sensibility of the elites might accord with that of the "lowest class" of the people.

*Napoleon had been a student in Brienne.

One hundred and twenty-five years later, a municipal dispute tore apart Lonlay-l'Abbaye,[9] a rural commune in the hilly area of Normandy at the foot of the Cotentin. The church tower, once part of an important Benedictine abbey in the heart of the Normandy *bocage*, had been badly damaged by the Germans in 1944. So for some years it was the siren on the roof of the town hall that let the agricultural laborers of the commune know that it was noon. In 1958 the bell tower was completely restored. A majority on the municipal council decided that the ancient Angelus would from then on suffice, and that the siren would be reserved for fires and training firemen.

The decision put the commune in an uproar. That year, the people of Lonlaye-l'Abbaye were far more deeply stirred by the dispute over the bells than they were by the thirteenth of May, the return to power of General de Gaulle, or the referendum. The inhabitants "of the villages," that is, of the hamlets and of any associated dwellings, called for the midday siren to be reinstated. The ringing of the bells, they claimed, could barely be heard by those working furthest from the church. Conversely, the "people of the *bourg*,"* together with a majority on the municipal council, valued the aesthetic qualities of the bells. Above all, they did not appreciate being deafened every day by the piercing sound of the siren.

This was a commune characterized by religious fervor and situated in the heart of a region seen by André Siegfried as a land of "clerical democracy," and yet the "peasants"[10] proved to be more deeply attached to the civic sound of the siren, a municipal instrument that first and foremost belonged to the captain of the firemen, than to the bells announcing the religious ceremonies to which they nonetheless flocked.

The dispute reopened old wounds and demonstrated the depth of feeling aroused by local issues. The "country people" clashed with the "people of the *bourg*," the Gaullists with the former Pétainists. As the conflict unfolded, revelations concerning the private lives of some of the parties involved were used tactically. Old hatreds were revived, and long-con

*In nineteenth-century rural France the distinction between village and *bourg* was not clear cut, but one criterion for distinguishing the *bourg* might be the presence of a market or fair.

cealed grievances came to light. The "peasants" descended "upon the *bourg*," hurled abuse, and also a few stones. They secretly blamed the parish priest, the notary, and the doctor.

The archpriest of Domfront, a small town in the vicinity, presided over a dominical high mass and preached reconciliation, but to no avail. The reaction of society at large was again one of astonishment and bewilderment tinged with ridicule. *Clochemerle*, Gabriel Chevallier's novel, had appeared twenty years earlier, and had been a resounding success. *The Little World of Don Camillo* had likewise introduced many readers to the idea of battles between mayor and parish priest over a "bell tower." *France Soir* and *Europe Numéro 1* got wind of the affair, which ended in high drama. The mayor, who had been under pressure for weeks and probably had divided loyalties, died of a heart attack. The local worthies on the municipal council went in a delegation to a former deputy, a socialist, then residing in Lonlay-l'Abbaye, his native commune. They begged him to accept the mayoralty and thus to end a dispute that seemed to have become insoluble.

Over the last thirty-five years, I have often paused to reflect upon this affair that, to my intense bewilderment, I witnessed, and in which I was somehow a participant, if only marginally. I realize now, taking everything else into account, that there is nothing surprising about the paradoxical attachment of a population of believers to the lay and communal uses of a siren. The "peasants" of Lonlay-l'Abbaye were spontaneously rediscovering, in 1958, the gestures made by their ancestors in the Orne, who had fiercely defended the secular uses of bells at the dawn of the July Monarchy.[11] It is nonetheless true that opting for the sound of a siren may be taken as proof of a tilting of the culture of the senses, indeed of a reversal in modes of evaluation and of collective emotion. It is this reversal that constitutes the subject of the present book.

How are we to understand a world we have lost or, rather, a world we have just lost? How are we to study phenomena that, even though close to us in time, bear witness to a paradoxical distance? With this end in mind, we would clearly do well to pay particular attention to what is no longer current, to what is unusual, and to what is dismissed as absurd. Plainly we must attempt to study the genesis of meaninglessness, and then the evolution and diffusion of modes of incomprehension.

In this perspective, village bells, *once* the occasion of so many obscure and forgotten passions, would seem to be a highly pertinent object of study.

The rural peals of the nineteenth century, which have become for us the sound of another time, were *listened to*, and evaluated according to a system of affects that is now lost to us. They bear witness to a different relation to the world and to the sacred as well as to a different way of being inscribed in time and space, and of experiencing time and space. The reading of the auditory environment would then constitute one of the procedures involved in the construction of identities, both of individuals and of communities. Bell ringing constituted a language and founded a system of communication that has gradually broken down. It gave rhythm to forgotten modes of relating between individuals and between the living and the dead. It made possible forms of expression, now lost to us, of rejoicing and conviviality.

Disputes over bells, which were so commonplace in this period, reflect a form of attachment—which has also disappeared—to symbolic objects. They laid bare an interplay of passions now incomprehensible to us. To control the voice of authority radiating from the center of a territory was a much coveted form of domination, although nowadays it seems a paltry thing. Numerous disputes in the locality hinged upon this privilege, which had so many ramifications.

The choice of such disputes for study suggests two further lines of inquiry. It provides us with an opportunity to investigate the roots of what might be termed a blindness towards history, and thus to look into the procedures whereby things are set apart and constituted as sleeping masses or dark continents hidden in archives. As Pierre Nora has observed, "we are today faced with a vast store of traces, which we neither understand nor inhabit."[12] This is especially true of campanarian* history, as the virtual disappearance of this epithet, once a part of ordinary speech, serves to show. It is not the struggle against loss and obliteration that is crucial, for there are probably sufficient documents extant

---

*campanarian: of or pertaining to bells and bell founding. The epithet is used throughout this book.

to permit study of some ten thousand disputes over bells in nineteenth-century France. Despite their avowed disdain for the task, government officials took the ringing of bells very seriously indeed and kept it constantly under surveillance. One of the defining characteristics of the period was a concern with general regulation, bells being a prime target.

Many studies have been devoted to the thousand or so bread riots that occurred in the nineteenth century, whereas disputes over bells have inspired no more than a handful of obscure articles. If the reading of sounds that I have here called an "auditory landscape" has disappeared it is because we have failed to listen in all humility to the men of the past with a view to detecting, rather than dictating, the passions that stirred them.

Campanarian history also allows us to indulge in the particular pleasure of studying a domain that contemporaries believed would be lost forever. The French people of the nineteenth century could never have suspected that their concern with regulation would make it possible for historians to consider, in some detail, the ambitions of their bell ringer, the grievances of their rural guard, and the claims of the winder of their clock. In short, they could have had no inkling that this same concern with regulation would one day justify the pleasure we take in imagining the astonishment of the dead.

VILLAGE BELLS

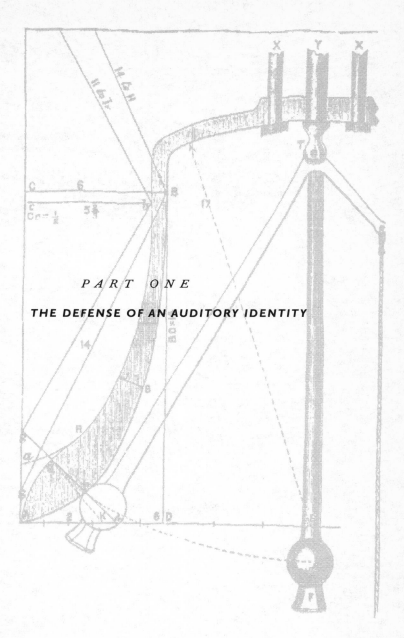

PART ONE

THE DEFENSE OF AN AUDITORY IDENTITY

CHAPTER ONE

An Impossible Revolution in the Culture of the Senses

The crucial issues concerning the history of bells in the nineteenth century first came to the fore during the Revolution. The leaders of the First Republic had sought to desacralize these instruments, to limit their strictly religious uses, to curb their sensory ascendancy, and to monopolize their solemnity. They also attempted to secularize and municipalize the peals, to subordinate them to the nation, and to insert them into a framework of citizenship. They therefore endeavored in various ways to deny communities their right to noise, to contest the need to sacralize space and time, and thus to alter the prevailing pattern of the culture of the senses.

Republican policies in this sphere were designed to curb the expression of everything pertaining to private life,[1] to counter the intensified attention paid to whatever served to distinguish the different stages in the life cycle, and to frustrate the people's strong desire to ring in celebration of rites of passage, which punctuated the existence both of individuals and of the constitutive elements of territorial communities. The most notable effect of such policies was to curtail the cult of the dead, a subject that has been studied by Philippe Ariès.[2]

The Network of Sounds

To grasp the initial impact of such initiatives and assess the changes occurring between 1793 and 1794 requires a preliminary effort of the imagination. It is not easy to picture the emotional power wielded by bells at the end of the Old Regime. We cannot be certain how frequently or how loudly the bells were rung, nor can we be sure about the number of peals, the complexity of codes, or the diversity of episcopal regulations. I will therefore limit myself to a cursory sketch here, not least because this topic is a little outside my own area of research.

Our efforts to understand also run up against a further obstacle, namely, that objective measurement of the frequency, form, and intensity of auditory messages does not allow us to reconstitute their impact upon the individual who heard them. The reception of such messages is determined at once by the texture of the sensory environment, the modes of attention brought to bear on the environment, and the procedures of decipherment.[3]

The nineteenth century is our observatory since it is the period from which our sources derive. Yet those who evoked the bells were haunted by memories of loss or deprivation, and by a desire for reconstitution. Accounts are therefore generally tinged with unabashed nostalgia. The very nature of the inquiry, and of campanarian literature itself, means that assessments are necessarily retrospective. Those left unmoved by the bells had no real motive for waxing lyrical about the sensual power of the bell ringing of the Old Regime. It was indeed in scholarly circles of the Consulate, fascinated by the rediscovery of a lost world of sound and by the refinements of Romantic sensibility, that the scale and solemn nature of the phenomenon were grasped.[4] Furthermore, this retrospective evocation occurred in a radically altered auditory environment, one rendered more aggressive—in the towns at any rate—by the puffing of steam engines, which could not help but exacerbate the sense of nostalgia.

Finally, campanarian literature employs an easily recognizable discursive strategy whereby the past of Christianity is represented as a golden age.[5] The present study is primarily concerned with representations of ancient bell ringing, and therefore with what they can tell us about the systems of evaluation current in the nineteenth century, which in their turn generated specific modes of behavior. Such representations are based on material facts that shed light on the physical attributes of sensory messages transmitted at the end of the Old Regime.

Nineteenth-century specialists in this field tend to dwell on what to them is an undisputed truth: "The belfries of our churches give us no idea of earlier rings [sets of bells], which would sometimes consist of twelve or even eighteen bells. So violently did the reverberation of all these bells agitate the air that . . . those listening suffered a *sort of vertigo* and minds were distracted from any other preoccupation."[6] Where authors evoke such "commotions" so forcefully, it is because they have a strong sense of their own distance in time from them, and of the collapse of a sensual ascendancy. Several stereotypes gave rise to or bolstered this viewpoint. The first derives from an old tradition according to which the possession of a vast number of bells once constituted an integral aspect of French identity. This claim was invariably sustained by references to the *Satyre Menippée*, to the *Gallia Christiana* and, still more often, to the harangue of Master Janotus de Bragmardo: "A town without bells is like a blind man without a stick, a donkey without a crupper, or a cow without cowbells."[7] Since medieval times, the reference to "ringing towns" had played a part in defining urban identity, and sayings current in the nineteenth century still bore the trace of this notion, or so we are told.

Given its concern with placing a high value on the emotional power of the bells of former times, campanarian literature also plied two other stereotypes, both of which were more attuned to Romantic sensibilities. The bells of yesteryear had the poetic power characteristic of popular rhetorics. They inspired numerous tales and legends, since the bell ringer, like the strolling fiddler, has down the ages played a part in the aestheticization of everyday life, a topic of particular fascination to many writers who had set out in search of the people.[8]

Specialists agree that, by the end of the Old Regime, the conciliar rules, which had restricted the loudest bell towers to the highest-ranked buildings, were no longer obeyed. Communities were at liberty to choose how many bells to have. As early as the seventeenth century, a number of churches in the Bray had four or five instruments, so that if the rules had actually been in force, they would have been elevated to the rank of cathedral.[9]

The abbeys covered the verdant wildernesses with networks of rings, although it is hard for us to gauge how far their sound carried. In 1784, L. Barbieux, a master founder from Tournai, set up his ovens inside the abbey of Saint-Armand-les-Eaux and cast thirty-eight bells for the community.[10] The abbeys of Normandy were capable of achieving a particularly high volume of sound.[11] Indeed the most significant changes to the auditory landscape and the most acute sense of loss and deprivation probably occurred in the Normandy countryside between the eighteenth and the nineteenth centuries. Old men in the 1850s, according to Dr. Billon, the pioneer of campanarian studies,[12] could still recall how loud the bells of Saint-Évroult had been. The strongest links in this chain of sound had been Troarn Abbey in the Val-Richer, which had nine bells in the seventeenth century—one of which weighed 3,600 pounds—and housed a school of bell ringers; Conches Abbey, whose seven bells people could remember hearing for two leagues in any direction; and Jumièges Abbey, whose great bell weighed 5,500 pounds.

Under the Old Regime, a "ringing" town was not necessarily an important agglomeration. On the eve of the Revolution, thirteen bells used to ring out on days of religious festivals in the small town of Saint-Pierre-sur-Dives. Some episcopal towns could likewise produce a sound disproportionate to the size of their populations. In 1789 the churches of Lisieux possessed forty-two bells between them.[13] "You've come from Langres, what do they there, pray tell? They ring the bells." The truth of this ditty is borne out by the case of Saint-Mammès Cathedral in Langres, where the bell towers contained seventeen bells in 1789.[14] Cambrai could likewise boast a disproportionately high number of bells, with the peal of the metropolitan cathedral then weighing 65,000 pounds. This powerful instrument consisted of nine bells, not to mention the twenty-three bells of the carillon, all tuned to the chromatic scale.[15] Mention is likewise still made of the five handsome bells in the north tower of the Cathedral of Châlons-sur-Marne, accompanied by fifty-six other, smaller bells, which made up the carillon and hung in the southern bell tower. Michelet assures his readers that Rouen once had possessed as many as five hundred bells—a great exaggeration—yet the claim itself bears out the significance given a source of sound that was lost, and that served as a symbol of a sensory environment that had disappeared forever.[16]

Several specialists in campanarian history endeavored in the nineteenth century to assess the power of bells within a given space. The attempts made to reconstitute the auditory environment of the past represent a historical fact of real significance in the present context. According to Dieudonné Dergny, the 161 parishes that would later form the arrondissement of Neufchâtel-en-Bray (Seine-Inférieure) had 231 "occupied" bell towers in 1738—161 parish churches, 54 chapels, 7 abbeys, and 9 priories. The web of sound permeating this space seemed *more dense* than it had been in the nineteenth century because the network of parishes was more closely knit. Numerous chapels and powerful abbeys also filled the void of sound characteristic of certain intermediate spaces. The same specialist calculated that within a radius of six kilometers, starting from Grandcourt, fifty bells scattered across nineteen parishes could be heard before 1793.[17] In the region of Condat-Murat alone, in the heart of the Auvergne, seventeen parish churches lost fifty-one bells during the Revolution. Taking into account those left for the use of the communes and those that did not belong to the parish churches, the bell towers of this small region would seem to have held over sixty-eight bells.[18]

The distribution of rings thus reflects the scale of destruction wreaked in earlier periods and the intensity of efforts made during the second half of the eighteenth century to complete, modernize, or tune the instruments. During the decades preceding the Revolution, the quest for a more refined sound resulted in many recastings, with decisions to this effect made by local assemblies[19] and assemblies of parishioners.[20] Veuclin, another specialist, remarked on the mounting "bell fever." During two different campaigns, one in 1778-79 and the other in 1784, the inhabitants of Bernay (Eure) thus managed to increase both the number and the power of their bells, to tune them, to make them more visible, and to have them ring the hours.[21] In the same period in Haut-Maine, very frequent castings and recastings took place.[22] Study of the initiatives taken during this period would undoubtedly help us achieve a deeper understanding of attitudes current in the Revolution. Up to July 1791, the modernization process continued, though at a seemingly slower pace and with altered procedures.[23] On 14 July 1790, the day of the Festival of the Federation, peals of bells, simultaneously and across the entire national territory, marked collective rejoicing with a volume, density, and intensity we may never know again.

A Period of Exchanges

Campanarian history during the Revolution has to take account of the multiple, staggered, and interlocking perspectives governing the treatment of bells. Given the complexity of the relevant legislation, the difficulties involved in actually implementing measures decided at the highest level, and the diversity of attitudes from region to region, my account here will have to be schematic. Besides, this is the only aspect of my research in this sphere that has proved interesting to modern-day historians.[24] I will therefore limit myself in this volume to a survey of the question.

The removal and destruction of bells was not a new phenomenon. Such things had been done long before 1791 and continued long after the Revolution. Thus in the sixteenth century, and doubtless before, the decision was made to melt down bells when invading armies were massing on the frontier. Hundreds of years later, this same sacrifice was ordered by the Emperor Napoleon following the Battle of Leipzig (1813). In 1870, the Bishop of Nancy authorized every parish in his diocese to take down all but one of its bells in order to cast cannon. The decisions made in 1793 thus need to be seen in a long-term perspective.[25]

The confiscation of bells forms part of an equally well-established tradition. In modern Europe, artillery commanders had rights over the bells of a conquered town and could distribute them as they wished or use them for casting cannon. However, permission was sometimes given to townspeople to buy back their bells. Nineteenth-century historians refer in this regard to the capture of Constantinople by Mohammed II and to the conduct of Charles the Bold. This practice lasted until long after the

Revolution. In 1807, for example, the townspeople of Danzig bought back their bells. During the Second Empire, a bronze instrument weighing five thousand pounds captured at Sebastopol was kept in storage for some years in the yard at Notre-Dame, while in 1863 General Galliffet seized some bells at Puebla. This right of war was even exercised in the twentieth century. Between 1914 and 1918, the Germans confiscated a number of bells in occupied territory. During the Second World War, requisitions were still more frequent.

Bells used to sound the alarm or to summon were a threat to the authorities. In the wake of an insurrection government officials might destroy an instrument in order to punish a rebellious community.[26] On 26 October 1548, the Constable of Montmorency had the bells of Vars (Charente) and the neighboring parishes smashed to punish the inhabitants for their revolt against the salt tax.[27]

By 1791 there thus existed a long chain of memories linking the loss of a bell to voluntary sacrifice, invasion, defeat, or punishment.

The Constituent Assembly hesitated for a long time over the use to which the bells from suppressed churches and monasteries should be put. The results of various experiments were scrutinized by experts,[28] but in the end the decision was made, early in the summer of 1791, not to sell the bells but to convert this supply of bronze into copper coinage.[29] This ruling, although initially restricted to Paris, was later extended to the whole national territory. Such, then, was the policy up until summer 1793. With the outbreak of war in April 1792, the smelting had become a matter of some urgency, so communes that so wished were authorized to reduce the number of their bells in return for an equivalent weight in copper coin.

On 10 August 1791, Minister Tarbé ordered the municipalities to compile a survey of available bells in their territory and a table of their presumed weights. In Metz they set to work immediately and completed the task by the end of August. Their inventory referred to 188 bells, including "la Mutte," weighing 192,000 pounds in all.[30]

Auctions were then held in the presence of the directory of the district, and various bids were made for the removal, smashing, or transporting of bells. The work was then carried out under government supervision. Bells of a modest size could generally be taken down by two men—a carpenter or a cartwright and a locksmith or a blacksmith. This was not the case with a large bell, which required the services of a specialist, generally a bell caster. In 1792, the smashing of both the second tenor bell from Notre Dame de Paris, weighing 25,000 pounds, and, the following year, the *Georges d'Amboise* in Rouen, required, or so it was said, whole teams of workmen.[31]

Once it had been taken down, the bell would be weighed in the presence of officials from the municipality and then conveyed to a storehouse. Those who had been awarded the contracts were then paid for their work and reimbursed for the deposit they had advanced at the outset. The operation involved not only the recovery of the bells but also the removal of the brackets, which were made of the same metal, and the fittings, all of which were immediately sold.[32]

The policies that were then adopted met with a range of contradictory responses and condemned the members of local communities to a conflict of loyalties. Requisition won the support of all who were prepared to accept, or even delighted in, the despoliation of the monasteries—indeed, of all who on principle approved of the implementation of measures adopted by the national representation. Yet satisfaction was not restricted to patriots. Partial confiscations led in this period to a significant degree of redistribution of property, which served to satisfy the aspirations of local communities, to allay old animosities, and to fund the repair of cracked bells or to re-tune rings. Provided they paid thirty sous per pound for any excess weight, communes could in fact exchange some of their bells for others that were otherwise destined for the Mint; they were thus given an opportunity, paradoxically enough, to continue with a process of modernization begun during previous decades.

This practice accounts for the greater number of these transfers which, at the start of the following century, would give rise to so many disputes. Twenty-four communes in the area of Reims, at least twenty-three in the Moselle, and eleven in the district of Amiens profited from this opportunity. With the permission of the directory of the Sarthe, twenty-four communes in that department exchanged thirty-three bells.

On 16 December 1791, under pressure from the municipal officials and the inhabitants of Moncé-en-Belin, Father Lelardeux went to Le Mans, notwithstanding an attack of gout, in order, he wrote, to "swap our broken bells for others that were resonant and well tuned." He had had his eye on the three bells of Saint-Nicholas-du-Mans for a whole year, or so he said.[34] Upon his arrival, the unlucky priest learned that the coveted bells had already been promised to the commune of Ballon. After a "long and tedious argument," he extracted an agreement that whichever of the two communes managed to bring its broken bells first would win the day.

Father Lelardeux then went to the courtyard of the Abbey of La Couture, in which over forty bells had been stored in a haphazard fashion. "There were," he later wrote, "ten to twelve parishes due to carry away bells from the store in the afternoon; fearing a chaotic confusion of bells, I arranged for the ones I had chosen to be kept under lock and key in a coach house beside the abbey." Lelardeux then sent a messenger to urge that the bells of Moncé-en-Belin be taken down with all possible speed. Upon his arrival in the parish, the priest again wrote, in a similarly self-aggrandizing vein: "I had them loaded up immediately. The next day they were at Le Mans . . . at six o'clock in the morning. No one from Ballon was there." The bells from Saint-Nicholas were conveyed to Moncé and hung that same day. They "chimed . . . very melodiously" on Christmas Eve. "A fortnight later, rumors were rife that the inhabitants of Ballon were to come five or six hundred strong and seize our bells, which had previously been promised to them. One could just as soon imagine the wind carrying them off!"

Resistance to the taking down and removal of instruments features prominently in representations of bells in the nineteenth century. I am less concerned here, however, with the frequency of such displays of loyalty than with the fact of their being evoked retrospectively. The bells of the revolutionary period gave rise to many legends. The numerous narratives, whether genuine or imaginary, helped to anchor territorially defined communities, to render them more cohesive, and to intensify a local sense of belonging. Such narratives may also have served to exorcize the baneful consequences of sacrilege, or at any rate to assuage the remorse occasioned by assaults on the sacred deemed so grave as to be almost beyond forgiveness.[35]

During this first period, the most common form of resistance consisted of implementing the decrees of the central government in as desultory a fashion as possible. It was not a simple matter, given the weight of the bells, to preempt confiscation by burying them.[36] The preferred tactic was therefore to proceed as slowly as possible, and certainly at the district level this helped to gain time. This is how things turned out at Amiens, as we saw earlier, where the process only began on 18 September 1791 and continued very slowly despite reprimands from the departmental directory. A number of communes hoped simply to be overlooked, as was the case, for example, in the district of Boulay (Moselle).[37] The efficacy of requisitioning depended on a number of different factors, such as distance from the capital or from major cities that were headquarters for the *sociétés populaires*, ease of access to a given territory, and the zeal of particular administrators.[38]

We may gather just how slowly bells were sometimes taken down and transported by considering the complaints of Tarbé, the minister for taxation. There is further proof of such delays in a declaration made by the King, dated 20 November 1791, ordering that consignments to the *hôtels des Monnaies* be speeded up. By this date, in fact, removal and transport had not yet been completed in any of the departments. Only in twenty-four of them had one or more districts begun delivery. Fifty-nine departments had not reported back to the minister at all. Four days later Tarbé threatened to suspend all distribution of monies to those who had not carried out his instructions.[39]

The Reduction in the Sensual Ascendancy of Bells

Between summer 1793 and summer 1795, the First Republic had recourse to the old tradition of sacrificing bells to forestall invasion. The leaders of the new regime had not yet set about silencing religious signals, but they were already trying to curb the power to move and to deafen—which up until then had devolved upon the clergy—and to interfere with the sacralizing of space and time.

Over the course of 1792 a series of decrees had already called for a reduction in the size of rings. In the aftermath of 10 August 1792, the sacrifice of bells served as an especially fervent expression of civic devotion, and such offerings were regarded thus for some time to come. On 23–25 February 1793, in response to a request from the municipality of Lisieux, the Convention authorized communes to have a number of their bells converted into cannon.[40] Following a proposal by François Aubry, the representative for the Gard, the law of 23 July 1793 stipulated that all churches still in use should keep only one bell each, and that the other instruments should be taken to the *chef-lieu* in each district. In accordance with the law of 3 August 1793, the bronze from the requisitioned bells was assigned to the artillery. On 13 and 15 September 1793, the Committee of Public Safety decreed that the confiscated copper and lead, together with the bells, would be used for the manufacture of weapons. A number of later measures served to round out this piece of legislation. Thus in March 1794, the decision was made to requisition bell ropes, and on 26 Messidor Year II (14 July 1794), the Committee of Public Safety instructed municipalities to surrender the larger bells from their churches in cases where the smaller bells sufficed for secular functions.

Such measures dealt a grave blow to the value traditionally accorded by a community to the ringing of its bells although, let me repeat, they entailed a reduction in, not a suppression of, the religious use of these instruments. A policy of this sort required a pedagogic effort. Thus at every level administrators endeavored to explain the new legislation. In their view, the traditional uses of bell ringing constituted an affront to the principle of equality and to republican virtue. "These monuments to the *luxury* of our cities and to the vanity of their inhabitants," explained the public prosecutor [*procureur*] for the commune of Aumale (Seine-Inférieure), on 23 September 1793, "can be more usefully employed in bringing terror and death" to the enemies of the republic. Nothing but modest simplicity could uphold the equality stipulated by the law. Not only did the municipal council order that just one bell be kept, but it also insisted that no more than a single person be employed in the temple. Furthermore, bells were regarded as instruments of superstition. Yet this simple metal, "being but matter," the public prosecutor went on to say, "can have no relation to religion, which is wholly spiritual."[41] Finally, it was important to make as limited a use as possible of bronze since wherever the enemies of the Revolution prevailed, it would be turned into an instrument of fanaticism.

The metamorphosis of bells into cannon, a symbolic fusion testifying to the resoluteness of the nation, was seen as a patriotic offering, a purification, and an act of reparation. This act formed part of a wider "regenerative liturgy."[42] Declarations drafted by the districts of Chambéry, Villefort, and Beaucaire provide compelling proof of this point. "These clamorous bells that deafen us with their lugubrious and discordant sounds," we read in one such text, "will now only disturb the rest of the enemies of the fatherland."[43] Bells that had been spared were meant, when necessary, to sound the alarm, to summon, and to express the joy of the secular community. The aim was thus to turn them into instruments of citizenship, to make them messengers of the nation and voices of municipal authority.

Communes were far more reluctant to surrender their bells than their silverware. Analysis of addresses to the Convention between Vendémiaire and Thermidor Year II (September 1793–July 1794), performed by Michel Vovelle and colleagues, bears out this point. Admittedly, 2,027 out of the 3,728 documents refer to silverware, but any mention of offering bells occurs in only 350—barely 10 percent—of these addresses. In addition, they were a little later than those concerning consecrated vessels and silverware.[44] In the second part of this book I will go to some lengths to explain why generosity was greater in the one case than in the other.

Conversely, a whole series of different studies prove that, in virtually every region, the taking down and removal of bells was done during the winter of 1793–94. An inquiry directed by Michel Vovelle has shown just how effective such legislative measures were, and has shed light on the time scale involved. In many places, the taking down of bells turned into a demonstration of revolutionary fervor that hinged upon the "pedagogy of sacrilege." Some national agents, for instance in the district of Loudéac (Côtes-du-Nord), incited the crowds to loot religious buildings. On that occasion, the national agent from the commune of Mayeux seized the statues and "placed them under arrest in the bell tower," which had already lost its peal of bells.[45]

Although requisitioning was by and large successful, it met with many different forms of resistance. To begin with, there was the tactic of passive disobedience whereby local people refused to attend the auctions. Thus on 20, 21, and 23 September 1793, three fruitless sessions were held in Boulay, *chef-lieu* of a district in the Moselle.[46] Sometimes the authorities could find no volunteer to take down the bell or transport it, and therefore had to resort to "foreign" carters. In some regions it was deemed a sacrilege to take part in such operations. At Échallon (Ain), the entrepreneur hired for the task was forced to abandon it.

In the towns, collective demonstrations against the new measures sometimes took a more active form. Here is a very early example: The four bells from Beaulieu Abbey, which had been taken down on 21 July 1791, were seized by seven citizens claiming to belong to the parish. The National Guard refused to comply with the municipality of Le Mans, which ordered it to seize the contested objects. On 26 June, *femme* Leboeuf and the men around her "all but murdered"[47] those sent by the authorities. The scene was repeated the following day, with the workmen fleeing for their lives. The bells were not in fact "surrendered" until 28 June. At Bernay, on 8 August 1792, and then in Lisieux[48]—in spite of the original enthusiasm of the municipality—crowds sought to halt the removal of the bells. Those belonging to the parish of Saint-Germain, which had been stored in the town hall, were recovered by the crowd and returned to the bell tower. In the same town the people gathered in large numbers at the tower of the church of Saint-Jacques and expressed their defiance by ringing uninterruptedly for several days and nights.

In the countryside,[49] resistance often took on subtler forms. Communities felt they had been the victims of theft. As I have argued elsewhere, in the nineteenth century country people hostile to the Republic tended to associate it with despoliation.[50] Campanarian history may well have reinforced this stereotype. One may readily appreciate that when a new bell had been paid for by subscription, cast on site, and admired for the harmonious quality of its tones, resistance to its confiscation would be particularly intense.

Hostility to the taking down of bells took the form of noncooperation or protest. Consider in this regard the mood of the communes in the district of Bernay during the summer of 1792.[51] In this region requisitioning preceded passage of the law, but there was great reluctance to implement it. On 10 June the municipality of Saint-Léger-du-Bosdel decreed that the commune's two bells should be kept. On 24 June members of Plainville municipality "voted unanimously to keep [their bells]." On the same day the general council of the commune of Bec-Hellouin "and the majority of its inhabitants resolved to keep their bells." Scrutiny of council minutes at Les Jonquerets on 29 June and at Saint-Clair-d'Arcey on 25 September reveals that the same decision was made there.

In January 1793 the administrators of the department resolved to count the bells and, with this end in mind, sent out a questionnaire to the municipalities of the Aisne. Some villages offered no reply, while others made no attempt to hide their reluctance. A number of communes in the Charente, especially some of the smallest among them, were successful in resisting confiscation.[52] In the district of Amiens there were varying degrees of cooperation,[53] while in Bezannes (Marne) and in Cernay, in the region of Reims, resistance was so stiff that the authorities were obliged to make several arrests.[54] In the Sarthe, the inhabitants of a dozen communes refused to implement the decree ordered by the Convention. At Marolles-les-Braults, 250 soldiers and an artillery piece were needed on 7 October 1793 to take down the commune's two bells.[55]

When the district commissioners at Homblières (Aisne) sought to enter the church by force to seize the bells, a crowd barred their way.[56] The "intruders" were later driven back. So determined were the rioters that the soldiers dispatched from Saint-Quentin had to retreat, whereupon the former sought to protect their bells by taking them down, storing them in the town hall, and, finally, burying them. It took a company of dragoons to quell the rebellion. In short, it is only by extending the range of our inquiries that we can hope to build up a more accurate picture of the scattered centers of resistance, which generally met with little success. And we should not overlook acts of revenge; at Bourg-Saint-Andéol, the populace stripped the mulberry trees of the citizen who took down the commune's bells.

Retrospective accounts of resistance emphasize the qualities upon which prestige in the village rested. For the most part such narratives highlight cunning, an attribute that enhances the stature of those who do not have brute strength on their side. Thus throughout the nineteenth century, the commune of Saint-Cornier-des-Landes (Orne) prided itself on having kept its precious bells throughout the Revolution. Abbot Berthout, the priest from a nearby parish, recounted the story as late as 1887.[57] According to eyewitness accounts collected by the author himself, especially that of Pierre Duchesnay, who had died in 1842 and who for the best part of half a century "showed such pride in having played his part *in the salvation of the bells* of the parish," the inhabitants of Saint-Cornier were deeply attached to their peal. Its three bells had been cast in the *bourg*—the small ones in 1784 and the large one in 1789. Their manufacture had cost many "sacrifices," and they were said to be "the finest and the most harmonious in the region." People remembered the celebrations held to mark the blessing of the bells, and the godfather of the smallest one was the resident doctor in the parish.

In November 1793, the mayor, a republican, decided to follow the letter of the law and take down the bells. The operation dragged on, however, as the patriots staying at the local inn shirked the task. The former "custos" of the church, a post that had been handed down within the same family for almost two hundred years, managed to persuade them to drink perry*—cider was still rarely drunk in the area—which delayed the operation, since by then night had fallen. Pierre Duchesnay, the servant of the mayor's aunt, whose cart had been requisitioned, was delighted to discover that the vehicle he had brought to move the bells was now quite useless.

In the following days the people of Saint-Cornier prided themselves upon having succeeded where neighboring communes had failed so lamentably. A few weeks later, a commissioner from the revolutionary committee of Domfront, escorted by a "juring" priest and a wagoner, came to seize the bells in question. He seemed to be in somewhat of a hurry and remarked to the mayor that he should have razed the bell tower because it was an affront to the principle of equality. It was then that a former bailiff residing in the commune decided to "play a trick" on the authorities by installing in the bell tower one Gabriel Duchesnay, a journeyman woodcutter who was armed with an axe and instructed to feign madness. After a drink or two, the commissioner set out to capture the bells, whereupon he heard the woodcutter order him to go back down. "If you climb up and lay a finger on the bells, I'll cut you right down!" cried the madman. The mayor, who had gotten wise to the trick, confirmed that it was indeed a genuine madman and the commissioner had to withdraw.

For three years the surrounding countryside was in royalist hands and

*perry: an alcoholic beverage resembling cider but made from the juice of pears.

Saint-Cornier held on to its bells. On 2 May 1817, Gabriel Duchesnay died, and they rang the whole day long. Between 1807 and 1843, Father Patry told his parishioners this "edifying story" countless times.

The version given by Father Berthout spells out or hints at a whole range of values, among them attachment to the community's bells, village solidarity (notwithstanding differences of opinion) the efficacy of native cunning, defiance and braggadocio, the cultural significance of drinking, the slowness of temporal rhythms, the role of the sexton, the hostility directed at intruders from the *chef-lieu* of the district, the heroic qualities ascribed to the main actors in the story, and the retelling of the edifying narrative by the priest in charge. This glorifying of the "impregnable bells" instills in the reader a sense that there is a perfect fit between the desire for bells, individual attitudes, local customs, and the social structure of a village community located about ten kilometers from Lonlay-l'Abbaye, the epicenter of this book.

Berthout's text is narrated with skill and is intended to be edifying but, these qualities apart, it identifies, at least implicitly, the deeper issues that were at stake in the episode and, in particular, those concerning its inscription in systems of memory. The parish priest's familiarity with his parishioners enabled him to *transcribe*, in an academic idiom, a logic of collective action that found expression only in speech during that period.

Narratives concerning hidden or buried bells were commonplace in the nineteenth century. But such deeds, when all is said and done, seem to have been the exception rather than the rule. The narratives vaunt the preservation of markers of a community's identity through a return to the telluric and originary milieu of the casting. The crucial thing to note in the present context is that the act of burying implies a particular conception of the future, that is , it testifies to the conviction, or at any rate to the hope, that legal measures involving the requisitioning, destruction, or silencing of bells were only temporary acts of persecution.

Until the bells could be conveyed to a warehouse the authorities arranged for them to be stored by the church door; the municipal councils were then held responsible for them. In a small number of communes the inhabitants seized this golden opportunity and made off with the instrument. Such deeds, even when of a seemingly trifling nature, assumed epic proportions when told and retold throughout the nine-teenth century. In Ladinhac (Cantal), the bell that had been taken down was hidden at the mayor's home.[58] In Haute-Rengen (Moselle), the small bell was buried in a barn along with a stone cross. The inhabitants of Chémery-lès-Faulquemont buried their bell in a field. In 1793 the inhab-itants of Plappeville buried their great bell in the cemetery; they recov-ered it in 1796 and rehung it in their church tower. According to Samuel Bour, a substantial number of frontier communes managed to sell their peals abroad. The same is true of areas adjoining Switzerland.[59]

The inhabitants of Le Fleix (Dordogne) buried their bells on the banks of the Charente; they unearthed them in 1801.[60] It is said that the inhabitants of La Goulafrière (Eure), in the region of Bernay, secretly buried theirs in a heath within the commune. There is some doubt, how-ever, regarding the validity of the anecdote.[61]

In the Cantal, likewise, buried bells were less numerous than has been claimed. Nevertheless, Antoine Trin gives two examples. The old bells of Vieillevie, cast in 1582, 1678, and 1718, were buried in the sands of the Lot and unearthed at the end of the Revolution. Carlat managed to save two of its bells, cast in 1512 and 1633. Once again, nineteenth century narrative hinges on a display of cunning. The church housed four bells and the mayor therefore ordered that three be taken down. Under cover of darkness, a group of local people hid the first bell in the bell ringer's cellar; the mayor's secretary took the second to his own house, while the third was hidden in the church roof. The following day, the mayor req-uisitioned a "cart," filled it with "dummy" objects, covered it with a tar-paulin, and drove it toward the district capital. Amid the bustle and con-fusion of the storehouse at Aurillac, he managed to get a receipt for this fictitious delivery.[63]

Transportation also provided opportunities for exchange. The inhab-itants of communes along the route taken by wagons were sorely tempt-ed to swap their single bells for other instruments of greater volume. Sometimes they would go as far as to "abduct" an instrument. Some bells were simply abandoned along the road by the wagoners. The inhabi-tants of Montsaugeon (Haute-Marne) were thus pleasantly surprised to discover the bell from Til-Châtel (Côte-d'or) on their territory and quickly hung it in their church tower.[64] At Illhaeusern (Haut-Rhin), over sixty bells were abandoned in this fashion on the banks of a river,[65] and twenty-six remained on the road at Gerstheim (Bas-Rhin) although they should have been transported to Sélestat.[66] Early in 1794 the bells from the region of Beaumont (Haute-Garonne) had been stored on either side of the rue des Cordeliers. In December of 1795 the inhabitants came with carts to recover what they regarded as the property of the village community. Thirty-five bells were carried off during the single night of 21–22 December.[67]

In the nineteenth century some communes thus took great pride in the ruses they had employed in order to hold on to their bells. In addition, narratives about buried bells helped to enhance legendary conceptions of space by establishing the sacred nature of specific sites within the communal territory. Above all such episodes served to justify boldness. They highlighted the shrewd tactics that featured time and time again in local disputes. I shall now describe the longer-term significance of such acts, and try to grasp, for example, how they might be related to the tragedy of the wars of religion.

Before being conveyed to centers for the manufacture of copper coin, and later to cannon foundries, requisitioned bells were piled up in warehouses. There were fifteen such sites in Paris. Those bells deemed worth preserving by the *Commission des Monuments* on account of their archaeological value were stored in the cloisters and gardens of the former monastery of the Petits-Augustins, and then, from August 1793 on, in the hôtel de Nesle, rue de Beaune. Objects to be melted down were generally assembled in the church of Saint-Barthélemy, in the heart of the city, and subsequently in the church of Saint-Pierre-des-Arcis.[68]

The bells from the district of Amiens were stored in the former abbey of Saint-Jean[69]; those from the district of Reims were taken to Épernay, and then down the river Marne to the capital.[70] The bells from the Moselle, the Meuse, the Vosges, and the Ardennes were stored in Metz. Those from the Haute-Marne were stored in the courtyard of the former palace of the bishop of Langres.[71] The bells from the Cantal were assembled at Saint-Flour, Aurillac, and Saint-Thomas-près-Bort. Some were then conveyed to Limoges, others to Clermont-Ferrand.[72] In the district of Roanne, on the other hand, bells from suppressed churches were melted down in a workshop that made flans, which were then transported to Lyon where they were imprinted as coin.[73]

Transportation was generally accomplished in stages through a network of intermediate storehouses strung out across the whole territory. Some were established in what were no more than villages. From Autumn 1793, the bells were put to a different use, but storage procedures remained much the same. A considerable tonnage of bronze then had to be channeled toward the cannon foundries.[74] Samuel Bour attempted to compile a detailed inventory of the requisitioning carried out in the department of the Moselle, accepting that the results of such an exercise could only be approximate. By 22 July 1794, the department had sent 854 bells to be melted down, their total weight being 596,164 pounds. In addition, on 19 February 1795, there remained 542,659 pounds of bronze in storage. From this we can conclude that over 1,138,823 pounds of metal had been transferred to the capital of the department.[75]

Bour's research tends to bear out the global estimate generally accepted in the nineteenth century,[76] that one hundred thousand bells hung in sixty thousand bell towers were melted down over the course of the Revolution. It goes without saying that this is probably an exaggerated figure. If we extrapolate from the case of the Moselle, we risk overestimating the total volume of bronze since this department is situated in northern France, which had more bells than southern France. Be that as it may, around fifty thousand tons of metal were removed from bell towers, transported, melted down, or sold. Towns lost more bells than the countryside, so it was the auditory environment of townspeople that was most drastically altered. Rural communes with only one bell on the eve of the Revolution lost nothing, while those with two seem to have been more successful than others in avoiding requisitioning.[77]

The measures implemented between the summer of 1791 and the summer of 1794 profoundly altered the culture of the senses in rural France. In less than three years, the auditory environment, the systems for transmitting information, the signals used to summon the populace, and the methods of expressing collective sentiments changed radically.

Before going on to consider the third stage in revolutionary policy, which was dominated by the concern to silence the bells, I ought to give a brief account of dechristianization, an episode that is now well-known.

The closing of churches and implementation of the dechristianizing policy (which was enforced differently from place to place) between Pluviôse Year II and Floréal or Prairial Year II (January–June 1794) does not concern us here since it was a matter of short term changes. The substitution for catholic worship by the Cult of Reason followed by that of the Supreme Being, the celebration of new liturgies, and the turning of some churches into hospitals, prisons, or meeting places for *sociétés populaires* occurred over too few months for this episode to have had any lasting impact on the representations of and customs surrounding the ringing of bells. Certainly, authoritarian dechristianization provoked some displays of resistance that were orchestrated by bells. During the month of Nivôse Year II (December 1793–January 1794), the inhabitants of Condrieu (Rhône) rang the alarm when they feared their church might be closed down.[78] On 21 Frimaire Year II (11 December 1793), the bells in the canton of Meymac (Corrèze) called upon the people to resist the closing of their church.[79]

But it is more relevant here to consider the efforts made by certain representatives on mission—notably Dartigoeyte and Mallarmé in Toulouse, Châteauneuf-Randon in the Lozère, and Albitte in the Southeast—to destroy the monuments of fanaticism, especially since their attitudes prefigure those of certain magistrates toward the end of the nineteenth century. Failing to apprehend refractory priests in hiding, Châteauneuf-Randon had some bell towers in the Lozère razed. Since 1791, Albitte had been calling for the total destruction of châteaux and fortifications, and he now endeavored to implement the policies of the Convention as rigorously as possible.[80] He razed the bell towers because their size and height gave material form to the domination exercised by the advocates of fanaticism, and because they symbolized an affront to the principle of equality. For Albitte it was a matter of "reducing these proud monuments of superstition *to the level of the habitat of citizens.*" By striving to give expression to every aspect of the social and political revolution, even in the sphere of village architecture, he completed the suppression of the sensual ascendancy of bells and of their power to summon the populace. Albitte, who travelled from Marseille to Lyon and from Nice to the plateaux of the Jura, nonetheless seems only to have succeeded in this "leveling" in the departments of Mont-Blanc and, especially, the Ain.[81]

Identical projects were discussed and sometimes put into practice in several other regions, although with less conviction. On 12 Vendémiaire Year II (3 October 1793), the General Council of the department of the Oise decreed that "the bell towers of former churches no longer used for catholic worship should be destroyed forthwith," and the same applied to the "great" bell tower of the cathedral.[82] On 4 Frimaire Year II (24 November 1793), Téterel, a municipal officer for the commune of Strasbourg, put it first to the *société populaire* and then to the council, that the cathedral spire should be demolished because it constituted an affront to equality. In order to save the monument his colleagues pointed out that the operation would cost too much.[83] In the district of Toulouse, a decree dated Pluviôse Year II (9 February 1794) stipulated that the bell towers be destroyed. The ruling was put into effect in the capital city, but only selectively. Elsewhere, crosses on the tops of towers were simply replaced by flags of liberty.[84]

The Desacralizing of Space and Time

In its third stage, the bell policy pursued by the various revolutionary regimes was no longer designed simply to reduce the number of instruments but also to regulate their use. It was no longer a matter of attacking the bronze that symbolized communities. The new policy was designed to bring about a disenchantment of the world, and it therefore has to do chiefly with the history of affectivity and with that of the culture of the senses.

The intrinsic logic of republicanism dictated that the Convention, and subsequently the Directory, should silence the bells once places of worship had reopened. In granting the secular authorities a monopoly over public announcements, summons to the populace to assemble, divisions of time, and auditory messages whether joyful or solemn, the republic sought to free municipal existence from the sensual ascendancy and the auditory injunctions of the ecclesiastical authorities. Such measures complemented those designed to rid the public sphere of the visual signs of this same ascendancy. The same logic underlay the decision to restrict religious services to the interior of churches, the destruction of crosses, the banning of processions, and the prohibition of bell ringing. The desacralizing of space and time, the restructuring of municipal territories, the consolidation of the new revolutionary calendar and of national and republican emblems, and the concern to discipline noise and sound constituted a concerted effort at subverting ancient markers and practices by authoritarian means.

For seven years the central authorities sought to impose a ban on the ringing of bells for religious purposes. Conversely, they seem not to have been overzealous in promoting the secular use of the bell, even though it was the sole instrument capable of producing that simultaneity of gesture and emotion that Mona Ozouf regards, in my view rightly, as a revolutionary ambition taken to almost obsessional lengths. The authorities seem in fact to have feared the evocative qualities of the bell and the sacredness of the sounds it produced, but they were also faced with the awkward problem that while revolutionary sound was supposed to issue from drums, it could not carry as far as that of their rivals. They therefore had not only to ban the religious use of bell ringing, but also to desacralize any signals emitted by bells and to transform the emotions they aroused.

The task was by no means easy, for as the municipal council in the canton of Neuville-sur-Vamse (Aube) observed with some regret on 21 Germinal Year V (10 April 1797), "the people have always confused the signs of religion with religion itself and confused the act of worship with the instrument that was used in the past to announce religious services." Patriots had not managed to convince the people "that *the former bell* called an aristocrat to his dinner just as much as it called a Catholic to Mass, and that today one can just as well hear the Mass without noise as dine without noise." Mindful of this failure, the municipal council decreed that the bell should continue to ring "the opening of the primary schools" but, this concession aside, "for publications and proclamations, national festivals, celebrations, and other republican ceremonies, the drum would be used."[85]

Be that as it may, one might think that the experiment lasted a sufficient length of time to have succeeded. This third stage in revolutionary policy is therefore the most important as far as the present examination is concerned; it marks the high point in the endeavor to uproot and transpose the auditory ascendancy of bells, and to desacralize the spatial and temporal markers upon which individual and communal identities rested. It also reflected a desire to standardize signals across the whole national territory. For seven years, children were not able to learn the complex language of the bells, which, despite the reduction in the size of rings, had not really broken down prior to the Year III. Yet the campaign failed and in many rural communities the enforced silence could not destroy the memory of emotions previously experienced, or the nostalgia for the sensuality of the peals and the solemnity of ceremony.

Two fundamental laws were aimed at banning bell ringing for religious purposes. The law of 3 Ventôse Year III (21 February 1795), Article 7, restricted the use of bells to national festivals and ceremonies associated with the decadal cult*, and they could not be rung to summon worshipers to other services. The law of 22 Germinal Year IV (11 April 1796) specified the penalties for breaking the earlier law. Offenders incurred a prison sentence of from thirty days to six months, and of one year if they were repeat offenders. Priests incurred a harsher sentence of one year's imprisonment for a first offense, and deportation if they persisted in their crime. The law of 19 Fructidor Year V (5 September 1797) enjoined municipal officers to close bell towers, to fit new locks to the doors, and to keep the keys until a citizen responsible for secular bell ringing could be appointed.

In an important memorandum dated 29 Frimaire Year VI (19 December 1797), to which administrators continually referred subsequently, the minister for the general police listed the legitimate uses of bells and explained in greater detail just what the central authorities required. He was particularly hostile to the ringing of the hours of the working day. In his opinion the mere sound of a bell constituted "a powerful lever in support of fanaticism." A series of later texts reiterated the same prohibitions without adding much that was new. On 7 Pluviôse Year VIII (27 January 1800), the same minister further specified that if a

---

*During that phase of the Revolution there was a ten-day work week. On the tenth day, the décadi, there was a sort of civic ceremony. Municipal officers presided over a ceremony in which the texts of recent laws and tales of "deeds likely to inspire public spiritedness and virtue" were read. The cult, observance of which became obligatory toward the end of the Directory, was designed to undermine the Christian calendar.

municipal council, despite the fact that the keys were in its possession, failed to prevent the clergy or their friends from ringing, first the clappers should be removed from the bells and then those guilty of breaking the law should be brought to justice.

Prescriptive literature of this sort is very revealing. The list of secular uses of bells that were permitted or recommended shows us where municipal authority lay in the first half of the nineteenth century. In order to fully understand the claims made by prefects and mayors at the dawn of the July Monarchy,[86] we need to know the customs that over the years had gradually been introduced into the countryside since the Directory. It seems plausible to suppose that individuals over fifty years old, as mayors very often were,[87] could recall the use to which bells were put in this period.

To what extent was the injunction to silence the bells observed? This is an aspect of the question that to my knowledge has been relatively little studied, yet it has a greater bearing upon the present discussion than any other. In order to write a history of the tearing of the auditory web I must of course refer to primary sources. Unfortunately, however, I am concerned here with a subject of study that is hardly amenable to quantification. It is not obvious, for example, how we should interpret traces of an infraction in the records. Sometimes bells were sufficiently audible to be noticed by patriots, and local authorities were sufficiently vigilant to pursue the matter, but such cases offer us no means of assessing the number or gravity of breaches of the law. There is a real risk, then, that we may neglect the frequency of bell ringing for religious purposes and accordingly overstate the gravity of the scandal that such actions provoked.

From the scattered traces of infractions identified in thirty or so departments we can conclude very little. The geographical distribution of such offenses—setting aside of course those territories, by this time quite limited, that were outside the control of the republican authorities—bears little relation to the degree of the people's religious fervor insofar as such a thing is amenable to retrospective measurement by historians. Breaches in the enforced silence tend to reflect a campanarian sensibility, itself linked to previously existing ringing practices and to the range of local customs. We cannot hope to give an accurate analysis of the territorial distribution of infractions, which would require reference to anthropological data which in this context remain irremediably opaque.[88]

Study of such matters does, however, allow us to reach one obvious conclusion that may be phrased as follows. Despite all the pedagogic efforts of the authorities, a strong desire to ring was apparent in numerous regions scattered across the national territory. As the commissioner for the Somme concluded, "there is no disputing the fact that what hit the people hardest in the Revolution was being deprived of their bells."[89] In many places they went on using them, either intermittently or all the time.

Whatever weight is given to the testimonies regarding such infractions, I would set greater store on sources that testify to *the desire*, even where it was thwarted, experienced by communities. Any traces of requests for derogations are, however, few and far between. Once religious worship had been reinstated, some citizens of Sancerre requested permission from the departmental authorities to ring (23 Messidor Year III / 11 July 1795).[90] On 26 Frimaire Year IV (17 December 1795), sixty citizens of Aumale (Seine-Inférieure) asked if they might at least be permitted to use the small bell for religious ceremonies; their plea fell on deaf ears.[91] On 7 Prairial Year V (26 May 1797), the Mayor of Saint-Pierre (Eure) transmitted to the prefect the same, unanimous wish of the inhabitants of his commune, but to no avail.[92]

Clergy would in some cases resort to alternative sources of sound. In Castries (Hérault), on Sundays and feast-days, despite the laws concerning the decadal cult, a child went through the *bourg* announcing the services with a "horn that he sounded as best he could." In other localities, priests had "children go down the streets, with little bells in their hands, so as to replace aerial ringing."[93]

Bearing in mind the reservations expressed above, I will now consider the geographical distribution of recorded infractions or, at any rate, of denunciations or mere observances. It is in this domain genuinely difficult to assess the veracity or otherwise of what is said. In Pluviôse Year III (January–February 1795), the Angelus was rung at Ladinhac in the Cantal.[94] The ban on ringing seems to have been particularly ignored in Limousin. In Maisonnais and Cieux (Haute-Vienne), on 16 and 23

Germinal Year III (5 and 12 April 1795), when the reopening of the churches was not yet official policy, several citizens seized the bell ropes and rang the Angelus. On 8 Frimaire Year IV (29 November 1795), the municipal agent unhooked the clapper from the bells of Rochechouart (Haute-Vienne). This act precipitated a riot, with threats being leveled at the national guard. In the Year IV the bells were rung in virtually every department of the Creuse. Violations of the prohibition became so commonplace from the Year V onward that the administrators there grew discouraged.[95]

In the Haute-Garonne, resistance on the part of many rural people proved more violent still.[96] In Caraman on 3 Brumaire Year IV (25 October 1795), a mob demanded that bell ringing be reinstated. While the municipal officers read the law the rioters removed the chain from the bell, entered the church, broke down the door to the bell tower, and began to ring. The municipal officers, wearing their sashes of authority, harangued the crowd but were so loudly jeered that they fell back. That same month there was popular unrest at Lavalette, likewise precipitated by a desire for bell ringing.

Recourse to armed force proved necessary in this same department, particularly in the region of Cadours, on 5 Pluviôse Year IV (25 January 1796). A month later, on 2 Ventôse Year IV (21 February 1796), two hundred women assembled and rowdily called for bell ringing to be reinstated at Saint-Nicholas-de-la-Grave (Tarn-et-Garonne). They occupied the church and booed the municipal agent. A hundred infantrymen had to be sent to restore order. In the ensuing inquiry, the local population maintained a guilty silence. Several municipal administrations at canton level in the Haute-Garonne were subsequently suspended for having turned a blind eye to the use of bells.

In Messidor Year IV (June–July 1796), a good many communes in the Moselle rang the religious ceremonies.[97] This was also the case in Ventôse Year VI (February–March 1798). In Nivôse Year VII (December 1798–January 1799), there were many places in this same department where people showed little hesitation in ringing to mark burials, pilgrimages, and processions. In the Marne, as we shall see below, infractions seem to have been still more numerous. In Floréal Year V (20 April–19 May 1797), there was ringing throughout the canton of Piney (Aube).

The prefect of the Eure was adamant in declaring on 25 Brumaire Year VI (15 November 1797) that civil servants in various places had been tolerating the ringing of bells for religious services.[98] The municipal agent for the commune of Le Sap, *chef-lieu* of a canton in the Orne, warned the prefect on 5 Pluviôse Year V (24 January 1797) that the inhabitants were restless. He forbade them to ring, but in the neighboring communes people were "ringing the bell."[99]

In the Year IV and the Year V, in the rural areas of the Sarthe, the ringing of the Angelus could be heard almost everywhere. Baptisms and burials were also marked in many communes in that same department. In Cherré, on 3 Messidor Year IV (21 June 1796), some women rose up when the attempt was made to ban such use of their bells.[100] We learn of the repeated use of bells in May and June of 1797 in Pavilly (Seine-Inférieure).[101] On 6 Frimaire Year VI (26 November 1797), gendarmes trying to stop the bell announcing mass at La Chapelotte (Cher) were insulted by the crowd.[102] In June 1798, a minor insurrection broke out in the canton of Châteaumeillant. Thwarted in their wish to have a bell to ring for storms, the inhabitants insulted the National Guard and threatened them so fiercely that they were forced to withdraw. The parish priest, who spoke out against the riot, was also shouted down. The assembled farmworkers, anxious to prevent the hail from ravaging the harvest a second time, told him that "his mass was as ridiculous to them as he was."[103] The departmental authorities had to send in fifty gendarmes and the National Guard to seize the clappers of the bells and convey them to Bourges. In Pluviôse Year IV (January–February 1796), the prefect of the Hautes-Pyrénées likewise referred to the illicit use of bells.[104]

In some regions the custom of ringing the beginning, middle, and end of the day (the *points du jour*) may have proved confusing, with some listeners perhaps imagining that the Angelus was being rung. The case of the department of Ariège is significant here. From Pluviôse Year IV to Nivôse Year V (January 1796–January 1797), the departmental administration was constantly upbraided by Parisian officials for allowing the hours of toil and rest to be rung.[105] It was in this same region, as we shall see, that the mayors proved most resolute in their defense of the full range of secular peals at the dawn of the July Monarchy. This underlines the point that the intensity of such disputes depended less upon degrees of religious fervor than upon the concern to defend local customs.

Historians have with some justification suggested a link between this desire to ring and the determination of rural communities to assert their cultural independence in relation to a weakened clergy. It is worth noting that at times the priests, admittedly more vulnerable than others to sanctions, were opposed to the illegal bell ringing claimed as a right by their congregations. On 8 Germinal Year IV (28 March 1796), an illegal peal was heard at Brouennes (Meuse). The commissioner of the canton tried to have the bells silenced, but was taken to task and assaulted by the people. The parish priest, who had sworn the oath of 1791, disapproved of what his flock had done, and so removed the bell rope and locked the door of the bell tower. The priest in charge at Saint-Satur (Cher) was likewise resolved to stand firm against his parishioners, so he cut the bell rope and disguised the shredded ends. In such cases the desire for bells seems to reflect a "wish to reclaim the space of the village" rather than a "bid to restore the authority of the priesthood." It testifies in fact to a "spontaneous reactivation of popular customs that had been in conflict with the spirit of the Enlightenment."[106]

Throughout these seven years the administration displayed great resolution, in its discourse at any rate. In Pluviôse Year IV (January-February 1796), when the authorities in the department of Maine-et-Loire were informed that bells were being rung throughout a part of the arrondissement of Saumur, they decreed that the bells, with the exception of the clock bell, should be seized and smashed.[107] On 25 Ventôse Year IV (15 March 1796), the central administration of the department of the Marne noted that bell ringing was occurring in the "greater part" of the territory and ordered that the bell towers be kept shut. Nonetheless the ringing continued in the Year V (September 1796–September 1797); by the beginning of the following year, in Vendémiaire (September–October 1797), the use of bells had become general, at least in the *rural areas* of this department.[108]

The authorities in Saône-et-Loire were equally resolute, if not effective. On 12 Brumaire Year VII (2 November 1798), they decreed[109] that the bells in cantons that persisted in ringing would be smashed within ten days and that the metal would be sent to the foundry in Le Creusot. In

order to enforce these measures, the *gendarmerie* was put at the disposal of
the municipalities. On 1 Messidor Year VI (19 June 1798), the departmental administration of the Hérault ordered that the bells from Ferrières and
from Saint-Chinian, both communes that had flouted the law, be taken
down and dispatched to Montpellier.[110] Conversely, in regions at odds
with the Revolution, the administration sometimes proved more lenient,
some places even allowing juring priests to continue with bell ringing so
as to consolidate their position with the refractory clergy.[111]

Compliance with the regime's injunctions also varied with the political conjuncture. When religious worship was officially reinstated, on different dates depending on the place, the clergy and especially their congregations seem in some regions to have thought that bell-ringing could
be made to coincide with and celebrate the reopening of the churches.
This was the case in the Charente, to judge by the authorities' version of
events.[112] The municipal councils in this department considered it
impolitic to oppose this restoration (Nivôse Year IV/December
1795–January 1796). The administrators in the canton of Saint-Germain
asked the minister of the interior how they ought to respond. On 21
Nivôse Year IV (11 January 1796), the Directory's commissioner
attached to the cantonal council of Lucy (Meurthe) was also unsure how
to proceed.[113]

On 29 Prairial Year V (17 June 1797), the young Camille Jordan read to
the Council of Five Hundred the report drafted by the Commission
responsible for inquiring into the policing of religion. "Should we
authorize the bells to be rung?" he asked.[114] He answered in the affirma-
tive, having given much thought, as had his colleagues on the Commission,
to the range of diverse signs. Bells, which appeal to the sense of hearing,
were not, he judged, any more intolerable than were temples, which appeal
to our sense of sight. "[This] sign is the least dangerous of all" for it calls
and "constantly reminds" the magistrate to be vigilant. Those wishing to
ban bells should, in strict logic, proscribe "drums, cannon, musical instruments, voices, indeed, anything whatsoever that serves *to communicate
thought swiftly.*"

The chairman, speaking on behalf of the Commission as a whole, recognized that the law was being widely flouted in the countryside. This
was evidently an intolerable state of affairs, and it was imperative that the

scandal of continuous violation of a law that was simply not being respected be stopped. "These bells," Jordan declared, "are not only useful to the people; they are dear to it also." The bells delighted the senses. Jordan's peroration turned the usual discourses on superstition inside out: "How sweet a thing it is for human legislators to be able to satisfy the wishes of the multitude at so little cost! What greatness there is in such condescension! How then should we regard this philosophic superstition against the bells, if not as akin to the popular superstition of our village women in their favor?"

Camille Jordan's speech was widely acclaimed, earning him both great popularity and sarcastic jibes and jokes. Although the Council of Five Hundred did not follow his recommendations, what he said had an immediate impact in many different places throughout the country. After the coup d'etat of 18 Fructidor, however, Jordan was forced to flee, and the authorities were obliged to apply the law more stringently.

Camille Jordan's apology for the bells prompted rumors that the peals were to be reinstated, for example, in the Lot and the Cher.[115] In the rural communes of the canton of Meaux (Seine-et-Marne), "the bells that had been successfully silenced were once again beginning to make themselves heard since Camille Jordan's famous apology for bell ringing," but since 18 Fructidor, "state functionaries have had much more power to clamp down on abuses."[116] The cases mentioned above of bells taken down, smashed, or melted down, and the involvement of gendarmes in local disputes, all date from this period, which was characterized, as we have seen, by a stricter enforcement of the law.

The Triumph of Dissidence

Popular pressure, however, was not slow to gather momentum. In the Pyrénées, a peripheral region that had vigorously resisted many revolutionary measures, the legislation on bells seems from this moment on to have been particularly laxly enforced. General Desenfant, who carried out a tour of inspection of the region, wrote to General Augereau on 18 Germinal Year VII (7 April 1799): "*I have heard* that people were ringing the Angelus, the midday [bell], and the Mass almost everywhere I went *as if it were twelve years ago*," chiefly in the cantons "just next to the border."[117]

No matter how firm a tone the authorities adopted,[118] between the beginning of Year VIII (September 1799) and the passing of the law governing the regulation of bell ringing (18 Germinal Year X/8 April 1802), the dissidents steadily gained ground. Their triumph and joy at seeing their desires fulfilled are worth considering in more detail. From Pluviôse Year VIII (January–February 1800), testimonies to this effect proliferate. In that same month, bells summoned congregations to worship in several communes in the Pyrénées-Orientales,[119] and infractions of the law were frequent in the canton of Souillac (Lot).[120] In Nivôse (13 January 1800), the commissioner for the department decided to allow bell ringing for religious purposes in the Sarthe, although he could hardly have done otherwise. In Saint-Maixent, the mob threatened to shave the head of a citizen accused of having removed the clapper from the bell. After this piece of bronze had been recovered, "the peasants assembled, and rehung it,"[121] whereupon they rang the bell for Vespers despite opposition from the municipal council.

"Since the Regeneration of Liberty on 18 Brumaire," wrote the municipal council of Arsonval (Aube), "the people violate the law of 22 Germinal with impunity and ring in several communes of this canton." In Moutiers-en-l'Isle, on All Saints' Day, the bell "was rung continuously and in an altogether brazen, insolent, and scandalous fashion from about two o'clock in the afternoon until six o'clock in the evening." The Mayor of Piney "was much harassed in his commune, with everyone calling upon him to ring." "I cannot deny," he wrote to the Prefect of the Aube on 15 Prairial Year VIII (4 June 1800), "that in the majority of these communes, at daybreak, on holidays, and on Sundays I have seen and heard so clamorous a use of bells that it seems almost to vie with that known to us under the regime of the dominant religion."

In May 1800 in Chaumont (Loire-et-Cher), prayers and services were announced by bells.[122] A year later, on 28 Germinal Year IX (18 April 1801), the prefect of the department gave permission to ring the times for work in the fields. In Floréal Year IX (April–May 1801), the services were rung in several communes in Tarn and Eure-et-Loir.[123] Municipal rivalries led to more and more infractions. In Ille-et-Vilaine, some municipal councils claimed that their clock bells could not be heard far enough away, and used this as a pretext for ringing the Angelus. As we shall see below, this was a region in which summoning the courage to ring became a point of honor for the communes involved.[124]

On 24 Vendémiaire Year VIII (16 October 1799), the central administration for the department of the Eure admitted that the "*points du jour*" were being rung in Sainte-Colombe and Beaumont-le-Roger. The mayors of these communes had grown tolerant.[125] In the department of the Orne, in Messidor Year VIII (June–July 1800), the reinstatement of bell ringing for religious purposes took the form of a breaking wave. In the region of Argentan, bells summoned the congregation to religious services and even marked processions. "Violations spread from commune to commune," the subprefect affirmed.[126] Shortly afterward, on 13 Ventôse Year IX (4 March 1801), the subprefect of Domfront* said much the same. On 2 Nivôse Year IX (23 December 1800), the subprefect of Dinan (Ille-et-Vilaine) informed his immediate superior that ringing could be heard in Pleslin, Plessix-Balisson, and Tréméreuc.[127]

The reinstatement of the peals was not achieved in one fell swoop on the appointed day, as nineteenth-century Romantics fondly imagined. It was not a question of a sudden restoration but rather of propagation by capillary action, and with significant and enduring geographical discrepancies. The restoration of religious bell ringing practices was like a rising tide. The crucial discovery would be the process by which the desire to ring was satisfied in the local context—by what initial action, be it of protest, defiance, or cunning, the will of the majority was expressed. From now on, the vocabulary used by the mayors implied that, as far as they were concerned, the Revolution had ended. For historians it is of particular interest to discover how such a conviction spread; a study of breaches in the required silence of bells could serve as an index of this crucial change.

On 26 Thermidor Year IX (14 August 1801), the Mayor of Saint-Aubert (Orne) complained to the subprefect that Jean Sorel, "provider" for this commune, had undertaken on his own initiative to repair the

---

*It is important to grasp that a subprefect was responsible for an arrondissement, and it is by way of abbreviation that he was known as the subprefect of the town that was the *chef-lieu* of that arrondissement. This observation holds true for the entire present text.

statues broken in the Revolution. On 23 Messidor (12 July), he seized the key to the church, which was kept in the town hall.[128] From this date on, until the mayor prohibited it, "the bell [could be] rung evening and night."[129] In this particular case, it was neither the goodwill of the municipal administration nor the vexation of the priest in charge, but rather the actions of a particular individual that precipitated the restoration.

On 28 Germinal Year X (18 April 1802—Easter Sunday), the tenor bell of Notre-Dame, after some ten years of silence, rang in celebration both of the Concordat and the signing of the Peace of Amiens. A few minutes later, all the bells in the capital began ringing. That momentous day, which had seemed to mark the symbolic end of the Revolution, was to live long in memory.[130] But this magic lantern slide obscures the real complexity of the process through which the peals were restored.

As the reader will already have grasped, the restoration was not complete. On that Easter Sunday, the Parisian bells rang far more quietly than they had on 14 July 1790. The clergy could not endow their messages with as much solemnity as before. A single bell was incapable of stirring the senses as deeply as the interlocking and harmonious peals of a powerful ring.

Notwithstanding the impression given by Chateaubriand in a famous passage from *Le Génie du Christianisme*,[131]* the clergy was not given full permission to ring on that day. New regulations were set out in the law of 18 Germinal Year X (8 April 1802) stipulating that prefects and bishops should arrive at an understanding, according to their respective spheres of influence, as to how the bells might be used.[132] For some years circumstances varied massively from place to place. Everywhere, however, the decision was made to *reorder customs* and not to revert to the old regime of bell ringing.

In some parishes the clergy, in their hour of triumph, were free to ring as they pleased, especially to celebrate the return of emigré ecclesiastics. The authorities looked askance at this attitude, which combined defiance, joy, and thanksgiving in equal measure. In the aftermath of the law of 18

---

*The publication of this celebrated book, whose religious and cultural message epitomized the new mood in France, was planned, by Chateaubriand and Fontanes, to coincide with the signing of the Concordat.

Germinal there began a period defined by the prefect of the Gers in a let
ter to Portalis, dated 26 Floréal Year X (16 May 1802), as one of impa
tience and anticipation of a liberty to come.[133] On 12 Prairial Year XI (1
June 1803), a former notary complained to the prefect of the Eure-et-
Loir regarding the attitude of clergy in Bonneval. "Our former parish
priest," he wrote, "on his return from London," had set ringing the three
bells, which were anyway "very discordant" and two of which had been
hidden from the republican government. "As if to express utter disdain,
these three bells are rung for the Angelus on the preserved feast days and
also on the feast days that have been suppressed but are celebrated all the
same, and upon each occasion there are three lengthy peals of a full half-
hour's duration, and the same thing is done twice at Mass and twice at
Vespers, so that *half the day* is given over to bell ringing."[134]

In many communes it proved hard to decide what constituted a legitimate use of bells. Such uncertainties precipitated in various places the
first of the interminable conflicts by which village communities were
both divided and structured. In some cases the municipal council was
already adopting a distinctly haughty attitude and had no intention of
abandoning its prerogatives quickly. On 12 germinal Year XI (2 April
1803), the Mayor of Montchevrel (Orne) complained to the prefect that
the parish priest had rung at half past eight in the evening for the baptism
of an infant. Furthermore, he had rung "a peal" of bells, which had previously served as a signal for citizens to assemble. This affront to the
auditory code of citizenship had disturbed sleep and caused "anxiety" in
the commune; some men made their way to the church door, others to the
town hall. According to the magistrate, the municipal council had been
justified in complaining, and the higher authority in intervening—all the
more so given the parish priest's claim that he was now within his rights
should he ring in the evening and, above all, in full peal.[135]

In other places, the clergy deemed it more prudent to bide their time
and respect the decisions made by the authorities. On 26 Brumaire Year
XI (17 November 1802), parish priests in Saint-Malo and Saint-Servan
requested permission from the subprefect to ring the Sunday offices and
the three *points du jour*,[136] showing that, in that commune at any rate,
weekday and Sunday bell ringing had not yet been restored. Those making the request thought it politic to add that the bells were already back

in use in Rennes and almost all the rural communes of the department. As a consequence, "the field-hands of Saint-Malo are the only ones to miss Mass, for want of being clearly forewarned."[137]

Campanarian policy under every regime until the vote of Separation was governed by the principle of a *concerted regulation*, as formulated in the law of 18 Germinal Year X. This same principle was at the root of virtually every conflict that for more than a century set prefects against bishops, and mayors against parish priests and priests in charge. The policy of concerted regulation was designed to standardize practices to some degree while at the same time respecting local customs. More precisely, prefectorial and diocesan authorities together tried to define legitimate modes of ringing and to stipulate both how often and how long one could ring.

For several decades, the law was hardly respected, or so the small number of statutes signed by prefects and bishops during the early years of the century suggest. I have managed to find only thirteen documents of this type (Côtes-du-Nord, Sarthe, Manche, Eure, Loir-et-Cher, Seine-et-Oise, Aube, Pas-de-Calais, Hautes-Alpes, Drôme, Hérault, Hautes-Pyrénées, Tarn).[138]

Several aspects of these documents call for further comment. To begin with, the bells seem not to have been used for any occasion related to private life. These regulations restricted the auditory celebration of rites of passage. With the sole exception of Seine-et-Oise, marriages could not be marked by ringing. Just four texts (Manche, Sarthe, Seine-et-Oise, Loir-et-Cher) concede the use of baptismal bells. In the Manche, as we shall later see, the concession was justified by the fact that this ceremony marked simultaneously one's entrance into the life of a Christian and into that of a citizen. In the Loir-et-Cher the most that was permitted in such circumstances was the chiming of *one* bell for a maximum of five minutes. In the event of a death, one could ring for a longer period of time, but here too there was plainly a concern to curb traditional practices. In the Manche, "one shall not ring for the dead, but only to notify clergy and relatives of the hour of the office and of the burial, and for a quarter of an hour at most." In the Hautes-Pyrénées, one could ring for fifteen minutes prior to the raising of the body. For the viaticum, there was supposed to be a simple tolling and the traditional use of the handbell. Regulation in the Hautes-Alpes was more liberal. There one could ring for benediction and prayers for the dying and mark as well deaths, burials, and holiday services. In the Hérault, regulations stipulated that bells could be rung for burials and tolled ten times for death agonies.

It is worth emphasizing that past restrictions lingered, although in mitigated form, and that the attempt was made to restrict the marking of the main stages of individual and familial existence. Such attitudes proved in the end to be untenable, however, and the initial austerity, though desired by Portalis, was soon overturned by local communities.

The first concerted regulations also reflect a wish to restrict the number of occasions on which bells might be rung for religious purposes, and thereby to avoid a complete restoration of the diocesan clergy's ascendancy over sound. Everyone accepted the right to ring the Angelus three times, Mass, the eve of feast days, and public prayers ordered by central government, but that was almost all that was permitted. In the dioceses of Blois and Saint-Brieuc, one could ring the bells for catechism, but not for more than five minutes.

Where there were several bells, use of the largest was also strictly limited. For example, it was not supposed to be used for announcing low Masses. Care was taken everywhere to stipulate how long and how many times the bells could legally be rung. In the Manche, in the diocese of Bayonne, one could ring high Mass three times but in the Eure just once. The regulations governing peals were even stricter. In the Hautes-Alpes, the Sunday service would be announced about half an hour beforehand by a "simple peal" five minutes long, then by a "brief tolling" immediately before the ceremony commenced. Regulations for the diocese of Blois prohibited the use of bells at night and peals for storms.

A system of norms, if not practices, was thus delineated under the Consulate, but it was soon abandoned by subsequent regimes. This is a point worth emphasizing. The abandonment of the system may readily be explained by the fact that the regional authorities who had put their signature to such regulations were rarely heeded. As early as 18 Ventôse Year XI (9 March 1803), the prefect of the Eure complained that "in some churches, the bells are rung for burials, baptisms, and weddings, and for a long time on the eve of feast days and Sundays, and on the day itself."[139] In short, in this sphere it was simply not possible to establish "uniform, invariable order." On 18 Thermidor Year XII (6 August 1804), this same magistrate considered himself to have been superseded. The regulation was, he admitted, simply not being enforced. One could ring whenever and wherever one wished: "the people demand it and the mayors give their consent."[140] After so glaring a failure the prefect yielded and prepared a fallback position. It was permissible, he wrote to the Bishop of Évreux, to authorize the ringing of bells for baptisms, weddings, and burials, but it was vital that a tariff specifying how such occasions should be celebrated be drawn up and agreed upon by the two authorities involved. This would make it possible, he added, to shape "a custom that at present varies according to the place, *the whim of the citizens*, and the degree of acquiescence shown by the priests in charge." Prior to the signing of the concerted regulation in 1807 in the Pas-de-Calais, the old customs were restored.[141] Moreover, as we shall see later, the authorities under the Consulate and the Empire utterly failed to enforce the ban upon ringing on the eve, or the day itself, of suppressed festivals.

The restoration of religious bell ringing, especially where it involved the celebration of rites of passage, was gradual and measured; in one place it might be closely supervised, whereas in another it would be, in practice, free. Everywhere, however, shortage of instruments proved a constraining factor. The concern to regulate and standardize bell ringing, which was especially pronounced where the secular authorities were concerned, clashed with the desire of ordinary people to accord proper recognition to the stages of human existence, to religious services, and to the feast days of patron saints. In this sphere, as in others, the ambitious attempt made at the beginning of the nineteenth century to forge a regulatory framework capable of containing the expression of collective emotions and pleasures soon proved to have been nothing but a Utopian idea. I can discern here what I found in my research in the history of venal sexuality and what other scholars have discovered through study of the theater, dancing, gambling, drinking, and smoking. Where bell ringing is concerned, there was the added difficulty of imposing a uniform shape on practices across the whole national territory. In order to explain how a policy of leveling and restriction (still inspired by the values of those who had sought to promote republican citizenship) was rebuffed, we need to take into account differences in customs and in the vocabulary used for bells—in short the diverse ways of imparting information, regional variations in aesthetic evaluation, and the growing intensity of feelings within the sphere of private life. The vicissitudes affecting the restoration of bell ringing tell us a lot, in their own fashion, about the difficulties involved in attempting to impose a new order.

Through a host of disputes from the Consulate onward, range and duration were extended, a greater number of ringing styles were reintroduced, and the practice of using full peals became both more commonplace and more widespread. The bells recovered the ground they had lost and gradually even acquired a greater ascendancy over the domain of sound. The process was not linear, however, but was affected by political conjuncture and inflected by a number of factors that I should now analyze.

I shall begin by considering, for the time being and so as to be done with it, *the reconstitution of local peals*. One should not think that anything like a restoration plain and simple occurred. It was rather a resumption of the process of modernization begun in the second half of the eighteenth century. Insofar as there was now in the countryside an almost perfect fit between commune, parish, and a single peal of bells, I shall now try to relate this recomposition of instruments both to the reinvention of the parish and to the strenuous efforts made by rural municipalities over the course of the nineteenth century to overhaul their shared equipment.

In 1802, the majority of parishes had the use of just a single bell. One of the first objectives of the rural communities was to restore to their ringing its emotional ascendancy and its capacity to aestheticize everyday life. This endeavor coincided with the high tide of localism and with the antiquarian enthusiasm of scholarly elites for curiosities of every description.[142] The combination of increases in the wealth of particular communes, especially bitter local disputes, and many other factors served to justify or promote the work of modernization. The latter, which had begun before collective efforts had become focused on local roads, the renovating and displacing of cemeteries, the building of schools, and the setting up of fairs and markets, was supervised by the authorities.[143] For a bell to be recast or purchased the prefecture had henceforth to give its permission.[144]

The procedures involved in modernization varied greatly. First, communes set about recovering bells lost during the Revolution. From the time of the Consulate, the hunt was on and genuine wars broke out, as we shall see later.[145] Some communes reclaimed bells abandoned in storerooms, but usually in vain. Several Breton parishes managed to recover one of the instruments stored on the quays or in the Arsenal at Brest.[146] In Langres, the bell in the tower of Saint-Mammès Cathedral was repositioned to increase its range.[147]

Most attempts at modernization involved recasting, some justified by cracks or breaks, others by the desire for novelty, others by the wish to have at one's disposal a number of bells so as to reestablish the auditory rhetoric in all its complexity, and still others by the need to retune. There seems to have been less tolerance than before of bells that did not ring true. There was a longing for harmony, which was what led in 1822 to the recasting of the peal at Quimper Cathedral.[148]

The archives are full to overflowing with requests by municipal councils for subsidies, but these were rarely granted. The restored monarchy refused to implement the principle of reversibility or, in other words, to melt down cannon in order to manufacture bells. It is telling that the government, and indeed Louis XVIII, refused to restore in this fashion the single bell in Bayonne Cathedral, which had been shattered during Corpus Christi in 1816.[149]

The stages by which recomposition proceeded are hard to identify. Recastings and additions of metal or, in other words, frequent metamorphoses, make it exceptionally difficult to give an accurate account of any particular sequence or to conjecture what the sequence of operations might have been. We therefore have no choice but to rely upon the summaries drawn up by specialists engaged in campanarian inquiries during the second half of the nineteenth century. These specialists, however, underestimated the efforts made by local communities, chiefly because they did not take interim recastings into account, especially for the years between 1820 and 1855. The itinerant bell casters during this period had had to brush up on skills that had lain dormant for a dozen or so years and they were therefore often of mediocre talent. We are also more able to grasp why breaks were so commonplace if we bear in mind the neglect suffered by bells and belfries, the intensity of the local rivalries—which led ringers to attempt ever higher levels of sound, on All Souls' Day or the *fête du souverain*—and the frequency of bell tower fires, attributable in large part to the lack of lightening conductors.

To judge by inquiries into campanarian activity in the Ardennes, Moselle, Seine-Inférieure, and Isère,[150] some regions held on to their old bells far longer than others. Such disparities reflect the incidence of earlier acts of destruction and, in particular, the uneven implementation of revolutionary measures. The arrondissement of Roanne possessed thirty-four old bells at the end of the nineteenth century,[151] and the whole department of the Dordogne some two hundred and eight. There were significant numbers of old instruments in the Haut-Comminges and the Charente while in the rural areas of the Bray a very small number of bells from before the Revolution had survived. There were none too many in the Ardennes either.

If the bells were only slowly refurbished or replaced under the Consulate and the Empire, this was no doubt because repairs to places of worship and presbyteries seemed more pressing, because the authorities took a while to determine what the standard usage should be, and because of the nature of the regime. Conversely, the work of refurbishment and replacement was, not surprisingly, pursued with particular enthusiasm under the Restoration. The drive to reequip churches with their full set of bells was sustained by a nostalgia for the old regime (which accentuated the generosity of local notables), by the enhanced hold of the clergy over rural parishes, by their concern to channel festive activity, by the freedom granted them to ring as and when they saw fit, by the frequency of missions and, in a number of regions, by the public's intense enthusiasm for folklore. At the same time there was a resacralizing of the countryside, as Philippe Boutry has shown in the case of the Ain.[152] For many communities the acquisition, casting, or recasting of bells was a priority.

The reequipping of the bell towers seems to have proceeded at roughly the same rate under both the July Monarchy and the Second Republic. In the Moselle, Louis-Philippe's reign proved to be the most intense period for campanarian activity. It is worth stressing the increase in the number of instruments achieved under a regime that, when all is said and done, did not much favor a clerical ascendancy. The Second Empire was a period of consolidation. By that time the majority of rings had been modernized, so that reequipping was aimed at other objectives.

Bearing in mind the date of the inquiries I am discussing here, it is hard to assess levels of campanarian activity under the Third Republic. Nonetheless, everything points to its having slowed down, at least after 1880.[153] The desacralizing of space and time, the revolution in means of communication, the destructuring of rural society brought about by mass exodus and recomposition in terms of new equilibria, and the imposition of unfamiliar aesthetic codes together meant that the attention paid to bells gradually ceased to be a relevant index of collective sensibilities.[154]

Let me now try to summarize. At the end of the nineteenth century, bells were perhaps less numerous than they had been at the end of the old regime, but it would be just as well not to exaggerate this decline. Taking into account all that had been attempted since the Consulate, the diminution in stock is mainly attributable to the decline in the number of bell towers. Jean Nanglard, for his part, estimates that despite the quantity of churches built during the nineteenth century, the number of bell towers fell from sixty thousand to forty-five thousand between the end of the old regime and the end of the First World War.[155]

The great majority of bells were henceforth concentrated in the bell tower of a single parish church. While these temporal and spatial markers for the everyday life of communities were becoming desacralized, the bell tower came to symbolize, more so than before, the basic unit of rural society. Belated and paradoxical though it may seem, the force vested in the symbolic ascendancy of this stone monument bears emphasizing. In the department of the Ain there was between 1850 and 1880, as Philippe Boutry has shown, a collective desire for verticality. The building of steeples reflected a wish to "proclaim the glory of the area," and showed that a sense of locality was in the ascendant. The communes were forever trying to vie with or outbid one another, and the restoration of ancient buildings, whether Romanesque or Gothic, was only a last resort. Carried away by their enthusiasm, the builder-priests of this period abandoned puddled clay, bricks, and mortar for stone. *The improvement in the quality of the sets of bells* was part and parcel of this same drive, which was not motivated by precisely the same desires as the reconstruction undertaken in the early nineteenth century.

The bells in use on the eve of the First World War were on average heavier than in the past. They were also more solid and more tuneful. Almost all sets of four bells cast during the second half of the nineteenth century were perfectly tuned. By this time some regions could boast an impressive number of bells. The beginning of the twentieth century was the heyday of the department of the Moselle. Rings of three bells were extremely common in the country areas, and ones with four or even five were by no means rare. The bell towers in the villages of Bettviller and Freyming housed six bells at that time; there were seven in Montigny, eight in Saint-Vincent, and nine in Morhange. Some communes of modest proportions possessed modern tenor bells whose weight bore no relation, one might think, to the importance of their church. The great bell of Montigny weighs 4,568 tons and that of Saint-Vincent, 6,120 tons—weights that bear comparison with the tenor bells in the cathedrals of the old regime.[156]

The reading of such a summary allows us to better understand the great importance of the disputes over bells that punctuated the history of rural communes throughout the nineteenth century.

CHAPTER TWO

The "Abductors of Bells"

Local Pride

The "abduction" of one community's bells by the inhabitants of another did not arouse precisely the same feelings as had requisitioning by the revolutionary regime.[1] Commandeering by the nation-state had been viewed, at least in some places, as anonymous despoliation if not profanation. It was also viewed as an assault instigated from a distance by the central authorities on the control of space and time that a formerly privileged order had exercised. The abduction of bells, by contrast, attested above all to a desire to possess the wealth, power, and prestige of a rival community. The perpetrators plainly relished such acts, which served both to satisfy their greed and to undermine the sacral authority of their neighbors and rivals. This was especially true where local legend extolled the merits of a particular bell. Older instruments might, for example, be

credited with the power to shield a community from harm or be valued for
the aesthetic qualities of their sound.[2] In this regard such petty local quarrels differed markedly from disputes between secular and religious
authorities within the same community.

The capture of bells aroused fierce animosities, unleashing conflicts in
the mold of the sometimes bloody territorial rivalries which, as François
Ploux has shown, raged during the first two-thirds of the nineteenth century.[3] In this domain as in so many others, the 1860s marked a turning
point. Up until then, abductions had been of momentous significance.
The taking down of a bell would cause great distress, representing as it
did a threat to the prestige, reputation, and honor of the community.[4]
Collective identity was undermined and the individual's sense of belonging to a given territory was disturbed. In short, the abduction of a bell
aroused far more indignation than an ordinary theft would have. The loss
was a "humiliation," and more intensely so for those referred to at that
time by civil servants as "inhabitants" than for the clergy. I will begin by
describing some of the conflicts caused by an abduction and will then
explain in detail why collective responses to such acts were so intense.

Bell tower disputes were generally precipitated by an attack provoked,
or turned to their own advantage, by the ecclesiastical authorities. The
abduction of a bell united the members of a community in the defense of
an instrument which, according to tradition, had acted as a shield against
danger, had served as a link when needed between a number of different
claims, and had expressed the emotions of the populace. The resulting
sense of loss and anguish, however fervent and intense in its expression,
should not be seen as intrinsically religious; something quite different was
at stake. Such disputes also occurred in "dechristianized" regions and
could drive some to apostasy.

A reading of sources suggests that the abduction of bells caused such
bitterness that, even over the very long term, the deed would be remembered and resented. In mounting a defense of its bell, a community also
had no choice but to invoke history. Such controversies brought into play
two conflicting discursive logics or lines of reasoning. The deprived communities would invoke the inscription on the instrument, the entitlement
of the godfather and godmother, the date it had been blessed, the chronological history of the parish, and the heroic resistance shown during the

Revolution. In short, their cases would rest on archival evidence and memories of actual events, thus being historical in nature. By contrast, the authorities called upon to settle such disputes would simply refer to the law that had justified the original confiscation, which had by the same token revoked any previous title to the property. Disputes over bells were thus subject to two politically divergent interpretations. Such disputes may plausibly be compared to the debate over the sale of *biens nationaux* with the proviso that there the issue was ownership by the community and not individual property.

With such general and entrenched resentment it was harder to come to an "arrangement" in this sort of affair than in many others.[5] Such sentiments also fostered the desire to restore places of worship since it was hoped that restoration might lead to the recovery of the stolen bell and a revival of lost prestige. The intensity of the complaints and protests reflected the attempts then being made to reconstitute the rings of bells and to *modernize* communal space by repairing and rebuilding churches, or by improving their bell towers.

Civil servants in the prefectures recognized the importance of such feuds but they did not really grasp the underlying causes. They would poke fun at such episodes, dismissing them as though of minor significance, and yet they were well aware of the sorts of cataclysmic upheavals that might follow.

It is possible to identify three kinds of conflict, which varied in intensity from one period to the next. At the end of the First Empire and under the Restoration, communes would often dispute the ownership of "semiophores" hoarded by the community only a few years before. Sets of bells had not yet all been restored, so such conflicts still reflected a sense of dispossession. They became rare after 1830.

Disputes over the redrawing of boundaries between parishes and communes were to drag on for much longer. These changes did in fact precipitate a second wave of bell transfers. In the provinces such modifications to the map probably proved more traumatic than did the revolutionary measures. The latter involved the entire national territory and did not in themselves exacerbate rivalries between villages. On the other hand, alterations to the map introduced at the dawn of the First Empire, between 1806 and 1808, and gradually implemented in the following years, affected hundreds of small communities. They produced a shift in territorial markers and a blurring of identities, the most momentous aspect of which was the taking down of bells. Nostalgia for a particular instrument, torn from a silenced belfry and then rehung in the steeple of a church belonging to a community that was frequently regarded as a rival, indicated just how hard it was to reattach oneself or, if you like, to transfer one's identity. With all due allowances for differences in scale, such disputes tell us a lot about the psychological processes that were part of integration into the nation-state.

Disputes within communes, precipitated even when there had been no change in the administrative map, were rarer. Nonetheless, in a commune with several churches the bells sometimes served to crystallize tensions between various parts of a territory. Such disputes bring out the complex fashion in which identities interlocked[6] in a century characterized by the clash, in the minds of individuals, between the desire to be subsumed by larger entities and the wish to preserve an intangible inheritance that had enabled a territorial community to cohere.

Bell Tower Disputes Between Communes

Aside from the widespread destruction of bells, which were either melted down or smashed, the policies adopted between 1791 and 1802 brought about many transfers. Such measures affected the number of bells in existence as well as their distribution. I have already described the sorts of exchanges that took place in 1791 and the abduction of instruments in transit. But civil war too provided opportunities for the actual capture of bells,[7] particularly in regions disturbed by the uprising in the Vendée, by the struggles between Jacobin and Girondin sympathizers over federalism, or by the *chouannerie*.* In such contexts the abduction of a bell, given the symbolic significance attached to such a deed, was all the more tempting. According to the *ministre des Cultes*,* several communes in the Vendée had hidden their bells during the Revolution. "During the troubles," he noted, "the rebels found the stores and distributed the bells among the communes that had requested them without checking to see if they belonged to them, while other communes took possession of bells that they had found." Such illegal transfers later caused a storm of protest. But the communes that had benefited from these changes "maintained that the bells were a fair return for those taken from them and refused to hand them back."[8]

Shortly after ringing had been reintroduced, the victims of an abduction might invade the place where their bell had been stored with the goal of retrieving one by force. In the Year X, the people of Brié (Charente), "their church having been reopened . . . went back to La Rochefoucauld, returning thence with a bell" weighing six hundred pounds.[9] The inhabitants of Croix-Dalle (Seine-Inférieure), having witnessed the seizure of all their bells during the Revolution, took one from the church of Saint-Agathe. That commune seems to have been resigned to its loss.[10]

Sometimes disputes over ownership of a particular instrument formed part of a cycle of claims and counterclaims.[11] On 30 September 1819, the members of the parochial church council of Argenton-Château (Deux-Sèvres) called for the return of the bell that the inhabitants of Les Aubiers had taken from them in 1794. The latter admitted the abduction "but at the same time insisted that their action had been in reprisal; that during the unrest occurring between 1792 and 1795 the inhabitants of Argenton . . . [had] frequently encroached upon their territory in order to steal corn; that during some of these raids they had stripped some shareholdings bare, and even killed a number of men; that the people of Argenton stole from them the consecrated vessels and the silverware which they had hidden. Finally, in order to put a stop to the evils which were being visited upon them, and in order to *take their revenge*, they had *joined forces* with an armed contingent from the Vendée, which attacked, stormed, looted, and burned the town of Argenton. It was around this time that they captured the bell, which they still have."[12]

The reader will note that political alignments, perhaps for strictly tactical reasons, were here subordinated to a preexisting pattern of territorial rivalries.

---

*The *chouans*, active in the West of France (Brittany and the Vendée), consisted predominantly of peasants fiercely loyal to the church and the monarchy, who waged a bitter guerrilla war against the Revolution.

*The *ministre des Cultes* was the government minister responsible for all matters concerning the administration of public worship.

The prefect admitted as much. During the troubles, he went on to observe, the communes had waged a "cruel war" and each in turn had looted and burned, depending on whether "the party whose side it had embraced had the upper hand." There were, after all, "few cantons, communes or even private individuals who could not identify in their neighbor's possession some effects which had once belonged to them." That such descriptions were by no means unusual suggests that wrangles over bell towers symbolized the bitterness resulting from the large-scale dispersal and transfer of property, a process that was meant to be obscured by a specifically designed clause in the Treaty of La Jaunaye [1795].

In fact the impact of the Revolution on the pattern of territorial rivalries turns out to be highly complex. While the events of this troubled period did occasionally precipitate conflicts between some communities, the Revolution also allowed others to bury ancient hatreds. Bygone wars could at last be forgotten and the mechanisms of revenge could be checked. Just as an explosion may put out a burning oil well, the policies of the revolutionary governments—by tampering with divisions, reordering old allegiances or animosities, and bringing territorial claims and matters of national importance into open confrontation—managed to extinguish a number of conflicts. In 1815, for example, the subprefect of Mauriac wrote that the Revolution, "by directing attention to more important objects," had allowed people to forget and "set aside their old enmities."[13] The commune of Trizac (Cantal) laid claim to a bell then in the possession of the commune of Lanobre. The subprefect regretted that the claim had been revived since there was no longer any rivalry between the two formerly hostile communes, and the inhabitants of both could often be found at the markets in Bort. Yet ancestral feuds might always flare up again at traveling fairs or village weddings. About two years before, the subprefect recalled, three or four individuals had lost their lives in a war between Lanobre and Bagnols (Puy-de-Dôme), and he feared that the bells might call forgotten tragedies to mind.

Yet the disputes over bells which broke out during the Restoration rarely resulted in collective violence. In nineteenth-century France it was difficult to penetrate deeply into the territory of a rival commune and take down a bell without the backing of the mayor or parish priest. There were nonetheless many protests, claims, and applications to the courts. In 1810, for example, the inhabitants of Lencloître and the parish of Saint-Jacques de Châtellerault contested ownership of two small, three hundred pound bells.[14] In 1824, the people of Wailly (Pas-de-Calais) laid claim to a bell then hanging in a church at Montreuil.[15] That same year the parishioners of Saint-Martin-de-Teillet (Tarn) called upon those of the parish of Saint-Michel, in the commune of Dourgne, to return their bell.[16] In 1825, the members of the church council at Chaillac made known their wish to recover *their* bells, which were hanging in the belfry of Saint-Gaultier (Indre).[17] The following year, the commune of Saint-Malo laid claim to its bell at Saint-Servan and the mayor of Trévérien claimed the one that summoned the workers in the port.[18] In Le Cher, in 1827, Assigny and Subligny decided to make an "arrangement." The abduction of the contested bell had been perpetrated by the people of that commune in 1806, the heyday of the First Empire.[19] My own soundings in the Gers suggest that this type of conflict was then, curiously enough, frequent in this department. The archives in the prefecture record ten such disputes between 1806 and 1824.[20]

Between Meauzac and Castelsarrasin (Tarn-et-Garonne), matters were more serious. The feud there lasted almost forty years (1801–1839) and was fiercely fought. In 1801, when bell ringing was reintroduced, the inhabitants of Castelsarrasin lost no time in hanging in the tower of their church the bell from Meauzac, which was then stored within the territory of the commune. For thirty-eight years the victims of the abduction issued an endless stream of petitions and protests, but the prefects in the *chef-lieu* of the Tarn-et-Garonne, one after the other, rejected every demand.[21]

The disagreement between Herbilly and Courbouzon (Loir-et-Cher), which lasted fifty years, seems to have been a more complex affair. This dispute also involved the type of conflict I will consider later, and that to my mind should be regarded as transitional. In 1802 the parish of Herbilly was merged with that of Courbouzon. A few years later the process was reversed, and the commune of Courbouzon was merged with its neighbor. From then on, the two communities were at odds. The removal of places from the administrative map did not automatically destroy the inhabitants' sense of territorial identity. The joining of the parish to its rival caused a sudden drop in church attendance in Herbilly. In 1840 the hostility between the two communities crystallized in a dispute over bells. On 27 December the mayor of Courbouzon,[22] emboldened by the presence of gendarmes and two hundred troops from the garrison at Blois, proceeded to Herbilly in the company of a justice of the peace from the canton. He had the bell taken down despite the hostility of the local population. As a result, "virtually all the people from Herbilly stopped attending religious services at Courbouzon and a fair number of them went as far as to call in a Protestant minister or even attend his chapel, which was only five or six kilometers away."[23]

The inhabitants of the suppressed commune and parish rejected the "accommodation" worked out by the priest, who hoped to forestall collective apostasy. In 1847, the territory of Herbilly was split from Courbouzon and united with the town of Mer. Two years later Herbilly was raised to succursal status, and services could once again be held in its little church. What had been a local conflict at Courbouzon now assumed a triangular aspect.

On 6 July 1851, Herbilly claimed back its bell from Courbouzon, reviving the old feud. It so happened that the inhabitants of Courbouzon "had, according to the bishop, seen fit to treat their continued possession of the bell *as a matter of local pride*. To lose territory to the *small town* of Mer seemed to them an intolerable *humiliation*." The bell provided the people of Courbouzon with a pretext for venting their bitterness; they "threatened that if the authorities were to prevail they would stop at nothing, even going to the lengths of closing down their church, founding a Protestant chapel, et cetera . . ." While acknowledging the need to "bring to an end this deplorable conflict which has divided and always will divide the area,"[24] the municipal council and parochial church council of Courbouzon, despite the urgent pleas of the priest, refused to return the bell to Herbilly. They demanded at the very least a substantial sum in compensation. If things were to be left as they stood, the bishop admitted, "one would vex the people of Herbilly," who flatly refused to buy *their* own bell.

The two bell towers were a mere 720 meters apart. Within this restricted territory, events throughout the first half of the nineteenth century had been dominated by this feud. On 4 May 1852, the prefect and the bishop were disheartened enough to admit that, after fifty years of struggle, reconciliation was still impossible. The bishop in particular feared that civil unrest was imminent. The recent reestablishment of order and authority nevertheless made it possible to act with resolution. On 10 May the prefect referred the affair to Prince-President Louis-Napoleon while at the same time ordering that the bell be taken from Courbouzon and transferred to Herbilly. After the Council of State had offered its opinion (1 July), a presidential decree, dated 16 July 1852, ratified the decision. We do not know if this authoritarian measure successfully resolved this conflict which had been raging for a full fifty years.

The Taking Down of Bells and the Blurring of Identities

We may judge just how entrenched the ancient allegiances were by considering the intensity of the reactions to the redrawing of the map of communes, parishes, and succursals (28 August 1808), and by the implementation of the decree of 30 May 1806, which transferred the property of "merged" churches and presbyteries to the vestries of churches that had been preserved.[25] The mood of these local squabbles reflected a collective unease at the discrepancy between territorial identity, which was enduring,[26] and the fashioning of an administrative space ordered in terms of new markers that served to shift both center and boundaries. The redrawn map, which had uprooted or rather disoriented people, and which had modified the geography of prayer and refuge, altered everyday itineraries and, to a still greater degree, dominical ones.

Administrative reform, as we saw in the case of Herbilly, brought with it the horrors of "*debasement*." Each event such as the closure of a church, the taking down of a bell—which marked the loss as irremediable—in some cases the transfer of relics, vessels, and consecrated linen, and of chasubles and vestments from the altar, and the interruption of burials in cemeteries that were from then on to be abandoned, was of momentous significance to the community it affected. It is not hard to understand why the taking down of a bell (or bells), being so stark a symbol of this obliteration or "nucleation," should so often have been regarded as an "abduction." The removal of bells could undermine the diverse ways in which each evoked the past, affect their sensory memory of signals, and therefore their experience both of the space surrounding them and of temporal rhythm. By no longer ringing on All Souls' Day in the environs of a now deserted cemetery,[27] the independence of the dialogue between a community and its dead, who were still being buried anonymously well into the nineteenth century, would be obliterated.

For whole decades the sound of a stolen bell aroused regret. I shall have more to say later on the dispute between Monclar and Cucassé (the Gers). Here I wish simply to note the wording of a petition sent by the "leading inhabitants" of the second of these communities to the *ministre des Cultes*, on 27 December 1830. They emphasized the "*distress*" each felt at "*hearing their own bell ringing daily in an alien bell-tower.*"[28] The abduction in fact dated from 1811, almost twenty years earlier. In a letter to the subprefect dated 14 January 1831, the mayor of Monclar, the community that had benefited from the union, gave a lucid account of the procedure involved. "The *authorities*," he concluded, "*desired that the call* [of the bell] *should come to them from one bell tower rather than the other.*"

Several case studies, selected from a dozen or so departments and introduced here in the guise of clips, may help to give an impression of the issues and procedures involved. Over the course of these debates the petitions piled up, with the victims of the new dispensation invoking the harshness of the terrain, the threat of wolves, and the possible rape of wives and daughters who were now obliged to cross woods or forests.[29] According to these accounts, regular attendance at catechism classes became impossible in winter. Some churches in parishes that had benefited from the new arrangements proved now to be too small. Most important of all, congregations from the "merged" parishes no longer knew where to go between Mass and Vespers so they frequented the local tavern. In the diocese of Grenoble the inhabitants of four such parishes resolved to do without priests, arranging for penitents to ring their bell, hold services, and bury their dead.

Saint-Christophe-de-Valains had been reduced to a dependency of Saint-Ouen (Ille-et-Vilaine). In the early years of the Restoration the community that had suffered "debasement" lived in fear and prepared to resist. The *inhabitants* of Saint-Ouen, wrote the mayor of Saint-Christophe in May 1819, wished "to seize the keys of *our* church and to *close it down.*"[30] The wording shows clearly that the confrontation was viewed as a clash between two territorial communities and not as the outcome of an administrative decision. To judge by the mayor of Saint-

Christophe's testimony, "the inhabitants of Saint-Ouen" also wished to take possession of the vestments and seize the bell.

The tactics used also tell us much about the nature of the confrontation. On 19 December 1818, "at seven o'clock in the evening," the parish priest, the curate, the assistant, the members of the municipal council, and the members of the parochial church council of Saint-Ouen made their way "*by separate paths*," so as not to arouse the suspicions of their adversaries, to the home of the mayor of Saint-Christophe, who as luck would have it, "was out in the fields." As precious time was lost in finding the mayor and asking him to hand over the key to the church, and as he anyway "very politely" refused to comply, the inhabitants of Saint-Christophe were able to assemble. They had grasped that the people of Saint-Ouen had designs upon *their* mayor who, though appointed by central government, seemed under the circumstances to be the representative of the community. When facing the parish clergy, he became the defender of the church and the consecrated objects. Insults flew and "there was a real risk of coming to blows." The people of Saint-Christophe cried out: "You mean to steal our bell!" They invoked the dramas of the Revolution and the blood spilled in defense of the Church. They blamed the priest, who in their opinion had become the priest of Saint-Ouen exclusively, and accused him of lowered moral standards. In short, they expressed bitterness at seeing themselves dispossessed under the Restoration of what they had defended so passionately under the Republic. It was all "for nothing," they said, they had already "shed their blood, and given so much of their time and energy." Identifying faith with their community's place of worship the people of Saint-Christophe-de-Valains retorted: "We will always stand by *the* faith and *our* church." It was all to no avail. The prefect and the bishop decided against them. The best they could do was to come to an "arrangement," whereby the prefect would order that an inventory be compiled of all the "merged" property with a view to its subsequent return.

Also in 1819, the inhabitants of Landes (Seine-Inférieure) were somewhat more successful in fending off the claims of the commune of Richemont, with which they had been merged. Through an arrangement formulated by the prefect with the minister's consent, they had won the right to keep their bell, but only after several "tumultuous episodes."[31]

The inhabitants of Mervilliers (Eure-et-Loir) adopted a different approach, with the former mayor of the commune that had been suppressed in 1821 keeping the bell at home and refusing to surrender it to the municipality of Allains, the beneficiary of the merger.[32] In 1822, residents of the hamlet of Cuigny (Orne), another merged parish, protested vigorously but to no avail the "abduction" of their bell by the mayor of Moulins-sur-Orne.[33]

Suppose we pause for a moment to consider a dispute which pitted Vitot against Vitotel (Eure) in 1831. The affair was deemed sufficiently important to prompt general and wide-ranging discussion among several ministers. The commune of Vitotel, noted the prefect in 1831, had called "upon several occasions" for the return of its ancient bell, "which was transferred to Vitot after union for the purpose of worship had been introduced."[34] In 1825 a series of fires had brought home how useful the bell was: the alarm had been sounded at Vitot while a conflagration raged unchecked in Vitotel. In September 1830 the prefect, like his predecessor, refused to heed the protest. Two months later the people of Vitotel brought their case before the minister of justice, but his response was tardy. This long delay was interpreted as "a denial of justice," and several "[then] took it upon themselves to act without due authority to take back the bell from Vitot and return it to the church in Vitotel." The prefect was inclined to be lenient since Vitot already had a bell of its own, while the people of Vitotel had sacrificed a lot to restore their church. The magistrates in the court of original jurisdiction did not see things in the same light; they condemned the abduction and imposed heavy fines on the miscreants. "The people of Vitotel," remarked the subprefect of Louviers on 28 March 1831, "were sorely vexed,"[35] and he foresaw that they might well "take the law into their own hands." The historical record, however, tells us nothing further of this affair.

On 29 March of that year, the inhabitants of the hamlet of Neuville-de-Vitotel came into conflict in precisely the same fashion with the commune of Les Mousseaux. Their bell had been transferred in 1803 to the church at Les Mousseaux. In the years that followed, the people of Neuville had bought back their church and restored it. They then claimed "the bell, to them the most precious object of all,"[36] together with a figure of Christ and seven statues of *saints*. The prefect referred to this conflict when informing the minister of the seriousness of disputes over bells. "The lack of such an object, which *seems to them* [the inhabitants of the suppressed parishes] *so crucial*, stirs the local people," he wrote, "*to hatred* for the communes with which they have been joined for the purpose of worship, and this could well give rise to serious disturbances."[37]

I now want to return to the triangular conflict that, in the Gers, set Cucassé, Mauléon (a commune that had benefited from the union), and Monclar (another parish that had benefited from the union), one against the other.[38] This is a particularly telling instance of the blurring of identities evoked earlier. In 1811, Cucassé's bell was conveyed, perhaps without its inhabitants knowing, "in a furtive manner and very swiftly,"[39] to Monclar on a hastily hired wagon. A ciborium, an alb, a chasuble, two altar cloths, and six napkins were also seized and taken away. "Once this abduction was discovered, there was general consternation. . . . The people of Cucassé were several times on the point of betaking themselves *en masse* to Monclar in order to reclaim what had been stolen from them." It should be borne in mind that worship had resumed at Cucassé once the inhabitants had repaired and decorated their church. Monclar now had two bells whereas Cucassé and Mauléon had none. The second half of the 1830s was a transitional period during which the authorities would often yield under pressure. As a consequence, threats to recover the bell by force were spelled out more clearly. Nothing was done, however; the prefect and the bishop continued to decide in Monclar's favor.

In 1839, a dispute of a somewhat different kind split the commune of Moncorneil-Grazan (Gers), which had been created through the merger of three parishes. Grazan, one of the victims of this "union," was then the sole parish to have a cemetery, and therefore to ring in honor of the commune's dead. The inhabitants of the two other sections, Moncorneil-devant and Moncorneil-derrière, believed that in this sphere they enjoyed genuine rights of use. In 1839, Grazan's bell shattered and ringing in honor of the dead stopped. A wealthy family in the hamlet, however, having reached an agreement with the parish priest, had a new bell cast, thinking that all the inhabitants of the commune would make contributions to pay for it. The two Moncorneils refused to comply, claiming that they enjoyed free use rights of Grazan's bell.

Then it was war, with the donor (or partial donor) having the clapper removed from the new bell. The "people of Moncorneil" deemed this a *challenge* that could not be ignored. Threats, insults, and altercations followed. The mayor himself was taken to task. Complaints and petitions flooded in to the prefecture. Despite the apologies offered to the mayor before an *assembly* comprised of inhabitants of the three former parishes, no "arrangement" was possible. The bell served to crystallize all the slowly accumulated "animosities" and "jealousies."[40]

Some conflicts give us a still clearer idea of just how long a memory might last. Consider, for example, the enduring hatred that for forty-one years embroiled Texon, Lavignac, and Flavignac (in the Haute-Vienne) in a small-scale war.[41] Here too we are concerned with a triangular conflict but, in contrast with those considered earlier, each of the three parties seems to have played its own hand without forging any discernible alliance. In 1806, the small commune of Texon was abolished and combined with Lavignac in temporal matters, and with Flavignac for spiritual affairs. Two years later it was wholly merged with Lavignac. Texon's bell was then conveyed to the latter's bell tower. In 1829, however, Texon was removed from the temporal supervision of Lavignac and entrusted to Flavignac. A parallel change was effected for the spiritual sphere in 1836. In 1829 and in 1830, the inhabitants were so concerned about recovering their bell that they signed ten petitions that were sent to the prefect, the bishop, the *ministre des Cultes*, and the council of state—but all to no avail.

In 1847 the inhabitants of Texon had completed the repair of their church. On 5 October they laid claim in no uncertain terms to *their bell*. They then "betook themselves to Lavignac . . . brandishing various kinds of weapons, and they seized our church and abducted our bell,"[42] complained the president of Lavignac's parochial church council, although failing to mention that it was in fact Texon's old bell.

The bishop's and the prefect's sympathies were with Flavignac. Until a solution could be found, the prefect had Texon's bell seized and stored in the prefecture. The court of Saint-Yrieix sentenced "the people" of Texon to terms of imprisonment. Each of the contending parties then tried to influence the final decision. On 28 December 1848, the mayor of Lavignac sought to derive some advantage from the noteworthy electoral success of the prince-president in the region of Limoges by addressing him as "Monsieur Louis-Napoléon Bonaparte, President of the Executive and of the National Assembly [sic]."[43] The bell had been at Lavignac for over forty years, he argued, before going on rather cunningly to refer "to several laws and imperial decrees" that the Republic had in no way modified, and also to the article in the "Republican constitution" that confirmed the inviolability of private property. The Mayor, however, went unheeded.

At the beginning of the following year the bishop of Limoges made known his pessimism. It did not seem possible to him to "mollify the inhabitants of Texon, who will never recognize the rights of *another locality* over *their bell*, and will always ascribe the loss they have suffered to injustice."[44] The bishop feared that they might take the law into their own hands.

On 19 May 1849, the minister ruled in favor of Flavignac. Texon's bell was conveyed from the prefecture to a third bell tower. This measure would serve, in the minister's opinion, to put a stop "to the difficulties the former bell of Texon has caused between the inhabitants of this commune [a revealing slip!] and those of Lavignac."[45] He does not tell us whether the decision caused further animosity between Lavignac and Flavignac, although it may well have. It is hard to imagine that minds were set at rest within this triangle that had been disturbed for over half a century by a bell tower dispute.

This type of conflict persisted under the Second Empire. In 1856, the commune of Marainville (Eure-et-Loir), later merged with Denonville, protested against the transfer of its bell.[46] In 1858 after a wave of arson attacks, the population of Goupillières-Renfeugères (Seine-Inférieure), "in their exasperation, made plain their intention to proceed to Fresquienne *in order to reclaim* the bell *themselves*"[47] that had been abducted some years before.

A characteristic example of such festering memories and resentments is supplied by the dispute that at a relatively late date, between 1868 and 1872, set the two communities of Aize and Buxeuil (Indre) against each other. "Forty or fifty years ago," declared the municipal councillors of the first of the two communes on 27 May 1868, Aize's church was sold and its bell conveyed to Buxeuil, "in spite of fierce opposition on the part of a few people who then resided in the *bourg*."[48] It is worth dwelling on this last point since it was in fact "the people from the *bourg*" who alone were in a position, and therefore might feel so inclined, to resist incursions from potential abductors. It was thus "common knowledge" that one of Buxeuil's two bells belonged to Aize. The latter commune had rebuilt its church and desired to recover its bell.

The commune launched its claim at the dawn of the Third Republic. In November 1871, Aize was elevated to succursal status. At the beginning of the following year, the municipal council renewed its claim to its property and turned down the compromise proposed by the prefect. The conflict unfolded along altogether classical lines. A diocesan inquiry allows us to piece together a more accurate version of the facts, and therefore to rectify to some degree the council's own account. The episcopal authorities were at this time accustomed to relying to a degree on long-term memory and oral inquiry. Their conclusions were as follows:

> Local tradition has preserved the most precise and *most circumstantial* memories *of this crucial event*, namely that according to the unanimous testimony of the old men of Aize, the bell was transferred to Buxeuil in 1809 on the instructions of the abbot Dessards, the parish priest, on a vehicle provided by the estate of Fontenaux, actually situated in the village of Buxeuil; that the inhabitants of Aize had put up some resistance before allowing the bell to be taken down; that the transfer took place when the days were short,[49] and the roads in a very poor state of repair, and that for these two reasons the bell had to be kept overnight at Bois-Moulins—this last point being admitted by Buxeuil municipal council, which, in its deliberations of 31 March last, referred to the aforementioned Danois as the owner of Bois-Moulins who had transported the bell; and that, finally, once installed in Buxeuil bell-tower, it served to announce the hour for catechism.[50]

Throughout our investigations we have been struck by how long events associated with bells were remembered, and the above quotation highlights several aspects of this phenomenon. Sixty-three years after the incident, its details were still etched in the minds of those who had witnessed it. The episcopal inquiry attests to a chronological precision as to year and season, an ability to identify the actors involved, a capacity to remember their attitudes and, above all, the recollection that the bell was used to ring for catechism. The ability of local people to recall this last detail would have been much enhanced, however, by the fact that the "old men" of 1872 would still have been children in 1809. Local events bite deeper into a person's memories than do episodes occurring outside the group because the recollection is reinforced by a recording of details and circumstances.[51] On the recommendation of the bishop and the prefect, a decree issued by the president of the Republic, dated 21 November 1872, at last ordered that the contested bell—whose value in truth did not far exceed the modest sum of one hundred and fifty francs—be returned to the parish of Aize.

This was by no means the usual outcome. At the end of almost all such disputes the authorities tended to invoke the text of the 1806 decree. They would therefore generally rule in favor of the communes and parochial church councils that had gained from the mergers, and they were wary of ordering that bells be returned to reconstituted parishes. If ministers and the great majority of prefects took this line it was because they were afraid of triggering a chain reaction. As Argout wrote in 1831, care should be taken to avoid "stirring up a host of *small*, peaceful interests,"[52] or encouraging "the revival of dormant claims."[53] This was tantamount as often as not to endorsing the status quo. "Like you," wrote Argout once again to the *ministre de l'Instruction publique et des Cultes*, I think it prudent to leave things in the state in which I find them." [54] This was also the con-clusion to which ministers came that same year when considering the dis-pute between Vitot and Vitotel.

It was then that Paris became aware of the risks involved in going against localities. Like many other matters, disputes over bell towers served to prove that the same tactics could not be adopted on every occa-sion. As Argout once again advised, one should "restrict oneself to a spe-cial solution for each difficulty," a point of view that led to the abandon-ment of many of the cherished hopes of the Consulate and the Empire.

Prefects seem to have taken pleasure in the surprising discovery by the ministries of an endless stream of highly irksome claims and counter-claims in each locality. The correspondence dealing with such issues betrays a set of attitudes with which twentieth-century historians are familiar. When writing to Paris, prefects would once again emphasize the petty character of the conflicts and, seeking to place themselves on a different level, felt obliged to describe them as if they were mere trifles. Conversely, they derived some pleasure from pointing out to the ministry how significant local disputes in fact were. The ability to understand them presupposed an ethnographer's competence, and in this regard the prefects' accounts were consistent with the exploration of France undertaken during this period by the Parisian elites, which focused on the delineation of regional variations, the visiting of the many impressive monuments to be found on the national territory, and on the vogue for novels reflecting the conditions of rural life. The project underlying this book may also in some way be said to derive from such a perspective, which always involves deciphering events dismissed as trivial, either through ignorance or arrogance.

The Foundations of Rivalry, Hatred, and Resentment

In this regard, disputes between merged communes or parishes remain the most pertinent subject of inquiry. It sometimes happened that within a single administrative unit, a dispute set two bell towers against each other, crystallizing tensions that were tearing the community apart. In order to add depth to my analysis and avoid the monotony produced by excessive repetition, I now want to discuss at greater length a single case study. The dispute that divided Mirmande (Drôme) between 1845 and 1850 enables us to discern both the many levels at which rivalry was operative and the crosscutting alignments involved in a conflict of this nature. During those five years, the desire to have a bell structured the local dispute and determined the alignments of the contending parties on a territorial basis. And this at the very moment in this essentially rural region when national political divisions were being consolidated and secret societies were gaining a foothold. Democratic and socialist agitation on the one hand, and repression by the forces of order on the other, were increasingly in evidence.

I shall begin by sketching in the background. "The territory of the commune of Mirmande," wrote the prefect on 3 November 1849, "extends from the crest of a hill to the river Rhône, so that it is divided into two distinct parts, the hill and the plain. The plain forms a parish that goes by the name of Saulce[s], whereas the hill forms a parish known as

Mirmande."[55] According to the parish priest of Mirmande, Saulces had tended "always *to despoil the other in order to enlarge itself* at the other's expense, and to acquire more influence."[56] During this turbulent period the desire to increase one's power through territorial expansion was not restricted to nation-states.

In 1834 the parish of Saulces built a church and endowed it with a bell funded by public subscription, or so local people said. Their adversaries, on the other hand, claimed that it had been taken from an older church. In the next few years the dispute was conducted on two levels; the traditional opposition between the two parishes within the commune of Mirmande or, in other words, between hill and plain, was being replicated, at a deeper level, inside the parish of Mirmande. Indeed, the resourceful—or overweening, if his adversaries were to be believed—priest in charge, who was called Belle, decided that he too would build a new church that would vie with the parish church of Saulces. He had it built on the side of the hill close to the plain, a choice of location that he judged would serve as a sort of challenge to his rival below. This construction would, he hoped, serve as a counterweight to the new church on the plain.

The parish council explained how it had arrived at its decision. The old church "was perched at the top of the village, at its very summit, which can only be scaled by means of roads that climb twenty-eight centimeters per meter, its precinct is but 257 [square] meters, including the three chapels and the huge gallery. It is . . . obviously too small for a population of eighteen hundred souls, of which at least seventeen hundred are desirous of having a church down below."[57]

The priest's decision is best understood in the context of modernizing impulses that were shared by most clergy under the July Monarchy, and that often found expression in building projects.

From then on the commune of Mirmande was divided into three contending parties, namely, the party of the plain (Saulces parish), the party of the foot of the hill (new church for Mirmande parish), and, the village on the summit.

The municipal council was opposed to the building of the new church. It therefore refused to provide a site or grant a subsidy. "It foresaw that the old church situated in the upper part of the village and *in the midst of its inhabitants*, would be abandoned; which would bring ruin to that part of the village and *foster divisions*, and this expectation has not been mistaken; now that services are held in the new church, the interests of a certain number of the inhabitants are harmed because the upper part of the village is much less frequented: there ensue tiresome rivalries among the inhabitants and, above all, a deep *bitterness* towards the priest in charge, who is accused of planning to buy a new presbytery alongside the new church."[58] The building of a new church thus brought about a change in the amenities, and therefore in the topographic ordering of trade within the commune. "Bitterness," "divisions," and "rivalries" were the inevitable outcome.

Despite the municipality's opposition, the priest in charge managed to execute his plan although not without incurring debts. In July 1845, the bishop of Valence, who had never wavered in his support of his priest, transferred services to the new church, and banned acts of worship in the "upper" church (September 1845). The bell from the latter had been moved to the new tower. This was a momentous decision since the bell had formerly served to strike the hours on the communal clock. The bishop's ruling had effectively silenced the clock.

At the dawn of the Second Republic the upper church, having been deconsecrated for three years, seems to have been in a state of disrepair. It is worth noting that the mayor and his deputy together with the majority of the municipal council members elected in July 1848—all men of order according to the prefect—lived in Saulces, the lower parish. An alliance was then formed, under the aegis of the municipal council, between the people of the lower parish and those of the summit, and against Father Belle and the advocates of the church on the hill. The parishioners of Saulces called for the bell to be rehung in the upper church "because they say that, being the bell of the communal clock, it belongs to the whole commune, and that if those who have had the new church of Mirmande (parish) built wish to have a bell in it they should buy one, just as those from the parish of Saulces did when they had a church built."[59] The inhabitants, especially the tradesmen from the upper part of the village, were of the same opinion, but for other reasons. In short, "there ensued *much aggravation* on both sides."

The dispute then passed through four different stages. *Act 1.* On 27 November 1848, a group of inhabitants from the upper village—fifteen to twenty individuals according to Mirmande's parish priest, and according to their adversaries, the entire population—made their way to the new church on the hill. With the consent of the inhabitants of Saulces and that of the majority of the municipal council, they seized the bell and hung it in the upper church.

The parish priest, vested by law with sole responsibility for overseeing the ringing of bells, from then on stopped ringing services. The bells had fallen silent in the parish of Mirmande. The *ministre des Cultes*, in response to complaints from the parish priest and parochial church council, decreed on 7 May 1849, just six days before the elections to the Legislative Assembly, that the bell should be returned to the new church on the hill.

Act 2. The prefect, being informed of this decision, refused to implement it on the eve of a crucial poll. He feared he would offend the men belonging to the party of order, who were the dominant force on the council in the commune of Mirmande. The mayor, who was only notified by the prefect of the minister's decision on 16 June, declared his intention of seizing control of the Council of State. For six whole months the parish council and the minister pleaded with the prefect to implement the decision, but to no avail. On 3 November the prefect explained to the minister that in his opinion the situation in the commune of Mirmande was exceptionally grave. The commune was now split between two parties, namely, the "abductors of the bell" and their adversaries. Each party was as vexed as the other. "Those wishing to keep the bell in the bell tower of the old church are the more numerous, and have almost all the members of the town council on their side. Those who wish the bell to be placed in the bell tower of the new church are headed by the former mayor and the priest in charge of the parish of Mirmande."[60] He forgot to mention the members of the parochial church council, with the exception of the mayor.

In the prefect's opinion, passions were running so high that any attempt at reconciliation was impossible for the time being. Furthermore, no one wished to assume responsibility for executing the ministerial decision. Thus, the mayor preferred to step down rather than acquiesce, while the members of the parochial church council feared that taking on such a responsibility might jeopardize their safety. "For so trifling a matter," asked the prefect, "must we provoke a conflict that could well end in bloodshed? Or must we send in troops to safeguard this operation?"[61] For his part, he preferred to wait until tempers had cooled.

Act 3. On 13 February 1850 the minister once again called for his ruling to be implemented. "The people residing in the upper part of the village began ringing out of defiance despite the ban imposed by the parish priest. Being still in favor of averting open confrontation, the prefect entrusted the mayor of the cantonal capital, former deputy Arbalestier, with the task of reconciling the contending parties. Once he had completed his inquiry the deputy renounced his mission, fearing a "terrible outcome."[62] The bishop warned of bloody retribution and threatened the populace with court trials while the prefect "foresaw genuine misfortunes."

On 27 March the prefect consulted Bérenger de la Drôme, president of the Court of Cassation, explaining his anxieties and pressing him to extract a postponement of six months from the minister. "The current mayor and councillors," he assured him, "are committed to order; the inhabitants who are of their party are in general men of order also, but they are so incensed at the idea of their bell being taken from them that they are fully capable of excesses that the mayor, in his wisdom, could not contain."[63] The conflict between these men of order and the parish priest evidently concerned just the one locality. On 13 April Bérenger reassured the prefect that the desired postponement had been granted.

For six months "the party of abductors,"[64] that is, the people of the upper village, indulged in the pleasures of defiance and bragging. They rang for church services "with impunity" despite the daily protestations of the priest. They "boasted publicly" (in May) of having reached an agreement with the minister. In July "unrest increased."[65] The parochial church council had "the window locked through which entrance to the bell tower was gained each day so as to render impossible the irregular and illegal bell ringing that has so often *scandalized* the parish, but the aforementioned locks have been removed by scaling the wall and burglary." The ringing continued. According to the parish council, the "abductors" went "so far as to assume complete control of the church, entering it by scaling a wall and doing there whatsoever they wished. In order to prevent the parochial church council or the priest from entering, they have lately taken pains to change the keyhole of the lock in the sole existing door."

The bishop complained to the minister, protesting at "the triumph of arbitrariness and disorder."[66] It is worth pausing for a moment to consider just how great a challenge had been launched at the ecclesiastical authorities by the members of a community that had seized, for a whole spring and summer, the right to ring whenever it chose, thereby depriving the priest in charge of access to his own bell. This was simply unheard of. It was an extreme and unprecedented circumstance that alerts us to the gravity of the issues involved. The people of the upper village, that is to say the representatives of the old community and the advocates of the old site, managed for some months to wield control over the sacred bronze. The bishop recognized that implementing the minister's decision would cause some unrest but he thought that it would not involve more than a few stones being thrown, particularly by women.

Act 4. At the beginning of autumn, political debates at the national level led, paradoxically enough, to a resolution of the dispute. While the "abductors" held the village and the upper church, and through the support of the men of order continued to defy the parish priest, some inhabitants of the plain, especially those from the islands of Boix, had formed secret societies. Their machinations formed part of the "plot of Lyon,"* the history and repercussions of which have been studied in the context of Loriol canton by Philippe Vigier.[67] On 10 September the ringleaders were arrested by troops. Some of the inhabitants of the plain, however, sided with the prisoners, thereby precipitating the first stages of an insurrection. The forces of order soon checked this uprising and disarmed the inhabitants of the parish of Saulces.

Nevertheless, the prefect did not dare use the presence of soldiers to flush out the "abductors of the bell," who were ensconced in the upper village. He undoubtedly feared both the confusion that further disputes would bring and the bitterness of individuals who, he wrote once again, "are on our side." "The parish of Mirmande has been quiet and calm," the members of the parochial church council observed. They added on an ironical note: "However, the Right Honorable Prefect, who had that day a detachment of two hundred men to disarm a village of six hundred

*This was a local plot, purportedly directed at the moderate republican government, and orchestrated by the far left.

souls, feared to jeopardize public security by taking down the bell!!! [sic]"[68]

Yet the climate had in fact changed. The time was now ripe for political repression and the restoration of order. Henceforth it was harder to challenge the decisions of the authorities, and the new balance of forces emboldened them to resolve disputes swiftly. On 17 September the *ministre des Cultes* reminded the prefect that the six months had now elapsed. He judged that the dispute over the bell was bound to "foster ill feeling in the commune of Mirmande,"[69] which had featured for a few days in the national press. In Paris little heed was paid to the finer points of the conflict. At that distance and given the scale on which the ministry was working, the risk of further complications seemed glaringly obvious, even if in the prefect's own opinion nothing was less certain. It was, however, fear that the dispute might be exploited by the "reds" (or democrats and socialists) for other purposes that finally led to the adoption of harsher measures.

On 2 November the brigadier from Loriol gendarmerie, having been ordered to move the bell, failed at his first attempt. His second-in-command, "a very brave man" according to the prefect, refused to assist and proffered his resignation. The priest declined to "supply" workmen and tools. In short, the Brigadier said in his report, "no one wished to lend a hand." He continued as follows: "I had procured [sic] four or five men who at first obeyed me, thinking themselves obliged by law to do so, but they were swayed, by whom I know not, and the result was that it was impossible for us to find a single man prepared to take down the bell. All the inhabitants of Mirmande feared the ill will of others in this regard and so dared not risk the deed. We have decided to procure [sic] some workmen from another locality. . . . I plan to go there tomorrow *at daybreak*."[70] Given the dangers he had run, the brigadier asked for promotion.

The second attempt proved successful. The prefect carried the day. He succeeded in getting the bell transferred, he explained to the minister, by "*taking advantage of the fear* that decisive steps taken in Loriol canton, in the aftermath of a *kind of insurrection* occurring there . . . [have instilled]."[71] That said, he judged it advisable to pay for the work out of his own pocket for fear that a request to the municipal council would stir up passions.

Debates unfolding on the national stage thus made it possible to resolve an apparently insoluble dispute. The prefect took advantage of repressive measures directed at the "reds" to try to curb men of order— then in league with the "abductors" of the bell—who had set themselves up as the defenders of the ancient site of a village perched on a hill. In this interweaving of conflicts we can discern no interaction between the different levels. No one, in the vast pile of documents spawned by this affair, ever spoke of "reds" stoking the fires of the local dispute; no one so much as hinted that "abductors" of the bell or discontented parishioners had rallied to the Montagnard "plot" (the plot of Lyon). Only the minister, far away in Paris, raised such a possibility.

Once again, the dispute fed off territorial rivalries that ran very deep. The traditional hostility between the two parishes of the plain and the hill was compounded by the emergence of real hatred between the summit and its flank. The building of a new church had served to divide a space whose inhabitants had up until then felt solidarity with each other. For two whole years (November 1848–November 1850), Mirmande's bell had haunted the prefect and earned him stinging rebukes from the minister. During this troubled period the moving, silencing, or defiant ringing of the bell expressed the determination of the people living in the upper village. They were resolved to hold on to the instrument that symbolized domination of a territory. They had felt threatened by the new church, since its isolated but accessible site deprived their community of the favored position it had formerly enjoyed in relation to the parish priest. Throughout the whole dispute, the "upper people" were striving to hold on to a "sacral power."[72] With this end in mind they forged an alliance with the men of order on the municipal council of the plain, where they came across the "reds" engaged in a fight on an altogether different level.

The series of incidents described in the preceding chapters will, I hope, have given the reader some idea of the diverse forms taken by this all but unknown turbulence that wreaked havoc in the French countryside from 1791 to the early 1860s. We can readily grasp what the leaders of the Revolution were aiming at, and what was at stake in the campanarian policies of the years from 1791 to 1801. There is no gainsaying the passion with which communities stood firm against the forcible taking down of their bells. Nor can we deny the intensity of their desire to reconstitute their peals, to which end they would sweat blood and involve themselves if need be in interminable wrangles. I now wish to go beyond the sentiments expressed or intimated in campanarian disputes and try to discern the basis of such firm loyalties and intense emotions.

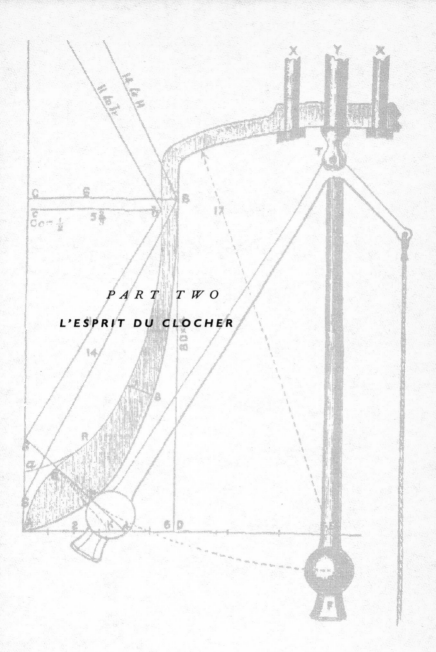

PART TWO

L'ESPRIT DU CLOCHER

CHAPTER THREE

Communities and Their Bells

A Symbolic Marker of Identity

On the eve of the Revolution, communities had been responsible for providing their own bells[1] and had attached great importance to their rings. In 1781, the congregation of Herpy, a parish on the Ardennais plateau, was very distressed to find that two of its bells had broken. According to the dean they expressed an "overpowering wish, before anything else was done, to see to their repair." This was because their sense of self-esteem was bound up with the bells, which were, "for that reason, *dearer to them than all else.*"[2] The intensity of such sentiments may readily be understood. In rural societies obsessed by the demarcation of communal identities, ever mindful of the defining features of groups and always ready to issue challenges, the bell is a unique object that serves as a natural symbol of a community's identity. The need for bells here

involves a series of interlocking logics conforming, first of all, to the hierarchy of parishes[3] and, later, to that of communes. Communities of any
significance could not conceive of being without a ring of bells.[4] In the
nineteenth century, bells were an integral aspect of municipal amenities.
Thus in 1809 the parish priest of Lencloître petitioned the Bishop of
Poitiers. He explained that his commune was the canton capital, the seat
of a justice of the peace, a registry office, a "gendarmerie," and that, furthermore, it boasted some "very fine fairs"; every Monday bustling markets were held there. Its church was "much praised."[5] All things considered, a ring of bells was surely indispensable.

A bell was a source of great pride. At the other end of the hierarchy of
communities, the inhabitants of Maintru felt highly honored at possessing
such an instrument since the hamlet in which they lived was merely a section of a commune.[6] The 1,500-kilo bell, acquired by subscription in 1858,
was the pride and joy of the parishioners of Sigy (Seine-et-Marne); those
living in the region were so impressed by its loudness and loveliness of
tone that they nicknamed it "the belle of the valley."[7].

The number of bells was also supposed to correspond to that of the
clergy. On 18 April 1821, the municipal council in Gahard, a small, "poor"
commune in the Ille-et-Vilaine, decided to devote the sum yielded by the
sale of a portion of its common land to the purchase of a bell. "Seeing that
we have but one in Gahard . . . everyone," the mayor insisted, " wishes
fervently for it, now that we have two priests; we are quite content but to
do things right we need . . . two bells."[8]

Communities were forever pondering how they might ring more loudly
than their neighbors or be heard beyond their own quarter or parish. The
loudness of a bell constituted a challenge. In the countryside the goal was
to have a peal that was not markedly inferior to the bells of the town.[9]
Such confrontations in sound belonged to a wider series of symbolic oppo-
sitions and contests between rival communes. Nineteenth-century campanologists deplored such rivalries since they led to pointless recastings,
which in their opinion amounted to vandalism. Each commune strove to
"emulate neighbors with new rings."[10] According to a now forgotten logic,
such recastings satisfied a desire to improve municipal amenities.

Where an area contained both Catholics and Protestants, the loudness
of bell ringing might well be a bone of contention even within the same

commune. In 1845 the Catholics of Aubais (Gard) launched a drive to fund the replacement of the church's old bell, which had been seized during the Revolution. The Protestants resolved to reply in kind and equip their own temple. In order to win a symbolic victory over their adversaries the Catholics then laid claim to a "double ringing." The vestry claimed the right to use the new bell that the local community—consisting of a mixture of worshipers of both creeds—had allocated to the municipal clock. The Catholics resisted every "compromise" put forward by the prefect and refused to admit that "the two forms of worship [were] completely identical."[11] Conflicts of the same type erupted in several neighboring communes. In 1854 and 1856 for example, Catholics and Protestants clashed over the use of a bell hung in the clock tower of Vabre (Tarn). The dispute, according to the members of the parochial church council, "threw everyone into a state of turmoil."[12]

We know from numerous testimonies that, in this period, hearing bells ring in harmony was a true pleasure to the ears. For example, on 1 June 1845, the rector of Publier (diocese of Annecy)* wrote to his bishop informing him that the three bells in his parish were "perfectly tuned." They rang "the major third." "The people are proud of them," he added, "and never tire of hearing them." Likewise the inhabitants of Pommereux, a commune in the Bray, considered it an honor to possess a bell that had been cast in 1833 in the village square, beside the communal school and opposite the forge; because it had a "special sound . . . its tremulous voice moved listeners whether they willed it or not."[13]

Hubert Dameras of Hannogne, in the heart of the Ardennes, kept a diary of local events. He took care to record castings and benedictions in the area and noted that on 24 November 1821, after having been broken by two clumsy carpenters the parish bell was recast, "the cost being borne by the local inhabitants contributing voluntarily to a fund." They decided to use the existing metal to forge a ring of three new bells. A few days later the new bells were heard for the first time. "The whole commune," as Dameras noted with satisfaction, "is indeed glad to hear our three bells, for they are well tuned."[14]

---

*Publier (and Annecy) were not a part of French territory until 1860, at which time Savoie was joined to France.

The silencing of a bell caused distress, and the threat of it constituted an impressive weapon in the hands of the clergy, as we shall see later. At the end of the Directory and the beginning of the Consulate, the prohibition on the religious use of bells began to break down.[15] The inhabitants of communes where there was not yet any bell ringing felt shamed by the boldness of their neighbors, who were not afraid to use their bells. On 10 Fructidor Year VIII (28 August 1800), the deputy mayor of the commune of Louvigné-près-Bais complained to the prefect of the Ille-et-Vilaine. Supported by the local justice of the peace and the commander of the national guard, the deputy mayor passed on the "request repeated almost daily by all the inhabitants that they be permitted once again *to delight in the sound of the bells*." He asked to do as the other communes that "*glory in their ringing* and insult us [because we cannot]." He referred to the trading by neighboring communes of "rumors, or even *insults*, that could well end in bloodshed." The case was all the more urgent given that such communes had often rung "in support of the brigands," who had been so prominent in that area, and who always sought to humiliate those who had "fought for liberty."[16] This testimony is of particular interest inasmuch as it suggests that a desire for bells could at times transcend party divisions. Opposition of this sort, wrote the prefect to the minister of police on 15 Prairial Year VIII (4 June 1800), should be ruthlessly crushed, if "uniform procedures" are to answer the "need to eradicate the causes of *rivalry*."[17]

Throughout the nineteenth century people felt it was humiliating to have an instrument whose sound did not carry, or to have too few bells. Dissonant bells could also be cause for collective shame, whether they were cracked, ill-tuned, "too high-pitched," or "baroque-sounding." A community would soon feel the need for "retuning." In 1832 the inhabitants of Commana (Finistère) decided to recast their bell because it "rendered the sound of divine office somewhat ridiculous."[18] That same year, the inhabitants of Saumont-la-Poterie (Seine-Inférieure) launched a drive to fund the casting of three bells. Unfortunately, "their discordant sound meant that they could not be kept,"[19] and it was decided in 1834 to melt them down and recast them. Much later, in 1873, one of the three bells in the town of Noyers (Oise) broke. In order to harmonize the bells the vestry decided that the entire ring would have to be recast.[20]

Members of a community—moved as they were by a common pride in

and loyalty to this symbol of their collective identity—much preferred to
recast bells rather than exchange them. In 1857 the inhabitants of
Neuville-au-Pont, a parish and commune that had been abolished in the
aftermath of the Revolution, took great pride in having successfully held
on to their bell. They planned to recast it and were firmly opposed to
exchanging it for "the castoff of some other community."

Nineteenth-century communities were faced with a dilemma; they
often had to choose between quantity and range of bells. Those with a
genuine ring of bells could attempt a carillon, thus aestheticizing the signal and transforming everyday life into art. A single loud bell, on the other
hand, made it possible to transmit an announcement further, and so to
symbolize the prestige of a community. In general, parochial church
councils and municipal councils opted for quantity. During the first two-
thirds of the century, they frequently chose to melt down the sole bell
remaining after the Revolution and, by slightly increasing the volume of
metal, to make a ring of three smaller bells from it. The authorities, on the
other hand, were concerned by loss of volume and fall in range. Being
preoccupied with secular peals, the prefects feared that the aestheticizing
of the religious signal might jeopardize the bells' other functions. [21]

A particularly telling example, and one worth discussing at length, is
supplied by the long, complicated dispute that divided Saint-Jacques-de-
Darnétal (Seine-Inférieure) under the Second Empire.[22] In 1804, the community's only bell was cracked. The municipal council and the parochial
church council, having consulted the assembled parishioners after Mass
on 26 December, had reached an agreement to replace the damaged
instrument with three new bells, "making up a ring." Long afterward, in
May 1863, the mayor, who was also the commune's benefactor, gave a sum
of twenty five hundred francs for the purchase of a bell weighing seven
hundred kilos. It was his express wish that it should repeat "with every
echo [his] joy and [his] gratitude" for the recovery of his wife [from a
grave illness]. He stipulated that *his* bell should be the first in the ring. On
5 July the parochial church council, voicing its delight at the donor's generosity, decided to recast the three existing bells. By adding some metal a
large bell could be cast. The parish priest launched a subscription for the
purchase of a third instrument that would weigh almost a ton; he guaranteed payment for it by offering some of his property as collateral. The

commune would then have a magnificent ring of twenty-two hundred kilos that would sound a major third. This "long-desired" ring would be "more in keeping with the size of the church and, more especially, with the needs of the parish." In order to be heard in every hamlet the " first" bell, according to artisans skilled in this line of work, would need to weigh 925 kilos, "the second," 694 kilos and "the third," 462 kilos. Under these circumstances the mayor's bell would no longer be the "first in the set."

Irked by this loss of superiority, the unhappy man "suspended the execution of his gift." The local population protested, objecting that "they had always had a peal of three bells," and that reducing it to two would be tantamount to "changing all the traditions and customs of the area." Being aligned with the mayor, the municipal councillors called for the reconstitution of a peal of three bells, the "first" of which would be given by him. The parish priest, for his part, would not allow the two other instruments to be hung even though they had already been cast and placed under the surveillance of the rural guard [*garde champêtre*].

For over five months no bells were rung in Saint-Jacques-de-Darnétal. Workmen in the neighboring factories complained because they were accustomed to resuming labor when they heard the five o'clock bell. On 30 January 1864, the prefect informed the *ministre des Cultes* that the dispute had taken on "a graver aspect." He went on to outline a "compromise" that would cause no offense to mayor or parish priest and would at the same time satisfy the inhabitants' desire for a peal of three bells. What is telling about this dispute is that inextricably mixed up in it are the vicissitudes of a classic conflict between mayor and parish priest and the articulation of demands that reflected the community's culture of the senses.

So concerned were the men of this period with collective honor that they sometimes took things too far. They might, for instance, acquire a bell whose weight was more than their bell tower could bear.[23] Furthermore, verbal exaggeration was the rule where bells were concerned, as specialists in this field have noted time and again. As early as 1750, the famous caster Philippe Cavillier claimed that if one weighed bells, "one would not find one that was precisely the weight it was supposed to be."[24] It was easy to exaggerate the weight and diameter of bells since they were so often invisible and therefore mysterious. Similarly, there is no counting the number of bell towers whose staircases, according to local inhabitants, consisted of exactly 365 steps.[25]

There was another logic underlying the constant attention paid to bell ringing that was purely symbolic. The harmony of bells seemed to guarantee that of the community. In 1884 the town council of La Croix-aux-Mines (Vosges) turned down the small bell that the parish priest had placed in the courtyard of the school so as to cease relying on the church's bell ringing to mark the beginning and end of classes. "We do not wish to have this *foreign bell* that does not belong to the commune, and whose shrill and irritating sound arouses discontent and universal and unanimous murmurings. . . . We can revert to our former ways and ring the bell that best suits us and is our property, *and when we were wont to ring it everyone was in agreement at La Croix.*"[26]

Bell-ringing, as we shall see, reflected the divisions and hierarchies by which groups were structured; at the same time, it ensured a degree of symbolic equality between individuals by imparting a rhythm to their lives and marking the completion of rites of passage. The right to "delight in the bronze" has been laid claim to time and again, even by free-thinkers at the end of the century, as I shall show later. Campanarian texts bear traces of such assumptions. In the Auvergne, "some bells of the planeze* carry an inscription testifying to the donor's formal wish that the bell ring for the poor as well as the rich."[27] Likewise, on the bell from Cussac (Cantal) cast in 1838, we may read as follows: "I shall ring for all without reward." In Brezons a tablet in the choir of the church lists twenty-two subscribers and ends with the wish that "the bells should ring for the poor as well as the rich." On bells at Tagenac (1862) and at Saint-Martin-sous-Vigouroux (1868), we may read that "the poor and the rich alike have a right to my services." Vestries, with the compliance of the municipal authorities, sought to impose a system of tariffs so as to take advantage of the vanity of those of higher rank. Such policies sometimes proved controversial.

On 11 February 1866, the mayor and municipal councillors of Réty (Pas-de-Calais) petitioned the *ministre de la Justice et des Cultes*. The pre-

---

*planeze: volcanic lava flow that imparts a tabular relief to the highly fertile soil in this part of the Auvergne.

vious year the inhabitants had acquired by "voluntary subscription" a second bell for their church. Most of the subscribers were "poor workers," and "only one condition was set, namely, that at the death of one and all, rich or poor, great or small, this bell should be rung without charge." This was the practice followed in the neighboring communes "where all the bells were rung free of charge whenever a member of the congregation died." Now, however, the petitioners objected, "all these good people have been duped"; the prefectorial and episcopal regulation, recently read from the pulpit, stipulated that one had to pay if one wanted two bells to be rung. So it was that "none but the rich, who can afford to pay for this right, would enjoy the sound of the bronze that is the property of all, and especially of the poor." This state of affairs caused something of a stir and led to "endless complaints."[28]

To arrive at a fuller understanding of the attachment of individuals to the ringing of bells and the intensity of a community's reaction to any encroachments, we need to consider the procedures involved in casting and recasting.[29] The symbolism attaching to the latter operation was particularly resonant. Through the use of old, already consecrated metal, one could achieve renewal and integration of the past at the same time. Recasting did not break the chain of time and did not, strictly speaking, constitute either a substitution or a succession. In both town and country, moreover, the inscription from the old bell would sometimes be repeated on the new bell.[30] The recasting of one or more elements of the ring gave communities the opportunity to add the names of reigning sovereigns or local magistrates to the engraved list of previous incumbents. Those who formulated such campanarian inscriptions had to engage with collective memory and thus reconcile a desire to be modern with the need to respect existing loyalties and preoccupations. So subtle was the symbolism of bells that they both perpetuated memory and expressed innovation. Their auditory message, being more commanding than the visual message of a statue, was by the same token invested with a more intense emotional power.[31]

Casting in the village

The bell caster would appear in the village in the spring, ready to do the community's bidding. Having recourse to the services of such a man was highly advisable since transportation could damage bells, which were fragile, delicately balanced objects. Crucially, on-site casting ensured that the recognized virtues of the metal from the old bell were preserved; it amounted to a transmutation without any loss of identity to a consecrated object that was often ascribed magical powers. The bell of the parish had marked the most important moments in an individual's life. On-site casting was preferred because it prevented breaches with symbolism and, in some sense, the disruption that acquisition of an alien object would entail. Local manufacture of bells continued to be the norm until the middle of the century; the following decade marked a turning point in this practice. In the Moselle, the very last on-site casting, that of the bell for Boulange,[32] dates from 1855. In the Charente the practice died out in 1860,[33] and in Périgord, around 1855. By the end of the century, on-site casting only survived in Corsica. A young bell caster tried to revive the practice in the Aude and the Hérault, but without much success. His venture was inspired by nostalgia for a bygone age, and was redolent of industrial archaeology.[34]

Most casters were migrant workers from Lorraine or, to be precise, the region of Bassigny.[35] A number of them lived in Breuvannes, a small commune in Haute-Marne. One can still read the names of the principal dynasties of bell makers on the pews of the parish church. Some casters (though far fewer in number) came from Picardy, Normandy, the Auvergne, and the Limousin. A small number were Italian, Swiss, or Belgian.

Bell casters tended to be self-employed, often in the context of a family business. Fathers and sons, or fathers-in-law and sons-in-law, would cover the region of their choice. Between 1822 and 1832, the Cauchois and the Barrards, who were natives of the Bassigny, "traveled" together through the arrondissement of Château-Thierry.[36] "Pockmarked" Barrard and François Barrard, known as "Ass's hide," accompanied their uncle, Nicolas Cauchois-Barrard. From 1835 to 1867, Barrard-Morlet, another member of the same family, returned year after year with his son Jean-Baptiste and sometimes his cousin as well, to cast at La Chapelle-Monthodon in the Aisne. His fame was such that he was able to marry his eldest son to the mayor's daughter. His mobile workshop, set up in the village square, became a permanent foundry run by his son, Barrard-Bertin, in 1842. For a quarter of a century the latter made from eight to ten bells there each year. The father, Barrard-Morlet, continued as an itinerant caster in Marne and Seine-et-Marne, but would periodically assist his son in La Chapelle-Monthodon.

From spring to autumn the caster would travel around, sometimes on horseback but usually on foot, armed with notebook, riveting iron, and some decorative die-stamps.[37] He would listen to the bells being rung, and be on the lookout for a crack or for "poor tuning."[38] He peered at bell towers to see if any bells were missing. He would play on the rivalries between communities in order to persuade several of them to commit themselves to a single casting to lower costs. A bell maker was a highly respected figure, valued for his arcane knowledge and the magical powers that were often attributed to him. Although significant progress in acoustics had been made since the seventeenth century,[39] thereby removing much of the mystery surrounding the campanarian art, at least in enlightened milieux, an itinerant caster would still pride himself on the prestigious secrets that had been handed down to him. Each bell maker had his own signature, so to speak, so that anyone with a trained ear could tell who had made the bells in the region through which he was traveling. Traditional procedures in bell making were so rigid—as were the iconography and the epigraphy—that the whole art smacked of archaism. This sense of stepping back in time was in striking contrast to the concern of communities to be modern and recast their bells.

It was no easy matter to get a contract, or "agreement," which was drawn up by the representatives of the vestry and/or the municipal council.[40] The bell caster would display the "certificates of satisfaction" given to him by previous clients; if it seemed appropriate, he might pay his interlocutors a "sweetener" to forestall rivals. Negotiations might involve several journeys, yet still come to nothing. If things turned out well, discussions would result in a deal being struck, generally at the local inn. Verbal agreements were common but tended to be backed up by a written contract during the nineteenth century. The outcome of highly contentious discussion, such a document would constitute an agreement of fearsome complexity. Aside from the essential clauses, provisions would be made for the wages of assistants, the apprentice, and the person engaged to keep watch over the future site.

Studies of campanarian history reproduce a number of such agreements, which make wearisome reading. I shall therefore give just one example, dated 31 October 1825, in which the municipal council of Saint-Sulpice-de-Mareuil (Dordogne) signed a deal for the casting of a bell of 731 kilos.[41] Aside from the 614 kilos of metal from the bell that was to be recast, the bell maker was to be provided with 1,500 oven bricks, 5 kilos of hemp, 4 kilos of melted tallow, 2 kilos of fresh wax, 1 kilo of cow's hair, and between 16 and 20 dozen eggs or 2 kilos of gum arabic for preparing the casting clay, together with some oak for the casting. It was agreed that the casting would take place "in town," and that the jacket in which the bell was to be draped on the day of its benediction would go back to the parish. The bell maker would be paid a fee of 300 francs, and 4 francs for each kilo of good commercial metal that he obtained from a local boilermaker.

It was left to the bell maker to decide precisely where the casting would be done.[42] A ditch had to be dug in front of the oven to hold the mold (or molds), and this required a terrain that was not damp, uneven, or stony. It was also necessary to build a covered shed to shield the ditch from rain. Although the ecclesiastical authorities forbade it, bell makers liked to cast in the cemetery surrounding the church. This was the case with Londinières, in the Bray, in 1824.[43] Otherwise the bell caster would choose the spot that suited him best in the village—perhaps the marketplace, a particular favorite, the main square, the presbytery garden or orchard, a meadow in the parish, a vacant lot, a ruined castle, a tilery, the area beside the public oven, a shed, a private barn, or the courtyard of a château, which was the site chosen in Chérisey (Moselle) in 1866.[44] If he had to, a bell maker would install himself at the innkeeper's or below the schoolyard. The discoveries of campanarian archaeologists have sometimes enabled us to pinpoint the exact spot where the bell was made. In July 1846, Jean Nanglard informs us, the bell of Saint-Cybardeaux (Charente) was cast, "near to the cemetery . . . to the left, beneath the walnut trees of M. Léopold Guilhot."[45]

Sometimes the parochial church council, the municipal council, or the two combined, or again, a single wealthy donor, paid the costs of the casting. Generally, if only to cover some of the expenses, a subscription was launched, or there was what the deputy mayor of Marigné (Maine-et-Loire) called a "gleaning."[46] It was a matter of honor to display generosity on such occasions. Sometimes a bell would be inscribed with the names of those who had contributed to the fund. They would thus be remembered kindly by posterity, with the most generous heading the list. To meet the expense, the municipal council would sometimes sell off a strip of woodland or a plot of common land. In 1828 the municipality of Luppy (Moselle) paid for the casting of its bell by giving up twelve trees from the estovers. The commune of Foulcrey, in 1850, and that of Launstroff, in 1857, did likewise.[47]

Many documents in the archives of the Gers[48] testify to the determination with which attempts were made within this department to satisfy the yearning for bells. Certain communes all but bled themselves dry. Some (for example, Cadeilhan, Mauroux, Espaon, and Puylausic) sold common land, some cut wood (in Monlaur-Bernet and Caupenne; in Termes two hundred oak trees were chopped down), while others (for example, Montegut-Arros) sacrificed their estovers. Still others sold government stock (Pujaudran). Yet others asked the prefecture to approve a special levy. Most communes decided to raise funds by subscription (Maumusson, for example). Several municipalities became indebted to the bell caster (Traversères-l'Hôpital). To cut costs, several communes came to an understanding and cast together. In every case the documents speak of an expense judged by all to be "indispensable" and "most pressing." None could bear the thought of having to "make their way haphazardly to services."[49]

Those failing to make a contribution might incur penalties. A sheet affixed to the church door in Saint-Louis-lès-Phalsbourg (Moselle) listed all those who had contributed to the purchase of the bells, with the sums paid up until 1 July 1845. Each person could, where necessary, ask for the amount shown to be adjusted. Gifts ranged between one and one hundred francs, with most being from five to ten francs. It was made plain that those who abstained would not be able to use the new bells.[50] In Saint-Jean-Kourtzerode (Moselle), the baptismal register recorded that nine parishioners, among them the mayor and the schoolmaster, had refused to make a contribution to the casting carried out in 1872. "The great bell," the document informs us, "will never be rung [for them] unless they have first paid the parish priest the sum of fifty francs . . . as fixed during the sermon at the parish mass eight days before the closure of the subscription."

The casting was not always funded by the whole community. Sometimes local associations would make a gift of an instrument. The small bell in the town of Leucamp (Cantal) that was cast in 1806 bears the following inscription: "I was made by the young," and below it the names of nineteen *lieutenants* and seventeen *lieutenantes* were listed.[51] In this region several bells were paid for by immigrants who were temporarily or permanently residing in the town. In 1837, "the natives of Cézens living in Bordeaux" gave a loud bell to their church, while in 1840 one of the bells of Saint-Clément was offered "by the children of the parish who reside in Paris." Much the same occurred at Brezons in 1844, and at Saint-Martin-sous-Vigouroux in 1868. Four years before, a bell named "Eugénie the Parisian" had been blessed in the church at Pierrefort. This is not the only evidence we have of an alliance between migrants from Cantal and the Imperial regime. The great bell at Lieutadès, cast in 1863 in a field by a bell caster from Rodez, was paid for with a collection from the "Parisians" and with an additional gift from the emperor. Such displays of generosity call to mind or prefigure forms of paternalism current in the second half of the century.[52] It was the custom of confraternities in Normandy to pay for the bell they had installed in their bell towers, but in this case a different procedure was followed since these associations later claimed ownership rights and free use of the instrument.

It was not uncommon for a commune to appeal to the generosity of neighboring parishes that lay within earshot of the bell they hoped to cast. This was what the people of Berg (Moselle) did in 1835.[53] As we have seen, some communities agreed to share a casting to cut costs. In 1833 Antoine, his son, and his brother-in-law cast thirteen bells in one go in Maizy, in the Aisne. In 1838 in the Trois-Moutiers, in the Vienne, Decharme father and son cast sixteen or seventeen bells on site in a single session. When they had commissions on that scale, however, bell casters generally preferred to make several castings in succession.

In the majority of cases, regardless of the procedure adopted, the local community played some kind of role in the creation of a new bell. The memory of such displays of solidarity fueled their anger at being denied the right to ring. As we shall see later, the right "to be rung" was regarded as irrevocable by all who had been present at the casting of a new bell and had made a contribution or played a part in its creation.

Participation in the "gleaning" was not the only way for the inhabitants to involve themselves in the casting; the process entailed many other collections. Since eggs were sometimes deemed necessary for the luting loam, the bell ringer was supposed to collect them. The whites were thought to lend smoothness and lightness to the casting clay, while the yolks enabled the bell caster to wolf down lavish omelettes. In 1839 when a bell was cast at Saint-Martial-de-Valette (Dordogne), "over fifty dozen eggs were given to the bell-caster."[54]

The collecting of objects intended to increase the weight of the metal to be cast was a more serious affair. By donating old copper cauldrons, pewter plates, worn saucepans, misshapen candlesticks, firedogs, mortars, and bronze coin, each person might hope to play a part in the making of the bell that would announce their death or the baptism of one of their descendants. Bearing in mind the extremely diverse nature of such gifts, we may better understand how heterodox the alloys were and how common it was for bells to break. We cannot be sure what the precise ratio of copper to pewter was in bells cast in the first half of the nineteenth century, but countryfolk seem to have been less strict in this regard than townsfolk. In the second half of the century, however, contracts stipulated that the ratio of copper to pewter should be between 78 percent and 22 percent.

Memories of events involving bells[55] ran back so far into the past that we are able to gauge the scale on which gifts were made when a set was cast or recast. In 1917 when Samuel Bour observed the refitting of the bell in the town of Basse-Vigneulles (Moselle), "the men who were present," he wrote, "assured me that their ancestors, in 1710, had brought to the bell caster, Potier de Créhange, whatever the village had in the way of objects made of silver,"[56] copper, or pewter. Memories of ceremonies were likewise very vivid. In 1900 Joseph Berthelé quizzed the old men living in the canton of Château-Thierry, many of whom he insisted could remember castings and "baptisms" of bells from the beginning of the nineteenth century. One of them remembered that in 1834 a ring of three bells had been blessed in the commune of Courboin.[57] Unless we take into account the existence of memories covering such a long stretch of time, just as they do in the entirely different sphere of marriage alliances, we cannot hope to understand the intensity of affairs involving bells, and we risk missing the import of bell tower disputes.

The itinerant bell caster's workshop, being set up in the middle of the commune, was the center of attention. The caster would make "a deep impression on one and all. The curious gathered round, but kept their distance, as if reined in by a reverential fear."[58] The bell maker, like other metal workers, would tend to drink large quantities. Being therefore a regular customer at the tavern or inn, he would gradually get to know members of the community. Sometimes the local people would take it upon themselves to feed him. The parish priest might then announce in his Sunday sermon who for the following week "should provide victuals for the bell caster, and which day they [would have] to receive him at their table."[59]

Once his oven was set up, the bell caster had to dig a trench, beat it flat, and line it with stones. Once he had puddled the clay he had to make and position the molds, set up his ground plan, and prepare inscriptions to decorate the bronze. The mold had to be heated to the point of complete dessication or it would not be able to withstand the heat of the molten metal. Throughout the whole operation the fire had to be stoked in order to cook, day and night, the core, the dummy bell, the cope, and the "head," that is to say, the constituent elements of the mold.

The villagers would help the bell maker throughout, supplying him with the carts itemized in the "agreement." They would saw wood and feed the oven with it, move the mold or molds into position and bury it (or them), and break up and weigh the metal from the old bell or that supplied by the donors. They worked the bellows. They rallied around when the time came to disinter the molds. Such tasks enabled the villagers to strengthen their gradually woven ties with the artisan and make manifest their collective participation in the casting of the new bell.[60]

Finally the symbolic moment of the actual casting arrived, generally at night. In Hannogne (Ardennes) on 28 July 1790, it took place at eight o'clock in the evening (still in sunlight), that is to say, towards the end of the day; in Londinières (Seine-Inférieure) in 1824, around one o'clock in the morning.[61] The operation, which required heating the oven with the prized oakwood, unfolded in the presence of the entire village. In particular, many children would witness the spectacle, and it would linger in their memory. Some bell casters held that menstrual blood endangered the success of the operation, a belief that social anthropologists have often encountered. This is why, to mention just one example, it was the custom of François Peigney in the 1850s to have the girls and women removed.[62] At this solemn moment, Joseph Berthelé recorded, "the libations and the bellows stopped. A priest in his vestments [came and] blessed the metal while the public knelt." The prayers stipulated by diocesan ritual for a successful casting were then said.

We are assured that at this point gold coins or family jewels were sometimes thrown in to impart a crystalline sound to the bell, but it is hard to know whether such claims are truth or legend. It is said that some bell casters, mindful that such metals were better kept out of the alloy but not wanting to lose a windfall, arranged for coins and jewels to escape the smelting so they could be recovered at the end of the operation. Be this as it may, in many places the inhabitants are convinced that this was the origin of the silvery sound of their bell.[63] Some also believe that the addition of a precious metal prevents the cracking of the instrument through frost. For my purposes, however, the essential is to appreciate how much this addition of gold and silver, lavished by families at the moment of casting, symbolically enhances the participation of the community of the living and the dead, and founds the desired attachment to the sacred object.

The risk of failure was great, further justifying prayers for the success of the casting. The mold might give way, the cope rise up, air bubbles might ruin the metal, the weight of the bell might not turn out as anticipated, and its note therefore might prove disappointing. In Issac (Dordogne), the bell cast in 1851 in the town hall courtyard was a success only with the third casting.[64] For all the above reasons the priest in charge, after saying prayers, would sprinkle holy water on the molten metal. When the mold had been broken and the operation deemed a success, the priest would intone a *Te Deum*. The evening often ended with a drinking bout either at the inn, the presbytery or in the mayor's own home. In Breuvannes, the bell casters' commune, this was known as "killing the dog."

The bell then had to be fettled, filed down and burnished with fine, damp sand, and weighed. In the countryside weight was often judged by eye, mainly because few communes had scales. This lack of precision fostered exaggeration and misdescription. Where the operation was well-funded, however, the bell would be weighed at the nearest "public scales."

Before being hung, the qualities of the new instrument were subjected to skilled evaluation. In Bourges in 1842, the population was divided as to the worth of the new set of bells and the topic was hotly debated in the local press. The vestry office resolved to consult "the judgment of the public."[65] For twelve days it had the bells rung in full peal every evening at five o'clock. Finally the tenor bell, "William-Stephen," was accepted, but the new bell, Caroline, was rejected because it was supposed to ring "*fa* sharp" but what one heard was a *mi*. When members of the vestry office, the bell ringer, and experts appointed for the occasion were able to reach an agreement, a "certificate of satisfaction" was issued to the bell maker. When this was not the case, the bell had to be recast. On 27 August 1827, after a long appraisal, a bell in Espaon (Gers) was rejected because of its "deplorable sound"[66]; the failure was all the more regrettable given the "very silvery" sound of the other bell in the church. Conversely, on 3 October 1844, the Mayor of Nastringues (Dordogne) issued a certificate to Martin of Breuvannes for a bell "with which," he wrote, "we have been generally satisfied."[67] Sometimes, as we have seen, the general rejoicing seemed worth recording. "On 25 November 1821, Saint Catherine's day, at ten o'clock in the evening, they were wholly successful,"[68] noted Hubert Dameras in his journal, with regard to the bells cast that day in the commune of Hannogne.

When the operation was finished it was time to settle up. Payment in kind in the shape of deliveries of wood, coal, or wine, though still frequent on the eve of the Revolution, seems to have died out over the course of the nineteenth century. On the other hand it was not uncommon for the community[69] to pay the bell maker in installments, requiring him to make additional journeys.

The church did not consider blessing of the bell to be necessary, yet the practice was generally observed. During the ceremony, through the symbolism analyzed at great length by liturgical specialists, the offerings, the lustration, the anointings, and the fumigation, the bell became a sacred object. Unless one keeps this separation from the profane constantly in mind one stands no chance of understanding the issues involved in conflicts over bell ringing throughout the nineteenth century. The public had been accustomed to personifying the bell, and would spontaneously compare lustration to christening, which would require the presence of a godfather and a godmother.

In December 1868 the commune of Sougé-le-Ganelon (Sarthe) was in an uproar. The mayor and the parish priest had failed to agree upon a godfather or godmother for their bell, nor had the intervention of a senior priest from La Fresnaye served to calm ruffled spirits. The priest "took it to be his duty to proceed with a blessing of the new bell according to the formula prescribed by Catholic ritual, on a Sunday, before the assembled congregation, but without a godfather or godmother. It was for this reason that the inhabitants, claiming that they had a *bastard bell* lacking the inscriptions they would have wished for, refused to accept it."[70]

Of course within a given community the choice of godfather and godmother could prove controversial, a matter I will return to later. For the time being I will simply note that the decision was made by the churchwardens or the municipal council, or simply by the parish priest and/or the mayor. The bronze of numerous bells merely mentions the inhabitants of the commune.[71]

Campanarian inscriptions recorded social hierarchies and sometimes reflected power struggles within the community. I shall return to this point later. There might, however, also be an invocation, a dedication, and/or a baptismal name. Such procedures for personifying a bell that, I repeat, was always seen as a unique object with its qualities and particular virtues, deserve close study since they reflect the collective representations of a community. In the nineteenth century it was rare to invoke God, the Trinity, or Christ in inscriptions on bells. Conversely, campanarian epigraphy provides confirmation of the many studies that have emphasized the spread of the cult of healer saints in rural France at this time, and the rise of Marian devotion in the country as a whole. What was crucial was the desire to shield the community from harm, for which purpose the mediation of the Virgin and the saints seemed then to be the most effective means at hand. Such was the case in the Moselle and in the Dordogne, to mention only the most meticulous campanarian surveys that have been conducted.[72]

Nonetheless, it is important not to exaggerate the importance of the epigraphical implications. In popular parlance bells were only very rarely referred to by their "baptismal" names or their dedications. Country people tended rather to speak of "the big," "the middle," or "the little" bell, or of "the first," "the second" or "the third." In sizable towns, however, nicknames were used, and these would sometimes stem from a legend accounting for the prestige of the bell. Most of the cathedral tenor bells had nicknames.[73]

The blessing of a bell provided an opportunity for decorating public spaces. In Forges-les-Eaux (Seine-Inférieure) in 1853, the ceremony was preceded by a procession through the streets of the village.[74] In Guernes (Seine-et-Oise) in 1864, a triumphal arch was erected at the entrance to the commune; another arch stood inside the church.[75] At the end of the century when somewhat provocative demonstrations were being staged by zealous Christians, the blessing of bells sometimes assumed a particularly ostentatious form, especially in the towns; anti-clericals were roused to anger and controversy was stirred up in the local press.

During the ceremony the bell, which was draped in lace reminiscent of christening robes, was hung amid the garlands festooning the choir of the church. On the way out it was the custom to rain sugared almonds on the crowd.[76] Popular celebrations often brought the day to a close and continued as the notables feasted after the blessing. In short, the "christening" of a bell provided an opportunity for an official festival whose routine sequence of rituals was modeled upon that of every other public display of rejoicing.

The crucial task here is to grasp just what the sacralizing of bells implied. In the middle of the eighteenth century Father Rémi Carré had expounded the doctrinal position very clearly, and clergy subsequently followed all his injunctions to the letter. First, blessing ensured that a bell could never, under any circumstances, seem to be a toy or mere source of entertainment. One should not use them "arbitrarily or indiscreetly,"[77] ring with "lascivious and profane airs" better suited to the theater, or "let women ring, except in nunneries."[78] The blessing banned, as far as was possible, all profane bell ringing. This takes us to the root of numerous disputes, the basic pattern of which merits further analysis. The refusal to bless a bell, for example, long remained a formidable weapon in the hands of the clergy. It might put the safety of the entire community at risk and create a breach through which a host of dangers might irrupt and afflict it.[79]

After 1860[80] bells were cast in factories. The Bollées family acquired a virtual monopoly in the center and west of France, while three bell casters from Villedieu-les-Poêles (Manche) and the Farniers of Rambervillers (Vosges) also controlled a significant share of the market. The transport revolution and the growing propensity of the most prominent artisans to remain in one place led to the concentration of industrial casting in particular areas. Procedures became simplified and standardized and the practice of coming to an "arrangement" gradually died out. Industrial casting enabled the parish priest or mayor to decide for himself whether to recast and so more readily avoid being controlled by the community. At the same time factory manufacture led to higher quality and more refined forms of decoration. The longevity of instruments was also guaranteed. The disappearance of the itinerant bell caster, the absence of risk, and the subsiding of collective emotion aroused by nocturnal casting all conspired to render bells banal. All the evidence suggests that everything in this sphere pertaining to the history of sensibilities suffered a drastic impoverishment during the last third of the nineteenth century.

The First Republic had itself waged an unprecedentedly wide-ranging campaign for the destruction of bells. Nothing rivals its attempts to promote desacralizing, the eradication of "fanaticism," and "superstitions," and the imposition of a strict division between the secular and the religious.[81] Yet such efforts had not really diminished the symbolic value and emotional power of bells and may, through the paradoxical effects of deprivation, have instilled new life in them. The First Republic had not reduced the part played by bells in the construction of individual and collective identities. In this regard the end of the 1850s marks the crucial turning point.

Nonetheless, until the dawning of the twentieth century and despite the perceptible decline of the preceding decades, *l'esprit du clocher** was still more than a metaphor. Up until that date the voice of bells played a part in the "sonorities serving to constitute existence and a working community," to quote Pierre Laurence.[82] If we are to stand any chance of fully understanding that voice we must strive to overcome our habitual neglect of this sphere of sensory experience and take account of what was then a careful listening to auditory messages that would of course have been repeated time and time again. The history of bells is closely linked to the history of our modalities of attention.

In order properly to grasp the fading and subsiding of messages emitted by bells—which constitute an important page in the history of our culture of the senses—I propose now to analyze the part played by these instruments in the construction of the social, temporal, and spatial markers for individuals living within range of their sound.

*esprit de clocher: While the term is ordinarily translated as "parochialism" or "localism," its sense is best rendered by the Italian equivalent, *campanilismo*. Note also that the closely related *querelle du clocher*, or bell tower dispute, is sometimes rendered as "parish-pump politics."

CHAPTER FOUR

The Auditory Markers of the Village

Bell, Space, and Territory

CENTER AND BOUNDARY[1]

The emotional impact of a bell helped create a territorial identity for individuals living always in range of its sound. When they heard it ringing, villagers, townsfolk, and those "in the trades" in the centers of ancient towns experienced a sense of being rooted in space that the nascent urban proletariat lacked. Bell ringing was one of a range of markers obviating the quest for an identity of the sort that defined the very being of the proletarian[2] who, as a migrant, was isolated in a condition that all too often resembled exile.

The bell tower prescribed an auditory space that corresponded to a particular notion of territoriality, one obsessed with mutual acquaintance. The bell reinforced divisions between an inside and an outside, as one might infer from the pejorative use of terms such as *l'esprit du clocher*. Marcel Maget has identified a set of concentric circles containing a zone of mutual acquaintance, a zone of marriage alliances, a zone of leisure activities, and a *zone of hearsay* that define social acquaintance in rural societies.[3] The range of a bell should be analyzed in very much the same terms.[4]

This auditory space is not much affected by the acceleration that swept the nineteenth century along, and entails no tendency toward mobility and speed. Listening to a bell conjures up a space that is by its nature slow, prone to conserve what lies within it, and redolent of a world in which walking was the chief mode of locomotion.[5] Such a sound is attuned to the quiet tread of a peasant.

The territory circumscribed by the sound of a bell obeyed the classical code of the beautiful—the schema of cradle, nest, and cell. It was an enclosed space structured by the sound emanating from its center. The bell tower was supposed to be situated in the middle of its auditory territory. Received wisdom has long rested on the assumption that such bounded spaces, inasmuch as they served to perpetuate the notion of walking distance, were in stark contrast to the coherent space of the nation and republican citizenship,[6] and that the advent of democratic regimes presupposed the construction of a new kind of territoriality. We are obliged, however, to qualify such claims once we scrutinize the imaginary attributes of the space upon which the triumph of republicanism was based. The landscape enshrined in the official ideology of turn-of-the-century France was construed in terms of classical harmony; it consisted of village cells, each permeated by the sound of bells. The Third Republic succeeded in rebuilding this reassuring notion of territory in its own image. It might be truer to the terms of the debate staged in those years to speak of the construction of a space, the basic structure of which was preserved while an attempt was made to desacralize its key markers, namely, bell tower, public square, crossroads and all the sites where public announcements might be made or the inhabitants might assemble.

The range of a bell, inscribed in a classical perspective of harmony, served to define a territory that was haunted by the notion of limits as well as the threat of their being transgressed. The crucial functions of the bell tower were to raise the alarm and ensure the preservation of the community. A sort of correlation was thereby established between bell and boundary, and between bell ringing and processions. Both served to define a space with readily perceptible limits.[7] Another correlation thereby arose between the loudness of a bell and the extent of a parish or commune's territory. It was important to ensure that no part of that territory remained obdurately deaf to public announcements, alarms, or commands, and that there were no fragments of isolated space in which the auditory identity was ill-defined and threatened to impede rapid assembly.

Bells shaped the habitus of a community or, if you will, its culture of the senses. They served to anchor localism,[8] imparting depth to the desire for rootedness and offering the peace of near, well-defined horizons. This is borne out by the correspondence between the historical literature on bells and the structuring of the space across which their sound carried. The histories were invariably the work of local antiquaries obsessed with their "*petit pays*," and they took the form of fragments or tiny essays cut to fit the episodic nature of everyday life. Such research, of which there is a huge amount,[9] represents a history of the minuscule; the narrowness of its scope and its scattered state precludes its ever being raised to the level of a more prestigious, all-embracing history.[10]

In the nineteenth century, at least in the countryside, bell ringing defined a space within which[11] only fragmented, discontinuous noises were heard, none of which could really vie with the bell tower. After all there were as yet no airplanes, which nowadays are capable of competing with, overwhelming and, above all, *neutralizing* the sound of bells. Aerial sounds have been desacralized. Since the dawn of the twentieth century, bell and cannon have ceased to be the sole rivals of the mighty thunderbolt.

The continuous noise of the internal combustion engine, electric motor, or amplifier were also unknown. People liked, therefore, being sporadically deafened, primarily by the ringing of bells, but also by the sound of cannon being fired or the explosion of "firecrackers," all of which were regarded as indispensable compliments to public rejoicing. The charivari, or "rough music" we tend to regard as unwelcome disturbance, was all the more appreciated for its breaching of a habitual silence and for its links with the structure of the auditory landscape. Let me reiterate, however, that nothing in a milieu of this kind could vie with the bell.

Owing to the regularity with which they were rung, bells played a part in the periodic "sacral recharging of the surrounding space."[12] Whatever the degree of religious fervor of the local population, the church served to define a small space at the very heart of the village that was generally respected.[13] From this center of padded silence emanated the sound waves that extended their "sacralizing" hold over an aerial space undisturbed by any other din.

Since the dawn of the Catholic Reformation the church has aspired to such a mastery of airborne sound. It has tried, although not entirely successfully, to hierarchize bell ringing. According to norms laid down by Carlo Borromeo in the sixteenth century,[14] a cathedral was supposed to have between five and seven bells while a collegiate church might have three, and a parish church two, or at the most three. Monastery bells were not supposed to drown out those of a parish church. Ringers were expected to respect the "rules of deference" that reflected the hierarchy of edifices. The Council of Toulouse (1590) prohibited the "ringing of bells in any church before those of the Cathedral or of the mother church [sic] had given the signal."[15] Such refinements had been unknown during the Middle Ages but equivalent norms nonetheless existed. When a church was first founded its filial status was emphasized by its being permitted just the one bell.[16]

In truth, there was such a quantity of bells and such a love of peals in modern France that it was very hard to maintain any control over the messages they emitted. Doctor Billon, the man responsible for inaugurating the campanarian survey in 1853,[17] found that in the eighteenth century it was the custom to accord preeminence to cathedrals. In the following century this principle of deference in the sphere of bell ringing seems to have been observed in the episcopal towns. A romantic traveler perched on a hill could readily make out the aerial music that emanated from such places that used to be known as "ringing" towns.

A bell was supposed to be audible everywhere within the bounds of a specified territory.[18] As we have seen earlier, this implied adjusting the loudness of a ring of bells so that it could cover the surface area of the parish or commune and surmount any obstacles in the terrain. "We have found," Rémi Carré noted in 1757, "that bells may be heard further on the plains than in the mountains, and that bells in the valleys may be heard still further than those on the plains."[19] A mountainous terrain called for both a loud bell and early announcements. The 1837 regulation stipulated that in the valleys of the Pyrénées the offices might be rung a full hour before the service was due to start.[20] The 1885 regulation deemed even this advance notice insufficient in the Haute-Savoie.

The archives are full to bursting with complaints that a ring of bells did not cover a given territory. Consider the department of Finistère. On 19 June 1808 the inhabitants of Ouessant unsuccessfully petitioned the prefect, requesting a bell "whose sound could be heard in every corner" of the island.[21] Three years later the Mayor of Plouider reminded the same magistrate that his commune had given four bells during the Revolution, among them "the loveliest in the land," which "could be heard from a great way off."[22] Plouider, however, now only had one very soft bell that could not cover portions of "mountain" and *sea* supposedly lying within its range. Once again, in 1892, the inhabitants of Plounéour-Lanvern complained that they could not hear their only bell more than a kilometer away from the town, and that it rang a *sol* though "the wish of the local population" was to hear a *fa*.[23]

A large number of complaints about the failure of bells to carry concerned ringing in secular contexts. The clergy reserved the loudest and most solemn bells for announcing religious services, leaving only the small bell used for low masses for other kinds of ringing. Sometimes a community would therefore claim the right to use the largest bell under all circumstances.

In 1880 the priest in charge at Ceffonds (Haute-Marne) refused to ring the curfew with the great bell although this was what the town council had requested. In his view, custom decreed that it should be rung by "the second." The dispute divided the commune for several years. At first opposition to the priest led the council to withhold the bell ringer's fee to stop the ringing of the curfew. In November 1884, however, emboldened by the new political circumstances, the municipality began reinstating the practice, this time " with the largest bell." The mayor appointed a bell ringer and the municipality decided to offer him remuneration for this task alone. The parish priest complained to the authorities and the dispute then led to a heated exchange between the subprefect and the bishop of Langres. When challenged by the *ministre des Cultes*, who had been alerted by the bishop, the prefect sought to justify the mayor's point of view. He stressed that the "second" bell was "none too loud," and that the affair had erupted around five years ago when the hamlets far from the center of Ceffonds repeatedly complained. Today, he said, the great bell was in use "to the general satisfaction of all." In his opinion the size of the commune fully justified the innovation. The dispute ended in May 1886 with victory for the municipality.[24]

In 1900 the commune of Lagrave (Tarn) was divided by a dispute of this kind. According to the mayor, a number of day laborers and landowners asked that "the great bell" be rung at six in the evening to mark the end of the working day. The bishop endorsed the parish priest's refusal to ring with that instrument. The commune had a clock whose bell chimed every hour on the hour and the two clerics deemed this perfectly adequate. The dispute was becoming bitter, the bishop stressed, and was being exploited by anticlericals. The mayor asked the *ministre des Cultes* for permission to mark the end of the working day with the great bell. A refusal would be bound, he said, to undermine his position, that of the municipal council, and therefore that of the republicans at the next election.[25]

One of the functions of a bell was to orient travelers or navigators within the space covered by its sound. Local customs, as much in the mountains as in coastal areas, but also in hilly regions, on the fringes of forests, and sometimes even in flat country, bear traces of the protection offered by such instruments. The monks of Grand-Saint-Bernard used a bell located forty minutes from the monastery that rang to orient straying travelers.[26] In the mountains of the Auvergne "it is the custom to ring the bells from five to six o'clock in the evening, and until eleven o'clock at night whenever the countryside is covered in snow."[27] The bell in Aubrac rang every evening for the same reason.[28] In some communes of the Puy-de-Dôme, "the Angelus is rung at eight in the evening, for a long time." In the canton of Saint-Béat (Haut-Garonne), the bell began ringing at ten o'clock at night in winter for the same reason. This practice was also followed at Haudricourt (Seine-Inférieure), a wooded, very hilly commune. Likewise the mayors of the Meuse, who had refused the prefect's request made in 1852 to ring at ten o'clock on summer evenings,[29] acknowledged that it was useful in winter to let the bell be heard at nine o'clock to reorientate travelers who had lost their way in the forest.[30]

Along the coast where there was no lighthouse, and everywhere when the fog came down, it was bell ringing that served to guide—and sometimes, it was said, to lead astray—disorientated sailors. In Dieppe (Saint-Valéry-en-Caux) and Bourg-d'Ault (Seine-Inférieure), the bells were rung in bad weather. In 1864 Tréport municipal council had a bell installed on the jetty.[31] In Sables-d'Olonne there was a rescue bell. It was placed "high on the bell tower dome" and "it rang in time of storm." In 1881 the parish of Ile-Tudy (Finistère) requested a second bell "to be better able to signal to sailors the precise location of the coastline in times of thick fog, which obscured the lighthouses."[32] The minister granted the sum required.

THE PATH OF THE GOOD ANGELS

Bells were supposed to preserve the space of a community from all conceivable threats. This prophylactic virtue was perhaps the one that aroused the fiercest passions; alone it justified the deep attachment to bells until the symbolic tie between ringing and communities began to unravel.

There was perfectly respectable theological justification for this function, as expounded by the abbot Jean-Baptiste Thiers in the *Traité des cloches*, one of his posthumously published works. Invoking the church fathers, John Chrystosom in particular, as well as the key texts of the Catholic Reformation, Thiers distinguished faith in the preservative virtue of bells from the cluster of superstitions that he set out to denounce in order to purify beliefs.[33] As far as he was concerned the formulas used in the benediction justified belief in the preservative virtue of the sacred bronze.

Demons dwelt in the air and were responsible for the spread of plagues and epizootic diseases. They precipitated swarms of insects, unleashed storms, provoked floods, and produced frosts. Above all, their aerial presence prevented prayer.

The point is that the demons were horrified by the sound of bells; they had only to hear them and they would let witches fall on the roads to the sabbath, and take flight. Bells were credited with the power to drive away thunder, thunderstorms, and tempests, and cleanse the air of every infernal presence. "Such effects are not achieved naturally," Jean-Baptiste Thiers elaborated, " but through the divine virtue impressed upon them when one blesses them, or when one rings them against these meteors."[34]

Bells also possessed the crucial power to summon angels. Belief in this virtue may be traced back to the angelology of the Catholic Reformation, which says that the universe was peopled with large numbers of supernatural beings.[35] These "holy undulations of the consecrated bronze," the abbot Sauveterre would write many years later, are chiefly intended to "open up a passage for the good angels."[36] Jean-Baptiste Thiers observed that bells were rung "to invite the angels to join in the prayers of the faithful." As a "palace of heaven," the church is by nature "the residence of angels,"[37] as John Chrystosom and, much later, Carlo Borromeo, never tired of repeating.

Bells had the power to break up the maleficent clouds that impeded the perpetual movement of angels and prevented contact between heaven and earth. There is nothing surprising, then, about the way campanarian epigraphy returns again and again to the same themes. Right up until the middle of the nineteenth century the bronze of the bells still proclaimed their protective virtues, which were inscribed on the older instruments and engraved upon the new. The phrase *Fugo fulmina* or "I drive away thunderbolts" is the inscription on the bell in Vebret (Cantal); the local inhabitants' trust in it is such that they have nicknamed it "Saouque Terre de Vebret."[38] The term *Sauveterre* is frequently found in the region, for example in Marcillac-la-Croizille and Concèze in the department of the Corrèze. The tenor bell in Forcalquier, in the Basses-Alpes, was nicknamed "Maria Sauvaterra." "Wherever my voice goes, none shall perish by storm" we read on two bells at Montain (Tarn-et-Garonne). Likewise in Saccourvielle (Haute-Garonne) and Sulac (Gironde), where the inscriptions liken the voice of the bells to the voice of God, which has the power to subdue tempests.[39] In Périgord[40] there are countless allusions to such a protective power. The phrases *pestem fugo* and *nubem fugo* feature in Sarlande, Coulaures, Bergerac, and Faux, in each case on bells cast between 1864 and 1883. I should also mention a number of other phrases such as *fulgura pello*, *fulgura frango*, *fulgura compello*, *nimbum fugo*, and *impetusque tempestatum pello*. A tenor bell made for the church of Saint Stephen in Périgueux in 1863 bears the inscription *daemones fugo*. Elsewhere it is the protective virtue as such which is designated, notably by the words *tuba salutaris*.

In 1868 the tenor bell at Saint-Mammès Cathedral in Langres was recast. The new bell still bore the inscription *nimbum fugo*,[41] which led the astronomer Camille Flammarion to voice his objections in *Le Siècle*. Two years before, in his *Causeries*, Edmond About had warned with irony that simply to repeat ancient phrases would be to risk a loss of meaning. He wondered whether the archaeologist of 1965, upon reading such inscriptions, might not naively assume that all Frenchmen under the Second Empire still believed in the magical properties of bronze.[42] I shall take this as a cue to turn to the question of actual practice in this period.

In the eighteenth century there is evidence everywhere for the customs associated with such beliefs, so there is no need to labor the point. In Ambert (Puy-de-Dôme) the inhabitants of the countryside would come when there were thunderstorms and ring from six in the morning to six in the evening. The townsfolk would take over for them during the night. "The parish priest would give in his Sunday sermon the order to ring in cases of bad weather."[43] Parishioners unable to play their part were supposed to arrange for someone to take their place, paying for this service a fee of between fifteen to twenty *sols*. In some villages the schoolmaster was responsible for organizing the bell ringing under such circumstances. In Sennely-en-Sologne "they rang three times a day and sometimes hourly," especially between 25 March and Ascension Day, to ward off thunderstorms and evil influences.

In 1772 the fury of the local people was so great that the bishop of Metz was forced to retract, at least in part, his ban on ringing during thunderstorms and springtime frosts.[44] This practice was then one of the bell ringers' customary obligations. If we read "the regulation governing the ringing of the bells at Cormicy," dated 1767, we find that "the ringers shall be expected to ring whenever there are thunderclouds, day or night."[45] Likewise, in 1792 Mr. Vinot was hired by the municipal council of Plappeville (Moselle) to carillon during thunderstorms."[46] In 1789 the parishioners of Auzouer complained in their *cahier de doléances** that "since our parish priest has banned the ringing of bells when the thunderstorms come, the wretched parish has been quite flattened by hail."[47] As we have already seen, resistance to the silencing of the bells by the First Republic was often due to deep attachment to the practice of ringing during storms.[48]

Such practices were consistent with the "deep temporality" presupposed by the daily struggle with the devil,[49] yet the more enlightened bishops were irked by them. Enlightenment rationalism and the concern of élites to set a distance between themselves and the system of popular beliefs[50] together fostered the view—despite the arguments of Jean-Baptiste Thiers—that the protective properties of bells should be branded superstition. Such notions were thought to be often found coiled up within even the most dogmatically pure beliefs.

This new attitude of distrust led to the adoption of two distinct approaches. The first involved suggesting natural explanations for a property so often attested to. For example the power of bells could be accounted for in terms of neo-Hippocratic explanations of airborne contagion, theories of infection, and in some ways, the new field of pneumatic chemistry that was growing out of the analysis of the constituent elements of air. A bell's sound, the worthy abbot Pluche recognized, could perhaps "mechanically penetrate" a cloud.[51] This scientific explanation had been advanced long before but Jean-Baptiste Thiers rejected it out of hand. Nonetheless, the Illiers affair had reinforced the hypothesis. On 17 May 1703, as Parent recorded in a 1710 issue of the *Journal des Savants*,[52] the Beauce was devastated by massive hailstones. The residents of Illiers, however, "rang so vigorously that the thunderstorm split above their parish and divided into two parts, each of which went its own way. The result was that this parish alone, in the midst of thirty others that did not have such good bells, suffered virtually no damage." Blavignac assures us that similar stories were told almost everywhere.

The sound of a bell, according to some Enlightenment scholars, might serve to "rarefy" the air; it would stir up health-giving currents capable

---

*cahiers de doléances: grievance lists, drawn up by each of the three "orders" in each electoral district at the time of the elections to the Estates-General in 1789.

of disturbing, and therefore *correcting* the atmospheric mass. In short, the sound waves from a bell possessed properties that some ascribe to cannon. Elsewhere I have shown how coherent such theories were.[53] In the case of bells, however, this sort of explanation was far from convincing the majority of enlightened minds.

During the second half of the eighteenth century, advocates of the Enlightenment preferred to emphasize the risks involved in ringing during thunderstorms and would compile lists of the accidents that had occurred. It was far more common at this time for the dangers of electricity to be denounced than for the purificatory properties of bells to be celebrated. Abbot Pluche, without denying the capacity of bells to pierce a thundercloud with their sound, assured his readers that on five separate occasions he had seen lightening strike bell towers in which people were ringing.[54] He said he had been informed of twenty such accidents; the number of bell ringers struck by lightening was, according to him, beyond count. Churches that remained silent during a thunderstorm seemed better protected from catastrophe than were the ringing churches. Some also noted that ringing bells in the mountains could set off massive avalanches.[55]

Such considerations may account for the tightening of sometimes ancient prohibitions. As early as the sixteenth century, several regulations had banned ringing during thunderstorms[56] in, for example, Lausanne and the canton of Vaud. In 1747 the Académie Royale des Sciences spelled out the dangers of such a practice and, as we have already seen, an episcopal statute of 1768 banned bell ringing during thunderstorms and springtime frosts in the diocese of Metz. On 15 May 1781, a circular signed by a councillor at the court of Nancy called upon parish priests to acquaint their parishioners with the truth in this matter. Finally a judgement of the Parlement de Paris, dated 29 July 1784 and ratified in 1787, "prohibits all persons from ringing the bells during thunderstorms."[57] The regulations published by prefects and bishops at the beginning of the nineteenth century reiterated this ban.

The episcopate was now willing to regard the sound of the bell as *a prayer* addressed to God, calling upon Him to dispel the thunder. Whereas people had always believed, the abbot Sauveterre objected in 1859, in these "mysterious signs of its metal that were supposed to guarantee its efficacy with God," here the sound of the bell was interpreted as no more than a "discreet invitation to prayer."[58] The abbot was right to stress how much the scope of thunderstorm bell ringing had been reduced.

In truth, there are numerous accounts of opposition shown by local people to such disciplinary measures. Among the clergy themselves and in the ranks of the theologians there was stiff resistance. Admittedly, Monsignor Giraud, bishop of Rodez, in a pastoral letter on bells read in November 1841 and designed to serve as a point of reference, urged his listeners to view bell ringing as prayer and to stop resorting to bells the moment the thunder began. Conversely, other ecclesiastics remained loyal to the old beliefs, basing their position on the ritual of blessing the bells and the study of their symbolism. They regarded the old beliefs as forms of resistance to modern rationalism. In 1838 the learned François Arago furnished them with an unanticipated weapon. "In the current state of science," he wrote in *L'Annuaire du bureau des Longitudes*, "there is no proof that the sound of bells renders thunderclaps more imminent and more dangerous, nor that a loud noise has ever caused a thunderbolt to fall."[59]

Be that as it may, people almost everywhere went on believing in the preservational property of bells.[60] According to Blavignac, peasants were often heard to say: "in such-and-such a year, on such-and-such a day, and at such-and-such an hour, no sooner had our bell begun ringing than we saw the hail receding."[61] In 1865 Dieudonné Dergny confirmed that the practice of thunderstorm ringing was still widespread in the nineteenth century, particularly in the Midi.[62] Scrutiny of archival documents bears out the truth of this claim. A resident of the commune of Courlon claimed in 1834 that the practice had in fact "become ever more firmly entrenched since 1807; on 23 August 1807, a terrible thunderstorm, an atrocious hail wiped out the entire agricultural yield of the area, submerged several houses, lifted off their roofs; the residents who had not rung on that day have come to regret it bitterly. Thus, ever since that time, the inhabitants have forewarned one another by turns to ring, day and night, when a thunderstorm is looming, and no municipal authority would dare to reform this type of bell ringing, for fear of drawing down upon it the wrath of the populace."[63]

In Labrousse (Cantal) a bloody battle erupted in 1831 between the residents of the upper village and those of the lower village; "the former wishing to ring the bells, and the latter claiming that [for this reason] they were forever suffering thunderstorms." There was bloodshed[64] and the church was laid under an interdict. In 1837 the mayor admitted to the prefect that he dreaded a repetition of such a drama. In this department the practice survived until the very end of the century. On 10 and 11 July, wrote the Mayor of Roannes-Saint-Mary in 1896, some thunderstorms afflicted the region; "bells were rung so as to halt or *divert* their advance." On this same date the prefect reprimanded the Mayor of Leucamp for permitting ringing during a thunderstorm. Those who did not ring, as had been the case formerly with the residents of the lower town in Labrousse, believed that the practice was effective since they complained of being the victims of their neighbors who had rung. In 1897 the Mayor of Marcolès informed the prefect of his grievances, which were phrased so as to make it plain that he shared this belief.

In 1846 the practice of ringing during thunderstorms seemed ineradicable in the Puy-de-Dôme. In the commune of Chauriat-par-Vertaizon the ban introduced by the parochial church council in 1817 was never respected. In the region as a whole, M. du Miral observed in a letter to the *ministre de la Justice et des Cultes*, "very few parish priests oppose these forms of illegal bell ringing because they believe that they pay homage to religion."[65] However, he continued, many of these "troublemakers do not believe in God."

In 1839 the prefect of the Gers denounced the dangers involved in ringing during thunderstorms and likewise regretted that "*in most communes* a deplorable prejudice [should cause this] practice to prevail."[66] The parish priest of Lavardens refused to interrupt such ringing: "formerly, in the parish . . . a similar ban [was] imposed by the administrative authorities in the department [and] the people proceeded *en masse* to the bell tower during a thunderstorm, broke down the doors, and rang, regardless of the ban."[67] He feared further unrest and argued that one should settle for tolling the bell on such occasions.

The results of a survey ordered in 1845 by Monsignor Rendu, and conducted by parish priests in the north of Savoie, confirmed the attachment of the local population to thunderstorm ringing. In this region belief in the prophylactic properties of bronze was reinforced by the flourishing cult of Saint Theodulus, whose principal attribute was a bell. In Flumet, according to the rector, the phrase inscribed on the instrument "says" that the storm bell "contains relics of [its] patron, Saint Theodulus. In the church there is a painting of Saint Theodulus with the demon at his feet, his head beneath a bell. . . ."[68] In Savoie, whenever a bronze bell was cast it had for centuries been the custom to incorporate into it a fragment from the bell of Sion, which was said to have been transported by the devil under the saint's orders.

In La Chapelle-d'Abondance as in several other parishes, the residents required the parish priest to add his prayers to the storm ringing. This practice was regarded as a form of exorcism. When he hears the first peals of thunder, the rector of this parish writes, the priest must "run to the church door dressed in his surplice with his sprinkler in hand."

The answers given by parish priests to an episcopal survey ordered by Monsignor Dupanloup prove that the practice of "having the bells rung during thunderstorms"[69] was then commonplace in the Orléans diocese. Here too, prayer was associated with bell ringing. When it thundered the parish priests would hasten to the church and read the story of the Passion while the bell ringer carillonned.

Politics sometimes insinuated itself into the banned practice, extending the scope of meteorological bell ringing. In the commune of Vahl-lès-Faulquemont (Moselle)[70] it remained the custom until 1845 to ring every evening after the Angelus throughout the month of May to protect fields and orchards from spring frosts. Young people between ten and fifteen years old took on this task and, according to the parish priest, made a fearful racket in the bell tower. That year the priest decided to prohibit the practice, but this harsh measure was then denounced by the mayor as a politically motivated decision. The first of May, Saint-Philippe's Day, was in fact a national holiday that parish priests and servers were supposed to announce the day before by ringing all the bells. It was to be celebrated the following morning in the same fashion. The parish priest of Vahl-lès-Faulquemont naturally denied that his motives had been in any sense political. It is therefore impossible for us to interpret his severity.[71]

In Choiseul (Haute-Marne), to judge by the mayor's account (who banned this same practice in 1862), the parish priest piously observed storm ringing because it represented a significant source of income. He "was very determined to preserve this custom for which he levied, just as he did for his telling of the Passion, a sheaf of corn from the dwelling of each agricultural worker."[72] No other testimony refers to a surreptitious tithe of this kind.

Up until 1870,[73] claims Samuel Bour,[74] author of the most scientific of the campanarian surveys, the population of the Moselle continued to believe in the protective virtues of bells in thunderstorms. They ascribed powers to bell ringing that went well beyond mere meteorology. The residents of this department believed that bells possessed therapeutic properties. In Breidenbach they were still convinced that someone afflicted with warts would be cured if he washed in mud while the death knell was tolling. A doctor from the Moselle, having broken a leg, had to have it amputated; "throughout the operation all the bells of Forbach were rung." One could view this act as simply a call to prayer.

Jean Nanglard supplies many examples of the belief of the local populations of the Charente in the curative properties of bells. At Saint-Amant-de-Bonnieure the old bell was held "to communicate through its rope the property of protecting vulnerable children from rickets. A mother would hold her little patient with the rope draped beneath its armpits and pray to Saint Amant to intercede in the child's favor."[75] This source further emphasizes the bond between the bronze of the bell and the cult of the saints, whose powers as healers were widely acknowledged in the Charente.

Demons abhorred bells, hence the belief, recorded once again by Samuel Bour, "of which I had often heard tell in my youth, that transporting milk outside after the evening bell has rung is to render it vulnerable to the influence of witches."[76] In Réding the liquid was thought to turn black and spoil. "Similarly, if one took some leaven to a neighbor after the evening bell had rung, one was supposed to remove a small portion to rid it of the influence of witches." Bour had many times heard it said "that one must never leave the stable doors open after the evening bell has rung," since evil spirits might block the cows' milk. "Indeed, for many, the evening bell marked the hour at which evil spirits and ghosts were at liberty to pass through the darkness of the night and to do harm."

Here, however, I am straying beyond the limits of my chosen topic.[77] While such practices were designed to protect auditory space, we should not neglect another function performed by bells, namely, that connected with the organizing of a community's temporal markers.

Interwoven Rhythms

The relations binding bell ringing to the flow of time consist of an interweaving of aims, meanings, issues, and conflicts, all of which call for careful analysis. We need here to take into account the complex organization of auditory signals in the nineteenth century along with peoples' many different experiences of time. The temporal architecture of life, the habitus, and the culture of the senses have altered so much that there is a grave risk of our losing the meaning of this history altogether.

One of the most obvious processes, of which scholars have long been aware, is only indirectly of concern to us here. I am referring to the shift from a "qualitative time" to a "quantitative time,"[78] and therefore to the tension between announcements respecting the flow of the continuous, measured, precise time of the clock, and the marking through bell ringing of a few, privileged moments in the year, the week and the day, the repetition of which served to anchor the sense of immobile time. I shall have more to say later concerning the depth and intensity of the conflicts that pitted the bell against the gong of a clock and caused the ancient privileges of the bell ringer to clash with the novel claims of the "winder." Control over quantitative time conferred increasing power upon the winder, especially in "clock regions" such as northeastern and east central France.[79] It precipitated a host of local disputes, chiefly over the guarding of the presbytery, the holding of keys, and the accessibility of bell tower ropes.[80] The clergy did not deny the usefulness of the clock and its striking of the hours, but they looked with distrust, especially in the countryside, on the introduction of measured time, the implacable regularity of which led insidiously to the desacralizing of the days.

What concerns us here is the role of bell ringing in the temporal architecture of communities at a time when public clock and private clock alike were rare, and everyday use of a watch was still the preserve of a tiny élite. "Most residents have no clock," observed the Mayor of Velaines (Meuse) on 28 March 1852,[81] although such instruments were more widespread there than in most other regions of France. "The great majority [of farm hands] do not have a watch," wrote the Mayor of Recoubeau (Drôme) in 1890.[82] Furthermore, ownership and use should not be confused, especially in this sphere. At the beginning of the twentieth century a field hand who owned a watch would scarcely "wear" it at all, except on Sundays. On 25 August 1907, the Mayor of Les Bottereaux (Eure) remarked upon the fact that "the laborers generally do not bring their watches for fear of losing them in the harvesting."[83] Conversely, since nuances are crucial in such matters, it did not take many laborers in the fields wearing a watch for it to become something to which the group might refer. In 1866 the parish priest of Autrécourt (Meuse) wrote regarding "agricultural laborers": "*Several* nowadays accord themselves the readily granted luxury of a portable watch. . . . consequently, it is enough to catch sight of *one* woman making her way back [at eleven o'clock] to prepare the midday meal, prompted by one of these watches, for the other women to take the same road," inasmuch as "work-gangs toil within sight of one another."[84]

The study of the part played by bells in the construction of the temporal markers of individuals and communities represents a page in the history of the habitus, and of the way in which it is attuned to biological rhythms. Such a study helps us understand how existences were once shaped. The sound of bells dictated the meaning of delay, the sense of being ahead or behind, and the forms assumed by haste. The act of getting dressed on Sunday mornings and preparing for one's entrance on the public stage was punctuated by bells and governed by a jerky estimation of the flow of time. The regulations agreed between bishop and prefect regarding the spacing, duration, and grading of announcements were fixed with a degree of precision that might surprise us. Until the end of the nineteenth century prelates did what they could to have the bells rung on Sundays and feast days several times, and for at least half an hour before morning and afternoon service. The prefects, on the other hand, tried to restrict every manifestation of this auditory ascendancy.

When dealing with so complex a subject of study one should be wary of being snared by too unambiguous an interpretation. The act of listening to bells and the various modes of attention it entailed were subject to imperceptible slippages in meaning, and to substitutions so subtle as to all but elude us. These were linked in turn to the confused spread of new

rhythms and increasingly to the requirement that everything be understood in terms of continuous clock time. A listener hearing both the
striking of the hours and the more solemn pauses marking services or
ceremonies had to cast his response in terms of a double temporal system. It is very hard for us to reconstruct the gradual transfer of emotion
achieved at the expense of a cyclical notion of time—the sacred nature
of which was attested to by the changing colors of priestly vestments—
and to the advantage of remorseless, continuously flowing time. Yet in
every case it was the signals emanating from the bell tower that at the
same time reflected and shaped this virtually imperceptible process.

A bell ringer had to avoid confusing the reiteration of signals evoking
immobile time, which established a sacral ascendancy, with the punctua-
tion effected by the gong of a clock or the sounding of the alarm and the
making of public announcements—forms of bell ringing that were
strictly conjunctural and served the material interests of the community.
In short, nineteenth-century bell ringing simultaneously sustained the
traditional architecture of existence and responded to the ever more
clamorous demands of modernity that were driven on by the need to
come to terms with all-embracing systems for the measurement and evaluation of time.

PRECISE TIMEKEEPING AND SENSE-IMPRESSIONS

I propose to divide this part of my study into two stages. First
I wish to consider together the process by which the bell gradually yielded to precise timekeeping, its enduring loyalty to a cosmic time determined by the perceptible duration of day and night, and the persistent
diversity of local customs. In those communes lacking a clock—and until
the end of the century they were in the majority—the bell ringer would
go by the sundial, although the postman might sometimes give him more
precise information.[85] In some regions, although a minority, no attempt
was made, during the first half of the century at any rate, to set the hours
of bell ringing with any precision. The crucial thing was to go by one's
sense impressions. The concerted regulation signed in 1804 in the department of the Tarn stipulated that the evening Angelus should be rung "at

sunset."[86] In 1834 the bishop of Aire specified that tolling should commence "toward nightfall."[87]

Generally speaking, residents expected cosmic rhythms and those of bell ringing to correspond. On 24 February 1806[88] the bishop of Montpellier issued a regulation setting the morning Angelus at five o'clock for Eastertide, at half past five in the summer, at six o'clock in the midseason and at half past six in winter. He thereby hoped to tie in the times of the Angelus with those for the opening and shutting of churches. This measure provoked a storm of protest; in this "country" it was the custom to go by the sun. The Mayor of Montagnac (Hérault), with the backing of the prefect, required the Angelus to be rung in the morning at three o'clock in summer and at four o'clock in winter. In December 1844 the mayor of Breuvannes, the homeland of bell makers, voiced his concerns to the prefect of the Haute-Marne. "The priest in charge," he wrote, "has the Angelus rung morning and evening in an unsuitable fashion since they ring them in the morning two hours before dawn, and likewise in the evening, two hours after dusk. This state of affairs has caused much muttering among residents."[89]

It had been customary, noted the Mayor of Berthouville (Eure) in 1901, to implement the change in the hours of bell ringing, both in spring and in summer, almost imperceptibly. That year, however, the bell ringer decided to abide by the regulations and to make the change from one day to the next. The commune was in an uproar. Routines were disrupted by the brutality of a measure of time that did not tally with sense impressions. The debate was of great significance and merits closer scrutiny. The custom since time "immemorial," wrote the mayor invoking the "forever" of immobile time, had been to change the bell ringing schedule "around October." The "time lag in the morning and the gain in the evening [were] *gradually* altered, with the result that around 15 or 20 October the bell ringing [took place] *around* half past five in the morning and around half past six in the evening" in accordance with the law of 17 Messidor Year IX, which set the hours of work in the fields. The same procedure was followed in the neighboring communes (Bernay arrondissement) until well after the implementation of the 1885 regulation. In 1901, however, "an *attempt at a sudden change*" was also made:

"from seven o'clock in the evening, on 30 September last, the ringing of the bells has been moved, on 1 October, to six o'clock in the evening. The same applies in the morning." "This attempt met with strong protests." The mayor remarked upon "the negative effects of this sudden change"; he therefore "so arranged things that a return was made to the old customs." The municipal councillors were *unanimous* in backing his decision to "change nothing."[90]

Although this episode reflects the attitudes of a minority, at least if we consult the text of the regulations, it shows clearly how at the dawn of the twentieth century France remained a patchwork of customs and systems of temporal markers; it highlights the *resistance* that was felt toward the surreptitiously introduced dislocation between cosmic time and that of global society, which had not long before, in 1891, become official time.[91]

The handful of incidents in the nineteenth century precipitated by the discrepancy between the ringing of bells to punctuate the daily routine and the impressions of one's senses are the culmination of conflicts extending over whole centuries; their multifariousness indicates the importance of the issues at stake. In this regard the case of the communes near Auxerre is significant. Since the fourteenth century, landowners in the town had disagreed with the vine growers and the journeymen, laborers who lived in the country, over vesperal ringing. The landowners wanted work to go on until sunset in summer whereas the vine growers and laborers felt that their toil should end well before dark. Over the centuries the difference led to "deeply entrenched hatreds."[92]

In March 1392, a regulation issued by Charles VI in the form of letters patent, confirmed by decree of the Parlement in 1393 and again in 1447, required vine growers and day laborers to work until sunset. But this ruling quickly proved inoperable. Workers first won back as much time as they needed to get home without "stopping on their way" before the setting of the sun. Subsequently the cathedral peal that enabled the laborers to keep time could be heard not only before sunset but earlier and earlier. In the eighteenth century the bell giving the signal to stop work was rung at six in the evening, a full two hours before the designated time.

In 1887 the custom was still followed. The bell sounded "at the setting of the sun, when this star disappears over the horizon before six o'clock, and invariably at six o'clock when it sets later, which is the case from 13 March to 21 September." In the same fashion, laborers had over the centuries won the right to have the announcement of the "shortened Mass" delayed, although it was supposed to ring "when dawn was visible in the chapel of Notre Dame des Virtus." The end of this service in fact served to mark the start of the working day.

It is worth pointing out that throughout France the Angelus was rung at different times in summer and winter. In only one case have I found someone expressing reservations about this shift, which was endorsed by all the regulations. On 20 April 1891, the Mayor of Domloup (Ille-et-Vilaine) regretted that the Angelus was not rung at the same hour in summer and winter; in his view, as transmitted by the prefect to the archbishop of Rennes, "this arrangement would to some extent inconvenience the farmers, who are accustomed to calculating the working days of those they have hired in terms of the relevant peals."[93] The mayor was in favor of setting a single hour and ringing the Angelus at six o'clock, morning and evening, regardless of the season. As is apparent, the request reflected a wish to be modern, and not a concern to defend an existing custom. The archbishop of Rennes then set up an interesting inquiry, which revealed that those working the land were not of one mind. Some in that commune favored the single hour while others remained *loyal to the very ancient custom* of changing the bell ringing times in spring and autumn.

I should elaborate on this point. Shifting the times of the Angelus according to the season was a matter of tradition as well as a procedure designed to accompany the movements of the sun, not to gainsay them. The duplication of time signals was not designed—in contrast with present-day practices—to obscure, let alone deny synaesthetic perception of the shift; the change in times of the Angelus served to tie the length of the working day to that of the actual day. It was a seasonal procedure, in accordance with the evidence of the senses, that allowed a closer adaptation to the rhythms of the cosmos and served to justify the coincidence between the movements of the sun and awareness of the matutinal and the vesperal.[94]

To conform to the results of the surveys conducted earlier, the first published regulations governing bell ringing, jointly agreed to by prefects and bishops, tied the change to the celebration of the two festivals of Easter and All Saints' Day. The series of regulations agreed upon in 1884–1885[95] placed the shift in the majority of cases on 31 March and 30 September. Let me emphasize this desacralizing of markers, which was accepted by the episcopate, and which was designed to achieve a closer fit between the date on which the hour changed and the date on which the equinox fell.

Analysis of all the concerted regulations of the nineteenth century has much more to teach us. Throughout the century the custom prevailed of ringing the morning Angelus at four o'clock in summer and five o'clock in winter; the evening Angelus was rung at nine o'clock in summer and eight o'clock in winter. Under the July Monarchy there were sixteen concerted regulations published that specified the hour of the Angelus and, of these sixteen, fourteen followed the schedule outlined above.[96] Of the sixty-three concerted regulations published between 1884 and 1885 I have managed to find—not to mention nine standardized regulations covering times of services that contain identical prescriptions[97]—thirty-four stipulate that the morning Angelus be rung according to the above schedule, and fifteen leave the parish priest at liberty to choose between four and five o'clock. Forty-two of the sixty-three regulations specify that ringing in the evening should be at nine o'clock in the summer and eight o'clock in winter.

Although their rationale is not always easy to discern, regional disparities nonetheless exist. We can make out pockets of *matutinal bell ringing*, which are to be found in mountainous regions (half past three in summer in Haute-Savoie) but also in areas with a gentler terrain (Côte-d'or, Tarn: three o'clock or four o'clock in summer, and four o'clock or five o'clock in winter), and which tend to be in the north, the east (regulations for the Haut-Rhin, for the territory of Belfort; the customs of the Meuse), and the center (Nièvre, Corrèze).

In some departments seemingly scattered at random across France, ringing would be later than elsewhere, though here again the rationale is obscure. In the Deux-Sèvres, the Vienne, the Marne, the Loire, and the Rhône, the regulations stipulated in 1884 and 1885 that the Angelus be rung at five o'clock in summer and six o'clock in winter. In the Vaucluse and the Savoie ringing in winter was fixed at half past five. There were some ten departments, likewise scattered across the national territory, in which the regulation stipulated that ringing was to be at ten o'clock in the evening in summer and nine or ten o'clock in winter.

Customs often varied from commune to commune so that within one department one might encounter pockets with stronger or weaker matutinal rhythms. The 1884 regulation specified that in Charente-Inférieure some communes, in contrast to their neighbors, were given to ringing the Angelus before four o'clock in summer.[98] The regulation from this same date for Loire-Inférieure[99] allowed the parish priest to modify the schedule to fit the size of the commune and that of its population. Earlier ringing, morning and evening, was permitted in some villages in that department. Despite their doubtful legal status, the municipal decrees decided upon between 1907 and 1910 (in the aftermath of the law of Separation of Church and State in the departments of the Eure and Eure-et-Loir) highlight such disparities from commune to commune.[100]

One could perhaps deduce the time allotted to sleep, or at least to nighttime rest, by calculating the time between the ringing of the *"retreat"*—not to be confused with the evening Angelus[101]—and the morning bell. This would leave six to *seven* hours in summer (from ten or nine o'clock in the evening to four o'clock in the morning)[102] and eight to nine hours in the winter. Such a calculation seems plausible where summer is concerned. Conversely, in those areas where it existed, the winter *veillée** brought neighbors together until about nine, ten, or eleven o'clock.[103] Under such circumstances sleep could not have lasted longer than six, seven, or eight hours, even in winter. Countless testimonies in fact suggest that in rural areas it was the custom to go to bed earlier in summer than in winter because of fatigue from work in the fields.

In some cases the seasonal shift in ringing times was considerable. To judge by the municipal decree of the mayor of Verdun[104] dated 14 October 1907, the bells could be rung from three in the morning until nine at night between 1 May and 1 October, and from half past five until half past eight the rest of the year. This implied that the stipulated period

---

veillée: a gathering on winter evenings of peasants, generally neighbors or kin, for sedentary labor, relaxation, and edification. There might, for example, be spinning, knitting, embroidering, and the plaiting of baskets and, in addition, singing and storytelling.

of silence and undisturbed rest amounted to six hours in summer and to nine hours in winter. It is tempting to correlate such figures to the nychthemeral rhythm of the population, but it would be rash to assume such a correlation.

I will end this brief survey with a number of provisional conclusions: (1) Standardization of usages and rhythms was only very slowly achieved, so that on the eve of the First World War the process was far from being complete. (2) Well before the hours were officially defined by law (1891) there was a growing concern in rural areas to have the bells' messages relate to a more precise system of timekeeping. (3) Nevertheless, the seasonal shift in the Angelus remained, and we know that morning, noon, and night the ringing of bells dictated the daily rhythms of country life. At the dawn of the twentieth century, customary usage did not yet reflect the blithe disregard for the sun's movements that structures our own awareness of time.

The crucial aspect of my inquiry, however, is situated at another level where I seek to analyze in the sphere of bell ringing the efforts made to reconcile the signals of a "sacrally organic time with the secular time of the modern epoch"; or, considering the question from a diametrically opposed point of view, I try to assess the varying degrees of tension between these two notions of time and identify "blurring, where it has occurred" or conversely, "persisting separation."[105]

Conflict (which was by no means unusual) or attempted reconciliation are situated at three different levels of temporality, namely, liturgical time, ceremonial time, and the everyday rhythm of the hours.

THE SCANSION OF THE LITURGICAL YEAR

I will begin by considering the time that is founded on the cyclical aspect of the liturgical year, which involves "so perfect a correspondence between the drama of redemptive history and the annual astral cycle that it has virtually become unconscious," and which requires, when all is said and done, a "rejection of the continuous, homogeneous time of calendar and clock."[106]

When the use of bells in the context of worship was restored at the dawn of the nineteenth century, it was officially restricted to Sundays—

Easter Sunday and the Pentecost being among them—and to the four permitted festivals of All Saints' Day, Christmas Day, the Ascension, and the
Assumption.[107] The other dates formerly celebrated by a respite from
work, namely, Epiphany, Corpus-Christi, the Feast of the Holy Apostles
Peter and Paul, the feast of the patron saint of each diocese and that of
the patron saint of each parish, and the Feast of the Birth of the Virgin,[108]
were now relegated to the status of "devotional festivals" to be celebrated on the following Sunday. They were now officially known as "suppressed festivals," that were distinct from obligatory festivals. This general reorganization of the year's festivals was meant to achieve two objectives, namely, to subvert by stealth the clergy's ascendancy over the local
population, and to reduce the number of holidays. "It matters that the
people work," wrote Portalis in 1806 in a letter designed to justify the new
policy,[109] "since work is for them the best support for the virtues."
"Suppressed festivals" were after all days on which work could be done.
As Portalis went on to observe, "the bells should not be rung on such days
as they are on holidays," for otherwise "the people will conclude that they
should cut short their labors; that would be to mislead them and to act in
a manner directly opposed to His Majesty's intentions." It was Portalis's
view that one should curb the power inherent in the sound of bells, which
could by itself lead the masses to cease work.

And indeed this is precisely what happened. During suppressed festivals, the prefect of the Haut-Rhin insisted on 19 June 1812, priests would
distract the people from their labors: "There is always some pretext or
another; birthdays, blessings, or octave prayers are forever calling the
people to the temple, and *he who remains at his labors when the bell rings is
deemed irreligious.*"[110] This confirms, if confirmation were needed, that
the ringing of a bell was then construed as a command.

The primary sources are explicit on this point.[111] Clergy should
refrain from celebrating suppressed festivals. They should not have bells
rung in peal on such days. At most, they might use the small bell that
announced low masses. By the same token, parish priests and priests in
charge should abstain from announcing the solemn celebration of "devotional festivals" from the pulpit.

This position, however, was to prove untenable. Admittedly, the
authorities had endeavored to enforce the law. In Nivôse Year XII

(December 1803–January 1804), the prefect of Loir-et-Cher showed great firmness in attempting to stamp out abuses brought to his attention.[112] In 1812 the prefect of Finistère, in accord with the bishop of Quimper, called upon mayors and parish priests to come to some sort of agreement and enforce the law.[113] A number of mayors found that such affairs offered them an opportunity to curb the clergy. For example, in 1806 the mayor of Saint-Chinian (Hérault) denounced the custom "of major ringing of bells" on days of "suppressed festivals" or confraternity festivals. "The people were [in fact] persuaded that the suppression of festivals was chimerical since the church was celebrating them. . . . and consequently they thought that they were obliged to observe the *religious immobility* prescribed for such occasions." "The people are muttering," noted the churchwardens of the parish, "since such celebrations are permitted in neighboring departments and in several communes in our own department."[114] This proves, again if proof were needed, just how ineffectual such prescriptions were in the heyday of the First Empire. In 1807 the priest in charge at Saint-Juéry (Tarn) observed the ban on ringing for "suppressed festivals," but noted that they were ringing in all the neighboring communes. His parishioners accused him of wishing "to stand out."[115]

Under the Restoration the expansion of religious bell ringing kept the repressive intent of the secular authorities at bay. During the July Monarchy, on the other hand, conflicts over bells focused, at least in some regions, on the thorny question of "suppressed festivals." The clergy in fact recognized here an opportunity to issue a *challenge* to the municipal authorities who, in their opinion, had become pretentious and meddling. It was in some such terms that the prefect of the Moselle interpreted the wish of the bishop and clergy of Metz to increase the number of occasions upon which bells were rung for religious purposes, particularly on "suppressed festivals." Someone out to denounce such moves wrote on 11 September 1845 to the prefect, recording that, "on the eighth of this month, the day of the Nativity [of the Virgin], a festival that was not preserved, *all* the bells of Metz were ringing *the whole day long*."[116] It is "with pride," declared the mayor of Saint-Georges-sur-Eure in 1836, that the parish priest rings the suppressed festivals.[117] On the morning of 9 December Louis the Great [sic], rural guard for Nonancourt, made a formal statement respecting "the use of the bell *in peal*"; he further stated that in the afternoon *two* bells summoned the local population to Vespers.[118] The commune was preoccupied for almost a year with the question of whether or not to ring on suppressed festivals. In Rugles events took a truly serious turn. In 1834 the mayor complained that the younger priests, unlike their elders, liked to provoke the municipal authorities by having bells rung on such days. In an area with factories this led people to "abandon work," and thus to "*debauchery*" and "dissolute conduct in the home,"[119] all unintended consequences that one was led to suppose came from using bells. The parish priest defended himself, claiming that he rang with due ceremony on days celebrated as feasts by confraternities,[120] just as the entire region did. It happened that such days sometimes coincided with suppressed festivals.

In June 1831 the mayor of Landivisiau (Finistère) clashed with the parish priest over the question of banned ringing. It was the verger's practice at this time to ring the "*main Angelus*" with the great bell. The mayor, in a conciliatory spirit, allowed him "to ring a peal, but only once, with the curfew bell." The parish priest objected that "all the bells are rung at Morlaix," and refused to comply. Besides, he went on, it had always been the custom to ring Landivisiau's bells on suppressed festivals. The prefect, being anxious to avoid a direct confrontation, forbade the mayors to give any orders related to this issue.[121] Let me give another example of the impotence of the secular authorities in such matters. On 3 February 1832, the Bishop of Saint-Dié refused to respond when the prefect informed him that people were ringing suppressed festivals in Neufchâteau. As far as the bishop was concerned, the solemn use of bells was a prerequisite for the proper performance of a ceremony.[122]

In 1831, 1832, 1836, and again in 1840, members of the government were in broad agreement; whether Finistère, Seine-et-Marne, the Orne, the Sarthe, or the Mayenne was involved,[123] ministerial rulings invariably urged *tolerance* and *respect for customs*. All that mattered was that preserved festivals and "devotional" festivals be announced differently and that the clergy should not treat them as obligatory. The pragmatic policies of the July Monarchy were designed above all to "avoid direct confrontation." "*Experience has shown* for as long as the Empire lasted," noted the Minister of Justice on 28 February 1839, "that it was impossible to achieve the complete suppression of the festivals in question; the wishes and customs of the masses have constantly prevailed over government intervention."[124] This seems a belated admission that liturgical time was in fact firmly rooted in popular practices.

There is plenty of other evidence to bear out this point. Regardless of the degree of religious fervor in a given population, the ringing of the major divisions of the liturgical year imparted a rhythm to the life of the community. These traditional practices may sometimes have inspired mistrust, even hostility, in members of the clergy, but they seem to have been deeply rooted. Unfortunately, in this sphere too, the scattered nature of the evidence defies summary.

According to Arnold Van Gennep, the custom of ringing Advent, known in some regions as "Little Christmas," was widespread in the French countryside. In his opinion this part of the year possessed a kind of "folkloric autonomy." In the Charente Advent had "from time immemorial" been announced every evening by ringing, tolling, or peals *ad libitum*.[125] Some attributed prophylactic properties to this ringing since Advent was regarded as a dangerous period. The practice was particularly widespread in the Angoumois. "No sooner had the tolling started than everyone fell silent. . . . the bell towers of the neighboring villages then gradually responded. It was the young people of the village who set the bells ringing for half an hour, then there was silence, likewise for a half an hour, and the ringing would start up again, continuing until morning. Each village had a different way of ringing, and the old men knew how to distinguish between them."

Precisely dated sources bear out the existence of such practices in the nineteenth century. In the Cantal it was traditional to "carillon"—in this case to ring a peal—during the nine, ten, or twelve days before Christmas. In Chaudes-Aigues the ringing was moved forward half an hour each day so that in the end it coincided with the bell announcing midnight Mass. The ringers spun out this carillon for as long as they could, taking breaks for drinking and card games.[126] On 14 December 1841, at half past eight in the evening, they rang in this fashion in Tourniac, against the priest's express instructions. "Exhausted by this noise, [the latter] found no other means of stopping it save that of firing two pistol shots in the general direction of the bell ringers. By a stroke of good fortune only the bells were hit."[127] In 1822 the priest in charge in Aiguines (Var) refused to celebrate midnight Mass and decided to carry the ceremony over to seven o'clock on Christmas morning. During the night, however, some young people climbed onto the roof of the church and set the bells pealing from eleven until two o'clock in the morning.[128]

In some places the bells were rung on Saint Sylvester's Eve to announce the end of the year.[129] In Blangy (Seine-Inférieure) the bell was set ringing at eleven-thirty on the evening of Shrove Tuesday to show "that the period of penitence was about to begin."[130] In the diocese of Amiens in 1865 the bells were rung every Friday at three o'clock in the afternoon to recall Christ's agony. Just a few years before, the bells of Roncherolles-en-Bray and Sommery (Seine-Inférieure) were rung a few moments before midnight on Easter Saturday to announce the Resurrection.[131] In 1841 the mayor of Parnes (Oise) protested at the parish priest's ban on ringing at midnight and Easter Saturday, contrary to what had been the custom "for centuries" in the parish.[132]

During the night of 1 and 2 November in particular, folklore's hold on the ringing of the major divisions of the liturgical year was most evident. This trespass aroused the ire of some members of the clergy and had done so since the seventeenth century and the unfolding of the Catholic Reformation. The church feared that the bells might be broken and, above all, that the bell tower might be turned that night into a place of debauch. It hoped to put a stop to the dances, drinking sessions, and feasting—to all the "impertinences" of the evening of All Souls' Day.[133] This was a conflict that continued into the nineteenth century. We should not forget that in many respects this period saw the triumphant diffusion and internalization of the precepts of the Catholic Reformation.

The community thought to regulate through its own customs the ringing of the bell that greeted and placated its dead on the occasion of their yearly visit.[134] Many priests in charge feared that this was merely a racket inspired by superstition. In spite of this disapproval the lengthy ringing on the eve of 1 November, eve of All Souls' Day, was then a widespread custom. "The night peal," insisted a resident of Courlon (Yonne) in 1834, "took place on 1 November from six in the evening until eight . . . and on the actual day [of the Dead] from five in the morning until nine."[135] Numerous villages in the Moselle[136] at the dawn of the twenti-

eth century would still ring what they termed "the *veillée* of the dead."
They began by ringing the "mortuary" [bell] on All Saints' Eve until
around nine or ten o'clock, depending on the commune. The bell started
up again the next morning at four or five o'clock. In some places they
rang the whole night long. Along the Seille valley this ringing was said
to "ease the passage of souls to heaven." In some parishes the bell was
used throughout the whole octave. On 2 November it was generally the
young people who rang. Having "pulled the bell," they would go around
to all the houses in the village, eating, drinking, and asking for money.

At the end of the century the ringing of the dead still took place in
Normandy. The bishop of Évreux insisted that "the local people are
deeply attached to it."[137] At that same time this type of ringing was a
"general custom" in Corsica, where regulations stipulated that one
should ring until ten o'clock on that particular night.[138]

Some of the conflicts precipitated by "ringing for the dead" arose out
of the authorities' wish to limit the duration of a practice that was in their
view excessive. "It was the custom [in the commune]," wrote the subprefect of Gourdon (Lot) on 2 November 1808, "to have the bells rung for
three or four hours on the eve of All Souls' Day. This prolonged ringing
disturbed the rest of the living." The deputy mayor wished "to put a stop
to such abuses"[139] and therefore ordered that the bell be rung only
between eight and nine in the evening. The bell ringer turned a deaf ear
to this injunction and set to work before the appointed hour. The deputy
major had him "put in prison for a few hours." The subprefect ruled in
the municipal magistrate's favor, and all the more so given that All Souls'
Day was a "suppressed festival."

The members of the parochial church council fought back, however,
arguing that ringing "from nightfall until around nine o'clock in the
evening" was a custom "going so far back in time as to belong to an
epoch past remembering." The deputy mayor banned any ringing before
eight o'clock. However "at seven o'clock the bells of the other parishes
were set ringing [and] several citizens enjoined the lessee of the bells at
the church of Saint Peters to do likewise." At stake was both the honor
of the parish, which was being humiliated by its neighbors, and the quality of the reception accorded its dead. Finally the prefect yielded to the

bishop's entreaties and allowed "the people," who were "deeply attached to their routines," to observe their old customs.

Most disputes were nonetheless precipitated by the desire of mayors not to ban such customs but to compel the clergy, who were mistrustful of all nocturnal bell ringing and opposed to every intrusion of youth inside the bell towers, to maintain them. On 28 January 1833, the bishop of Amiens complained that the mayor of Bussy-lès-Daours (Somme) had the bells rung for several hours, so as to "bestow more *solemnity* upon All Souls' Day."[140] The mayors of Ault and Vignacourt had the bells rung "for five hours in succession without notifying the parish priest first."[141] On All Saints' Day in 1842, the rector of Commana (Finistère) resolved that this "ringing in full peal would be restricted to a relatively short period of time so that the vergers could limit to a very small number the hordes of young people who would come, most of whom treated the occasion as a picnic." His concern was to ensure decorous conduct and "the well-being of the bells."[142] The mayor, however, enjoined the verger "to have the bell ringing on All Souls' Day executed as in the past, that is to say, ringing a peal until ten in the evening." In his defense the mayor invoked "various rumors" and "mutterings" emanating from certain "highly respected persons in the commune," who were opposed to any changes "to a custom handed down from *father to son*." The bishop observed that the mayor was guilty of a second infraction since he had rung a peal when "for the ringing of the dead, one should limit oneself to ringing the passing bell."[143]

Some local customs required bell ringing to announce religious events during the week. In the Ardennes it was still the custom in 1886 to ring every Saturday for an hour, in full peal, what was called "*le grand midi*," to announce the approach of Sunday.[144] On 10 July 1886, the Mayor of Viel-Saint-Rémy instituted proceedings against ringers following what was, in his view, an unauthorized custom. The parish priest objected to the justice of the peace that such had been the practice since time immemorial. Nevertheless, the ringers were sentenced by the police court of Novion-Porcien to a fine of fourteen francs. The archbishop of Reims, Cardinal Langénieux, appealed against this judgment in the Court of Cassation, his view being that it was a custom "enshrined in tradition" and "followed in almost every parish in the department." On 12 May 1887, the Court gave a ruling on the "*grand midi*" affair, quashing the decision of the police court of Novion-Porcien and finding in favor of the prelate. The list of authorized ringing times given in the regulations was, in his opinion, "regarded as indicative and not restrictive."

CEREMONIAL TIME

"Liturgical time," Alphonse Dupront wrote, "contains within itself another level of time that is at once more readily perceived and less easily grasped, namely, *ceremonial time*. . . . The rhythms, cadences, shapes, and processional sequences of a ceremony satisfy many of the deepest needs of the soul."[145] The nineteenth-century episcopate devoted much attention and care to the maintenance, even the elaboration of this, a time that lay within celebration. Harassment by auditory signals helped to inspire the emotion shaping this ceremonial time, whose heyday was under the Old Regime. Although the context is urban, consider by way of example the bell ringing schedule at Bourges cathedral on the eve of the Revolution.[146] The edifice then held four large bells and some eight other medium-sized or small ones. On feast days the "cockerel," whose function was as the name suggests—to rouse the faithful—rang from three o'clock on; it also served "to call the ringers of the great bell" who would then ring a peal they dubbed the "long" for a half hour. The "long" was intended to awaken parishioners living too far from the cathedral to hear the "cockerel." They then rang the "*Manaux*" or "*Monaux*', a carillon of small bells hanging in the old tower. "When the *Monaux* had fallen silent, they rang the *halt*, which indicated *that one had to halt*, set aside whatever one was doing, and make one's way to the church; and, finally, the *entrance to the service*, which was announced by the ringing of all the large bells." As was often the case with bell ringing regulations from this period, there were very precise guidelines as to how one should ring, when one should start ringing, and how long one should ring.

In the nineteenth century, the state endeavored by means of concerted regulations to ensure the clarity of signals, the correct ordering of messages, and a strict division between secular and religious bell ringing.

In addition it sought to curb the anarchic proliferation of the tollings and peals that served to define ceremonial time. By reading such regulations we can gain a sense of the range of tactics deployed to set limits to the sequences of sound deployed in ceremonies. Sometimes the number of calls and, more often, the kind and size of bells used, the manner of ringing—be it peals or simple tollings—and still more often, the duration of the ringing, were strictly regulated. Consider for example this last point. At the dawn of the nineteenth century, shortly after religious bell ringing had been restored, permitted rings were somewhat brief. Around the middle of the century they tended to last longer, very often as much as half an hour. In the series of regulations drawn up in 1884 and 1885, which followed the model laid down by the *ministre des Cultes*, the ringing relating to ceremonial time was generally cut down to around ten minutes. In the aftermath of the Separation of Church and State, many mayors decided to limit this type of ringing to five minutes, three minutes, or even one minute. In 1908 Goujat, a radical socialist deputy for the Nièvre, restricted authorized ringing at Cosnes, where he was mayor, to five minutes.[147] In 1907 the Mayor of Le Luc (Var) forbade the parish priest to ring for longer than two minutes. That same year the mayor of Montagnac (Basses-Alpes) decided to cut religious bell ringing to thirty seconds.[148]

Some mayors instructed rural guards to stand on the parvis of the church, timepiece in hand, to catch the parish priest or his bell ringer in breach of regulations. In short, the history of bells teaches us something about the inculcation of a sense of what a minute, or indeed a second was, a process described by Eugen Weber.[149] To achieve a genuine understanding of this apprenticeship, we need to reflect upon the progressive weakening of the sense of duration determined, not by the movement of a clock, but by the recitation of various prayers. The length of some peals had been regulated in this fashion, as many gestures and pauses may also have been. In Auxerre in 1887, to announce the curfew the verger had to ring the large bells thirteen times, then the small bell for "the duration of a *pater* and an *ave*."[150]

The sound of bells often served, as we have seen, to mark the itinerary of processions. In some dioceses, successive chimes kept absent parishioners informed of the high points of the service and invited them to join in thought with those who were present. Six regulations published in 1884 and 1885 authorized the ringing of the sermon and the elevation. Such peals might still lead to conflicts between mayor and parish priest, although without calling the former's religious fervor into question. On 31 January 1838, the mayor of Hestrud (Nord) had the bell rung at the *Magnificat* despite the priest in charge having banned the practice. In the very middle of the service the priest withdrew into the sacristy. The mayor followed him and the two men belabored each other with insults despite the fact that they were standing in the midst of children from the choir.[151]

THE WEB OF EVERYDAY SOUND

Where temporal markers and rhythms are concerned, it was the web of everyday sound that caused the most tension. Few practices have aroused so much passion and fomented so much hatred as the daily ringing of the Angelus. In order to arrive at a serious understanding of this phenomenon we need to present the points of view of the various protagonists. In the eyes of the clergy, who were responsible according to the law of 10 Germinal Year X for regulating bell ringing, the Angelus—and more particularly its tollings—was first and foremost an invitation to prayer. Since 1724, indulgences had also been attached to prayer, provided that one recited it kneeling and to the sound of the bell.[152] On 3 April 1884, Pope Leo XIII laid down certain conditions. Henceforth to qualify for indulgences one merely had to recite the prayer "at a moment approximate to the hour at which the Angelus is rung."[153] In short, the tolling of the Angelus partook of the Church's endeavor to "give the faithful the support and energy of each day"[154]; like Books of Hours, *Imitations of Christ*, spiritual writings of various kinds, and beads and rosaries, they restored to everyday time its religious intensity and reflected a determination to master the hours and control their tiniest interstices.

In this regard, it is worth noting that over the course of a day the bell would not only exhort the faithful to recite the Angelus but, in addition, would sometimes call upon them to use their beads or rosary. The latter type of ringing featured in regulations found in the Aveyron and the Landes in 1885.[155] In some regions bells imparted a rhythm to the reading of the prayer book; in others the bell ringer summoned the congregation to evening prayer. Such was the practice at Pin-la-Garenne (Orne)[156] during Lent and Advent until the mayor decided to ban it on 4 November 1832. The parish priest protested, and in the end prevailed. According to the prefect, the custom was observed almost everywhere in the department.

It sometimes happened that on his own initiative a parish priest would resolve to ring to summon his congregation to prayer, although in so doing he risked being rebuked or fined. In the spring of 1842 the priest at Baussaine (Ille-et-Vilaine) had the bells rung for a few minutes at eight o'clock in the evening for some forty days. He meant "to warn his parishioners not to forget the *souls in Purgatory*, above all those of their deceased relatives." He had the bells rung "so that in every house, upon hearing that sound, they would recite five *paters* and *aves* for the deceased, particularly *for those of the parish*."[157] Once again the bell ensured a simultaneity of prayer; on this occasion it served to reaffirm the bond between the living and the dead of the community. When Ernest Renan's *The Life of Jesus* was published, the bishop of Marseille ordered that, as a gesture of reparation, the passing bell should be rung for three minutes each Friday in every church in the diocese.[158] So as not to stray too far from the topic in hand, I want now to return to the daily messages imparted by the bells, that is to say, the Angelus.

It was *matutinal* ringing to which the clergy attached the most importance. This bell shared some of the attributes of the "cults of the early hours of the day" and of "the quest for a new dawn,"[159] which were key elements in popular piety. Man should give thanks to God at the precise moment that the star, by its light, begins to create the world anew. The morning Angelus, if one follows the symbolism of bell ringing,[160] evokes at once the Annunciation, the Incarnation, and Jesus's triumph on Easter morning. The bell invites one to treat awakening as a rising up, recalling that of Christ from the tomb; it calls for the consecration of the new time it announces. This accounts for the intrinsic value of the matutinal in the clergy's eyes, and the passion with which they strove to defend it from an insidious system of evaluation that tended to undermine it. As we have seen, parish priests and priests in charge associated ceremonial rejoicing with the ringing of bells very early in the morning. It was as if religious festivals, in contrast with the moral turpitude of those who prowled by night, presupposed particularly early rising. More or less consciously, this moral reading of biological rhythms formed part of a process of "disciplinary acculturation,"[161] and of the attempts made since the dawn of the Catholic Reformation to combat the dangerous freedoms of *otium*.

Conversely, the clergy sought to put up defenses against the snares and phantasms of the night. As we have seen, they generally arranged for the evening Angelus to be rung at twilight. This peal, a symbolic reminder of the death of Christ, evoked the pain and tears of the Passion, or even the end of time.[162] It was a call to contemplation and in many places the clergy were determined to make the bell of the vesperal Angelus the last of the day. The secular ringing of the curfew or "retreat" aroused such controversy because it breached the nocturnal silence enjoined by the Angelus, even though the secular ringing was itself designed to "moralize" the night.

In Cottévrard, a commune in the arrondissement of Dieppe (Seine-Inférieure), an immemorial custom "dictated that" according to the incumbent, "the six o'clock Angelus [was] *the last sound* of the day" and seemed to be "a kind of '"retreat.'"" But on 5 November 1857, Mr. Isidore Dubos, the sexton, "having presented himself at half past six to name a child, was requested by the priest in charge, after the ceremony, not to ring, considering that the bell had already announced the Angelus; Mr. Dubos ignored this request and began to ring himself."[163]

The priest complained to the public prosecutor about the illicit half hour, but to no avail. Fearing that the balance of his parishioners' daily routine was in jeopardy, he referred the matter to Minister Rouland. On 30 June 1858, the minister, ensconced in his office in Paris, failed to grasp the significance of the affair and simply advised the priest in charge to replace the sexton.

The ringing of the midday Angelus, which was of crucial importance to peasants, seemed to matter less to members of the clergy. Furthermore in some (but not many) regions, the Lot[164] for instance, it was not the custom to ring at this time of day. In Guindrecourt-sur-Blaise (Haute-Marne), in 1873 midday was only rung on Saturdays.[165] The symbolism of the noontide Angelus appears imprecise. For some exegetes, ringing when the sun is at its zenith celebrates Christ's Ascension. For others[166] it is a reminder of the moment he entered into his agony. In all events the midday Angelus was often rung at half past eleven or eleven. Such was the custom virtually everywhere in the department of Eure-et-Loir. At Blangy, in the Bray (Seine-Inférieure), the noontide Angelus was rung at eleven o'clock on market days.[167] On the banks of the Bresles the bell tolled at half past eleven. A second peal, secular this time, sounded thirty minutes later; it was called the "twelve o'clock." In many places[168] the gap between the middle of the day and the "midday Angelus" justified the insertion of a secular peal.

Secular bell ringing, however, embodied a completely different conception of time. As the decades passed, morning awakening became desacralized. The hedonism of rising late in towns, a habit that was aristocratic in origin, was gradually embraced and even claimed as a right; behavior like that of the handsome cousin who fascinated or scandalized the members of the Grandet family in Balzac's novel, gradually ceased to elicit surprise in the provinces. Claiming the right to rest[169] undermined the diatribes directed at matutinal slumber and warm beds. By the same token a new interpretation of the dawn bell became current. For more and more citizens what had been a sacred peal was now regarded as an unwelcome din. At the same time, sleeping late and night life, given added luster by the routines of the elites and rendered more viable by improvements in streetlighting, acquired some of the prestige attaching to modernity.

The conflicts over the morning and evening Angelus arose out of divergent conceptions relating at the same time to the culture of the senses, ethics, and politics. The mayor's authority lay, to an extent that should not be underestimated, in his being able to ring in the evening even after the Angelus, in the right to stop the parish priest from using the bells at an hour deemed too matutinal, or in his readiness to impose a secular peal at eleven o'clock or midday. For the townspeople such powers likewise seemed to promise emancipation from the clergy. What was at stake in all these conflicts was control of the community's biorhythms and the management of time allotted to toil and repose.[170] These disputes also touched on social morality since in the last resort what was at issue, in the clergy's view anyway, was the moral worth of a parish. To do battle for matutinal rising or vesperal silence was to combat the machinations of the devil.

Three types of conflict will serve to define this war over temporal rhythms. The first concerns the interpretation of the Angelus and the duplication, where it occurred, of the peals known as the *"points du jour."* The second arose out of the municipalities' struggle against excessive matutinal ringing. The third was caused by the clergy's hostility toward the nocturnal ringing of the curfew or the "retreat."

a) In communes where one rang only once each morning, noon, and night, there could be disagreement over *the interpretation offered of peals* since some would assume they were hearing an Angelus while others would hear them as secular signals, which not long before had been the sole legitimate form of ringing under the First Republic, at the height of the dechristianization campaign. A number of mayors in the Haute-Marne, the Meuse, the Vosges, and the Côte-d'or refused to recognize the polysemous nature of bell ringing; to do so would be tantamount to acknowledging the sacralizing of the rhythms of human existence under the aegis of the parish priest or priest in charge. As far as such municipal magistrates were concerned, it was first and foremost a matter of secular peals. In Brittany, on the other hand, where a secular sensibility seems to have been less developed or pervasive, the tollings and peals that imparted a rhythm to the days caused almost no controversy. They were spontaneously regarded as religious messages.

In the Meuse and the Vosges the municipal authorities set particular store by the midday peal. When, therefore, the priest in charge stopped ringing the Angelus, some communes introduced a secular "midday" peal. The lack of a bell at this moment jeopardized the organization of the whole day. Since ringing at noon had stopped, some parishioners from Dombrot-le-Sec (Vosges) explained to their parish priest in 1891, a great number of "farmers *tarried* in the fields, being unaware of the time, and were consequently unable in the evening to finish tasks of greater urgency than had been those over which they had tarried in the morning."[171]

Elsewhere the *duplication* of peals would sometimes cause controversy and lasting animosities. In January 1810, Cardinal Cambacérès, archbishop of Rouen, threatened to lay the parish of Buchy (Seine-Inférieure) under an interdict because the mayor had decided "to ring a half of a quarter of an hour at the beginning, middle, and end of the day," at times just slightly staggered in relation to the Angelus. The parish priest, for his part, forbade the sexton to ring "the mayor's times"[172] or risked dismissal. In the end the minister ruled in the priest's favor, with the understanding that consultation between the two authorities would prevent any duplication of this type recurring .

In some regions such dualism had become tradition. In the department of the Nord, the 1843 regulations stipulated that the custom was to ring at eleven to alert the laborers in the fields irrespective of the Angelus. This was also the case in the Aube. According to the mayor of Grandes-Chapelles, ringing at eleven o'clock between 1 June and 1 September was an "old custom."[173] Elsewhere some municipalities strove to introduce duplication. In the middle of the century a number of mayors in the Meuse wanted the bells to be rung at eleven during haymaking, harvest, and sowing times in order, the Mayor of Autrécourt[174] explained on 2 August 1866, "to alert all those who are in the fields and who need to go home and fetch something for the harvesters to eat," and to announce to the womenfolk the moment for preparing dinner. But, the parish priest objected, "the bells were not solemnly blessed in order to call all the world to soup." In 1884 the subprefect of Mirecourt (Vosges) further claimed that the municipalities in his arrondissement should have the right to ring for harvesting and haymaking "for a quarter of an hour at most," "at ten or eleven o'clock in the morning and four o'clock in the evening."[175]

Yet it was once again in the Haute-Marne that the problem engendered the most intense conflicts throughout the century. One example should suffice. In December 1843, the parish priest of Humberville[176] altered the time of the evening Angelus. It would henceforth be rung at nine o'clock, the hour of the curfew, and no longer at eight o'clock as had been the custom. Traditionally, however, "the Angelus and the curfew had been rung at different times in Humberville," as I would add, in many places. The mayor, with the backing of the prefect, deplored the intolerable confusion caused by the parish priest, who clearly aspired to a vesperal monopoly over religious bell ringing. The two peals, he quite correctly observed, "have nothing in common either in their causes or in their ends." "I would much prefer it," wrote the prefect to the bishop of Langres, "if the two peals were everywhere to be kept entirely distinct," as they were, for example, in the vicinity of Chaumont. In addition it was his wish that the Angelus mark the hour of rest, which was five o'clock in winter in the countryside, and that a secular peal, "fixed by English law and maintained by custom," should announce the hour of curfew at eight or nine o'clock in the countryside and at ten o'clock in Chaumont, as had been the practice in that town since 1830.

In 1886 the department of Côte-d'or underwent a real crisis over the Angelus,[177] or rather over what in the rural areas was termed "the ringing of the *points du jour.*" The mayors requested permission to intervene in cases where parish priests had stopped ringing the statutory Angelus. The bishop of Dijon, however, was opposed to such a step. He feared the resulting desacralizing of these peals as well as the daily intrusion of the commune's bell ringer into the bell tower. In addition, he hoped that the municipalities would agree to fund the Angelus, although up until then they had refused. In 1886 the parish priest of Coulmier-le-Sec stopped ringing the Angelus with the excuse that the municipality was refusing to pay for it. The mayor took advantage of the situation to bring a new ring of bells into use, entrusting them to the schoolmaster. The conflict was eventually referred to the minister.

In the aftermath of the vote on the Separation of Church and State the battle over duplication took on national dimensions. In the departments of Eure and Eure-et-Loir it served to crystallize antagonisms arising from the regulation of religion, although the positions of the protagonists had altered since the Second Empire. In many communes parish priests had over the years given up ringing the Angelus. According to the prefect this had already happened in the majority of parishes in the Eure by 1884.[178] The mayor of Prouais (Eure-et-Loir) alluded to "the Angelus formerly in use in every village, but long since gone in ours."[179] As in Coulmier-le-Sec (Côte-d'or), so too here the municipalities refused to fund religious peals. For the clergy, then, suppression of the Angelus had been an economy measure.

Having noted the disappearance of the Angelus, several mayors in the Eure-et-Loir decided to ring for the resumption of activities in the morning, for the midday meal, and for the cessation of work in the evening. Some parish priests, distressed at seeing a peal, of which they had not long ago been the "regulators," being desacralized in this fashion, resolved, much to the annoyance of the hostile municipal councils, *to restore the Angelus*. Until the Council of State annulled the decrees establishing the *"points du jour"* issued by the mayors (1911), the duplication of peals gave rise to dozens of disputes in this department. I shall give just one example here.

In Saint-Martin-de-Nigelles the ringing of the Angelus had fallen into "abeyance" four years earlier. The mayor decided in June 1911[180] to have the bell rung *in full peal* by a lay bell ringer, at quarter past eleven to "announce to the agricultural laborers that it was time to return from the fields." The priest in charge thereupon reinstated the ringing of the Angelus at five in the morning, at noon, and at eight o'clock in the evening. He then suggested to the mayor that they might come to an "arrangement." To avoid duplication the priest would have the good grace to ring the Angelus at quarter of twelve while the mayor would stop ringing at quarter past eleven. The municipal council, having met to discuss the problem, turned down the proposal and decided to maintain its peal.[181] The parish priest, intent upon resacralizing the custom, then arranged to toll the Angelus just when the municipal bells were ringing. The mayor threatened to ban the ringing and planned, moreover, to prevent the parish priest from ringing too early in the morning and too late in the evening. I should add that the pastor, perhaps out of defiance, often rang at half past four in the morning and after half past eight, in the evening.

In every one of these disputes the position adopted by central government was now clear,[182] namely, that the mayors had no right to set the times of the Angelus. From 1911 onward they were forbidden to introduce those peals known as "resuming work," "rest hour," or "stopping work," since they were not on the official list of signals at the disposal of "local government."[183] In short, it was not part of the mayor's duties to impose a rhythm on the life of the community in which he was supposed to guarantee law and order.

b) The rejection by municipalities of excessive matutinal awakening occasioned another series of disputes over the control of the temporal architecture of everyday life. Once again the debate became especially heated at the dawn of the twentieth century. Between 1907 and 1910 in particular, countless mayors tried, although without much success, to prohibit the parish priest from ringing before the time stipulated by the municipality. The series of statements taken down during this period by rural guards make for more entertaining reading than any other primary sources in the archives concerned with the regulation of religion. Conflicts of this nature kept the Court of Cassation busy, although it generally endorsed the conviction of recalcitrant parish priests; they were likewise referred to the Council of State, which hurriedly quashed the municipal regulations, one after the other, on the grounds that they were in breach of the Law of Separation of Church and State.[184] Such episodes may again seem trifling to us but they prompted much heated comment in the press. Every single conviction or disclaimer, no matter how minor, was seen as a symbolic disaster[185] and the passionate involvement of the protagonists astonishes us.

c) The ringing of the "retreat" and/or curfew gave rise to a third kind of conflict. In fact, their forms were not easily defined in the nineteenth century and they varied from region to region. Yet in every case these secular peals were distinct from the evening Angelus, which was sometimes known as the "recall."[186] Originally, curfew and "retreat" indicated that the time had come to retire to one's hearth. At this signal one was supposed to leave taverns or inns as well as the house of one's neighbor or any place where a *veillée* was being held. Upon hearing the "retreat" one closed the shutters. In the Moselle, as we have seen, this bell announced the irruption of demons into the village, in some sense opening up the night to witches and their evil spells.

During the second half of the century, while the traditional division of the day—now under threat from other rhythms—began to fall apart, the ringing of the curfew spread. This bell, however, scarcely had any other function but that of signaling the official closing time for taverns and endorsing the authority of the proprietor, who might then show recalcitrant customers the door. In communes without municipal clocks the innkeeper, even if he had a pendulum clock, relied on the sound of the bell to tell him when to shut the premises. In 1859 the proprietors of Arches (Vosges) petitioned the prefecture. They asked for the "retreat" to be rung since, without a public clock "regulating the hours of the day *for one and all*,"[187] they could never be sure *exactly* when to close up shop. "Closing time can vary depending upon the extent to which the clocks of

police and residents agree." Furthermore, discrepancies between private-
ly owned clocks had to be taken into account.[188] Initially the demand for
accuracy led to a proliferation of peals.

The clergy was in a dilemma; as we have seen, they did not welcome
any ringing after the evening Angelus. They had to admit, however, that
the "retreat" bell helped limit debauchery and served to guarantee moral
order in the parish. This function was particularly evident in communes
that only rang the "retreat" on Sundays and feast days. At the dawn of
the Second Empire the mayors of the Meuse, despite their hostility to the
routine deployment of such peals, acknowledged their usefulness on days
when no work was done.[189] In June 1862 the municipal council of La
Martyre (Finistère) decided to ring a curfew in the evening on the first
Thursday of each month, when a fair was held in a neighboring commune. This measure, the deputy mayor insisted, was a matter "of public
order and morality, given that, on their return from La Roche fair, which
is held on that day, a large number of overexcited individuals linger in the
taverns until a late hour, leaving their animals to suffer outside these
pubs, and causing their families anxiety."[190] This is a telling remark that
serves to remind us that in stock-breeding areas, diurnal rhythms were
dictated by animal biology. Townspeople would also get little rest if
horses were pawing the ground outside the door to the inn.

I will not attempt a history of the curfew here since it was a very old
custom. Blavignac traces the practice back to the eleventh century and, as
we have seen, it was generally in use at that time in Normandy.[191] The bell
that rang the "retreat" was called the "Cache-Ribaud" in Rouen, the
"Chasse aux Ribauds" in Gascony, and the "*Crovefeul*" in Burgundy. The
ban bell was often used for this purpose. In the eighteenth century in
Paris, the "canons' curfew" was rung every day at seven in the evening,[192]
although in this case, admittedly, it was confused with the Angelus. In
Strasbourg a bell reserved for this use would then ring the "retreat."[193]
Under the Old Regime there was a logical connection between the city
bell and the ramparts, and between the ringing of the "retreat" and the
closing of the city gates.

In the nineteenth century the curfew was a firmly rooted tradition. In
1901 it was rung every day in Sarlat (Périgord) with a bell specially cast
in 1825 for the purpose.[194] The custom was witnessed in the Drôme in

1844[195] and in the Aisne[196] in 1852. At that time, in spite of some resistance during summer, the "retreat" was rung, I repeat, in virtually every commune in the Meuse; the prefect gave orders for it to be rung. The inhabitants of Consigny[197] (Haute-Marne) petitioned in 1848 to be permitted to retain this peal, which offered them "a measure of public safety given that the commune was surrounded by woods and rocks [and] . . . [that] the long winter nights [are] often dark and the weather bad." In 1867 the "retreat" was still rung in Ploudaniel, in Finistère.[198] In Grand (Vosges) in 1873, the duration of the "retreat" depended on the weather, with the bell being rung from 1 October to 1 March at eight o'clock "for half an hour when there was snow and the light was poor, and for a quarter of an hour in moonlight."[199] In 1896 the ringing of the curfew was noted in the Côtes-du-Nord.[200] This is no more than a small sample. Regulations signed in 1884, 1885, and 1886 gave official authorization for this usage or for the "retreat," in forty-one different departments.

The "retreat" bell thus seems to have become more commonplace during the second half of the century.[201] As we have seen, it answered to the new need for accurate timekeeping. "If the curfew, which in our countryside [the Bray] had all but fallen into disuse, has been reintroduced in *many places*," wrote Dergny in 1865, "this is due to the all too rapid rise in the number of cafés and other gaming houses."[202] In regions where the "retreat" and the curfew were currently in use, they occasioned almost as many disputes as the Angelus. In either case the issue was control of collective rhythms.

In Senon (Meuse) it "had long been the custom" to ring the "retreat" at nine o'clock in the evening in summer and at eight o'clock in winter, "save on Sundays and holidays, when," the mayor specified,[203] "the "retreat" is rung at nine o'clock throughout the year." In 1849 the parish priest decided to oppose this practice, which he felt was too late in winter. One Sunday he therefore "barricaded" the church door to prevent the verger from ringing. "The next three Sundays," recorded the mayor, "the parish priest himself rang the "retreat" at eight o'clock, and on the fourth he stopped ringing it and once again barricaded the door." The priest claimed that the bells should not have been used after eight o'clock. "This regrettable dispute threw this community of some eight hundred souls into turmoil." "The children were forever hearing their parents complaining and muttering," and as a consequence ceased to respect the parish priest.

The mayor wished to ring the "retreat" at nine o'clock in winter for "reasons of humanity, public order, and sound administration." Besides, this was the approach adopted in the surrounding area. A commune "once so peaceable" was now torn apart. On 20 January 1850, the parish priest voiced his anxieties. He wrote to the mayor suggesting that "in view of the general unease" it might be advisable "to call in the gendarmerie for tomorrow, [for] fear of disorder." The affair was only resolved when the minister ordered the two protagonists to come to some understanding.

In the Haute-Marne the ringing of the "retreat" was a highly contentious issue. This was the case with everything relating to the segmenting of time in that department. In 1860 the mayor of Giey-sur-Aujon demanded the right to choose precisely when to ring. The parish priest rejected the times chosen by the mayor. He wanted the "retreat" to be announced at eight o'clock in winter, not at nine o'clock.[204] Between 1880 and 1886, as we have seen,[205] the commune of Ceffonds was split by a dispute over the ringing of the curfew, although on this occasion it concerned not the schedule but the size of the bell.[206]

A single conflict might sometimes entail a complex interlocking of debates regarding several forms of bell ringing in a community. For the sake of clarity I have tried to separate the various points at issue. Here, however, is a case in which various aspects of ringing were inextricably intertwined.

In November 1867, the parish priest of Chatonrupt (Haute-Marne) decided to stop ringing a bell for school classes, although it had been an established usage since "time immemorial."[207] The mayor held that this secular ringing should be "a peal" while the parish priest wanted it simply to be tolled. The municipal council ordered the schoolmaster, who was already responsible for the communal clock, to ring at a quarter to eight in the morning and at "a quarter to one." To enforce this ruling, five or six municipal councillors accompanied by the deputy mayor came "to ring a two to three minute peal for school."

The commune was thrown into turmoil. If a peal was rung both for classes and for mass, which began within minutes of each other, there was a real risk of confusion. The commissioner of police for the canton of Joinville was informed and conducted his own inquiries. According to him "the local inhabitants wanted school to be rung with a peal," but with *a different bell* to prevent confusion with the bell used to announce services. Unfortunately it so happened that the only two viable bells "produced roughly the same sound." This conflict, according to the commissioner, "*disrupts* and sows a regrettable dissension among the residents of Chatonrupt . . . since this issue first arose, around a year ago . . . animosities have grown daily and plunged spirits ever deeper into a *bitter* and *interminable* struggle." Discussions were "frequent and continuous," and all the more so given that the parish priest sought to restrict the ringing of the curfew—likewise a custom since time immemorial—to a simple tolling.

The commissioner suggested a possible "arrangement" to the prefect. The mayor would settle for "having school tolled" and the parish priest would agree to have the curfew rung "as a peal," as was the tradition in that region. There was much to be said for this solution, not least because a tolled curfew might be confused with an alarm bell and bring people hurrying in from neighboring communes.

The prefect lost patience. "It is time to end a dispute," he wrote on 17 January 1868, "that has caused bitter controversy and set residents each against the other." He asked the parish priest to renounce his innovations and abide by the traditional practices. His resolve in this matter had been strengthened still more by the priest's display of hostility toward the Imperial Regime on the national holiday of 15 August.

It would be tiresome to extend this section of my inquiry any further. The number of disputes, the reader will perhaps object, is modest by comparison with the number of communes in France as a whole. If, however, one reads the archival sources carefully, one cannot help but be struck by the multifariousness of the debates, by the heated nature of the disputes, and by the persistence of rivalries if not hatred; in short, by the scope of the auditory messages that served to set the temporal markers of the community. *The sense that bell ringing was a necessity* engendered habits of *intense listening*. In order to arrive at a true understanding of such disputes, it is important, once again, to be wary of the psychological anachronism arising out of our current, decidedly casual attitude toward bells.

The Proclamation of Social Divisions

READING THE BRONZE

The bronze of bells and peals of honor expressed social hierarchies and reflected social mobility. They served as a record of shifts in dominant values and of transfers of authority.[208] For historians interested in the social foundations of power, campanarian epigraphy offers an abundant corpus. In villages, or urban *quartiers*, no inscriptions were more numerous, more considered, more concerted, and often more contentious than those seen on bells. Yet no phrases were more mysterious, since the bell tower remained inaccessible to most of the population and such texts, though carefully weighed, languished in a semidarkness that rendered them illegible.

Nevertheless, as we read through the abundant corpus of inscriptions engraved in relief on the bronze, we are able to discern, in the context of each region, the hierarchy of prestige and domination as well as the relative efficacy of the various authorities. It bears emphasizing that in order to arrive at a real understanding of clerical pretensions and municipal claims, one should banish the simple notion that they stood face to face with faith on one side and unbelief on the other.[209] The fluctuating balance between secular authority and ecclesiastical power,[210] between the profane and the sacred, and between the lay and the religious underwent an incessant but sometimes furtive process of rearrangement within communities characterized by a degree of religious fervor where the citizens shared the same beliefs. Campanarian epigraphy helps us pin down this often subtle balance.[211]

There are collections of all the extant dedications, mentions of godfatherhood, and "baptismal" names inscribed on nineteenth-century bells for the Ardennes, Moselle, the Bray (Seine-Inférieure), Isère, Cantal, Charente and the Dordogne.[212] Partial surveys have been conducted in Normandy and the Pyrénées,[213] but this is only to mention the major studies. A researcher working unaided could not hope to give a quantitative treatment of this vast corpus, and besides, the uneven impact of destruction in the revolutionary period, or of the recastings undertaken in the nineteenth century weaken the scientific pretensions of such a study. I shall therefore present only the most obvious conclusions drawn from reading these works and stress the processes identified by the researchers.

On no other official monuments do references to women—except where they are symbols—feature so prominently as on the sacred bronze of bells. Generally they are in a subordinate position. In such inscriptions the name of the godmother follows that of the godfather; it is he *who chose her*. Moreover, the majority of women accorded such an honor owe it to being wife, daughter or, more rarely, mother of the godfather.

Mention of children on bells was more surprising; it was a rare and belated phenomenon. At the end of the century, shortly before the introduction of private communion, the attention paid by the church to the early years of life sanctioned, although belatedly, the rise of a sentiment identified some years ago by Philippe Ariès. There arose a custom whereby the children of the parish might collectively be the godfather. This was the case in the Dordogne.[214] One of the bells cast in 1882 bears the following inscription: "I am the angels' bell. For godfathers and godmothers I have the children from Nontron from one to seven years old." In Champagne in 1890, a bell that was also dedicated to the holy angels "had for godfathers all the small boys of the parish and for godmothers all the little girls." The new bell of Eygurande (Dordogne) reads: "The godfathers and godmothers [are] the children of the first communion of 1 June 1899." Likewise an inscription on the bell in Cabans informs us that it was recast through the good graces of the children of the parish.[215] On bells from the Bray dating from the latter half of the century it is not uncommon to find the names of the sons or daughters of the godfather and godmother, who are then regarded as "little godfathers" and "little godmothers." This seems to be a way of expressing the hope that a line of notables might be perpetuated.[216]

The traditional élites plainly left their mark on the bronze, a fact that is in no way surprising. Between 1814 and 1830, especially, while ancient formulae were being reintroduced and titles of nobility and honorific references[217] were proliferating on bells, the attempt was made, in this domain as in others, to effect a social restoration, although it varied in extent from region to region. We cannot help noticing the phenomenon in the Bray and it was plainly operative in Périgord, although there was barely a trace of it in the Ardennes. It served to inspire the nobility's generosity toward the patrimony of specific communities, as Michel Denis has shown in the Mayenne, and Claude Brelot in Franche-Comté.[218]

By the very end of the century the bronze of the bells had ceased to count for much, and the secular authorities no longer had any real ambition to have their inscriptions added. Campanarian epigraphy became the preserve of a nobility nostalgic for bygone glories and of a small élite of zealous clerics. We should not let ourselves be misled by the ascendancy of categories more and more deeply rooted in rural society that remained attached to honorific procedures increasingly devoid of meaning.[219]

Madame Armande Félicité Barbetet, the godmother of the bell at Saint-Lucien (Seine-Inférieure) cast in 1858, lived in the château of La Hallotière, her own property; she "is the benefactress of the *area* in general, and of her own parish in particular."[220] The commune of La Hallotière had granted her in perpetuity a plot in the cemetery near to the church. Her husband was buried there. "The pious donor has had a chapel built for her own private use. Because a section of the wall has been taken down, she can attend services in the church, of which the little oratory seems to form part." Here the sponsorship of the bell serves to complete and, in some way extend, the presence of notables, which is in some sense guaranteed within the parish church. This form of sponsorship at once reflects and reinforces the ascendancy aimed at by the region's great families, whose genealogies and coats of arms Dieudonné Dergny, with his obsessive desire to renew the chain of time, takes such delight in detailing.[221]

It sometimes happened that a local community fervently wished to reserve for its benefactors the honor of sponsoring the bell. In 1869, 103 residents of Marignié (Maine-et-Loire) protested the Saint-Sulpice parochial church council's choice for godfather and godmother of persons "who have not done good in the parish." This decision was detrimental to the Carrier *family*, who had given proof since time immemorial of the utmost devotion to the community. The signers of the petition declared: "*We want*, recognize, and choose M. Joseph Carrier and Mme Philomène Carrier, his mother, as godfather and godmother of *our* bell."[222] In this way a majority[223] of a community's members could assert their power to choose, and demonstrate the importance attached to the election of those honored enough to preside over the "christening" of the bell.

During the nineteenth century new forms of sponsorship arose. The Bonaparte dynasty saw to it that it was itself featured on the consecrated bronze. In 1809 following a proposal from the mayor, the municipal council of Lombez (Gers) dedicated the principal bell in its parish church to the "great Napoleon" as a token of "its love, gratitude, allegiance and respect." The council delighted in the thought that the bronze would resound down the generations: "Long live Napoleon the Great."[224] Manufactured during the reign of Saint Louis, the bell broke as it was celebrating the entrance of the French into Vienna. Under the Second Empire, imperial bells were cast in series and generously dispatched to the departments.[225] This procedure forms part of the staging of imperial authority, a topic analyzed in various works in progress. At the same time the names of officials began to feature in campanarian inscriptions, even under the First Empire. In 1807 the bell of Brioux (Deux-Sèvres) had the subprefect for its godfather and the subprefect's wife for its godmother. In Secondigné (Deux-Sèvres) in 1811, the godfather was the subprefect of Melle and the godmother was the mayor's wife.[226]

I have already referred to the inscriptions that attributed the ownership or sponsorship of the bell to the local residents or an immigrants' association. While on the topic of democratization of campanarian texts, I should mention how common it was for godfathers to be identified simply as "farmers,"[227] even as early as the First Empire and the Restoration. "In the year of 1824, on 25 August,"[228] we read on the small bell at Compainville (Seine-Inférieure), I was blessed . . . and named Joséphine by Étienne Legoix, farmer, and by Joséphine Leclerc, wife of J.-B. Duputel, landowner at Compainville, in the presence of François Cauchois, mayor and farmer in the aforesaid place, and of the members of the municipal and parochial church councils. I owe my existence to the diligence and zeal of residents of Compainville."[229]

In the Ardennes this type of inscription was more common than in the Bray. According to Henri Jadart, references to "upstanding families of landowners and farmers"[230] greatly outnumber those to members of the nobility; only two such instances occurred in the canton of Asfeld. From the inscription on the "middle" bell at Hannogne, "baptized" in 1850, we learn that the godfather was a "farmer's son" and the godmother a "farmer's daughter."[231] In Taizy the godfather and godmother of the bell cast in 1823 were "workers of the region."[232] Campanarian epigraphy reflects the hold of the democratic spirit on the region. One could list other examples. According to Jean-Pierre Jessenne, from the end of the eighteenth century, but still more in the aftermath of the Revolution, sponsorship of bells reflected the social power of the farmers of the Artois.

The most interesting cases involve the inscription on bells of those who claimed to exercise authority in the village. It is hardly worth lingering over the names of parish priests, which are often mentioned. Conversely, it was now rare for the names of the churchwarden, bell ringer, or cantor to feature on a bell. The only conflicting evidence on this point is furnished by Samuel Bour who quotes several examples from the Moselle. The cantor's name appears on the bell at Landroff, which was cast in 1811; the name of the master of the choir-school appears on the bell at Lidrezing, which was cast in 1832.[233]

It had been the custom under the Old Regime to inscribe the names of consuls, syndics, or the mayor beside those of the parish priest and the churchwarden; in the nineteenth century inscriptions featuring the name of the leading magistrate were very common. Such names sometimes functioned as a reference point for a system of dating. A mayoralty would then appear alongside a pontifical and/or royal reign. All the bell in Nanteuil-de-Bourzac (Dordogne) had by way of inscription was: "Has been cast in 1817 under the mayoralty of M.E. Modenel."[234] It was common, however, for the mayor's name to appear on its own without any temporal reference, as was the case with twelve bells in Périgord.[235] Some biographical detail might, however, be appended to the name of the magistrate, generally touching on the start of his period in office. On the bell in Mauzac (Dordogne), which was cast in 1865, we read "M. Joseph Aubry, mayor since 1818,"[236] while on the bell recast in 1829 in Bassing (Moselle), the mayor's age—he was fifty-one—was given.[237]

Sometimes the name of a prominent municipal magistrate and the members of the local community appeared together. On the great bell of Saint-Loup-en-Champagne (Ardennes) the bell makers had inscribed: "This recasting was made possible by the generosity of a very great majority of *heads of family* from this commune, who *have chosen* M. Étienne Batteux, mayor, as my godfather, who has himself chosen Mme.

Jeanne Trichet, his wife, as my godmother."[238] In this particular case, campanarian epigraphy allows us a glimpse at the cascade of village elective procedures in the heyday of the July Monarchy.*

The prestige of things municipal is also reflected in the listing of council members. Such lists feature on the bell in Jussy (Moselle) that was cast in 1806,[239] on each of the three bells in Saint-Fergeux (Ardennes), recast in 1847,[240] and on the bell in Grumesnil, recast in 1841.[241] From 1830 on, the name of the deputy mayor featured prominently alongside that of the mayor in inscriptions. At least this is one of the most obvious findings to emerge from a study of the accounts given by researchers. Conversely, it was rare for the deputy mayor's name to appear without that of the leading municipal magistrate. The formula inscribed on the bell in Gomont (Ardennes) that was cast in "the year 1831, first year of the reign of Louis-Philippe I, King of the French," suggests a particular concern to pay homage to an individual. The godfather is described as a "*rantier*" [sic] while the godmother was the mayor's wife; it is further stated that they gave their name to the bell "in the presence of the deputy mayor."[242]

It was possible for the list of municipal council members to appear on a bell without mention of the mayor or deputy mayor. Sometimes reference was made at once to rank and to level of generosity shown. The bell in Rouvray-Catillon (Seine-Inférieure), which was recast in 1854, bore a list detailing the amount contributed by the various subscribers: the parish priest, 260 francs, the mayor, 110 francs, the deputy mayor, 110 francs, etc.

It is somewhat surprising to find that in many places the name and Christian name of the *schoolmaster* appear on the bell, an honor perhaps due to the fact that he often performed the duties of bell ringer. The inscription on the bell in Avaux (Ardennes), cast in 1816, links the names of mayor, deputy mayor, and schoolmaster.[243] On the bell in Guessling (Moselle), which dates from 1848, the schoolmaster's name is accompanied by that of the parish priest.[244] The inscription on the bell in

---

*On 30 July 1830, Louis Philippe, duke of Orléans, was acclaimed by the crowd in Paris, in the square of the Hôtel de Ville. This episode precipitated the founding of a new constitutional monarchy, known subsequently as the July Monarchy.

Le Thil (Seine-Inférieure) reads "cast in 1815 through the diligence, and *under the auspices* of M. Boulanger, schoolmaster of Le Thil, with the help of the residents of this parish."[245]

For all the dryness of such inscriptions, they seem imbued with a yearning to satisfy ambition, quench a thirst for recognition, and safeguard honorific capital, whether individual or familial. Bells give us a sense of how conflicts arise. The drafting of inscriptions gave local authorities the opportunity to boost their prestige by finding a place for themselves within a cascade of references—a sort of pyramid of powers and statuses. This may well have been the case with the mayor of Saulx-Saint-Rémy (Ardennes); when its bell was cast within the commune itself in 1817, the following lines were inscribed upon it: "To the glory of God in 1817 . . . under Pius VII, Pope, Louis XVIII, King, François Cassiaux, of Saint-Thomas-en-Argonne, parish priest, P. Guilhaume Riflart, mayor, Maurice Badu, deputy mayor."[246]

Inscriptions sometimes embodied a desire for the harmonious accommodation of each and every claim. One may read on the middle bell in Le Thour (Ardennes), "I was cast in 1834, *through the efforts* of M. Jean-Baptiste Nivelle, parish priest; Joseph Fergeux Sorlet, mayor; Nicolas-Catherine-Olive Philippot, deputy mayor [note the inclusion of all the Christian names]; Pierre Malhomme, municipal councillor for the commune of Le Thour; and *at the expense* of the residents and of the parochial church council."[247] The godfather was the viscount of Virieu and the godmother was his wife.

Sometimes where many bells had been cast it was possible to satisfy several ambitions at once. The case of Rethel in 1826 is relevant here.[248] The first bell had the archbishop for godfather, the second, the subprefect—who was a chevalier of the royal order of the Légion d'honneur—the third, the mayor, a doctor, and a surgeon, the fourth, a mill owner and a member of the general council. This hierarchized grouping was wholly characteristic of the Restoration.

Needless to say, the precise wording of an inscription could sometimes divide a commune. In Haudricourt (Seine-Inférieure) in 1858, each of the contending parties held a banquet to mark the "baptism" of the bell.[249] In 1864 Magny-en-Vexin (Seine-et-Oise) was bitterly divided. The mayor held that the godfather and godmother of the new bell should belong to "families that have remained aloof from the recent electoral struggles." The parish priest, however, chose Maurice Richard, a deputy for the constituency, and the wife of a spinning mill proprietor who was the opposition candidate for the general council. In short, the preferences expressed were in the subprefect's view a direct "reflection of the struggles that for the past eight months have divided the area." "The affair of the bell," he added, "has become a political matter." "It is very serious," he concluded, "[for] if the parish priest were to prevail . . . behind the contingent question of the bell . . . the entire party aligned with the present administration, and the friends of government, would be defeated; by the same token, the mayor's influence would then be outweighed by that of the parish priest."[250] The affair was even mentioned in passing in the national press. The embarrassed prefect declared that he would either appoint the godfather and godmother himself or dispense with the inscription altogether.

Eight years later a conflict erupted in Libaros (Hautes-Pyrénées). The mayor and municipal council planned to compose an inscription for the new bell, which had been funded by public subscription. They, therefore, gave the bell caster his instructions. The new parish priest and his parochial church council were, however, opposed to this initiative and to any allusion to the commune on the new bell. They wanted the original text reinstated since it had been drafted by the priest—"leader of the contributions," that is, principal donor—and approved by "the people assembled in the church." They requested that the bronze be inscribed as follows: "This bell is the fruit of the charity shown by residents of the parish of Libaros, canton of Galan, Hautes-Pyrénées." The parochial church council and the priest let the new bell into the church but they would not allow it to be hung until the municipal inscription was erased. If it were not they threatened "to cast out the bell."[251] The *ministre des Cultes* in the end ruled against the mayor on the grounds that a commune had no call, in his opinion, to interfere with the drafting of a campanarian inscription.

THE PEAL OF PRIDE

The promise "To be rung in one's own lifetime" went even further to satisfy the thirst for prestige than the knowledge that one's name was inscribed in the semidarkness of a bell tower. Thus the ringing of the "bells of honor" was a fiercely defended tradition. Under the Old Regime, and quite apart from the peals that constituted one of the elements of baroque pomp arranged for by private citizens at funerals, it had been the custom to ring in honor of the lord and the members of his family, and of the bishop and the parish priest. A decree by the Parlement of Toulouse, dated 1743, required the parish priest of Saint-Martin-Gimois (Gers) to have the bells rung for forty days at the death both of its lord and master and his wife.[252] On 3 July 1703, the parish priest of Herpy bequeathed three pounds to the sexton " to ring for a whole month after his demise an evening *lesse*" with the great bell and "to ring for a whole year on fine days at the first stroke of matins, with all the bells great and small, for the space of a quarter of an hour."

On the eve of the Revolution villages and towns echoed the sound of these peals, bearing witness to an enduring society of orders. Article 48 of the law of 10 Germinal Year X, however, silenced these displays of obsessive concern for individual status. Social historians have not taken into account the scope of this massive and drastic reduction in the social discourse of bell ringing. The regulations jointly agreed to by bishops and prefects severely curtailed the use of *bells of honor*. Nevertheless, many parish priests and mayors, wishing to celebrate whomsoever they pleased, overstepped the mark and, by so doing precipitated other disputes over bells.

Bell ringing was one of a series of practices that reinforced existing social divisions. A number of parishes were torn asunder, as we shall see later, by disputes over the order of participants in processions and, above all, over *pews* of honor.[253] The town hall and presbytery were often at odds over such matters. It is also worth noting the exceptionally close links that existed, as it happens, between pew and bell. In the tower of the church in La Chapelle-d'Alagnon, near to Murat in the Cantal, there is an inscription from 1828 that reads as follows: "M. Pierre Valeri de Saurret du Jarousset, priest, and honorary canon of Saint-Flour, has paid for the bell on condition that the owners of the château of Le Jarousset shall have the right to a pew in the church of La Chapelle."[254]

First, let us consider the legitimate uses of honorific ringing. Bells might, for example, be rung to welcome the bishop or vicar general when

paying a visit to the parish, or to celebrate the prelate's return to his episcopal town. As the regulation of 6 November 1806 specified, "*all the bells*
shall be rung upon the arrival of Monsignor the Bishop of Quimper
when he has been absent a whole month from his capital."[255] Under the
Old Regime one of the bells in Avranches cathedral served no other purpose but to solemnize the bishop's return.[256]

Napoleon loved the sound of bells above all else.[257] It is therefore not
surprising to find the decree of 24 Messidor Year XII requiring *all* bells
to be rung when the first consul, and subsequently the emperor, entered
the territory of a commune.[258] Throughout the century the obligation to
ring a peal of bells at the passage of the sovereign and members of his
family was maintained and, it seems, observed. The survey conducted in
1884 and 1885 at departmental level to discover whether mayors approved
or disapproved of ringing in honor of Jules Grévy, were the occasion to
arise, shows that there would have been little opposition to it. At most
there was a touch of reluctance here and there.[259] The decree of 16 June
1907 concerned with "secular honors" likewise stipulated that "at the
entrance of the president of the Republic into *each* commune, *all* the bells
[must] ring *a peal*." The observance of this injunction during the numerous journeys made by Raymond Poincaré in 1913 and 1914 was much crit-
icized in the pages of *L'humanité*. The editors saw it as a symbol of
renascent "reaction."[260]

When the sovereign visited it was not only the communes directly
affected that saw fit to ring. The inhabitants of Saint-Riquier-en-Rivière
(Seine-Inférieure), whose bell was "one of the loveliest sounding in the
region," "could find nothing more apt to do, upon Louis XVIII's return,
than to ring for a whole day." So lustily did they ring that the bell broke,
bringing their rejoicing to an end. Yet the commune in question was not
on the king's itinerary. In 1829, during a journey by Charles X through
the departments of the East, all the bells in the region of Nancy were
simultaneously set ringing.[261]

The other honorific peals, now illegal, gave rise to many problems. To
go by archival documents, a parish priest would only rarely have the bells
rung simply because he wished to celebrate the presence of a personage
he thought to be of note. Nevertheless, it is impossible to judge how
commonplace such a practice was since there are only traces of it when

the perpetrator was denounced. In 1835 the parish priest of Cerizay (Deux-Sèvres) was accused of having rung a carillon "so as to celebrate the *arrival* and the *passage* of the wife of M. de Chauvelin, brother-in-law of M. de La Rochejaquelein." The parish priest admitted "to having been well pleased" that "Mme de Chauvelin heard the sound of a bell, of which she had been godmother, and for which she had in part paid."[262] This interesting remark points to the symbolic identification and emotional tie linking the notable's wife to the bell bearing her Christian name.

Samuel Bour, incidentally, has recorded a fact which I shall simply repeat here without being able to say whether it was a habitual practice. Around the middle of the nineteenth century, Dr. Guthmann, a doctor held in high esteem by his patients in the Moselle, was taken very ill and conveyed to Metz. Each village, wishing to make its sympathy for him known, rang the bells as he passed through.[263]

The ringing of a peal to mark and celebrate the arrival of the prefect or subprefect caused much debate, even though the regulations made no provision for such an honor. In the Vosges this peal was current until the drafting of the 1840 regulation.[264] In August 1859, the mayors of the two cantons of Maure and Pleurtuit (Ille-et-Vilaine) gave instructions for the bells to be rung upon the arrival and departure of the prefect. According to the archbishop, those parish priests who refused to comply were subjected to "threats and very nearly to violence" at the hands of the municipal magistrates. Minister Rouland delivered a stinging rebuke to the prefect and expressed his regret at "these deplorable conflicts." "No secular authority," he went on, "should tolerate its being accorded honors that, in the temporal sphere, are the prerogative of his Imperial Majesty."[265] On 11 May 1869, the municipal councillors of Fontaine-l'Abbé (Eure) denounced the parish priest, who had refused to ring when the subprefect of Bernay came even though the mayor had instructed him to do so. Needless to say, the prefect, pressed on this point by the bishop of Évreux, in the end had to rule in the cleric's favor.[266]

Oddly enough, this type of conflict seems to have become rarer under the Third Republic whereas the peals for the fourteenth of July, for the Angelus, and for secular burials occasioned innumerable disputes. Nevertheless, it is perhaps worth recording that in 1901 the parish priest of Parnes (Oise) chose to loop up the bell ropes to prevent the mayor from ringing to celebrate the arrival of republican dignitaries. In reaching up to grab the rope the unfortunate magistrate slipped and injured himself.[267] On the regulation signed in the Manche in 1885, we read that where the tradition was already established, it was permissible to ring for the prefect's first visit,[268] suggesting that in some communes in that department the practice of honorific ringing did exist. Once again, at least as far as bells were concerned, the territory became a patchwork of local usages.

Of more immediate relevance to us here are the disputes over honors bestowed upon local authorities. The "rectors" from Finistère enjoyed such power and prestige that they felt able to ring when they saw fit. In October 1831, the Mayor of Pont-Croix took his grievances to the prefect: "The bell ringer took the liberty of ringing *in full peal*, at six o'clock in the morning, for at least a half an hour, to celebrate the return of the parish priest, and this at the bidding of the curate, he has told me."[269] In Créancey (Haute-Marne) in September 1876, it was his own departure that the parish priest had rung. The sexton was ordered to give four *lesses* of a "lugubrious sound" which, according to the mayor, "threw the commune into a state of alarm."[270]

In 1860 the Mayor of Lannilis (Finistère), vexed at being denied the right to honorific peals, pointed out that a carillon had celebrated the arrival of the rector in the parish. "Ever since then," he went on, "every year, on the *eve* of Saint-Yves, his birthday, a *great Angelus* has been rung in his honor."[271] In the departments of Brittany and Basse-Normandie, priests in charge seem to have rung as and when they chose without paying the regulations much heed. On 2 May 1817, the parish priest of Saint-Cornier-des-Landes (Orne) marked the death of his heroic sexton by having the bells rung *throughout the day*.[272]

The municipal authorities were as uncompromising in this sphere as the clergy. In many regions it was the practice to ring an honorific peal when a mayor or municipal council was installed. According to the prefect, this was the case in the Orne in 1833.[273] In 1884 honorific peals of this type were still current in the Vosges and in eighteen communes in the Manche.[274] Some parish priests were opposed to the practice, however, so conflicts arose, especially under the July Monarchy.

On 24 April 1845, the mayor of Brasparts (Finistère) complained to the subprefect of Châteaulin. Contrary to established usage, the priest in charge had refused to have the bells rung to celebrate "the recent installation of the deputy mayor."[275] Much later, on 12 January 1875, the mayor of Milizac complained to the subprefect. "An incident, occurring on Sunday the tenth," he wrote, " has made me the laughingstock of the whole commune." The parish priest interrupted the verger as he was beginning to ring in honor of the installation of the municipal council. When, however, he mounted the pulpit and gave the reasons for his ban, his words "caused some residents *to burst out laughing*." The mayor was a notable who traded in livestock. According to the prefect, he could count on over 25,000 francs in rent; he was a "tried and trusted conservative." He had succeeded his father, himself mayor of the commune for forty-six years.

In 1881, shortly after the Republic had prevailed, three similar conflicts erupted in the same department. According to the mayor of Kernével, parish priests would ring for the installation of those they called "the good Lord's mayors" and deny the bells to those they regarded as the devil's mayors. The rector of Sizun, without even referring the matter to the newly elected official, set the bells ringing in honor of the mayor's installation whereas the parish priest of Kernével denied the plaintiff an honorific peal.[276]

On 25 January 1881, the mayor of Esquibien informed the prefect of his intention to ring on the following Sunday to mark his own "appointment" together with that of the deputy mayor. He knew that the rector had decided to shut the bell tower to preempt this honorific peal. He therefore asked the prefect's permission to "bring up a ladder in order to reach the bell-ropes."[277] That same year the parish priest of Saint-Uniac (Ille-et-Vilaine) denounced the municipality for "having had a passing bell rung in honor of a former mayor"[278] without having asked his permission. On Sunday the seventeenth, wrote the deputy mayor of Landudal in a letter to the prefect dated May 1896, *"we gave the order for the bells to be rung in our honor as is the custom* in the area," but the verger "ordered everyone down from the bell tower."[279] In this commune, according to the complainant, the parish priest would ring at the death of persons known by him to hold conservative opinions but withheld the honor from republican councillors. At the opposite end of the national territory, the mayor of Moyemont (Vosges) decided in July 1884 to mark his own installation by ringing without informing the priest in charge.[280]

Throughout the century the government ruled against municipal authorities, reminding them that bells rung in honor of mayor, deputy mayor, or councillors were contrary to regulations. Nevertheless, in a number of communes the ringing continued. In all these disputes, as in those over honorific pews, mayors and deputy mayors had to give way in the end. As we shall see later,[281] they were even denied the right to mark municipal council meetings by ringing—another usage that could be regarded as honorific.

There was another way for a bell ringer to celebrate an individual and proclaim, where necessary, powers and hierarchies. This involved modifying the use of bells that solemnized rites of passage or celebrated the memory of the deceased. I have in mind here *peals of pride*, which were claimed as a right by some families. The "unanimous knell," rung by all the bells in a given town, like the emblazoned pall, constituted in the eighteenth century one of the elements of the baroque funeral services studied by Michel Vovelle and François Lebrun. In actual fact this practice was already being contested on the eve of the Revolution by élites concerned about showing discretion and breaking with the more spectacular forms of funerals. In 1812 the prefect of the Haut-Rhin gave a clear account of the history of the practice. "*This kind of honor*, being formerly reserved for *persons of distinction*, is nowadays lavished upon anyone who can meet the expense. The priests take great pains to present the death peal as a religious duty, so that the poor man and the rich man alike, one out of fanaticism and the other out of ostentation, pay this tribute." The prefect thought that "the bells should only announce a *public mourning* when society loses one of its members who has given outstanding service to the state, that it is unseemly that the demise of the most obscure of men should be announced with as much ceremony as is that of a magistrate, and that at all times of day we should disturb a numerous population to announce that an artisan, often unknown to his closest neighbors, has ceased to exist."[282] This text, which deserves to be quoted in full, seems to reflect at the same time a wish to forestall an egalitarian use of bells, a rejection of the privileges of birth and money, the cult of the great man who has served the city well, and a sense of a division between public and private.

At any rate, the prefect of the Haut-Rhin went on, the recent destruction of many bells made it harder to mark distinctions that had once been articulated in terms of rank. Under the Old Regime the "great peal" and the "small peal" were easy to recognize. Since the restoration of religious worship Colmar could only call upon two bells "so that there could not be too much difference between peals reserved for persons of distinction and those accorded to private persons."

The former procedures, though preserved here and there, gradually took on a vestigial quality. In 1872 the mayor of La Roche (Haute-Savoie), a region that had only been incorporated into France in 1860, wrote that, "according to an old custom, the bells of our little town announce the demise of members of the nobility and clergy with *knells of lamentation*, which are repeated on the day of burial." However, he hastened to add, "this usage, standing condemned by the principles underlying our society, no longer has any reason to exist, and public sentiment calls for its abolition." He therefore called for the suppression of the "knell of lamentation" on the grounds that it was a "special peal,"[283] and the parochial church council concurred.

Several of these honorific peals[284] survived here and there in the countryside, which is, after all, the focus of the present study. In 1886 the residents of Poumarous (Hautes-Pyrénées), disagreeing in this regard with the parish priest, wished for a peal to be rung on the great bell for the burial of an adult, and *both* for that "of an adult who was, or who at any time in the past had been, a town councillor."[285] Such, they went on, was the custom in several neighboring localities. This was anyway simply a restoration, since the death of a councillor from Poumarous had once been marked in this fashion.

Despite vestiges of such practices, the use of bells was becoming more democratic, a general tendency that is consistent with our analysis of the extension of godparenthood. Parochial church councils, however, intent on exploiting vanities and social ambitions in order to boost their all too meager revenues, set about recreating distinctions, although this time they would rest on wealth alone. Over the course of the nineteenth century the practice spread of modulating the size and duration of peals to match the generosity of the family in question. The regulation agreed to in 1885 between the archbishop of Rennes and the prefect of Ille-et-Vilaine reflected such a policy. A burial called for six peals: two "on the eve, after the midday and evening Angelus, the third on the day itself after the morning Angelus, and the three others before, during, and after the ceremony."[286] The number of bells and the duration of these peals depended on "the class" of the deceased.[287] The archives contain hundreds of such tariffs drawn up by parochial church councils and approved by the prefect. They are as monotonous as can be.

Occasionally, however, some resistance was shown.[288] In 1865 the commune of Void (Meuse) was divided over such policies. The municipal council, when it met on 14 March 1865, wanted burial to be the same for all, rich or poor. In particular, it called for three bells to be used for everyone. Paupers felt that distinctions in this sphere were "an insult to their poverty." On 4 November the parish priest of Void presented his own case in a long letter addressed to the bishop of Verdun. On 5 March, as a pauper was being rung with two bells, the mayor had communicated an order through the rural guard for the three bells to be rung. This, then, would be a "great peal." The parish priest, who was at that moment at the altar, had put up some resistance but had then advised the bell ringer to obey the magistrate. Such was the episode that unleashed the conflict. The parish priest made himself out to be the defender of "honorific peals." He went on to explain that families were at liberty to choose. When a child was to be interred, many wanted only a single bell. For the past thirty-six years only two bells had been rung for paupers. The other members of the congregation opted for a "lavish peal." According to the parish priest, the rich valued such honors. As he saw it, one would do better not to confuse "natural equality and civil equality with social equality," which he regarded as the "negation of every honor, of all hierarchy, and consequently of society itself." Void's parish priest said he could not understand how the municipal council could speak of an "insulting, humiliating, and irksome measure" when generalized use of the third bell would in fact imply the "subversion of the foundations of society."[289]

Parish regulation of peals, where it existed, often reflected membership of confraternities. In this fashion hierarchies arose within the community. According to a text composed by the parochial church council of Loubressac (Lot), the great bell was rung for all the deceased. When, however, the dead person had been a member of the Confraternity of the Holy Sacrament, one "pulled" the second bell as well. Conversely, if he belonged to the Confraternity of the Rosary the small bell would accompany the great bell. When the dead person had belonged to both confraternities he had the right to all three bells. In 1855 the parish priest decided to increase the annual subscription paid by members of the Confraternity of the Holy Sacrament. The fee, now one franc instead of twenty-five centimes, served to exclude a number of parishioners who were consequently much offended.

On Sunday 2 September 1860, Adeline Bombezy was buried. She belonged only to the Confraternity of the Rosary and so had no right to the second bell. A group of women, indignant at the thought of their friend being thus deprived, went into the church and took it upon themselves to ring all three bells. The parish priest was unable to make them stop. The rural guard and sergeant finally managed to expel them from the sanctuary. With the help of a young farmer the women renewed their attack and rang once again. The parish priest refused to proceed with the removal of the body while regulations were being flouted. The following night some cabbages were taken from the presbytery garden. In Quercy this seems to have been the usual way of displaying hostility toward the parish clergy.[290]

In spite of the obstacles put up to block its deployment, it is worth noting how keen the desire for *honorific bell ringing* was, especially in societies where everyone knew everyone else. By the same token, we should note how intense the disappointment was when requests were turned down. The bell was one of the "semiophores" so coveted by the new nineteenth-century élites. For a factory owner who wished to found a lineage, but also for a well-to-do farmer or a wealthy "laborer," campanarian inscriptions promised to render their names eternal. This was all the more so given that, as we know, the history of bells is closely linked to the procedures of "long memory" through which social representations, in villages at any rate, were ordered. The members of rural communi-ties, sometimes the residents of mere hamlets, mayors, deputy mayors, "councillors," and notables by birth or fortune were plainly moved to hear a bell symbolically proclaiming their rank, prestige, and honor.

To be denied the symbolic gratification of ringing "a peal" may have seemed cruel, if not humiliating, especially in regions where this form of solemnization—being so firmly rooted in local custom—was taken very much to heart. This seems to have been the case in the west, north, and east of France. It is hard for us nowadays to grasp the impact of bell ringing, let alone of silenced bells, on the social world. This brief foray may perhaps encourage others, at least I hope, to pay fresh attention to these peals that occasioned so many conflicts and such deep bitterness; they did so much to anchor, through emotion, contrasted systems of social representations.

Through bells an individual was better able to apprehend the identity of the group to which he belonged. They helped him locate himself in space and time. They audibly proclaimed to him the order of the society within which his life unfolded, and made manifest the power of the constituted authorities. Yet this was not the whole story; in the countryside bells were the most important medium of communication, and their history is chiefly concerned with this fact.

CHAPTER FIVE

The Density of Truth

*T*he life of a community presupposes the reading of other auditory signals in addition to those that impart a rhythm to time, defend a territory, give expression to hierarchies, or identify personages deemed worthy of honor. Bells also serve to make announcements, exhort people to assemble, sound the alarm, and express general rejoicing. Under the Old Regime, ways of ringing were so various that the residents of each parish had to undergo a highly specific apprenticeship[1]. Although the authorities in the nineteenth century sought to introduce a degree of uniformity within the framework of the department, each community still had its own code of bell ringing that was understood by each of its members but was hermetic, at least to some extent to "foreigners."[2] Successive governments acknowledged the persistence of these "immemorial customs" that prelates and prefects had more than once attempted to record, while also trying to identify their origin. I want now to describe in broad outline the language of bell ringing.

The bell ringer had a crucial role to play here. Without a clear system of peals it was impossible to notify the members of a community of the appropriate times for performing specific tasks, for assembling, or for rejoicing. Auditory signals had to be limpid and, above all, *devoid of any confusion*. A number of heated disputes were thus precipitated by incoherent announcements and the resultant disruption of the community's temporal architecture.

Regardless of the setting the language of bells, which structured information and communication within a given community, had to obey certain rules that never varied. First, religious bell ringing had priority over any other kind. The parish priest or incumbent had to be informed whenever a bell was used for secular purposes. As we have seen, one could not ring before the morning Angelus or after the evening Angelus unless circumstances were exceptional. Lay bell ringers, where they did not double up as religious bell ringers, were supposed to avoid any *simultaneum*; they were not allowed to set a bell ringing in the intervals left by a religious peal. They were not supposed to ring during a service. The regulation for the Dordogne (1884) stipulated that, given this statutory inferiority, "secular peals shall be suspended from Easter Thursday at nine o'clock in the morning until Easter Saturday at noon."[3] To be more precise, secular peals should not be mistaken for religious peals.[4] Whatever the circumstances, the bell ringer was supposed to hold back for a while. On 5 May 1889, during the centenary celebrations of the meeting of the Estates-General, several parish priests in the Loir-et-Cher refused to allow the peals announcing the festivities to be rung "immediately after the Angelus." The bishop of Blois backed them. He "would allow [at best] that an interval of a few minutes was left between the ringing of the Angelus and the secular peal." The *ministre des Cultes* accepted and asked the prefect "to see to it that the confusion mentioned by the diocesan authority does not prevail, particularly on the occasion of the national festival."[5]

The language of bell ringing was governed by a second principle, namely, that the "*peal*" and often the use of the great bell were reserved for public announcements that were the direct responsibility of the parish priest or priest in charge. The clergy held a monopoly over signals of solemnity and were for this reason sensitive about all celebrations of national festivals, even when they did not disapprove of them. Such occasions entailed the use of auditory messages that were simultaneously secular and solemn. The mayor, who was responsible for keeping the peace locally, was authorized under certain circumstances to order the bells to be rung. But he was only permitted to use a single bell; he generally had to keep to the smallest and settle for having it tolled. As was pointed out at the prefecture of the Orne in 1840, some care had to be taken not to confuse the "sound of the bell" with the "sound of bells."[6] According to a regulation signed in the Haute-Marne on 6 March 1832, "public assemblies shall be . . . announced by the sound of *a* bell, which shall only be tolled and not rung in peal."[7]

The desire to avoid any confusion between secular and religious ringing was matched by a concern to differentiate between announcements, signals, and summonses. Both preoccupations influenced the bell ringing schedule submitted in 1846 by Monsignor Parisis, then bishop of Langres, to the prefect of the Haute-Marne. He proposed ringing three peals to assemble a congregation—one peal "when it was only a question of distinguishing between particular parts of a service, of *announcing without a summons* a religious ceremony, or of giving the signal for some religious act to be performed on its own"[8] (for example, a prayer), and simply tolling on secular occasions.

In order to grasp the subtleties of this language, we require a good understanding of what distinguished the various ways of ringing. In order to toll[9] one was supposed to use a rope to draw the clapper directly onto the bell, or set the bell in motion in such a way that the clapper only struck the inside edge, and always on the same side. There was, however, another way of giving the listener an impression of tolling that involved tapping the outside of a motionless bell with a mallet or ordinary hammer, despite the risk of breaking the instrument. In Guerville (Seine-Inférieure) the bell ringer would, if need be, combine these various ways of tolling so that when a wedding or a baptism was to be announced, "with one hand he simply struck the bell with its clapper and with the other [he struck it] with a mallet."[10]

Ringing in peal entailed making the clapper strike either side of the moving bell in turn. The bell ringer tugged gently on the rope until the clapper began to strike the metal. Then, "during the peal [proper he] should pull perpendicularly, let the rope fall in front of him in a semicircle or let it slip through his hands and not hold on to it."[11] Above all, he should take care not to be swept off his feet and risk cracking his skull on the frame of the belfry.

Carillonning, or playing a melody using the elements of a ring, required more bells—at least four according to Antoine Trin—than most churches possessed. Some bell ringers in the Bray nevertheless managed to create the illusion of carillonning. They tied up the clapper of their bells and introduced into them some "iron rings placed at suitable intervals." "In this way they produced enough notes," according to Dieudonné Dergny, "to play a few short melodies."[12]

I should further point out that ringing was not done the same way in the north as in the south. In some southern regions, as in Spain and Italy, the bells were made to somersault.[13] Being generally of quite small dimensions, they were hung in such a way that they made a circular movement that rendered them more visible to the naked eye.

The reader will no doubt have guessed that the principles governing the use of bells were far from being observed in every case. Styles of ringing could prove contentious, as was the right to use the bells. The municipal authorities, the mayor, the deputy mayor, the members of the municipal council, and the lay bell ringer, who was often the schoolmaster, endeavored to gain as much access to bell ringing as they could, to ring for long stretches at a time, and with several instruments. Above all their ambition was to use the great bell.

The parish clergy sought, as much as possible, to prevent the municipal authorities from ringing, preferring to see them stick to the bass drum and side drum. At any rate, they wanted to debar them from using the largest bell and from ringing peals. They also held that the mayor should only perform his official duties between the morning and the evening Angelus and abstain from ringing during services. As we shall see later,[14] there were two main ways in which the parish priest might best his adversaries. He could either withhold the key to the bell tower or rely on the obedience of the statutory bell ringer.

Be this as it may, clarity was in all circumstances absolutely crucial.

Confusion could result in an unnecessary gathering or even a catastrophe. On 26 Floréal Year XIII (16 May 1805), the "sexton's" son in Appenay (Orne) made haste to ring the tocsin to signal that a property belonging to the former mayor was on fire. After a few minutes the priest in charge rushed into the bell tower; he "bid him carillon instead[15] on the grounds that a carillon was used to sound the alarm in his region."[16] I should add that the priest was a native of a commune some twenty kilometers from Appenay. Thinking that a baptism was being announced, the laborers in the fields, who had begun to make their way back to the town, resumed work. The former mayor's property burned down.[17]

Conversely, on 4 December 1821, the sexton in Rétiers (Ille-et-Vilaine) rang a baptism in such a fashion that the local residents came running, with those from the surrounding communes close behind. The listeners believed they had heard the tocsin.[18] Likewise in January 1893, the eighteen–year–old daughter of the bell ringer in Clinchamp (Haute-Marne), with the help of several of her friends, tolled the three bells to mark a wedding. Misled by this deviation from the accepted code, the "laborers in the fields" thought they heard the tocsin and "returned with all possible haste to the village."[19] The ringers were heartily amused. The prefect, however, was much displeased and ordered the mayor to have the rural guard notify the "sexton" of his dismissal.[20]

The Old Regime Of Information

THE AUDITORY REGISTER

Bells informed the community of the completion of rites of passage. This was the most frequent, and perhaps the most listened to of all the forms of annunciatory ringing. Mutual acquaintance, the precondition of communities, implied constant attention, and the ceaseless readjusting of one's knowledge of others, and of family biographies in all their detail. The act of listening to the bell that told of rites of passage and the legibility of its messages were crucial aspects of a process of everyday elucidation. Without it a group risked dissolving into the indefinable.[21]

In the aftermath of the Revolution, ringing that announced rites of passage was still regarded as secular and religious at the same time. Article 4 of a concerted regulation, signed in the Manche on 14 Prairial Year XI (3 June 1803), was worded as follows: "At the baptism of a child the bells may be rung for a few minutes only to make the joy one feels in a republic at the birth of a citizen, and—in the militant and triumphant church—at the adoption of a child into the family of Jesus Christ."[22]

The baptismal peal was subsequently turned into an exclusively religious practice until, at the end of the century, free thinkers strove to desacralize the ringing of rites of passage.[23] The bell of baptism, we read in a petition dating from 1840 and signed by a hundred or so residents of Longny-au-Perche (Orne), marks our "joye at seeing a soul wrested from the clutches of the demon."[24] This text reminds us that it is anachronistic to suppose that such peals simply involved a wish to celebrate the joy of a birth.

At the end of his own survey, Arnold Van Gennep, although he unfortunately failed to give a precise date for the practices in question, concluded that ringing lasted longer for the baptism of boys than for that of girls, that the great bell was used for boys and the small bell for girls, and that styles of ringing likewise differed. Generally, three peals announced the baptism of a boy but two peals that of a girl. Bastards and foundlings did not enter by the main door of the church; sometimes they were confined to the sacristy. Whatever the sex of the child the bells were not rung on the actual day of the baptism. It was meant to pass unremarked, and these children were not supposed to be "socialized after a Christian fashion."[25]

The survey initiated in 1845 by Monsignor Rendu in the diocese of Annecy testifies to the existence of such practices even in the mid-nineteenth century. In Cuvat the bells were not rung for the baptism of bastards. In that parish—likewise in Publier and Ballaison—the bell would not sound for children who came "into the world before the sixth or seventh month of marriage." In Publier the nuptials of "a girl who had gone astray" were celebrated "noiselessly." Yet as the rector of Cercier wrote, it was a "great dishonor" if baptisms and weddings were not carillonned. The above testimonies all show how important bells were in managing the symbolic capital of individuals and families alike.[26]

Perhaps no peals were listened to so intently as those marking death agony and death itself. No others required such clarity. In some parishes under the Old Regime this announcement was the exclusive preserve of a special bell to which parishioners sometimes attached a funereal nickname. In Reims it was called the "barking of death" or the "death-bark,"[27] and elsewhere it sometimes bore the name "bell of tears."

This funereal instrument informed the members of a community that one among them *was in his death agony*. It called on them to take part in the "greeting of the death agony"[28] or at least recite the prayer for those in the throes of death, "so as to mitigate the rigors of that terrible passage."[29] The handbell used to accompany the route of the viaticum served almost everywhere to confirm what the bell had already announced. The ringing was designed to save the deceased from the distress of solitary agony and belonged to baroque mortuary tradition.[30] The *knell of passing away* would follow and then, on the appointed day, the announcement of the religious ceremony preceding the burial itself. Under such distressing circumstances the bell had a threefold function serving first to announce the death agony and then the death; to issue a call to prayer; then, somewhat later, to enjoin the members of a community to gather together in pious assembly. At the end of the nineteenth century[31] freethinkers wanted bells to be used to *announce* the demise of their friends, but they did not take this to mean that the deceased had undergone a conversion. The sound of bells had for them lost the meaning formerly vested in the polysemic ringing regulated by the clergy.

No bell ringing code was as refined as that marking the death agony and death itself. It was of the utmost importance to avoid any confusion. The sound of the bell was more expressive and imbued with greater emotional intensity than the reading of the notification of death, above all in cases of sudden death. In the countryside the death knell was often anticipated. In societies characterized by mutual acquaintance one generally knew who was going to die. The auditory announcement of an unexpected death heard at the same moment by every member of the community, would thus have made a deep impression.

The interval between the bell for the death agony and that marking the death itself allowed all to collect their thoughts as they sadly awaited the misfortune to come. In some communes in the Moselle[32] they rang "in mortuary fashion" as soon as the death took place; in others after "the next Angelus" so that the sad news was delayed and rumor spread unchecked; in still others this peal was repeated after every Angelus.

Ways of ringing differed from commune to commune. In Morhange the death knell was tolled three times after each Angelus. In other communes in the Moselle one struck the clapper of the great bell three times to announce the death of a married man, but that of the second bell three times if a married woman had passed away. When the deceased was unmarried the same rules applied except the third bell was used. In some communes the code required that one ring in the same fashion but nine, six, or three times. In others, where traditions were more egalitarian, one tolled nine times for all the deceased, invariably with the great bell. In yet others one struck once on the great bell, once on the middle bell, and once on the small bell for a man, and in the reverse order for a woman. Such announcements using the death knell sometimes served as a prelude to the peal, which itself varied according to the gender and age of the deceased. For children who had died before their first communion, generally only one bell, the small one, was used. No bells were rung for those who had died before being baptized.

The refinements of the code, given in simplified form here to avoid confusing the reader, were just as elaborate in the Bray (Seine-Inférieure). "At Neufchâtel, death itself was announced with fifteen strokes of the bell for a man, twelve for a woman, and six for a boy or girl. In Bully, Esclavelles, and Bures, one tolled thirteen times for a man, eleven for a woman and . . . seven for children. In Gournay, death itself was announced with twelve strokes for a man and eight for a woman."[33]

Ways of ringing after the announcement of death and the use of "*tins*," "regrets," and "tollings" once again varied according to gender and place. Dergny's survey, conducted under the Second Empire, brings out the extreme complexity of the code and the need for members of a community to serve an apprenticeship—once you stepped outside your own commune the signals would seem scrambled.

In Neuf-Marché and in part of Argueil canton, one tolls thrice times three for a man and twice times three for a woman. . . . in Dancourt, nine "*tins*" for a man—one stroke on each of the three bells repeated three times; for a woman, six only—one stroke on each bell, two times . . . in Grandcourt one tolls nine strokes for a man and the same number of times for a woman, but for the latter the final three are tolled in succession with no pause. In Vieux-Rouen and in Fry, when someone dies one rings a peal, while a person in the bell tower strikes that same bell with a wooden mallet. This usage is still current in a large number of parishes in the county [sic] of Eu. . . . In Croisy-sur-Andelle, someone with one hand strikes twice on the bell with a mallet while with the other he strikes a third stroke with the clapper of the bell.[34]

Ringing for children who had died before their first communion likewise varied from place to place. "In Dancourt the small bell is tolled thrice times three for a boy, thrice times two times for a girl. In Neuf-Marché, three "*tins*" only for a girl, four for a boy . . . in Grandcourt, nine alternating "*tins*" for a boy, and thrice times three "*tins*" in succession for a girl . . . in Monchaux, they ring the middle bell for a boy and the small bell for a girl."[35]

In the Bray the demise of a parish priest was announced by the "toll of regret," which was rung every hour for three quarters of an hour; during the final quarter of an hour the third bell was rung in peal. In 1831 this peal, which had been established usage under the Old Regime, was restored in order to announce the dean of Gournay's death.[36]

By contrast, bell ringing at funeral ceremonies and burials was not designed to announce and was consequently more uniform. These peals were normally governed by regulations specifying the tariff for the various classes of ceremony. The listener, who would already have known the identity of the deceased, generally learned the rank and fortune of the departed and the level of generosity shown by his family. As we have seen, some were led to voice their anger at this inequality. Sometimes the clergy would deny paupers any peal whatsoever. A hundred or so residents of Longny-au-Perche petitioned against this circumstance in 1840.

In that commune the poor "are obliged to have their loved ones buried in silence."[37]

The custom was to bury children *"non sono lugubri, sed festivi."* In the Moselle the ceremony was generally announced with the ringing of a small bell in peal. Sometimes the small bell was rung for a girl and a larger one for a boy.

Although the signals for burial were relatively uniform compared to the great diversity of ways in which death was customarily announced, some communes in the Bray in fact had their own particular "mourning peals." One such peal was called "the *lame one* while another was named the *Swiss March*. In several parishes . . . the name *épeinte* was given to a peal of bells rung in mourning." In Gournay this peal was known as "the lost bell."[38]

The regulation signed in 1886 by the prefect of the Ardennes and the archbishop of Reims stipulated that "peals commonly called *lesses*" could be rung if families so wished. They served to announce the demise "of relatives who were foreigners." This usage was in fact judged to be "immemorial" in the diocese.[39]

The announcement of the death agony and the death itself, being modulated to take sex and age into account, reflected prevailing representations of man, woman, and child in rural society. Almost everywhere there was a distinction,[40] with the announcement being almost invariably shorter and/or less solemn in the case of a woman. The size of bell reflected the sex and age of the deceased. This explains why so many parishes decided to recast their one and only bell to turn its metal into three instruments of different volumes. Actions generally ascribed to pride also stemmed from the need to make the language of bell ringing clear and precise.

Later I will consider the none too successful attempts made by some mayors to take control of the bell announcing rites of passage. I would like to mention here, however, one particularly significant example that brings out the underlying logic of the aspiration to keep a community informed of *the whole range* of events punctuating the private life of each of its members. On 12 June 1908, the mayor of Beaubray (Eure) decided by decree to "announce to the public, through the ringing of bells, the important events in the secular life of individuals." Henceforth he would have the bells rung "to announce a birth, an *adoption*, a marriage, a *divorce*, or the death of a person from the commune, regardless of whether such events were secular or religious."[41]

THE "TOWN HALL SERMON"

We have already seen, in relation to the Angelus and the use of a bell for the Festival of the Dead or in stormy weather, that a number of peals, though regarded as intrinsically religious, prove on closer inspection to be polysemic. They were often seen by the mayor and councillors, and the young, if not by residents in general, as practices that might with luck elude the clerical monopoly. Some peals, on the other hand, belonged officially to the secular sphere and were overseen by the authorities responsible for keeping the peace. It is these that I propose to consider now.

Where announcements are concerned, such claims on the part of secular authorities are the culmination of a long history, which likewise forms part of the history of bell ringing. As is well known, the auditory prevails over the visual. Radio is more persuasive than a newspaper or a voiceless image. In the nineteenth-century countryside the sound of bells bestowed certainty upon those who listened to it. In a universe of information dominated by the flexibility of rumor, the bell conferred the density of truth on events. It proclaimed, or powerfully recalled, the existence or approach of the sovereign, with the same peals used to announce the word of God. It legitimized authority. It alerted listeners to danger and risk. It accompanied the public reading of laws and lent weight to administrative decisions. In the last case it reinforced the authority of posters.

Consider, then, the various ways in which municipal authorities could make their decisions known. Article 11 of the law of 18 and 22 May 1791 "entrusted to the mayor the responsibility for specifying the places in which are put the posters of the laws and decisions of the public authority,"[42] but it prohibited such billposting on the walls or doors of churches. Such announcements, it was claimed, in fact undermine public order; they "obstruct passersby because people crowd around to look at them"; "they provoke heated conversation and more or less intense debate, which disturbs priest and congregation at their worship." In short, due respect should be paid the division between the secular and the religious since it corresponds to that which had constituted the sacred and differentiated it from the profane.

Nevertheless, the practice of posting decrees on the doors or walls of churches spread. After the law of 3 May 1841, it was even permissible to post prefectoral rulings, jury lists, and decrees regarding expropriations there.[43] During the first two-thirds of the century many rural communes were deprived of actual town halls. In such cases the term would refer to the mayor's own place of residence. The jurist Parieu strongly advised municipalities without municipal buildings to erect "in the church square a post or pillar upon which shall be placed a board for billposts."[44] This advice does not seem to have been much heeded. Many mayors, even if only out of defiance, had the billposts stuck on the main door of the church. In short, the sacralizing of administrative announcements—or in other words the relative secularization of the door or walls of the church brought about by municipal billposting—belongs to the same zone of conflict as the struggle over the keys to the bell tower.[45]

The triumph of the Republic after the 1870s did not lead to a radical transformation in usage. According to article 15 of the law of 29 July 1881, the natural place for a poster was the town hall, or some hall serving that function. Where there was no other suitable site the mayor could now opt for billposting on the outside of the church.[46]

To understand why some municipal authorities would choose not to have recourse to a profane space or a secular edifice, we need to consider the initial procedures involved in making an announcement. The standard practice at the beginning of the nineteenth century was to read official texts *after the service*, outside the church. A number of mayors wished this act to be performed as near as possible to the religious edifice and, crucially, accompanied by the *sound of the bell*, or at least a handbell. A *boundary-stone* close to the church or the *pedestal of the cross in the cemetery* adjoining this edifice served as rostrums for the leading municipal magistrate. The clergy showed no hesitation in multiplying the number of announcements delivered from the pulpit, and would obviously have wished to limit the impact of what in Finistère was called "the town-hall sermon." Given that both parties nursed the desire to exercise a monopoly over secular announcements, conflict was occasionally inevitable.

In 1812 the mayor of Coësmes made his dissatisfaction known to the prefect of Ille-et-Vilaine. The rector, he avowed, made any number of different kinds of announcement from the pulpit; he even read out some "bills of sale in which pigs featured." Conversely, he would not tolerate the mayor having the "*échelette* rung around the cemetery in order to assemble the people at the gravestone." He had said to the sexton that "everything pertaining to bell or handbell was his." The mayor resolved to take one further step; he had the bells rung before giving some official texts their public reading. "After this scene he [the parish priest] went to the main door of the church and mockingly tore off the poster of the decree I had put there before the Sunday morning Mass."[47]

In January 1851 the prefect of Ille-et-Vilaine rebuked the mayors in his department. "In many communes," he wrote, " they have turned the pedestal of the cemetery cross into a rostrum,"[48] leading the rectors of the cantons of Dol and Plaine-Fougères to register a collective protest.

The affair that erupted in Lannilis (Finistère) was still more revealing. Up until 1860 it had been the tradition there to ring when the residents were to assemble for the "town hall sermon." Given that the regulation was in his favor, the rector decided that year to acquiesce in or reject this practice depending on whether the mayor was in his good graces or not. After a quarrel between the two authorities, "the [town hall] sermon was no longer announced except by the tolling of a handbell in the public square as the congregation emerged from the high mass. The use of so paltry a means seemed to put the municipal authorities in a ridiculous and demeaning light."[49] The mayor therefore urged the parish priest to restore the former usage. The priest relented. "I got the church bells," recorded the mayor, "but instead of nine strokes the [town hall] sermon was now only announced by six or seven strokes and I do not rightly recall which." The rector "set great store on this reduction." The mayor, however, made known his reluctance to rely in this fashion on the priest's "good graces." He therefore asked the prefect if he might be allowed to revert to what, following the old usage, he sometimes termed the "peal summoning [the people] to the town hall sermon" and sometimes the "announcement of the sermon." Every fortnight for almost a year the mayor of Lannilis called upon the subprefect of Brest to rectify the situation. As he wrote on 11 June 1861, "there is something humiliating about the situation in which I now find myself, and it constitutes an affront to my dignity as a mayor. I desire *at all costs to extricate myself.*"

Affairs of this sort were commonplace in the Orne during the heyday of the July Monarchy. Over the course of 1839 and 1840 alone the mayors of Boissy-Maugis, Lonlay-le-Tesson, Montgaudry, Saint-Honorine-la-Guillaume, and Chemilly claimed the right to maintain the established practice of "pulling the bell" at the end of church services, even if "only for one or two minutes"[50] to give notice of the decrees of the prefect, subprefect and the municipal assemblies as well as the registers of direct taxes and public health measures. As the mayor of Les Monceaux observed in 1840, ringing the bell represented a savings since the municipality could consequently do without a drum. This magistrate asked the prefect for permission to take one of the church's two bells and place it "in the town hall."[51] The mayor of Lonlay-le-Tesson noted that since the announcement bell had been abolished no one came to listen to the official decrees being read; "the publishing of them had therefore become pointless."[52] As the deputy mayor of Le Grais pointed out, it was the bell "that brought everyone near," so "if you were to remove this freedom it would become quite pointless to publish anything." The commune of Verrières had some drums in its possession but no one, the mayor observed in 1840, knew how to use them. "The drum," declared the mayor of Origny-le-Butin that same year, *is not best suited to the bourg.*"[53]

Conversely, parish priests were willing, with very few exceptions, to have the bells rung or let them be rung in peal when momentous events affecting the nation were announced.[54] In the Hérault, but possibly in other departments as well, the bells were rung when Bonaparte was made first consul for life in August 1802.[55] Momentous events in 1804, 1830, and 1852 were likewise announced with peals from all the bells in the Moselle. In 1814 the return of the Bourbons was celebrated in the same fashion, as was that of the Eagle, flying from bell tower to bell tower in 1815.[56] The births of the king of Rome in 1811, the duke of Bordeaux in 1820, the count of Paris in 1838, and the prince imperial in 1856, were all rung in the communes of this department, as was the marriage of the duke of Berry. At the death of Louis XVIII in 1824 "the bell [called] Mary in [Metz] cathedral was rung for forty days, each time for about an hour." "For the duke of Orléans, who died in 1842, [*la*] *Mutte* was tolled every evening for a fortnight."[57] Moreover, we know that many mayors throughout the national territory used bells to announce the demise of Félix Faure in 1899. Parish priests who refused to ring on this occasion were rebuked.[58]

Needless to say, bells announced great victories. In the Isère, battles won between 1805 and 1808 were all celebrated with the sound of bells. Despite the breach between emperor and pope that had begun in 1809, military successes continued to be rung. This auditory effervescence needs to be borne in mind if we are to stand any chance of genuinely apprehending the emotions of the population at large during the Napoleonic Wars.[59] The same was true after 1814. In that year, from Bordeaux to Toulouse and from Toulouse to Paris, the duke of Angoulême was everywhere greeted with the sound of bells, drums, and fanfares.[60] To take just the case of the Moselle, the successes of the war in Spain were rung in 1823. On 14 July 1830, the bells of this same department carillonned the capture of Algiers. During the Second Empire, peals simultaneously announced and celebrated the victories of the regime.[61]

On all such occasions the bells, which were ringing in unison, served to integrate communities into the space of the nation. They caused hearts and minds to thrill to the rhythms of the wider society. The ringing of the bells in November 1918 represented the culmination of a long history of collective emotion, deriving from a culture of the senses whose specific qualities have yet to be properly analyzed. Historians of the political would do well to take account of such matters.

The Injunction to Assemble

The sound of a bell was also a summons. Secular bell ringing enjoined listeners to assemble.[62] The original function of the instrument, as Jean-Baptiste Thiers recalled in 1709, had been to summon monks and, later, congregations to various services, day and night. I have already described some of the forms employed to convoke religious services, which were themselves structured in terms of liturgical time. It now remains for me to give an outline sketch of the secular peals that called upon the populace to assemble. Curiously enough, historians barely mention what was in fact the key means employed to mobilize crowds in the nineteenth century.

This use of bells was traditional, especially in the former *pays d'états*, as the prefect of the Basses-Pyrénées observed in relation to his own department. "There was a whole host of issues that could only be decided upon with the assent of all the inhabitants, as was the case with, for example, matters relating to sales, farms etc. . . . the villeins, aldermen, etc. [were] summoned by the sound of the bell." When the communes had stopped "running their own affairs collectively [the reader will notice the impression given here that with the introduction of the commune as an administrative unit and censitary suffrage, democratic procedures went into decline], the ancient method of summoning was kept for assembling the people, especially when all the inhabitants had to be assembled."[63]

Successive governments were well aware of the great importance of this custom. Its undermining would have threatened the cohesion of the community and the most basic aspects of its functioning. The secular peal for summoning a community had to be tolerated. All attempts to abolish the practice met with stout resistance, which was not drummed up by interested individuals but flowed directly from territorial identities. In many regions those who laid claim to the secular use of bells as a right invoked the prestige attached to auditory messages but were at the same time adamant that drums would not do. These peals, which were independent of liturgical and ceremonial time, were almost always regarded by those concerned as immemorial practices; in their eyes they derived from an immobile time which, were it to be maintained, offered the best possible guarantee that whatever it was that constituted collective identity would survive.

For the sake of clarity I will distinguish between a dozen or so secular peals that served to summon. The first concerned the meetings of the municipal council, and magistrates had no difficulty justifying it. "Since time immemorial," wrote the mayor of Poullaouen (Finistère) on 16 March 1853, "it has *always* been the custom in the commune, whenever the municipal council has cause to meet, to arrange for the verger to ring the bell once to announce the arrival of the president and at the same time the opening of the session, and that so as to hurry along members still

making their way to the council chamber, and to alert those who are waiting in houses in the *bourg*."[64] The previous evening, however, the parish
priest had banned this traditional peal. It would be altogether too "humiliating," the mayor felt, to acquiesce. This custom survived for a long
time in Brittany; it was still found in the Côtes-du-Nord in 1884.[65] It
existed in other areas as well. In 1840, attempts to abolish the practice
were fiercely resisted by many mayors in the department of the Orne.[66]
The regulations published in 1884 and 1885 permitted peals for the sessions of municipal councils in seven different departments.

At the dawn of the July Monarchy, in every region of France, those
mayors most favorably disposed toward the regime acquired the habit of
ringing the bell to summon the national guard,[67] inspect it, drill it, elect
its officers, or have it participate in ceremonies involving the planting of
liberty trees and the "trooping of the colors." In the Charente in bad
weather, some mayors would ring and then drill the guard inside the
church.[68] During this period some liberal mayors would also ring for
every sort of "impromptu holiday." An example would be to celebrate
the "building of a house" or even "the erection of a simple hut."[69]

From 1835 onward the government attacked those secular peals of
which it disapproved. On 23 June Persil, *ministre de la Justice et des Cultes*,
expounded his arguments at length in a letter addressed to Thiers, then
minister of the interior. Such a use of bells ought to be banned because it
constituted "a sure means of promoting the schemes of mayors who
count on assembling the national guard at the precise times that services
are held, bringing them together to actually drill on the parvis of the
church so that most of the parishioners are prevented from attending services, whilst those who do attend are distracted by the noise from the
drum, by the commands, and by the noise produced whenever the
national guard meets. Let us give the mayors the option to summon it by
ringing the bell; the latter would then only ring for it, and not for divine
service."[70]

In attempting to define exactly what was at stake, the minister referred
to the symbolic significance of sounds in the war being waged between
secular and religious authorities. In his view, bestowing the bell upon the
mayor, who was already master of the drum and the din the national
guard made in the town square, would be to accord him too easy a victo-

ry. "More especially as, when one gives them access to the bells," Persil added, " municipal magistrates tend to regard it as a triumph, and ring out of pure defiance"; "some there have been that are so unreasonable that they will deafen the populace with ten to twelve hours of bell ringing . . . simply to defy the parish priest."[71]

The conflict continued until the end of the Second Republic. In January 1851, in a circular addressed to the mayors of his department, the prefect of Ille-et-Vilaine reproached them for having misused these controversial peals since 1830. To judge by this document, some of them threatened to debar recalcitrant vergers from proceeding with the collections they were traditionally allowed to make to supplement their own earnings; others amused themselves by ringing in the middle of the night.[72]

The advance of democracy had, initially at least, reinforced some secular uses of bells. After the implementation of the law on municipal elections (passed in March 1831) it *became* the custom in many communes to ring the opening and closing of the poll(s). In some places the bell was "pulled" to announce the count; in others the result was carillonned. These practices seem to have been widespread between 1831 and 1852, although they dwindled subsequently. In the Jura in 1840, electoral meetings were rung everywhere.[73] In 1839, the mayor of Sainte-Honorine-la-Chardonne (Orne)[74] recalled that the parish bell had been paid for by local residents. In his view this gave the municipality the right to have the second ballot rung. "The sound of the drum," he added, " was not sufficient to alert all the electors." In 1840 in the same department, the mayors of Sainte-Opportune, Saires, Champs, Préaux, Saint-Mard-de-Réno, and Berjou claimed the right to do as they had in the past and ring the ballots. The same claim was made by the mayor of La Chapelle-Montligeon, who pointed out that the interval between the first and second ballots amounted to three hours.[75]

The situation was much the same in the towns. The mayor of Alençon, the *chef-lieu* town in the department of the Orne, asked permission to ring when the electoral colleges met to elect deputies, general councillors, and councillors for the arrondissement. The bells kept pace with censitary suffrage. In 1840 the mayor of Bellême likewise emphasized the indispensable nature of this peal: "In Bellême, the *great* bell has always announced the opening of sessions and the *recall* at elections. . . . the *continuous sound* of the bell is far more effective in attracting the attention of the electors than a simple announcement with a drum, even when it is made in each quarter of the town in turn."[76] Details such as these belong to the history of modes of attention and demonstrate that, where it was a matter of summoning the inhabitants, bell ringing was more effective than drum rolls.

In the Manche, the Orne, the Eure, and the Sarthe,[77] ringing at elections proved highly controversial, under both the July Monarchy and the Second Republic. In the Manche, for example, a dispute culminated in bloody disturbances, with victory going, at least provisionally, to the mayors.[78]

On 20 November 1831, the mayor of Gaillon (Eure) informed his fellow citizens that he would ring to summon electors for the first ballot and, should the need arise, for the second ballot. "After casting his vote, each should go away," he wrote, "and come back when he hears the signal for the second ballot."[79] Between the two ballots, however, the parish priest forbade ringing. The second bell might, in his opinion, disrupt vespers. When the verger refused to carry out his orders, the mayor donned his sash and proceeded to the church in his official capacity. The parish priest once again refused to use the bell until vespers had ended. The mayor, with the backing of some national guardsmen, then resolved to use force, while in protest the priest abruptly interrupted the service and sent away the congregation. A similar episode, highly indicative of the respective attitudes of the secular and religious authorities, occurred in the Orne a few years later. The mayor of Bellou-en-Houlme complained to the sub-prefect of Domfront that on 10 June 1840, he had resorted to force to have the second ballot rung. Out of seventy-two municipal electors only seventeen had voted in the first ballot. The curate had shut the door of the bell tower and the priest's maidservant had refused to hand over the keys to the municipal authorities.[80]

Under the Second Republic, ringing at elections remained controversial in this department. The mayor of Argentan requested permission to use the *great* bell on such occasions, but the bishop of Séez objected. In his view the advent of universal suffrage and the advance of democracy implied that bells would no longer be used at elections. The argument is of interest especially because the practice actually did die out as suffrage was extended. "In former times," the bishop wrote, "elections were infrequent, summonses occurred on just one day of the week, and, given the very small number of electors, rarely continued into Sunday. In the future, however, this exercise is to be staged on a Sunday, with the law summoning all citizens to it. . . . will necessarily last the whole day; finally, it will be repeated far more often than was the case in the past." If bells were still to be used on such days, worship would be disrupted. During the recent elections in Argentan "twenty-seven summonses were rung."[81] For this reason, several communes had dispensed with bells at elections. The bishop asked that the same measure be introduced in every commune in the department. As he went on to observe,[82] there was no special way of ringing elections, and therefore always a risk of confusion.

This custom did not disappear with the advent of the Second Empire;[83] there is evidence for it in Brest in 1860.[84] In 1884, according to the bishopric of Coutances, it was the only secular peal still extant in the Manche.[85] At this same date elections were still rung at Trévérec (Côtes-du-Nord).[86] In 1884 and 1885, twenty-three concerted regulations attest that the custom was maintained.

It was rarer for bells to be rung in triumph to honor the victor of an election. In 1844, however, the practice was known in the arrondissement of Briey (Meurthe-et-Moselle), even in large towns.[87] It was also known in Tulle under the censitary monarchy. On 7 July 1831, the town witnessed a symbolic contest between the bell and the charivari handbell. "Around half past four in the afternoon" the mayor "gave orders for the cathedral bell to be rung to announce, *as was the custom,*" the "nomination" of M. Bedoch. "The ringers had already been summoned with three strokes on the bells. Then it was that several persons climbed the bell tower and detached the bell ropes." Around half past eight a "sizable gathering" of individuals armed with trumpets, saucepans, and *handbells* serenaded the newly elected man and his presumed electors. The crowd shouted, "down with the Carlists, down with the Jesuits, and down with the electors who voted for Bedoch!" At ten o'clock, "there was the *beating* of the 'retreat'" and the uproar died down."[88]

Patrick Lagoueyte has shown that celebratory ringing on the evening of an election was an established practice under the Second Empire.[89] Subsequently the custom seems to have died out and the authorities certainly frowned upon it. There were exceptions, however. "Upon receiving the dispatch informing me of the results in the (legislative) elections," wrote the mayor of Celles (Vosges) in 1885, "I had an artillery salvo fired, and at the sound of the first detonations the entire population of Celles assembled. . . . a resident went to the home of the bell ringer, who was blind, and said to him: "You must ring the bells." This the bell ringer proceeded to do, and with all the more alacrity since Jules Ferry, one of the winners in the ballot, had obtained for him welfare assistance equaling the sum of one hundred francs. Upon being rebuked by the subprefect the mayor was unrepentant, refusing to allow that a monopoly of the commune's bell should be granted to "so unworthy a creature as the incumbent of Celles."[90]

In many regions it was the custom to ring to announce the arrival of the tax collector. On 16 March 1836, the prefect stressed that it had been thus in the Loiret for some thirty years. In his opinion this peal was genuinely useful because "there is no other way to summon."[91] The bishop of Orléans, on the other hand, assumed the tax collector could announce his arrival through posters affixed to the church door on Sundays. The *ministre des Cultes* finally ruled that this usage, being so widespread, should be tolerated. In the Eure this practice had been known since time "immemorial."[92] Under the July Monarchy its usefulness even seems to have been still more widely recognized than before. There was a greater desire and need to be punctual, and it was also increasingly important not to waste time. Under these circumstances there was no other effective signal but the bell.

On 18 July 1835, the tax collector general for the Basses-Pyrénées registered a protest with the prefect over the ban on ringing to mark the arrival of his agents. This decision, he declared, would jeopardize the collection of taxes. It was hard for collectors to be punctual and taxpayers invariably forgot when they were due to come. The bell "reminded [them] of [their] obligation." Above all, "the peal . . . is again meant only to summon the taxpayers *at the precise moment* when they are supposed to pay their installments, so they only forsake their labors for the amount of time strictly necessary to pay their taxes." As the tax collector general emphasized, they were thus able to effect an "economy of time."[93] You could not hope for a more telling instance of the link between the bell and modern practices of judging time. When there is no peal, the tax collector went on, "the assembled taxpayers" have to wait for a long time, which offers them opportunities for gambling and intemperate conduct. Some will even "sacrifice the money . . ." originally meant for the tax-collector.

In 1832, the prefect of Landes advanced another argument in favor of this peal, namely, that it was linked both to the spread of democracy and to the new exigencies regarding the management of time. "The tax collectors are supposed to arrive in the communes at specified times, but since the laws have required them to assist with the compilation of the municipal and departmental electoral registers, as well as the register for national guardsmen, it sometimes happens that their itinerary is altered."[94] Since only the bells could announce their arrival they were able to be more flexible in their use of time.

Needless to say, this peal also gave rise to conflict. In June 1828, the parish priest in Lascazères (Hautes-Pyrénées), growing weary of hearing the peal in his church announce on the first Monday of every month the arrival of the tax collector, "tied up the bell rope" and placed it "under lock and key in the case of the clock."[95] On 2 November 1837, the municipal council of Urgons (Landes) protested vigorously at the abolition of the tax collector's bell. Taxpayers were unhappy; the functionary's visit "slipped their minds" and as a result they "were very often fined." Some "threats were made by a number of residents that they would not *contribute* to the repair of the bells if they were to break."[96]

In Montgaudry (Orne) during this same period, the tax collector marked his arrival on the final Tuesday of the month "by ringing the bells fifteen to twenty times," to announce "that it [was] collection day."[97] The mayor requested that this peal be maintained. He knew that taxpayers might well forget that they were supposed to come into town if it were abolished. In this department the bells were also used to mark the arrival of the official responsible for checking weights and measures.

The custom of "pulling" the bell upon the arrival of the tax collector lasted in some regions until the end of the century. In 1864 the prefect of the Aube wanted to dispense with it and asked the tax collector to rely on "the services of the drum." In 1885 the practice was still current in the Pyrénées-Orientales and was endorsed by regulation in that department.[98] In 1903 this same peal was still liable to cause controversy in Montcharvot, a commune in the Haute-Marne. There "the town crier, who had inherited the post from his father, and from his grandfather before him, was a child and still at school"; he could not announce the arrival of the tax collector. Consequently the collector "[himself] tolled the bell a couple of times"[99] to notify the town of his arrival, as was traditional in neighboring communes. The parish priest objected to this practice, thinking its sole purpose was to vex him.

There were many other secular uses for assembly peals. In 1828 the parochial church council in Bouilly (Aube) expressed its formal opposition to the use of bells "to summon plaintiffs to the court of the justice of the peace," which proves that the practice was still current. In some communes in the Nord, the Doubs, and Savoie, bells were used to announce expropriations and summon potential purchasers, or to "summon those enjoying rights of estovers to the meting out of a felling."[100] In Sarralbe the custom was to ring when "soup was distributed to the poor."[101] Elsewhere a bell was used to summon those engaged in public works or to give the times for what, in the Landes and the Hautes-Pyrénées, were still called "*corv*ées," meaning obligatory services on the roads and highways.

In December 1849, the parish priest of Labarthe-de-Neste (Hautes-Pyrénées) observed to the mayor that a drum would be better suited than a bell to the task of summoning "to the *corv*ée." The mayor paid no heed to this opinion and explained to the prefect that bad weather led to interruptions that sometimes lasted several days. Only the sound of a bell could obviate needless journeys to-and-fro, with laborers able to listen for a signal to gather that would be audible across the entire territory of the commune.[102]

In some regions the bell alerted residents to *the removal of refuse*. In 1844 in Epfig (Bas-Rhin), the bell announced the times at which the streets would be swept.[103] A peal of this kind precipitated one of the most famous municipal disputes over bells in the entire nineteenth century. The episode was set in the episcopal city of Coutances (Manche), and threw the offices of the minister into turmoil for months. In this town, or so the bishop said, the lay bell ringer was *"prostituting"* the bells by using them to give "the cleaners of refuse from the streets [the signal] to perform their duties."[104] The theme was not "fitting," and all the more so given that in Coutances the sound of the bell had been passed by "public allocation to the lowest tender."[105] The bishop had a barrier placed at the foot of the bell tower. This dispute, being referred to the legislative committee of the Council of State, prompted the formulation of a ruling to which all subsequent governments would refer.[106]

The ringing of the Angelus or the *"points du jour"* punctuated the working day of those in the fields but this was not the only application of bells to agriculture. In Savoie the "going up to the Alps" and the bringing down of the flocks were rung[107]; elsewhere bells marked the beginning of the harvest.[108] In many regions it was the custom to ring when the gleaners set out. From 1844 on this had been the custom in Lesboeufs (Somme). In 1872, however, the parish priest decided to end the practice. The mayor objected vigorously.[109] In 1884 regulations in the Oise endorsed the use of the bells to give the signal to glean.[110] In 1896 the mayor of Froyelles (Somme) still claimed the right to toll on such occasions.[111] In almost all wine growing areas the bell announced the beginning and end of the vine harvesting. The 1884 and 1885 regulations endorsed this peal in ten different departments.

Bells sometimes played a part in the commercial sphere. Although common enough under the Old Regime this usage was to become rare in the nineteenth century. Vestiges of the practice survived, however. In 1832 in the Basses-Pyrénées, the bell announced the moment at which stalls at the market were rented out.[112] "In some communes in the Haute-Saône it is customary to ring the bells when the markets open."[113] The prefect wanted to maintain this useful peal.

A far more common practice was that of tolling a few times on the church bell to summon children to school. In 1884 and 1885 this custom was explicitly endorsed by the regulations of thirty-eight different departments. In eleven of them one could even ring to announce and celebrate the awarding of prizes. In 1838 the practice of ringing to announce school classes was extremely widespread in the Haute-Marne. The bishop of Langres acknowledged and deplored it. "It is generally the case," he wrote, "that the schoolmaster, rather than ring himself, leaves it to his wife, or, what is worse, delegates it to a troop of children, sometimes of both sexes, who rush in a disorderly fashion to the church and so become from a very early age used to behaving irreverently in a holy place; one cannot help but feel that such abuses, *though they may go unremarked from afar*, must be fatal for public morality and alarming to a vigilant and zealous pastor." The bishop "called for the custom to be abolished or directly supervised by the parish priest."[114] Nevertheless, the usefulness of the "school bell" also increased as the demand for precision rose.[115]

This peal upset the parish clergy, and all the more so given that, as we have seen, it sometimes vied with the ringing of the Angelus and could also be mistaken for the peal calling the faithful to Mass. In 1845 the schoolmaster of Gourzon (Haute-Marne) avoided ringing at eight o'clock when the boys returned to their classrooms because the priest in charge celebrated Mass at that same hour; on the other hand, the bell was rung when the girls resumed their places after the service.[116] In December 1847, ringing the "beginning of class" was an "immemorial usage" in Bouzancourt as it was in the surrounding communes. The parish priest decided, however, to ban the practice; the curfew was likewise banned. The town council resisted. Resolving that the bell for school would be rung all the same, it entrusted this task to a lay bell ringer who contracted to ring at seven o'clock in the morning and one o'clock "in the evening." The council's instructions were that this bell should be "rung with sufficient force to be heard at the outermost edge of the commune." It also decided that the schoolmaster should no longer have to "take his pupils to church on Thursdays," or perform the role of cantor, as he had in the past. The parish priest, for his part, stopped ringing the curfew and then denied the rewinder of the communal clock, who was also the schoolmaster, access to the bell tower. In short, at the end of 1847 we are, the mayor wrote, "without a means of announcing the start of school classes, without a curfew, without a public clock," and without a cantor.[117] The populace "rose up"; a petition called for the parish priest to be replaced. Conflicts of this type erupted many years later in the neighboring department of the Marne, in Vauchamps, and in Bergères-les-Vertus.[118]

As I come to the end of this survey of the uses to which assembly peals were put I should add that sometimes bells were used to summon draftees when the recruiting board met, and that "the bell was pulled" to announce vaccination times.[119]

As the reader will have gathered, the intensity of the conflicts caused by secular peals used for announcing or summoning varied from one period to another. The boldness of the clergy on one hand, and the defensive tenacity of local communities on the other, tended to reflect political circumstances. Two periods in this history stand out. The first coincides with the early years of the July Monarchy when the secular authorities, often egged on by the prefects, launched a vigorous offensive. On 20 December 1831, the prefect of the Sarthe outlined his position as follows:[120] "Neither drums nor notices delivered to homes can replace the bells in the countryside, where habitations often lie very far apart one from the other, where no one has a very precise idea of the time, and where the municipal authorities generally lack the resources to keep persons individually informed by means of the written word. The bells can be heard from afar, prevent residents from wasting valuable time waiting, and are the only means to hand in the countryside for achieving prompt and packed meetings." It was not until an efficient postal service was established[121] that methods for summoning really altered and, with them, the attention paid to the sound of bells.[122] Yet members of the clergy were resolved to check the proliferation of auditory messages. They were also opposed to the perpetuation of customs and prejudices since, in their view, secular peals profaned the sacred bronze.

The proliferation of uses to which the bell was put—in evidence throughout the national territory in 1830 and 1831—was therefore followed in 1835 by a vigorous counterattack on the part of the clergy. This in turn precipitated defensive reactions from the municipalities, which regarded the new and more restrictive policy as an obstacle to modernity. Between 1835 and 1845 a number of disputes arose not so much due to this or that usage, but due to the concern to abolish or defend municipal bell ringing as such. A revealing example in this regard was the Frustelle affair, which erupted in the Hautes-Alpes in 1840. "For all time[123] there had been a bell known as 'la Frustelle' on Mount Saint-Jean, in the middle of the merged communes of Saint-Jean and Saint-Nicholas. It hung in a bell tower that had once been part of an old, now demolished church.

It was placed such that its sound could be heard in virtually every hamlet within the vast territory of this parish. Every day this bell rang the times for resuming and breaking off from work in the fields. In cases of accident, such as a fire or some other especially serious event, it served as a tocsin or alarm. It also rang when there was electoral business in the commune. This state of affairs had never been disturbed until, in December 1838, a young and imprudent parish priest in Saint-Jean and Saint-Nicholas took it into his head to boost the peal at his church by adding 'la Frustelle' to it." The municipal authorities having turned down his request, "the parish priest resolved to have the bell abducted furtively at *night*; [he] had it carried off and hidden in his own presbytery, where a raid by the authorities brought it to light." "I cannot begin to tell you," wrote the prefect of the Hautes-Alpes when relating the affair to the *ministre de l'Intérieur et des Cultes*, "how greatly vexed *the whole area* was."

The mayor lodged a complaint against the imprudent parish priest, now a receiver of stolen goods, who was found guilty. "The bell was rehung in its old bell tower" until the minister, in accordance with the law, decided to put it at the priest's disposal. "The young clergyman had gotten the better of the municipality, yet the populace was so vexed that no one dared lay a finger on the bell, which had now been returned to its original place." Wishing to restore "peace to the area," the vicars general, standing in for the bishop, hoped for a "compromise." "Mayor and priest agreed that 'la Frustelle' would remain in its old home provided that the municipal authorities refrained from having it rung with the religious sound of the Angelus, and that it would be used for all of its other established usages." When the bishop returned to his diocese, however, he rejected all compromise (23 May) and called upon the prefect to execute the ministerial ruling.[124]

A few days later the parish priest once again "abducted" the bell, but this time in the daytime after having officially notified the municipal authorities of his intentions twenty-four hours before. On 27 May the commander of the cantonal gendarmerie, at the request of the mayor—who thought that he could still count on the prefect's support—sent two of his men to help the magistrate "effect the recapture of the bell, an instrument that had been the cause of so much conflict."[125] The prefect was not sure how to react and feared "a serious clash" between residents.

That is as far as our knowledge of this episode goes. But the vicissitudes described above show very clearly how determined the opposed parties were, how attached the local people were to the secular peals, and how deeply vexed they were by any abduction of a bell.[126]

I have managed to identify four centers of spirited resistance to the clerical counteroffensive that spanned the national territory. The first corresponds to the far southwest of the country and has its epicenter in the arrondissement of Orthez in the Basses-Pyrénées.[127] During the summer of 1835 the municipal councils in this region swamped the prefect with petitions against the regulation of 28 June, which had abolished a number of immemorial usages. There was widespread public protest. The elected representatives put the most stress on *urgency*, as they understood it. In this region parish priests, mayors, and bell ringers in some cases lived far from the church; should danger threaten, or an accident occur, local residents would themselves mount the bell tower, a practice that the clergy now intended to ban. In short, the municipal councillors for the arrondissement of Orthez wished to defend, along with so many other liberties,[128] their right to ring as and when they saw fit. According to the mayors of the canton of Sauveterre, banning this practice would condemn "residents to no longer being able to understand each other in an infinite number of different circumstances"[129] for want of an effective signal for summoning. In this area, where it was the custom to ring for many occasions, rioting seemed a distinct possibility.

Resistance was not markedly weaker in the Landes. Here, as in the Hautes-Pyrénées, the regulation signed on 28 January 1837 prompted a number of protests. In this department the loss of the right to ring for town council meetings was felt to be particularly humiliating. The council of Urgons rested its case on the recent history of bells, with councillors underlining the fact that in 1801, when the inhabitants moved the town hall bell to the bell tower of the church, they could never have imagined that they would one day be banned from ringing for their meetings.[130] The bishop of Bayonne felt, however, as we have seen, that communes wishing to ring should simply purchase a bell to be used exclusively for secular purposes.

The second center of resistance corresponds to a vast region comprised of the Manche, the Orne, the Mayenne, the Sarthe, and the Eure.

Throughout this zone municipal authorities gave vent to their bitterness at the new regulations, which were felt to be deeply wounding. In the Manche, as we have seen, there was unrest. In 1834 the prefects of the Sarthe and the Mayenne sided with the municipalities since to their mind secular peals formed part of "local custom." In 1837, however, both prefects and municipalities had to yield to pressure from the minister. Nevertheless, it was in the Orne that disillusion at this time seems to have been deepest. In this composite department discontent appears to have been widespread.

A third center of protest against the reduction in number of secular peals is discernible in the Nord, with the arrondissement of Avesnes as its epicenter. In 1844 the mayors of the cantons of Maubeuge and Solre-le-Château, dissatisfied with the regulations for bell ringing signed the previous year, together took their grievances to the prefect. The case they made was rooted in history:

> In Maubeuge, and even under the Empire and the Restoration, we announced the arrival of troops with a particular peal just as soon as they could be glimpsed from the bell tower; we rang the retreat, not just on Sundays but every day; we rang the bells to mark the installation of municipal magistrates; we rang them for the opening of the fair; for public celebrations; they were entirely at the magistrate's disposal; the opening of the electoral colleges was announced by the ringing of a bell; the same means were also used to announce bids for property belonging to the commune or to the poor etc. In our rural communes, residents were summoned in former times to the distribution of estovers etc. by the sound of the bell; expropriations, the sale of property belonging to minors, or that of indivisible properties invariably took place in the presence of mayors and deputy mayors and we were summoned to them by the sound of the bell; this was also the case with voluntary bids, as thousands of reports drafted by our forefathers attest; it was in line with this usage that, up until your ruling of 23 June 1843, the bells were rung when the notaries invited bids in a rural commune when something was to be done for that commune.

Just as custom dictated that residents be summoned by the ringing of a bell to hear police regulations read, so too have they been summoned to listen to the reading of official decrees; to attend assemblies serving to secure prestations for the roads; to drill, although this is at present infrequent, in the national guard, and to pay taxes."[131]

In the East, some regions in the Lorraine were likewise agitated by this question. In 1840, shortly after the concerted regulation had been signed by the prefect of the Vosges and the bishop of Saint-Dié, the mayor of this commune stiffened the resolve of the municipalities to resist. He unleashed a public protest against a document the secular authorities felt to be humiliating. "The affair" seemed to him "very serious."[132] The mayor of Rambervillers deplored the fact that he could no longer ring when the streets were to be swept.[133] This level of anger helps to explain how, at the dawn of the Second Republic, government commissioners in this area hurried to rescind the 1840 text.

Clergymen in the area around Metz, beside themselves with indignation at what they considered excessive claims made by the municipalities since the beginning of the July Monarchy, resolved to counterattack, although a little belatedly. In 1845 the bishop of Metz expressed his indignation to the minister.[134] The municipalities were even ringing, he said, "to mark the return of flocks, or to locate male animals that have strayed"; the bells were at "the disposal of the mayor, the tax collector, the schoolmaster, and even the village shepherd"[135]; in Gros-Rederching "the *corvées* and the public sales" were rung.[136] The parish priest had tried to resist and his door and windows had been shattered at night with blows from an axe. According to the parish priest in Aboncourt,[137] the bells were rung "to hire out pigs" and "in Pentecost to hire out dances"; "on 9 May they were rung to announce the sale of common land on the parish roads." The curate in Kuntzig wrote that the bell was pulled "to hire a bull or pig, to sell clay in the streets, for harvest, for the arrival of the tax collector, to sell a dance at a festival."[138] The subprefect of Thionville,[139] on the other hand, supported the mayors in his arrondissement. In his view immemorial usages were at stake. Besides, some communes in the region had no drum.

From the list I have given of centers of resistance one can gauge how important secular peals were in former *pays d'états* (in the arrondissement of Orthez and the department of the Nord), in regions where usages involving the community were especially prominent (Lorraine), and in those where rural populations, although in other respects given to religious fervor, tended to bridle at anything that might undermine their cohesion (in Basse-Normandie, Maine, and other regions where the *chouannerie* had been a force to be reckoned with).

The reign of the annunciatory and summoning bells lasted the first two-thirds of the nineteenth century. The rise of a new need for precision, a more acute sense of urgency, and a confused demand for quantitative time all preceded the spread of clocks, the building of the railways, the mass use of a mail, and the purchase of fire engines, all of which would satisfy this expectation of modernity. The heyday of the bell was in this interval, which extended from 1801 to the middle of the 1850s. During this epoch, as we have seen, it still tended to be cast on-site and was consequently well-suited to symbolizing territorial identities.

We are thus better able to understand why the authorities were so concerned to regulate bell ringing. In spite of pressure from some prefects who blindly defended the rights of the mayor, the policy of successive governments followed much the same principles applied during this same period to "suppressed festivals." Ministers tended to show great prudence. They were forever repeating that parish priests and priests in charge had sole responsibility for regulating bell ringing; in this regard they invoked the terms of the ruling made by the legislative committee of the Council of State in 1840. Gradually, as we shall see later,[140] they succeeded in fending off the mayors' claims and according preeminence in these disputes to the presbyteries. At the same time, however, there was much that was realistic about this policy. Ministers called upon the clergy to show tolerance towards local customs, which were often immemorial. By the same token, they asked that some record be made of them, and this was sometimes realized with the help of the episcopate. Ministers under the July Monarchy often displayed in this regard an acute sense of locality. In this domain, as in so many others, this period is noted for the proliferation of territorial *inquiries*, which were inspired by a deep sense of the historicity of collective modes of behavior and the realization that it was impossible to blindly subjugate them to the brute will of central government. A realistic policy, predicated on the notion of taking one small step at a time, led imperceptibly to parish priest and mayor exchanging their respective positions with regard to bell ringing.

At the time of the inquiries that paved the way for the signing of the concerted regulations in 1884, 1885, and 1886, the secular uses of the bell were recorded. I have represented on a map (p. 391) those that were retained by both prefect and bishop, despite the bishop's frequent reluctance. The reader will note that a graphic representation of secular peals suggests an analogous line of interpretation to that given of conflicts under the July Monarchy.[141] The distribution of authorized secular peals indicates where communities were solidly established, and where traditions concerning announcements and summoning were deep-rooted.

Several zones with an abundance of such peals are clearly discernible: (1) the Jura mountains up to the frontier of Alsace (Jura, Doubs, the territory of Belfort) together with the adjacent regions, (2) the east of the country (Meuse, Meurthe-et-Moselle), (3) the North from the Somme to the Belgian frontier, (4) the Alps (Isère, Savoie, Haute-Savoie) and the Pyrenees (Ariège, Hautes-Pyrénées and Basses-Pyrénées). Although less sharply defined, one can also make out (1) a region that corresponds more or less to the Rhône country (Rhône, Vaucluse, Gard) and extends into Languedoc, (2) a part of the Armorican massif (Manche, Ille-et-Vilaine), and (3) a few departments in the central West.

Elsewhere the secular peals that figured in the model outlined by the minister were not kept, meaning either that they were no longer in use or that the bishop proved so persuasive that they were suppressed.

Be this as it may, the conflicts over secular peals that erupted at the end of the century assumed a very different shape than those analyzed above. Between 1890 and 1910, during the years immediately preceding and following the passing of the Law of Separation, the mayors—now enjoying longer periods of office and consequently more independence from the prefecture than in the past[142]—pressed their claim to ring vigorously. When such conflicts broke out the mayors were flanked by councils that were better educated than in the past, and abreast of the great debates stirring the nation. Municipal grievances were now more cogently formulated. But *what was really at issue was not so much the cohesion of a community, its management, or its functioning, but rather the symbolic manifestations of ascendancy*. At the dawn of the twentieth century bell ringing was no longer, save in exceptional circumstances, truly indispensable; a number of the secular uses of the instruments were already redundant. *Disputes over bells had essentially become conflicts over matters of belief*, with anticlericals, freethinkers, and atheists being pitted against clergy, clericals, and zealous Catholics. The most embattled mayors were motivated by an intense *desire to desacralize* the bells, and by the same token, the rhythms, space, and signals of their communities. They wanted to deprive the clergy of its power to deafen, feeling it to be humiliating and intolerable.

This second offensive on the part of the secular authorities focused on the peals rung for the Angelus and those announcing and celebrating rites of passage. I discussed the first of these usages earlier and I shall refer again to the conflicts arising from the desire to ring the secular certification of private life. This said, it seems appropriate at this stage to point out the radical difference in the issues, perspectives, and attitudes involved in either case. One must not take apparently similar actions as proof of identical intentions.

I have found no trace in nineteenth-century France of any usage reminiscent of *the bell of infamy*. Under the Old Regime this bell served to summon the community to where a person was to be tortured or put on public display to bear witness to the public nature of the punishment and confer due solemnity upon it. In Angers in the eighteenth century the great tenor bell in the cathedral would toll nine times before the public penance and execution of a condemned man "to summon the people to witness such an action." In Geneva at the end of the century, when a girl of ill repute was whipped in the courtyard of the place where she was detained, the ringing of a bell announced the beating.[143]

There was, however, an exception. In the diocese of Aire the bell rang when public executions were staged. Yet this practice only had a bearing on the religious sphere. "The faithful will be alerted beforehand," read the text of the 1837 regulation, "by a *particular peal*, so that they may take themselves to the church to pray, but the ringing will stop the moment the condemned man leaves prison."[144]

The Propagation of Alarm

From the restoration of religious peals to the outbreak of the First World War, there was one use of bells that was never really contested, namely, the alarm peal. In 1884 and 1885 every department acknowledged its usefulness. It never occurred to anyone to deprive bells of their function of announcing fires, which had been the legal basis for the secular use of bell ringing. Where there was no other practice of this kind, as was the case in a number of communes in the Eure, the Eure-et-Loir, and the Côtes-du-Nord, the paramount *necessity* of a tocsin was nevertheless emphasized. This was the justification given for reinstating suppressed parishes; they often endeavored, despite the law, to keep one of the bells from their church for warning against catastrophes. The same was true of succursals where the presbytery was inhabited.

The tocsin belongs to the language of bells in the West. It was not rung everywhere, however, in the same manner—or to be more precise, in the same rhythm—but it was defined almost everywhere by hurried, redoubled, and discontinuous strokes.[145] This was an abrupt, irregular peal that was heard intermittently and was executed, whenever possible, with a small bell. The alarm bell was hurried. It seemed to urge on and instill anxiety. It is highly likely that it made hearts beat a little faster. Its pauses caused listeners to hold their breath and prick up their ears. By contrast with the other secular peals, the alarm transcended the territorial limits of the community. The tocsin of neighboring communes or parishes was obeyed. Furthermore, one of the qualities of this peal was its tendency to propagate itself to extend the area over which persons might be summoned or might gather. The tocsin was designed to spread alarm and fear. Bells ordinarily transmitted news from a central point radiating outward.[146] The tocsin, however, was an exception; it transmitted its message by propagation in the same fashion as rumor, with which it was to some extent allied. It lacked the quality of calm certainty possessed by the other peals, and still contained that element of anxiety characteristic of what Alphonse Dupront has described in relation to pilgrimage as panic culture. The hurried sound of the little tocsin bell, the polar opposite of the solemn tenor bell, belongs to an Old Regime of information—one brought to an end by the siren.

To be effective in towns, the language of the tocsin had to be precise and shed some of the simplicity that has been somewhat too hastily ascribed to it. The regulation enacted on 2 January 1792 divided the city of Metz into six areas. Chimney fires, it stipulated, would be rung as "'peals' [not the correct term] of six paired strokes of the bell tolled at intervals of two strokes; general fires by peals of twenty strokes tolled hurriedly. In either event the area affected would be identified" by means of a code based on the number of strokes. "When there was a fire in the outskirts of the town, ten hurried strokes were tolled on La Mutte." "The bell ringers from the various parishes in which the fire had broken out would also ring, identifying the area affected by ringing the specified number of strokes."[147] This regulation was simplified in 1802. Metz by then had only four areas divided into three subsections, each with an alarm bell.[148]

In the countryside, knowledge of the sound and manner of ringing characteristic of each bell situated within earshot enabled listeners to pinpoint the alarm. In the Moselle there were countless ways of ringing the tocsin. In Languimberg "one struck twenty slow strokes on the bell when there was a chimney fire; redoubled and hurried, in twos, when there was a general fire." "*Hurriedly* repeated and *intermittent* strokes announced a fire in many villages in the arrondissements of Sarrebourg and Forbach. In Bouzonville they used . . . an iron mallet, striking in turn and *hurriedly* the two largest bells." In Contz-les-Bains they tolled the three bells *as irregularly as possible* "by striking the clapper hard against the edge of each of them." "Elsewhere they would strike slowly, one stroke after another, but pausing after a given number of strokes. In yet other places, they would 'tie up' two bells . . . and ring the great bell in peal,"[149] but very irregularly to distinguish the ringing of an alarm from that of the passing bell.

This diversity, which hampers all attempts to give a precise definition of the tocsin, made it easier for listeners to locate the epicenter of the danger. The identities of communities were in part constituted by, and perceived in terms of, their particular approaches to ringing the alarm. The ear had to be trained in this regard, though perhaps less so than for the interpretation of the passing bell. Knowledge of this language served to justify and deepen intercommunal solidarity within the "*pays*" or locality, a territorial unit that was then fundamentally important but has too often been neglected by historians.

The tocsin of course announced the intrusion of outsiders and the imminent threat or anticipated occurrence of natural disasters of every

kind, be it fire, flood, shipwreck or storm. We have already seen with
what alacrity thunderclouds and frosts were rung, although in such cases
many preferred to ring *a peal* since an alarm bell could also offer protection. Many bell ringers believed that efficacy was directly proportional to
volume of sound.

When fires swept across Normandy in 1830[150] the tocsin proved its
worth in the countryside. For nearly a year it extended an auditory web
across all of Basse-Normandie. Convinced that gangs of arsonists were at
work, and using a trumpet blast for a signal, the country people set about
organizing their own defense. Patrols were formed in each village. No
sooner was a "stranger" glimpsed than the tocsin would be rung and
between one hundred and three hundred people would assemble. Several
parish priests, accused of having delayed the sounding of the alarm, were
roundly insulted. In some communes the other peals were suspended to
avoid confusion with the one announcing an intrusion. One mayor advised
those within his jurisdiction to go about their business in silence, listening
for any suspicious noises. Elsewhere the opposite tactic was followed, and
rough music was used to drive off the arsonists. Hearing played a key role
in this strange battle. One individual, because the familiar sound of his
broken clog was recognized at the site of a calamitous fire, was condemned
to death. Throughout this protracted affair in Basse-Normandie the villagers clearly took some pleasure in spreading the alarm.

Bells served to control the movement of individuals across the whole
region. Peasants were quick to stop Parisian police agents—"spies" as far
as villagers were concerned—if they tried to infiltrate. Prefects, however, did not like this defensive system founded on the tocsin, and we can
readily understand why. The intrinsic ambiguity of the tocsin, where it
served to draw attention to a human threat, has been noted numerous
times. The logic is plain enough. Many insurrectional movements were a
response to a reflex of fear and defense; a bell announcing a threat and
precipitating a defensive assembly could readily turn into a signal for
insurrection. The *emotional power* of the tocsin in such circumstances
transcended that of any other source of information. The alarm bell,
being the signal of a threat, implied that plots were afoot or that treason
was involved, and called upon listeners to take up arms and assemble. It
"roused" the people. Even in the early eighteenth century, Jean-Baptiste

Thiers denounced the dangerous power of bells and was prepared to justify the preventative or repressive measures adopted to curb them. It is for this reason, he wrote, that the Turks do not admit them into their empire and deny them to Christians living under their sway.[151] Removing bells serves to calm the people. This was why, again according to Thiers, the monarchy in France had withdrawn the peals from the insurgents of Marennes in 1547, and emptied the bell towers of Bordeaux in 1547 and those of Montpellier in 1574.

The fact that bells only summoned "the rabble" made such steps all the more justified. Their powerful and dramatic tones served under such circumstances to frighten "gentle and peaceable souls" while whipping "the mad up into a fury."[152] Thiers recalled how in Bordeaux the bell ringer who had set the bell ringing on the day of a riot had been hung from its clapper. In Gand Charles V had the bell that had summoned the populace smashed, "leaving only a fragment that rang in a cracked and tuneless fashion," serving as a daily reminder to listeners of the failure of their revolt. Right in the middle of the nineteenth century, on 2 December 1851—the night of the coup d'État—Maupas had the churches of Paris occupied so that no one could ring the tocsin. As an additional precaution he even ordered that the ropes be cut.[153]

There is no disputing the connection between bells and massacres. To write the history of the alarm bell would be to write that of the bloodiest episodes in modern times. I shall therefore not attempt the task here. It was highly astute, however, of Janine Garrisson-Estèbe to entitle her narrative of the drama of 1572 *Tocsin for a Massacre.*[154] Blavignac underlined the role played by bells in the massacre of 10 August 1792, while the pages of Chateaubriand and Michelet evoking the tocsin used in the September Massacres are well known. The power of bells was then attuned to bloodthirsty fury. It was likewise the sound of the tocsin that swelled the Parisian insurrection of June 1848. According to the *Gazette des tribunaux*, Thérèse, in her celebrated disguise as one of the Amazons of the people, had abandoned the barricades and "mounted the bell tower of the church of Saint-Séverin."[155] This anecdote, whether based on fact or not, reflects the important role of acoustic entreaty in the unfolding of the drama.

Peals that sounded above massacres served to justify the violence by authenticating the danger. A tocsin combined announcement, alarm, and summons in one bundle along with, I would add, a kind of rejoicing, so plainly did it play a role in massacres. In short, the tocsin, the most poly-semic of the peals, played on a gamut of emotions including fear, exhil-aration, panic, and horror. That it lent itself to different, coexisting inter-pretations renders this key element in a now forgotten culture of the senses all the more complex.

Far from Paris, the center of the national territory, unrest in villages was invariably (until the middle of the 1850s anyway) signaled and inten-sified by the tocsin. There is no point in attempting to compile a list. In 1789 the revolution in the countryside and the panics of the Great Fear unfolded to the sound of the alarm bell. By way of example, it was the tocsin that same year that inflamed the *bocage* of Basse-Normandie between 19 July and 20 August.[156] The popular "emotions," that in some places between 1830 and 1848 greeted the change of regime and filled the power vacuum, were announced and propagated by ringing everywhere. I referred to this phenomenon earlier in the case of the Limousin and Périgord, where the tocsin was associated with rumors of fire. For rural populations, whether merely wary or openly insurgent, revolution and subversion were cast in the image of fire.[157] But the most graphic instance of the power vested in the tocsin in the nineteenth century is supplied by the riots precipitated by the "forty-five centimes" tax imposed in the spring of 1848. Around Ajain (Creuse)[158] the movement radiated outward from a few hamlets—territorial units that had no bells. The first step taken by the insurgents was to go into town and ring. It is hard to see how without bells such a movement, buried in a zone lacking substantial agglomerations, could ever have consolidated itself and expanded to the point of drawing crowds in its wake and emerging as a massacre. A few days later the Parisian insurrection unleashed a repetition of the Great Fear in the outskirts of the capital. In Dreux and the neighboring com-munes they rang the tocsin.[159]

This peal likewise lay behind the most serious bread riots.[160] The fren-zied tolling of a bell set in motion and shaped communal anger; it served to proclaim collective demands. The use of the alarm bell conferred upon such movements the legitimacy presupposed by the notion of a "moral economy."[161] The polysemic nature of the tocsin accentuated the ambiguity of uprisings that, as they unfolded, expressed simultaneously a rejection of economic legislation, a respect for the local authorities, and a determination to defend the best interests of the community.

On 4 June 1817, market day in Montargis, the high cost of grain led to rioting. The buyers began to share out the corn. The subprefect then ordered the alarm to be sounded for the national guard to assemble. The crowd was well aware how important it was to control auditory signals. The town crier, wrote the subprefect, "had his drum punctured by the people."[162] The postmaster general recalled the hesitation displayed by some; the same auditory message could both summon the forces of order and assemble the rioters. "The people," he wrote to the subprefect, "began by preventing the tocsin from being rung, which could have taken the place of the drum. They then captured the church and rang the tocsin themselves."[163] The subprefect then gave his version of events: "I heard the tocsin ringing. I had sent a picket of national guards to the doors of the church, where they were disarmed. I then entered the church on my own, climbed the tower and, sword in hand, brought down those who were ringing."[164]

The rumors of insurrection that spread through the surrounding countryside were, to begin with, borne by the tocsin. The authorities accused beggars, malefactors, and boatmen of having intended to "seize control of the bells" and of having "given, by ringing the tocsin, false alarms and thus assembled the population of the countryside in one spot."[165] The magistrates and examining magistrates in the *cour prévotale*,* who began their inquiry on 9 June, charged beggars with having set events "in motion" and having "proceeded to the bells."[166] The commune of Nargis "was attacked by thirty beggars who wished to ring the tocsin." "They are still there," wrote the subprefect of Montargis. "I am going to send an express messenger with instructions to have the bell's clapper removed."[167] Elsewhere "it was people from the locality" who captured the tower. In Gien the rioters forced the bell ringer to hand over the keys.[168] In Dammarie, "a very small commune, on Sunday morning

*half civil, half military courts, against whose judgments there was no right of appeal. These courts were very active in the early years of the Restoration, a period of "legal terror."

the eighth of June" the tocsin was rung by a hundred individuals demanding grain.[169] This auditory petition constitutes yet another use of the bell, one that I have not mentioned before. In Châteaurenard the parish priest refused to let an "unbridled mob" ring the tocsin, so the mob resolved to "make its way to the town hall."[170] It is worth noting the sequence of events. Early in the nineteenth century the first impulse virtually everywhere in this "locality" was to "proceed" to the church, sound the alarm, and give a summons. Voicing a grievance, entering into negotiations, and arriving at a compromise then required contact with the mayor. In Barlieu (Cher) the troublemakers simply threatened to ring the tocsin, calculating that this would be enough to sway the municipal authorities.[171]

Sometimes, however, the rioters approached the town hall first. On the night of 5–6 June "two or three residents of the small commune of Feins *forced the deputy mayor*, in the mayor's absence, *to have the tocsin rung* and to follow them" as they paid a visit to the homes of the landowners, whom they accused of hoarding grain.[172] In refusing to ring themselves, the rioters were clearly trying to bestow the legitimacy of a municipal measure on the tocsin, and therefore on their subsequent actions.

The authorities took ever more precautions to prevent the tocsin from "propagating" riot. The subprefect of Gien instructed the mayors in his arrondissement to put the bell towers under guard, while the subprefect of Montargis likewise called for vigilance in this respect.[173] In Paris the minister of general police was well aware of the importance of the issue. On 5 June he instructed that those who had punctured the drum and those who had rung the tocsin should be regarded as "fomenters of disorder," and hunted down. "These acts of rebellion," he added on 10 June upon hearing of the "resort to the tocsin" in Montargis, "should be made an example of, and punished with all due severity."[174] The bell provided the authorities with a simple means of identifying the guilty and shifting collective responsibility onto a handful of individuals.

On the third of July the *cour prévôtale* arrived at a verdict. Five individuals were sentenced to death. Four of them were executed on the following day, without anyone considering the possibility of a royal pardon. One of those executed was only sixteen years old. He was "guillotined even as a crowd of citizens was demonstrating on his behalf. This child,

an anonymous correspondent recorded, was given thirty *sols* by a citizen
to climb the bell tower while the tocsin was being rung and tell the others to stop making noise, given the fatal consequences that might result.
He therefore climbed up hastily and was stopped on his way by a gen-
darme."[175] Two other individuals were sentenced to deportation for having, by ringing the bell, " incited citizens to wreak destruction, massacre,
and looting."[176]

Village brawls, which were very common in the Lot during the first
half of the nineteenth century, likewise were fought to the sound of the
tocsin. The alarm bell informed villagers of provocation, alerted listeners to the outbreak of local wars, and called for reinforcements. On 2
December 1827, fifty or so young people from Cornac set out to defy the
residents of Bretenoux. In the ensuing fight staffs were used and stones
were thrown. Two shots were also fired. The commune under attack rang
the tocsin.[177] On 13 July 1834, the bell in Gramat sounded the alert.
Several townsfolk had been attacked at an inn by people from Rignac, a
hamlet in the same commune. A woman seized the drum and sounded the
alarm. A crowd broke into the town hall and grabbed the national guard's
rifles.[178] On 17 February 1836, Ash Wednesday, some young people from
Touzac went to Vire-sur-Lot with their faces covered. They led a horse
upon which they mounted a straw dummy as a deliberate act of provocation. At the same time the other residents of their commune gathered on
the heights overlooking Vire and hurled insults. In order to defend themselves from the coming invasion the victims of this act of aggression rang
the tocsin and assembled.[179]

On 7 December 1836, the bells sounded the alarm in Thégra and
Lavergne. The inhabitants of both communes prepared for war. They
armed themselves with rifles and scythes, then proceeded to the hamlet of
Bertrand where they had decided to do battle. This time the gendarmes
managed to prevent a confrontation.[180]

A brawl erupted on 29 September 1818 between some inhabitants of
Marminiac and some "people" from Cazals, who had met at the Salviac
fair. The former judged that they were too few to win a victory so they
dispatched some emissaries to sound an alert in their commune. In a flash
over forty people, including some women, assembled with rifles, scythes,
and sticks, and proceeded toward Salviac.[181]

The only responses to invasion, exclaimed Barère in 1793, are "national defense and the tocsin." He thus emphasized the power of the bell to sound the national alarm.[182] That same year, and then three times during the nineteenth century, the tragic sound of the tocsin gave notice that the enemy was approaching. It is many years since Henry Houssaye emphasized the role played by the bell at the start of the French campaign in 1814.[183] It was much the same in 1815. It was by means of the tocsin that General Debelle assembled the five hundred members of the national guard who successfully blocked the duke of Angoulême's march on Lyon on 29 and 30 March. As the duke was retreating in the direction of Pont-Saint-Esprit the tocsin rang continuously on both banks of the river. This made it possible to deploy the guard and some demi-solde (soldiers on half pay) from the region against the duke. On this occasion it really was a question of the military use of the alarm bell.[184] All the communes in Eure-et-Loir rang the tocsin, one after the other, during the winter of 1870–1871 to announce the arrival of the enemy. On 2 August 1914, and then again in September 1939, the bells of France were rung to announce that war had been declared.

In an entirely different context, the tocsin sounded here and there in 1906 in parishes whose residents had decided to resist the listing of objects of worship decided upon after the legal separation of church and state. In Parçay-Meslay (Indre-et-Loire) the Catholics took refuge in the parish church, where they built a barricade of chairs and pews tied together with wire. The obstacle was two and a half meters high and four meters wide, and took the authorities a full two hours to dismantle. Throughout the operation the tocsin never stopped ringing.[185]

It would be worth devoting more space to the metamorphoses of fear, aroused by peals and rumors. Throughout the century the bell served to impart a proper solemnity to the emotions of the village; it reinforced the actions of municipal authorities when they seemed to stray beyond the bounds of legality; it turned mere aggregates into genuine assemblies.[186] The auditory staging of insurrections enhanced the sense of solidarity and lent a greater urgency to decision making. The participation of each bell—recognizable by ear—in a given "locality" helped to maintain communal identity within the larger context of an insurrection.

If there was much anxiety at the thought of losing a bell this was because it was so vitally necessary for defense against floods, lightening, and fire, and against the intrusion of brigands or hostile armies. For a community to have no bell was not simply a matter of being deprived of an auditory symbol of its identity. It seemed quite simply to be threatened with dissolution if it had no means of sounding the alarm or giving a signal for inhabitants to assemble. Without a bell assistance would be slow in coming, rumors would be hard to confirm, and rites of passage could only be celebrated "in silence." A bell tower without bells served as a constant reminder of a painful lack, and we can therefore readily understand the alacrity with which communes set about reconstituting their peals after the Revolution.[187]

Control Over Peals of Joy

Furthermore, the bell was also the privileged interpreter of collective rejoicing. Never in the nineteenth century would a community mark its joy without bell-ringing.[188] It is an artifice of our exposition to have distinguished between the announcing of an event and the joyful sounds by which it was announced. It is obvious that the bell signaling the arrival of a sovereign, the restoration of a dynasty, the birth of a prince, the winning of a great battle, or the signature of a peace treaty was also a message of jubilation. Successive governments in the nineteenth century nevertheless endeavored, in this domain as in many others, to curb any excess. This control over peals of joy merits further comment.

The debate centered around two key issues, namely, national festivals and local festivals. The former were supposed to be rung, although a good many parish priests, as we shall see, refused to set all the bells ringing to celebrate events that they deplored, a regime that they detested, or sovereigns whose presence on the throne they did not much appreciate. Bell ringing thus became one of the central issues in village politics.[189]

On the other hand, the nineteenth-century clergy had long sought to oppose the complete secularization of festive activities. Bell ringing was a means to this end in that depriving an event of bells meant robbing it of its intensity and diminishing its joyfulness. After the Third Republic had triumphed it meant reducing the efficacy of organized festivals. The thick file preserved in the National Archives, which allows us to follow step-by-step the drafting of the bell ringing regulations agreed in 1884 and 1885, shows that the discussion was forever coming up against the problem of defining the precise nature of festivals.[190]

The episcopate was unanimous in its view that *the festivals of patron saints* should be rung just as they had always been, but it refused to set the bells ringing for *local festivals*, which were the exclusive preserve of the town hall. Ringing the former meant, first of all celebrating a saint, the patron of the parish and very often the dedicatee of the church. The bell ringer accepted under such circumstances the sacred nature of the bell. To use the bell for local festivals, however, the bishops repeated,[191] would be to profane it. In the clergy's eyes such secular celebrations, entailing no reference to the sphere of the sacred, were merely occasions for juvenile debauches and demeaning contests. Worse still, ringing for organized festivals was tantamount to guaranteeing the triumph of anticlericalism. It could even happen, observed the bishop of Mende, that some mayors would baptize "a banquet following elections," "a public ball etc.," as local festivals.[192]

In 1904 the mayor of Tréffiagat (Finistère) was only too aware of what was at stake. He decided to ring *its secular festival*, the program reading as follows: "At eight o'clock in the morning, the ringing of bells (if possible). At two o'clock, a bicycle race. At four o'clock, young persons' race. Throughout the afternoon, Breton dancing to the sound of the Breton pipes."[193] This initiative is of interest because it involves an attempt to integrate the bell into the municipal festival, thus relegating bell ringing to the status of one element among many in a municipal program. In short, the mayor of Tréffiagat meant to effect a radical desacralizing of the auditory expression of rejoicing. Moreover, his initiative reflected recent alterations to the Sunday routine. From the 1890s onward, across all of France, banquets, gymnastic meets, equestrian shows, and fashion competitions tended to fill, and thus desacralize the "Lord's day." The rise of entertainment, perceptible throughout society, served to undermine the primacy of the pedagogic intention that had been apparent in the previous two decades. In watering places therapeutic aims gave way to hedonistic practices. This development brought about a reinterpretation of festivals and village celebrations. The bell, whose dominical mission had been to announce simultaneously prayer, "a well-earned rest,"[194] and the joys of a traditional sociability, could not legitimately celebrate the new forms of entertainment. The prefect of Finistère turned down the plans and proposals of the unfortunate mayor of Tréffiagat, whose festival was therefore condemned to remaining "mute."

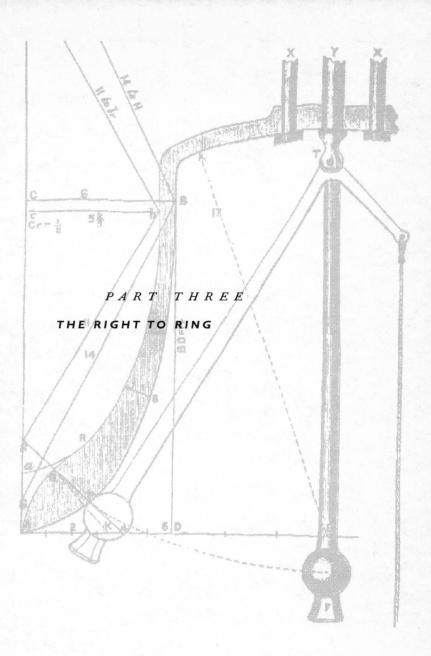

PART THREE

THE RIGHT TO RING

CHAPTER SIX

The Stakes Involved in Local Disputes

The Fear of Humiliation

The nineteenth century was a period when the village, a setting too often dismissed as being of minor significance, was beset by conflict.[1] Tensions and rivalries may never have been so numerous and so intense. A range of interlocking conflicts, which sometimes unfolded simultaneously at different levels and obeying disparate logics, fostered hatred and resentment. Analysis of the interweaving of rivalries, for all its difficulties, reveals villagers passionately involved in these local contests. It contradicts the stereotype of passive individuals incapable of calculation or reasoning, obsessed with the need for mediators, and at best prone to sudden, archaic rages.[2] The majority of these now all but forgotten local dramas seem, at least during certain periods, to have hinged on conflicts over access to bell towers and the use of bells.[3] Before describing the overall shape of such episodes I will give a brief account of what was at stake in these often highly charged struggles, and of the broader historical processes underlying them.

The symbolic power and territorial sway of the church on one hand, and of the town hall on the other, have been much studied.[4] But historians have rarely considered the two in open *confrontation*. Yet the rural town hall, as has too often been forgotten, was defined in opposition to church and presbytery.[5]

The village church was generally located where roads and highways converged; often it determined the eventual shape of a settlement. It was the point of departure and the culmination of any procession. It was also often the oldest monument in the commune and the one most heavily burdened with history.[6] A number of episodes in the Wars of Religion and the Revolution were set in churches. In this regard the parish sanctuaries were the only museums country people ever visited. The treasury, the old statues, the ex-votos, the valuables stored in the sacristy, the tombstones, and the proximity of the cemetery, at least in communes where it had not yet been moved, served to anchor this memorial function, which nineteenth-century clergy and donors sought to reinforce by building monuments or by adding commemorative plaques.[7]

The environs of the sanctuary were protected sites and would remain so after the Separation. The law of 29 July 1880 was expressly designed to prevent profane noises from disrupting services. Noisy trades were banned in the vicinity of the church; the fire from the smithy was kept at a reasonable distance, as were taverns, inns, and fair booths. "About the time of the Concordat," recalled Gabriel Le Bras, "the Council of State kept, around churches and on the site of deconsecrated cemeteries, a clear patch of ground and a circular path that in some places were called processionals."[8] Village children knew they were meant to avoid this silent and sacred precinct; their respect for it had been acquired with their first awareness of the territory of the commune.[9] In regions characterized by a degree of religious fervor, and in others during the "good [and therefore preserved] festivals," the "exit from mass" was the moment on Sundays at which persons would meet, and cousins, for example, would embrace.[10] Hence the significance of church doors. Official arrangements for entering the edifice were of some significance, and I shall return to this topic

later. Variations in informal customs respecting the same issue also merit
study, however. The wish to go into the church by the main entrance
could imply a desire to imbue one's actions with solemnity or raise one's
social standing. Conversely, entering by a side door could serve as proof
of familiarity and daily attendance, in short, as a subtler sign of honor.

The bell tower should not be confused with the church; it sometimes
consisted of a timber frame that was entirely separate from the ecclesiastical edifice. At the end of the century republican mayors often did their
utmost to enforce such a distinction. Nevertheless, in many communes
access to the church and access to the bell tower were one and the same, a
circumstance that gave rise to hopelessly complex problems over keys.[11]
The bell tower designated and constituted the center of the territory for
both the parish and the commune. It was therefore the most crucial reference point. It symbolized the domain of the law, the sphere of order,
cohesion, and sexual purity—the site from which the divine and sovereign word were heard. The centrality of the bell tower was contrasted
with the periphery and the murky zones of the boundary, a world of
impurity, disorder, and dissolution.[12] It exorcized the deepest fears,
whether of fever or unrest. "The forces sustaining village life and fur-
thering its glory thus took their bearings from its center and passed across
the main square in order to reach it and to irrigate it...."[13]

In the nineteenth century the bell tower stood in the midst of an
increasingly dense network of sacralized sites. Never were so many
chapels, grottos, calvaries, and perhaps stations of the cross built as during this period of decline in religious practice.[14] The bell tower symbolized and embodied elevation, and the aspiration toward the light. You
were compelled to lift your gaze. For Catholics as for freethinkers, the bell
tower was directly associated with prayer. A homology was established
between the massiveness of this psalm in stone and the smoke from the
incense which likewise climbed toward the heavens. By contrast with the
other symbols of elevation in the village—the temporary maypole
erected by the young or the conscripts' flagstaff, for example—the bell
tower had the advantage of possessing the "absolute density of stone."[15]

It would be a drastic oversimplification to take at face value these elements, whose solidity seemed in this period to defy the passing of time. In
the nineteenth century the bell tower was also a monument to modernity

and an object of collective pride. The clergy's aspiration to dominate these
edifices was thwarted by the territorial community, which regarded the bell
tower as its symbol,[16] was passionately involved in disputes over bells, and
was likewise intent on preserving its traditional customs and rites.

As the decades passed the growth of municipal consciousness, which
was one of the most pronounced features of the period, made bell towers
again the focus of intense interest; it served to exacerbate the disputes
they caused and the tensions they crystallized. Needless to say, this
heightened susceptibility varied from one "locality" to the next. I would
not even contemplate a sketch of the geography of campanarian sensibility here. It was, however, especially intense in regions where "religious
integration [was] closely associated with social integration."[17]

A close reading of the archival documents for this period shows that
most of the conflicts tearing communes apart hinged on the preservation
of a symbolic capital. Virtually all of these contests, which for too long
have been deemed insignificant, were dominated by the concern with
honor and *the fear of humiliation*. Mayor and priest alike dreaded being
treated like children by the subprefect.[18] Both feared being humiliated by
their rival, and these sentiments were shared by the municipal council and
the parochial church council. Defiance, harassment, mockery, and a desire
for revenge shaped communal conflicts in which pride and esteem were at
stake. This flowed from the very structure of a society founded on shared
acquaintance, and from the patterning of the zone of reputation. The
anonymity of today's great cities precludes our understanding a sensibility peculiarly responsive to all that undermines honor, or rather esteem,
and therefore representations of self, family, and community.

The Symbolic Restructuring of a Territory

Needless to say, power was also at stake since it interlocks with
pride and esteem. The right to order sounds reflected actual domination
of the space within which they could be heard.[19] Bells did not only serve
as auditory markers. They also played a part, as we have seen, in the *marking that served to constitute a territory,*[20] and that was indissociable from the
notion of surveillance.[21] The right to place political emblems on top of
bell towers was another aspect of this political control.

Anyone who held sway over bell ringing also had the power to deafen. Owing to the sheer loudness and ubiquity of the sound of bells they could quite literally force others to shut up. Deciding on ways of ringing was thus one of the refinements of authority. From the beginning to the end of the century many mayors dreamed of exercising this privilege, although they knew perfectly well that, according to the law, the parish priest had sole responsibility for regulating bell ringing. On 25 July 1846, the bishop of Langres complained to the prefect of the Haute-Marne that the mayor of Is "has just passed and, unbeknownst to his reverence the parish priest, has published *to the sound of a drum*, a decree specifying that the Angelus be rung morning and evening *at two bells* during harvest."[22] So serious did this affair seem to the prelate that he demanded that the prefect draft a regulation preventing any such usurpations occurring in the future.

To exercise control over the use of bells was to enjoy a monopoly over immediate communications or injunctions, and this was no small privilege at a time when the rounds of the postman or the rural guard alone enabled the majority of a community's members to stay informed. Whoever had the key to the bell tower had the means to propagate messages; only the bell could imbue the voice of authority with the requisite substance, and certainty. We need to differentiate this kind of passive information, which emanated from a central point and allowed no rejoinder, from the spreading of rumors.[23] The latter are transmitted by direct contact and personal interaction and, being endlessly embroidered, end up losing all certainty.

Whoever was responsible for regulating bell ringing could also decide to silence the bells, and therefore wield sanctions, both individual and collective. He could, after a fashion, introduce divisions into communal society. In May 1834, four parishioners from Saint-Martin-d'Oney (Landes) lodged a complaint against the parish priest, "who in no wise has the bells rung for everybody, and when he does ring, it is *according to his own caprice and whim.*"[24] The priest authorized peals of his own accord, deciding how much solemnity to bestow upon each occasion or how honors were to be distributed.[25]

One can readily understand how a community's representatives might have desired control over its bells without that preoccupation constituting a sure proof of irreligion. Disputes over bells long predated the conflicts arising out of anticlericalism at the end of the century, and they were less a matter of belief and religious fervor than of a struggle between the "stole" and the "sash," to borrow the terms used by the parish priest of Frenelle-la-Grande (Vosges).[26] For a long time and in many places, the rise of municipal consciousness was reflected foremost in claims to marks of honor inside the church. In this regard bell ringing disputes should properly be subsumed within a larger category of conflict. Godparenthood of bells and the wording of campanarian inscriptions could sometimes cause disputes. As we have seen, mayors, deputy mayors, municipal councillors, schoolmasters, parish priests, and churchwardens would sometimes clash over the words inscribed on the bronze. The same was true of *pews* and, more particularly, of the seating reserved for representatives of the municipality in the sanctuary.[27]

By virtue of the decree of 24 Messidor Year XII (13 July 1804), the mayor and councillors could lay claim to a place of honor in the church when they attended, in person and in full dress, services celebrated on government-sponsored festivals. Apart from these occasions the mayor, being ex officio a member of the parochial parish council by virtue of the decree of 30 December 1809, was entitled to the third place—after the parish priest and the president—in the churchwardens' pew, which generally stood in front of the pulpit.[28] A good many mayors, however, refused to sit alongside the parish priest when he was not officiating since it implied being relegated to third place. They laid claim to, and were often granted, a special pew, sometimes decorated in red velvet and marked with a label. This pew might even be kept under lock and key. The crucial point, as far as the mayors were concerned, was to be visible.[29]

The clergy, still engaged in a struggle begun under the Old Regime, sought to reappropriate the space of the chancel. In doing so they tried to drive all forms of encroachment deep into the nave. They aspired to mastery over "the new parochial market in honors."[30]

The demands of the municipality and the intransigent attitudes of the clergy inevitably gave rise to conflict. On 30 Vendémiaire Year XIII (22 October 1804), the parish priest of Plessé (Loire-Inférieure) "using brute force, had taken the [municipal] pew and hurled it against the font." On Sunday 9 April 1809, the mayor of Lacave (Lot) "entered the church in a rage and loudly asked the assembled people who had moved his seat. He grabbed hold of it, chose a place for it, and said it was there to stay no matter what decrees were issued." He roundly insulted the parish priest and "threatened him with a big stick that he twirled in his hands."

In 1810 the mayor of Bourg-des-Comptes (Ille-et-Vilaine), according to the priest in charge, had a "huge pew" placed in the church such that the congregation could no longer reach the communion table. On 2 May 1834, conflict erupted in Saint-Père. The parish priest had refused to admit the municipal council into the chancel even though it was the first of May. He was also adamant that if on this *fête du roi* he were to hear the sound of the municipal drum before the start of the service—and this might indeed be the mayor's riposte—he would refuse to say Mass.[31]

In December 1839, conflict broke out between the mayor and the priest in charge of Sainte-Honorine-la-Guillaume (Orne). The priest wished to relegate the first municipal magistrate to the churchwardens' pew. According to the mayor, however, " his place ought properly to have been in full view of that occupied by his reverence the parish priest or the incumbent. That, since the priest occupied the first stall on the south side, the mayor should have occupied the first stall on the north side, and that this is the custom in every town and in virtually every commune."[32] As usual, the prefecture ruled against the mayor. Men in his position were forever being humiliated in this kind of dispute. Such issues were of particular significance in regions characterized by religious fervor, where the space of the church was construed as a full space within which each person had his place, and where the staging of social distinctions was highly elaborate.

In the Tarn-et-Garonne as in the Lot, the problem posed by the municipal pew tended to crystallize village conflicts. "In the majority of parishes," wrote the bishop of Montauban in 1847, "there is a pew for the mayor, but this very often gives rise to difficulties."[33] The *ministre des Cultes* believed that mayors were simply there on sufferance, but the latter found it hard to accept that the parish priest could decide what place they should occupy inside the church. In 1840 the mayor of L'Honor-de-Cos complained that the vestry had reserved "the municipal pew."[34] In 1845 the mayor of Saint-Loup gave orders for his pew, which the parish priest had removed from the sanctuary, to be put back. In 1847 the mayor of Monbéqui wished to "restore" the municipal authority's pew to its former position. In August 1849, the mayor of Verdun-sur-Garonne charged the parish priest with having removed the escutcheon of the republic from the authorities' pew. In 1849, 1853, and 1854, disputes along similar lines erupted in Labastide-de-Penne and Lauzerte.[35]

Baron Rendu understood perfectly the nature and significance of such rifts. In a note addressed to the minister dated 8 February 1841, he wrote: "One should be wary. The inhabitant of a rural area keeps a watchful eye over the local authorities he obeys, above all when he has himself chosen them; he feels outrage if their powers are diminished or obstructed, and still more intensely if it is with a view to increasing those of ecclesiastics. . . ."[36] Even at this early date Baron Rendu advocated "building a door on the outside of the bell tower for emergency peals," and considered what tactics might ensure "the secular authorities the respect owed to them." He advised "balancing" the advantage enjoyed by the clergy with "a perceptible display of deference on the part of the parish priest toward the mayor, when the latter occupied the place reserved for him in the church; for example, *the holy water might be given him with particular marks of favor.*" "It is often the case," he went on, " that subtle displays of deference create a *climate of mutual esteem.* This advice was not heeded, the minister fearing that such courtesies might suggest a return to a seigneurial regime.

The municipal authorities also had sounds at their disposal,[37] but none that could vie with the mighty peals of the bell. Thus, ever since the nationalization of the church in force during the Revolution, they had endeavored, as far as was possible, to incorporate bell ringing into the schedule of secular announcements. As spokesmen for the community and the government, mayor and council made themselves out to be the defenders of local custom. The usages in question, which could include ringing for school, the arrival of the tax collector, the lining up of conscripts, the summoning of electors, council meetings, and for the times of toil, rest, and "retreat," were vigorously defended if they were an integral part of local tradition. This bitter determination—which I repeat, was not directly related to irreligion[38]—reflected, even when a town hall had yet to be built, a *growing desire for municipal autonomy* and a concern to curb the powers of the clergy.

The emergence of this aspiration may be defined in terms of two key moments, starting with the first decade of the July Monarchy. In the aftermath of the law of 21 March 1831, which made municipal councils elective,[39] they were regarded as, and indeed felt themselves to be, the representatives of their communities. As a consequence they were less prepared to tolerate clerical interference than they once had been. The rise of the municipal facilitated *the practice of local disputes*, which provided a perfect apprenticeship in village politics.[40] Even the configuration of such disputes had a history. For a long time the tiny local arena had been dominated by the conflict between inhabitants and the mayor and/or the councillors, who were appointed by central government. With the implementation of the law of 21 March 1831, the debate tended more and more to pit mayor, council, and inhabitants against the prefecture and the bishop's palace. At this level an apprenticeship in politics came first through running the affairs of a community. Yet between the beginning of the July Monarchy and the end of the Second Empire, modernity imposed increasing demands on this milieu. Local magistrates were passionately committed to the improvement or construction of roads and highways, the setting up of post offices, the creation of washhouses or garbage dumps, the moving of cemeteries away from the center, perhaps the building of schoolhouses and town halls, and even the acquisition of fire engines. Among these elements of modernity there were some that, as we have seen, were informed by the new sense of urgency, the quantitative measurement of time, and the need for accuracy and speed. All of these seemed to imply control over peals and the possession of a municipal clock, which would generally be installed inside the bell tower. In short, *the bells became, to a greater degree than in the past, an issue involving modernity*. This was all the more the case because of improvements in quality and, generally speaking, the increase in the volume of their sound. Communities became attached to their peals *for new reasons*. In this sense, one can claim that the heyday of bell ringing was in the early 1860s.

After that date the gradual intensification of the postal service, the spread of newspapers and posters, the proliferation of household clocks, and the quicker pace of everyday life tended to sideline auditory messages. The fading of such customs left little else but sacrality, emotion, and nostalgia. From the last quarter of the nineteenth century, I repeat, the steady decline in the pragmatic functions of bell ringing gradually drew attention to its symbolic properties and powers of evocation, which had subsisted and perhaps even been enhanced.[41] In short, "fin-de-siècle" disputes in this domain, which have quite justifiably been interpreted as signs of dechristianizing, secularizing, or desacralizing, also reflect changes in modes of consciousness and feelings of identification.

Whereas the structure of local communities was profoundly modified by the selective mechanisms of the exodus from rural areas,[42] the sphere affected by disputes over bells tended to shrink. Several processes accompanied this attenuation in the range of issues at stake, although the number and intensity of conflicts did not diminish. Since the passing of the laws of 1882 and 1884, the mayor had been elected by the municipal council. He was thereby brought closer to those under his jurisdiction.[43] His term of office was extended, and by the terms of Article 101 of the 1884 law he was entitled to one of the two keys to the bell tower. The fact of there now being two keys spelled the end of the clerical monopoly and was tantamount to a desacralizing of the monument. The bell tower would no longer be regarded as a place of worship but as a building distinct from, and independent of the church, and thus in some way a mere accessory. The bell, although it had been blessed, no longer seemed to be the equivalent of a sacred vessel.[44]

By the same token the municipalities, which were often involved in anticlerical agitation, now hoped to incorporate the bell tower and its peal into the symbolic restructuring of the territory brought about by the building of a town hall or the installation of statues of Marianne. As Jules Méline, a republican deputy for the Vosges, declared to the inhabitants of Julienrupt at an inaugural ceremony: "You used to feel like everyone else that a commune is only truly complete when three edifices, town hall, school, and bell tower are combined. The bell tower . . . is also the external embodiment and, so to speak, the beacon of the commune itself."[45]

The clergy braced itself to defend this, the last symbolic prize at stake within the territory of the commune. It in fact showed great determination, so that the last disputes over bells, though novel in their configuration, were hard-fought.[46] Olivier Ihl confesses to having been struck by the solemnity with which the municipalities, through their delegations, orchestrated these conflicts.[47] We should not, however, be taken in by this stern resolve and ostentatious staging; control of bell ringing, which had once been crucial to the functioning of a community, was tending increasingly, I repeat, to be no more than a symbolic prize, although not an issue of secondary importance.

It has become the custom to write as if the last third of the century saw a shift from community, territory, and custom to the national and, as if by the same token, an apprenticeship in the code of citizenship was thereby instigated. The reader will perhaps be familiar with the thesis of Eugen Weber, according to which peasants became Frenchmen,[48] or with Maurice Agulhon's emphasis on the republicanization of the municipal setting. Instead of thinking in terms of a shift from a sense of the local to a strictly national identity, it might perhaps be more accurate to speak of inveiglement. Republican electoral gains and the implanting of the new symbolic order were achieved without country dwellers losing all sense of their communal identity. The sense of belonging to a community, making allowance for its restructured aspects, and the sense of territory were anyway directly addressed by the Republic, and a strategy may be discerned at the local level. The huge mayors' banquets held in 1889 and 1900 seemed to symbolize this notion of federation; in the villages such events served to enhance the prestige of the municipal magistrates. "Do not therefore mock *l'esprit du clocher*," exclaimed once again Jules Méline, "for it is one of the constituent elements in the idea of the *patrie*."[49] It was possible to know about national divisions and interpret them while at the same time subordinating them to the locality, where in spite of everything, the issues regarded as crucial were still in evidence, inscribed as they were in the midst of the sites of life and death.

After this rapid survey of the key issues and the processes serving to modify them, I now want to examine more closely the general shape and evolution of the conflicts. I will analyze in turn the rewinding of the clock, the choice of bell ringer, the key to the bell tower, and the use to which the bells were put, especially during rites of passage and national festivals.

CHAPTER SEVEN

The Control of Auditory Messages

Chime, Mechanism, and Dial

Needless to say, ownership of rings of bells led to a considerable number of conflicts.[1] Each of the adversaries would attempt to seize the instrument in dispute, and one loses count of the bells sent surreptitiously by the parish priest to be recast or taken down and stored in the presbytery or the town hall. Not to mention those entrusted to the religious bell ringer or his adversary, the lay bell ringer. The conflicts bearing on the ownership, placing, rewinding, and dial of the communal clock are of more interest to us here, and were sometimes closely interconnected with these issues. Whatever claims the municipal authorities had on the interior of the bell tower were justified by their need to have access to this instrument.

We know the significance in medieval cities of a secular, mechanical time imposed by an instrument that served as a symbol of power and authority. We also understand the importance of the ties then interweaving the announcement of the hours with control of the everyday time of urban masses. Even before acquiring a clock a good many communes in the Moselle still, in the middle of the nineteenth century, possessed "their hour bell, which rang the most important hours of the day."[2] This was also the case in the Germanic territories. Conversely, I would remind the reader that the public clock seems to have spread quite slowly to many French rural areas. Nevertheless, as the decades passed, the dial and the chime seem to have driven out and rendered obsolete some secular and profane uses of bells. For individuals living within view of the clock, telling the time became superimposed on the whole range of auditory messages signaling the passing of the hours.[3]

The majority of country dwellers were nevertheless living beyond the zone of visibility of the clock dial; a significant number of them could not hear the chime of the communal clock either, and would only learn of it through the sound of other bells. There was therefore a division within the population that affected representations of time and the sorts of claims that were advanced. Being the best placed, the "people of the *bourg*" in particular called for more precise announcements of the time. In Auradé (Gers) the municipality decided in 1838 to purchase a public clock that would ring the half hours.[4] The inhabitants of the countryside requested, more and more insistently as the decades passed, that it be made possible for them to hear the striking of the hours. In some places, countryfolk living some distance from the town asked that the great bell be used as the clock's chime; in others they requested a *repetition* of the ringing of the hours, testifying to a shift in the practices of vigilance, which arose from a greater need for accuracy.

In short, behind the conflicts over clocks—which had to do with the sacred and the profane or the religious and the secular—there were other issues at stake that were associated with advances in the measurement of duration. The chime of the clock gradually imposed an empty, continuous, and neutral time, which contrasted with that of the peal, the bearer of a sacred time and announcer of festive or dramatic events. Nevertheless, this shift also caused some anxiety. One has only to think of the resistance shown by country dwellers in the nineteenth century to all strict measurements, whether they involved the counting of men,[5] weights, and monetary values, or, still more clearly, the systematic surveying of land. Attachment to the ringing of bells may perhaps be a part of this rejection of abstraction, which was regarded as a sign of the intrusion of new norms, and therefore as a threat. Paradoxically, the neutral time of the clock could seem to be a factor promoting the disintegration and impoverishment of the relationships through which communities were constituted. Precise measurement and the rigorous structuring of times and values might well have satisfied a desire for modernity and yet, in standardizing usages and surreptitiously integrating communities into a sphere of all-embracing norms, they also aroused an obscure anxiety.

The municipal authorities, as the bearers of a desire for quantitative time, had some solid arguments on their side. Clock time made local policing easier, at least in communes where the curfew was not rung. Innkeepers could read off their closing times from the municipal dial. Clock time could also be said to have promoted economic activity; it harmonized the rhythms of a community with those of the neighboring territories. The mayor of Tillac (Gers) noted in 1839 that the acquisition of a bell serving as a chime for the clock had become a necessity now that a mail coach was traversing the commune.[6] As far as bishops, parish priests, and members of the parochial parish council were concerned, the primary function of a clock was to enable services to start on time.[7] They argued that the fact of the instrument being attached to the bell tower lent it a sacred character—more especially so as it was generally associated with bell ringing given that one of the bells served as a chime. I would add that the clock was very often incorporated into the brickwork or timber frame of the tower.

The law was clear on such points and should by itself have silenced the disputants. As the minister of the interior declared in 1858,[8] "since a clock placed on the facade of a church is primarily intended for secular uses, the municipal authorities should have overall responsibility for its operation and maintenance."

The range of conflicts arising from such subtle issues almost beggars belief. Some had to do with the placing and control of the clock, others with the independence of the chime. In Rhétiers (Ille-et-Vilaine) village politics for over a third of a century may be read in terms of the fate of

the communal clock. Study of this case serves to show just how significant the placing of a dial or a clock mechanism could be. This delicate
question, which swiftly became an issue of major importance, determined
the various alignments. It becomes hard to judge whether the conflict over
the clock reflected the great national disputes or whether, conversely,
these disputes were merely used as tools in a local quarrel between the
parish priest and municipal authorities. From 1820 to the dawn of the
Second Empire the placing of the clock served to crystallize and fix the
tensions and animosities involved. The dispute stirred up passions to such
a pitch that in 1851, according to the subprefect of Vitré, it assumed grave
"proportions." If his testimony is reliable, the conflict spread beyond the
confines of the commune, becoming "a party matter throughout the canton."[9] Unfortunately the sources are so contradictory that we have no
way of assessing the relative strength of the two camps.

Since 1702, a very early date indeed, a clock had been installed in the
church in Rhétiers. When religious bell ringing was reintroduced under
the Consulate, the mechanism was placed in a gallery within the church
where, according to the prefect, it would not disturb the worshipers. In
1824, in agreement with the then mayor, the reverend Richard, newly
appointed as parish priest, removed the clock from the gallery of the
church and placed it in a pavilion built on the first floor of the tower.
According to the pastor, the case of the clock disfigured the church while
its sound disturbed the congregation. With the 1830 Revolution a new
mayor was able to prevail and, "being bent on revenge,"[10] if we are to
believe the reverend Richard, got the prefect's permission to return the
clock to the gallery. He set the process in motion on 3 May 1831, that is,
two days after the *fête du roi*, a national festival. The protests of bishop
and parochial church council were in vain. The political situation had
changed radically since the Restoration; anticlericalism now hold sway.
For the mayor it was a point of honor that the municipal instrument
should be visible, and its mechanism audible from within the sanctuary.

As is well known, the July Monarchy came in time to forget its origins.
In 1842 the reverend Richard, while enlarging the church, had the gallery
demolished and the clock returned to the tower. When the mayor lodged
a complaint with the prefect in 1843 the latter managed to arrange a compromise. Yet everything suggests that the leading municipal magistrate

was reluctant to agree to it. In January 1848, as the opposition to the regime was gaining in strength, he profited by the parish priest's absence to install a new clock in the church. In so doing he was presenting a real challenge to his adversary. Since there was no longer a gallery the mayor installed the mechanism directly on the pavement beside the church door. Moreover, by modifying the gearing he had the *great bell* operating as chime to his clock. He was thus issuing a second challenge—the enhanced visibility of the instrument symbolizing secular authority was complemented by an amplification of municipal sound.

On 9 February the parochial parish council demanded that the clock be removed on the grounds that the noise of the mechanism disturbed services. In addition, they said, the religious bell ringer was becoming entangled in the gear wheels and clock hands now blocking the stairs, and therefore could no longer get access to the bell tower. The crucial point, however, was that the noise prevented penitents from being heard and forced them to relinquish the mezza voce upon which the confidential nature of the confessional had depended. A few days later the regime fell. By the parish priest's own admission, the advent of the Republic imped-ed the formulation of such grievances; as he was later to write, for him "the time for action had passed."[11]

The members of the parochial parish council bided their time. In Rhétiers, however, 10 December—the date of Louis-Napoléon's elec-tion to the presidency of the Republic—seems to have been regarded as a turning point. On 11 December the parish priest decided to have a Te Deum sung. The mayor resented the prince's election, regarding it as a triumph for his adversary, and refused to attend. We should note, how-ever, that this mayor was in no sense an extremist; the subprefect of Vitré described him as a "liberal lacking in all arrogance." The wind had plain-ly turned in Rhétiers. On 6 February 1849, the prefect, upon being informed by the subprefect of the complaint lodged by the parochial parish council, instructed the mayor to remove the clock. The mayor flat-ly refused to comply with so humiliating an order. On 27 April 1850, the administration adopted a harsher tone, and a prefectorial decree autho-rized the clock's removal. Passions, however, had reached such a pitch that the departmental authorities dared not resort to force. The dispute dragged on. Finally in March 1853, the *ministre des Cultes*, mindful of the gravity of the dispute, ordered an inquiry and decided on the basis of its findings to act with prudence and restore the status quo. In his view, the parish priest should never have had the old gallery demolished.

I would be inclined to stress here the fact that all the protagonists regarded this affair as being of the utmost gravity. As far as the members of the parochial parish council were concerned, the communal authority was attempting to annex the parish church. It is instructive to note in this regard the symbolic weight attached to the presence of municipal objects inside the sacred site. Indeed, other elements beside the clock were sometimes involved. A mayor from the same area had had the gravedigger's pick and shovel stored there; the anxiety of the members of the parochial parish council was such that they reeled off a list of the intrusions that their adversary, in a nightmarish scenario, might inflict upon them. They wondered whether the municipal authority might not "place the clock wherever they saw fit: in the chancel, [and] then climb it while services were being held, just as a pastoral letter was being read out?"[12] The mayor might place picks and shovels, hand-barrows from the nearby roads, and "weights and measures from the market" in the church. This testimony evidently bears some trace of memories from the revolutionary period. Finally the members of the parochial parish council suggested that the clock be installed in the town hall as in the neighboring commune of Marcillé-Robert. It is worth noting this proposal to effect a degree of separation, thus abandoning any claim on the announcement of a quantitative time inasmuch as it appeared to be the mayor's prerogative.

There were many other affairs of the same kind, though they were often on a smaller scale. The department of the Haute-Marne was especially well-known for incidents involving clocks. Literacy had come early to this region, and telling the time seems to have been a skill developed in parallel to that of knowing how to read, write, and count. In 1853 the parish priest of Chancenay stopped the workman appointed by the mayor from installing a new public clock in his church. It should be noted, however, that this carpenter had out of defiance set to work on a Sunday. The priest in charge, "who was then taking a catechism class," "emerged from the chancel in his surplice" and berated the workman for working on the Lord's day. After vespers, in the absence of the parish priest, the deputy mayor, upon being informed of the dispute, had a locksmith force the door and ordered that the clock be moved inside the church. If we accept the parish priest's narrative, his adversary, "hat upon his head, pipe in his mouth, and using blasphemous words even in a holy place," had the desired change put into effect "in the midst of a troop of children and young people who had been drawn there out of curiosity."[13]

In 1868 the mayor of Chaumont accused the parish priest of stopping, or having someone else stop the clock at periodic intervals to assert his claims over the instrument.[14] Nine years later the parish priest in Humbécourt opposed the mayor in his wish to move the public clock, so that it might be repaired, since he had not received prior permission from the parochial church council.[15] In 1880 in Andelot a more serious conflict erupted, one that was reminiscent of the dispute in Rhétiers. That year the mayor had had a new clock installed in the bell tower of the church without asking the parish priest's permission. Worse still, he had a sky-light opened up, and this disfigured the church. In addition, dust from the building work had damaged the parish organ. These alterations were carried out *very noisily* during mass, forcing the priest to quit the altar. The parish priest in Andelot, as in Rhétiers, objected to the clock hampering the free play of the ropes used in bell ringing.[16]

In 1899 a conflict of this same type erupted belatedly in Estrennes, in the Vosges.[17] The former municipal clock was installed in a gallery of the church. The mayor had it moved to a higher floor. The priest in charge thereupon had the locks to the gallery changed and denied the rewinder access. Yet the clock's weights still hung there and could therefore no longer be checked by the person responsible. The authorities ruled in the priest's favor for, although he was required to give the mayor's agent access to the clock, no mention had been made of inspection of the weights.

There seem to have been still more conflicts over the chimes as such. The mayor of Saint-Mamert-du-Gard and the municipal council of Vergèze (Gard) had the clapper of a bell removed to keep it for the communal clock.[18] In November 1863, a dispute split Saint-Gervais d'Auvergne (Puy-de-Dôme).[19] One of its bells had been broken by the clock's hammer, and the parish priest and parochial church council took the opportunity to recast the peal to harmonize its various elements. They refused, however, to let one of the new bells be used as a chime. The mayor, who had a copy of the key to the bell tower, let himself in and had the hammer of the public clock placed against the side of the *great bell*.

Conversely, it was the municipality that in 1864 was set against the removal of the old bells chosen by the parish priest of Saint-Martin-en-Cailleux (Loire), who wanted to modernize the peal. The councillors argued that one of the bells served as chime to the public clock; that the peal was, in their view, the property of the commune; that, above all, the "storm bell"[20] had time and time again given proof of its protective powers. Over and above the conflict between town hall and presbytery it seems reasonable to suppose that this affair evinced a community's fear that it might be deprived of a marker of its identity.

On 11 December 1865, the mayor of Salmagne (Meuse) formulated another type of grievance. He complained that the sexton rang the bell while the communal clock was striking the hour. Local inhabitants were prevented from learning *the municipal time*, which the mayor *deemed more accurate than that of the sexton*.[21]

This said, one should not be misled by the abundance of sources referring only to conflicts. If one bears in mind the number of communes in the national territory, disputes over clocks can only have affected relatively few of them. In this regard, compromise and mutual concession were the rule. Most parish priests and priests in charge were prepared to let one of the bells in the set serve as chime to the public clock, which would be installed in the bell tower. The municipality might itself sometimes make concessions, although this was rarer. In Aubais (Gard) the communal clock had kept its chime during the Revolution while the church had been deprived of all its other bells. The decision was also made to fit this chime with a hammer, the rope for which hung in the sacristy; this allowed religious services to be rung on the municipal bronze. That was the state of affairs in 1845 when the bell, having been worked too hard, finally shattered.[22]

The Bell Ringer's Pride

In order to really understand the conflicts precipitated by the choice of bell ringers, or by their actions, we need to scrutinize the terms governing their recruitment, differences in status, and official duties. I propose to start with the religious bell ringer.[23] He was supposed to over-see access to the bell tower, clean the stairs, particularly when there had been heavy falls of snow, look after the bells, which had to be greased regularly, examine the suspensions, and ensure that no friction was obstructing the movements of the peal and that no part was attacked by rust. The bell ringer was supposed to supply ropes and look after them. It fell to him to buy whatever candles were needed for winter peals, espe-cially those required for All Saints' Day and Midnight Mass. Finally, he had of course to ring.[24]

In the majority of cases, the presbytery bell ringer, even when he was not responsible for secular peals, had another trade; he was often the sex-ton.In many regions—in the Orne for example—the two terms were syn-onymous. The sexton, still called "custos," was responsible for guarding the church; it was he who served at mass when the choir boy was absent, and he very often sang at church.[25] In addition, he accompanied the priest when the latter took the viaticum at night to a dying person. These duties were exclusively masculine.[26] In rural France at this time the recruitment of this assistant to the clergy was a matter of some importance.

To judge by the official texts, it was up to the parish priest to choose his own bell ringer. In practice, however, such appointments were deter-mined by a patchwork of local customs.[27] Furthermore, the terms gov-erning recruitment and the claims of the various protagonists varied with the political situation and the power of the secular authorities. It would therefore be an error to take normative statements at face value.

In many regions, perhaps even the majority, the bell ringer, like the sexton, was recruited by the parish priest. In some places, however, the mayors wielded considerable influence in this domain, especially at the dawn of the July Monarchy, a high point for municipal power.[28] Several communes in the Haute-Marne were torn apart by conflicts over the choice of bell ringer.

In the Hautes-Pyrénées the bell ringer was elected[29] and was general-ly responsible for both secular and religious bell ringing. In Souyeaux the bell ringer was chosen *by the heads of families*, who met on the first day of the year.[30] In Gardères the occasion was staged in a "chamber of the town hall."[31] In truth , in this region the procedure was a complex one that involved both an election and an auction. In Souyeaux we further learn that after a series of bids had been made, the heads of families elected "the most deserving."

This way of proceeding was common in the Haute-Marne, where it was termed a *"relaissée."* There, as in the Hautes-Pyrénées, the appointment and salary of the bell ringer were therefore indissociable. The latter was paid by the commune or the parochial church council, the sum being fixed at the *relaissée* or by "descending bids." Private individuals would not be put to any expense when they gave instructions for a peal to be rung. We gather that in 1848 the inhabitants of Consigny were opposed to the abandonment of this purportedly immemorial practice.[32] Their refusal led to the drafting of a petition and to some unrest until the administration gave in and accepted a "compromise."

In Braux (Haute-Marne) the parochial church council took responsibility, from 1850 on, for organizing the *"relaissée."* It was held on Low Sunday. This custom was well-established in the Haute-Marne, the Meuse,[33] the Vosges,[34] and the Hautes-Pyrénées, and survived until the end of the century. It was even reintroduced at a later date in some places. In February 1875 Damrémont municipal council met to come to an agreement on terms governing the *"relaissée."* In this commune the bell ringer, who was also the gravedigger, was elected for a period of three years. Before entering into his duties he had to pay a surety.[35] In Buchey in 1890 and again in 1894, the job of bell ringer and that of town crier were put up for auction, simultaneously.[36] The awarding of the post, which went "by Dutch auction and by inch of candle," was publicized in advance by posters and legal notices. It was held every five years.

This system also gave rise to many conflicts, which were sometimes very intense. As early as 1840 the parish priest of Montoussé (Hautes-Pyrénées) found himself at odds with the local community.[37] After mass one Sunday in January the mayor proceeded to a sale by public auction "to the lowest bid." The schoolmaster, who had taken the mayor's side, addressed the assembled people after the service. He declared that the appointment of the bell ringer was not up to the parish priest. The priest found the speech humiliating and lodged a complaint; the fact of the mayor "keeping [the key to the bell tower] in his own house" rendered the situation still more offensive. There was a repetition of this scene the following year. After the January election the mayor, the schoolmaster and, this time, the public health officer intervened publicly. The mayor, disappointed by the hostility of the parish priest, resolved from then on to withhold the bell tower key from the religious bell ringer, whom his adversary had appointed on his own initiative. As a consequence, the bells stopped ringing in Montoussé. Conflicts of a similar nature arose here and there when decisions had to be made regarding bell ringers who were destitute.[38]

By virtue of Article 37 of the decree of 30 December 1809, parochial church councils were obliged to pay the bell ringer "the accepted rate for each place," a ruling that left plenty of latitude. Where peals were ordered by private individuals, each vestry in principle drew up a tariff, which was supposed to be approved by local government.[39] Throughout the century the ecclesiastical authorities endeavored, often without much success, to standardize usages by establishing diocesan tariffs. In practice, bell ringers were remunerated in a bewilderingly wide range of ways.

Across the greater part of the national territory bell ringers would seem in fact to have been remunerated by the parochial church council and the parishioners, according to a tariff drawn up by the council.[40] Sometimes, however, the ringer would be paid by the users according to rates decided by the party concerned, often in consultation with the parish priest. Such arrangements, needless to say, could prove controversial. This is evident from the attitude of the bell ringer at the church of Saint-Pierre de Tarsac (Gers), who was accused by the subprefect of Lombez of being a "fleecer of youth."[41] On Tuesday 19 June 1839, four marriages had to be celebrated at the same time. The bell ringer, with the priest in charge's approval, shut the church door as the processions drew near. He announced that the wedding parties would not be allowed into the sanctuary until the godfathers and godmothers of the future spouses had each given him two francs. This excessive demand caused such ill feeling that "in the resulting tumult," the mayor reported, "the holy place was about to witness a brawl." "After *lengthy negotiations*" the magistrate managed to placate the wedding parties. The bell ringer was persuaded to open the doors for a round sum of ten francs, instead of sixteen. This then, was yet another instance of the customary shift from "tumult" to "arrangement."

As we have seen, the bell ringer, who was also responsible for secular peals, might well be paid by the municipality or the local residents. In some regions, the parishioners rejected the tariff set by the parochial church council since it generally entailed a cash payment whereas countryfolk, as is well known, preferred barter and payment in kind.[42] Furthermore, some regarded the tariff as a political tool in the hands of the clergy. In 1894 the priest in charge of Arthès (Tarn) was accused of having increased the amount payable for peals in order to avenge a republican victory at the polls.[43] Finally, it was felt that diocesan or parochial church council tariffs served to subdivide ceremonies into different classes, thus introducing harmful distinctions or reinforcing hierarchies founded on wealth.[44]

The remuneration of a bell ringer by the local community might be effected in several different ways. Sometimes the ringer would simply appeal to the generosity of parishioners, visiting them two or three times a year. Such door-to-door collections took place in the Tarn and the Cantal until around the end of the 1880s.[45] They were current in the Ille-et-Vilaine under the Third Republic. Some anticlerical mayors then sought to ban a way of doing things that, in their view, might be likened to begging, but several rulings in the Court of Cassation found against them.[46]

Sometimes the term "collection," which is polysemic, implies the collection of sums of money or quantities of foodstuffs fixed by local custom or by a regulation of the parochial church council.[47] In several communes in the Moselle, payments in kind continued right up to the end of the century. Sometimes it was the bell ringer who decided on the size of the "collection." "Several of those under my jurisdiction complain," the mayor of Monestiès (Tarn) wrote in September 1893, "that the carillonneur *demands* annually a bushel of corn for every head of horned livestock and fifty centimes from those who do not own such animals."[48] The parish priest spoke in the bell ringer's defense. The bushel here, he argued, is only five liters. When the attempt was made in the parish to abide by the diocesan tariff, no individual complied voluntarily. Any family refusing to pay, the mayor insisted, would forego all rights over bell ringing.

In many communes in the Hautes-Pyrénées the bell ringer, once elected, would conclude a contract (as we have seen) with the heads of families. In Souyeaux in 1896, each landowner with the right to cut firewood had to pay. In Burg in 1898, the carillonneur, who doubled as cantor and gravedigger, was paid "in corn, maize or potatoes for each household depending on its size"[49]—an arrangement that the prefect now rejected. In May 1895 Layrisse municipal council decided that the carillonneur should be paid yearly "at Christmas" a measure of maize per family. This amount would be halved in the case of the needy, whose names were listed. Newly established sharecroppers were exempted from paying the sums owed by their predecessors.[50] In 1892 heads of family in Calavanté had to pay two francs or "an acceptable quantity of wheat." In Siarrouy the commune paid the bell ringer on behalf of the poor.[51] In the Haute-Marne the *relaissée*, which was leased out, was often accompanied by a tariff in kind designed to thwart the more demanding bell ringers.[52] In Damrémont in 1875, each household, "in accordance with a custom established since time immemorial," had to give five liters of wine or seventy-five centimes to the contractor.[53] Nevertheless, it was not unusual for a bell ringer to perform his duties without any fee; it could be regarded as an honor, not as a burden, to have access to the bell tower and be permitted to use the bells. This was the case with a good many schoolmasters.

At the end of the century the procedures I have described were attacked from three different angles. Some bell ringers—and this was the case in Siarrouy in 1899, for example—now insisted on being paid in cash. Each bishop did his utmost, I repeat, to standardize usages throughout the diocese. Finally, central government wished to control a levy that it regarded as a kind of tax. During the 1890s the prefecture of the Hautes-Pyrénées called upon mayors to endorse local usage through rulings made by town councils. Payments, or their equivalents in cash, made by family heads were now supposed to be included in a commune's budget,[54] and the municipal tax collector would henceforth be responsible for their collection.

All these considerations meant that bell ringing could not be entrusted to a woman. The bell ringer, however, was entitled to some help, and when three bells had to be set in motion he had no choice but to use it. Such duties were often kept in the family. A bell ringer's son would learn from his father how to handle the ropes. Sometimes an official ringer would be assisted by his own daughter,[55] although this could pose problems. In May 1816 two inhabitants of Saint-Pé, in the Hautes-Pyrénées, petitioned against the "carillonneur." According to their version of events, "the latter is obliged to have his sister ring the bells and she, though about eighteen years old, does not and cannot perform this function as it used to be performed, in spite of the fact that some young people go up to the top of the bell tower, perhaps to help her."[56] In 1894 the carillonneur's daughter in Adé hurt her leg while ringing in place of her father.[57]

Throughout the century there was a fear that bell towers, being difficult to enter, might provide cover for surreptitious lovemaking. There was also a concern that *the youth might burst into* the tower and grab the bells. We have seen how tempting it was for this age group, which by convention was responsible for charivaris, to deploy the loudest auditory signals. The adults, on the other hand, sought to protect the bell towers from this juvenile meddling and would impose penalties if the need arose. In July 1837 Concombre junior, known as Rouzy, climbed the tower in Saint-Orse (Dordogne), rang without the parish priest's permission, and broke a bell. The seventeen members of the municipal council and "those most heavily taxed" *voted by secret ballot*, this last detail being pertinent to any study of the ways in which voting was learned in rural society. They were unanimous in their decision that Concombre senior should pay for the breakage.[58]

It was traditional during this period for widows who might otherwise be paupers to take on duties previously performed by their husbands. Some women became tobacconists, roadmenders, or even town criers. This practice explains why one might sometimes encounter female bell ringers. In 1841 the mayor of Serviès (Tarn) instructed widow Duran to hold on to the key to the bell tower that had been in her husband's keeping, and intended that she succeed him. He refused to recognize the new bell ringer, who had been appointed to the post by the parish priest.[59] In Rouffiac (Tarn) in 1903, a "poor woman"[60] was responsible for looking after the bells.

Sometimes a whole family might be regarded as holding the office of bell ringer. In Chambroncourt (Haute-Marne) in 1896, "the Tassin

family" assumed responsibility for all bell ringing that concerned the commune on the basis of "verbal agreements between *it* and the mayor."[61]

Since bell ringing was so often learned within families, the claim sometimes arose that the *duties were hereditary*, a notion that could cause conflict. In Colombey-lès-Choiseul (Haute-Marne)[62] in 1882, the bell ringer,
who enjoyed the support of the mayor, was named François Perny. He
had kept the secular peals for himself and was paid by the commune for
ringing them. The parochial church council also paid him twenty-five
francs a year to ring "the middays." His two sons quarreled over his lega-
cy. The elder son, Victor, had been appointed by the parish priest as
François's successor as far as religious peals were concerned. He also carried out the duties of sexton for the parish. He was paid in kind by the
local inhabitants. François Perny, however, very much wanted his son
Prosper, who was sixteen years old and lived at home, to inherit all the
peals for which he had formerly been responsible. He therefore
reproached Victor for a lack of courtesy toward him. The mayor agreed
and wanted to entrust the secular peals to Prosper. In the parish priest's
opinion, however, Prosper should only inherit the ringing of the Angelus
and the "care" of the clock. The dispute dragged on, with François, the
father, needing three months to negotiate an "arrangement."

You could not ring without knowledge, and therefore without an
apprenticeship. A peal was neither a toy nor a source of entertainment; it
was forbidden, as we have seen, to carillon profane airs or treat the bells
as theatrical instruments. Furthermore, without a degree of expertise
there was a real risk of shattering the bronze. There were some ringers
so unskilled that they had a reputation for being "wreckers." It was particularly important to avoid excessively long peals.

A good ringer was attuned to his instruments and knew how to impose
his will upon them without violence and as if by persuasion. His art lay
in matching the movement of the bell and that of the clapper while
manipulating several ropes at the same time.[63] Some artists were known
for leagues around. This was the case with, for example, the ringer from
Oulchy-le-Château, in the Aisne. Father Alexis, as he was called, tied up
the clappers of his bells to make them more sensitive. Holding a rope in
each hand and controlling a third with his foot, he leaned against the
frame of the belfry, shut his eyes in order to hear better, and then

"animated" "his bells," "puffing and blowing, exhausted and dripping with sweat." "I am a musician," he declared to the painter Frédéric Henriet, who was astounded by the quality of his peals. "I have composed and arranged a fanfare for the locality. I sing bass in the choir, I play the ophicleide, I know counterpoint, and I would have no difficulty in composing a march, an andante, or an allegro." "I have known my bells" for over fifty years,[64] he added. The inhabitants of Oulchy-le-Château were proud of the old man.

A bell ringer's pride was a complex phenomenon. Like any other artisan, he was proud of his expertise. In addition, he was in daily contact with the priest. He had access to the bell tower and, very often, to the sacristy. He could handle the books there, as well as some objects used in worship. As we have seen, he might have aesthetic pretensions, and this was particularly likely if to his other duties he added those of cantor or serpent player. It was he who expressed the joy, sadness, or alarm of the community. He regulated time through the rhythm of his signals. He was responsible for summoning the inhabitants and he symbolized punctuality in the village. His person seemed imbued with the mysterious forces of the bell tower. In a word, he participated in the sacred.

The bell ringer's prestige was in no way diminished by his also being a sabot maker, a wheelwright, a saddler or, more often, a schoolmaster. Needless to say, his status depended on the procedures involved in his appointment or his remuneration as well as his temperance. Bell ringers did in fact have a reputation for frequenting taverns, for theirs was thirsty work. Moreover, this was what worried members of the clergy, who for this reason alone were hostile toward the idea of impromptu bell ringers bursting into bell towers—they too would be prone to drinking large quantities. "According to information gathered in several different communes," the prefect of Ille-et-Vilaine noted in 1885, "the bell ringers, without any concealed intent to profane or to cause scandal, when they perform peals that last a long time [in this case for 14 July], bring cider for their refreshment."[65]

Graffiti in bell towers sometimes expressed pride in the performance of a duty. The bell ringers, although they would not see their names inscribed on the bronze of the bells, as were those of the parish priest, the mayor, the deputy mayor, or the schoolmaster, nevertheless endeavored in

some cases to leave a trace close by their bells. Inside the bell tower in
Herpy, in the Ardennes, one can read "the names of the bell ringers for
the last few centuries inscribed in the stone."[66] The earliest date was 1647
while other graffiti record the prices of grain in 1766 and 1801. Still others
tell of bells being melted down or blessed. This bell tower was thereby
made into a realm of memory.[67]

The bell ringer was plainly a figure of importance in the countryside,
above all where there was a degree of religious fervor.[68] His office predated that of the rural guard. All eyes were on him. He was forever being
assessed for his punctuality, his accuracy,[69] his expertise, and the size of
his tariffs. His comings and goings could by themselves lend credence to,
or precipitate rumors. He had formidable weapons at his disposal, namely, a refusal to ring and *sound as derision*, which was terribly humiliating
for a family at a christening and still more so at a wedding. In 1894 the
bell ringer in Arthès (Tarn) withheld the peals or, what was worse, "rang
in a derisory fashion"[70] when he was not paid as much as he would have
liked.

We are thus the better able to understand the nature of conflicts
between the two bell ringers. The ringer with sole responsibility for the
secular peals was answerable to the mayor and the council. He did not
have the same duties as his rival and he could not use the whole ring. One
of the bells, generally the smallest, which he merely tolled, belonged to
the range of instruments reserved for the use of the municipal authorities. I should therefore fill in the context to which it belonged.

In some mountainous regions, although this was less and less the case
in the nineteenth century, the mayor transmitted messages by means of
the *municipal horn*. In Orgeix, in the Ariège, "the schoolmaster would
announce school times by simply sounding the horn. The horn is still
used in several parts of France for secular and religious purposes."[71]
Some parishes announced Advent Sunday services by this means. In 1892
the new mayor, "judging that this manner of issuing proclamations gave
offense to many relatives," decreed that "the use of the horn is formally
banned in the commune of Orgeix."

In fact the quintessential municipal signal was *the drum*, which would
be entrusted to a person referred to by varying names depending on the
place—rural guard, town crier or "jack of all trades." It may prove

rewarding to pause for a moment and consider this instrument, the better to grasp the scope of bell ringing.

Somewhat condescendingly the clergy had surrendered ownership and use of the drum to the municipality. In their view it was the mayor's instrument. This opinion enabled the parish priest in Coësmes to claim that, conversely, bell and handbell "belong to him."[72] The sound of the drum was recognized as the quintessential secular signal. If in 1832 the parish priest of Nonancourt (Eure) denied the mayor use of the ring of bells it was, he wrote, to prevent the latter from becoming a simple drum.[73]

The clergy nevertheless objected when drum rolls disturbed services or when there was, in short, risk of a confrontation of sounds. In fact some anticlerical mayors relished such challenges. Under the First Empire the mayor of Caussade (Tarn-et-Garonne) would enter the church with the drum beating whenever he attended a ceremony with the national guard in attendance. Portalis, however, ruled that "the drum was to stop beating at the church door."[74]

At the dawn of the July Monarchy, as we have seen, a good many rural mayors drilled the national guard on Sundays in the square outside the church to defy the parish priest and make the drum reverberate in the ears of the assembled congregation. The sound of a drum brought back the military memories of the Revolution and the First Empire; it called to mind a period of domination by the secular authorities.[75] Yet many rural communes in the Moselle[76] and the Orne, for example, remained for a long time without such instruments. Moreover, the mayors used this lack as a pretext to justify their own claims to ring the bells, particularly at elections.

The clock in Rhétiers enables us to reconstruct a history of politics in the village. The same is true for some twenty years of the drum in Saint-Aubin-du-Pavail.[77] In 1790 or in 1791, according to the version of events given by the mayor in office under the Restoration, the national guard in this small commune in Ille-et-Vilaine acquired a drum. Each member had paid, he went on, "according to his rank." The neighboring municipalities then proceeded to do the same. The drum was handed down through the three captains who subsequently held the post, and was then kept at the mayor's house. At the mayor's death his successor "found the instrument at his father-in-law's house." Everything suggests that the drum, having been abandoned in the house of a private individual, was no longer in use. In 1810 or 1811 the young people of the commune, having been authorized to take up arms and "desiring to do as the other parishes were," resolved to redeem "the trust of their predecessors and relatives" so as to escort in a seemly fashion "the Holy Sacrament to Corpus-Christi." Ever since that ceremony the drum had been *stored in the sacristy "for the use of the town-hall."* On 22 August 1816, three days before the *fête du roi* [Saint Louis' Day], the new mayor—who presumably had clerical sympathies—the deputy mayor, and the bell ringer refused to hand the instrument back to the former mayor, who was now claiming it. I do not believe that this highly symbolic set of circumstances, whereby instruments were abandoned and then intercepted, can have applied to the majority of drums. Nevertheless, it tells us much about power relations in this region of Brittany at the dawn of the Restoration.

Throughout the national territory it was the mayor who appointed the individual responsible for beating the municipal drum. Sometimes, as we have seen, these duties were put up for auction with those pertaining to bell ringing. It is possible that some sort of hereditary right to the post of watchman or town crier was implicitly recognized.

In some cases the mayor could resort to one or more communal bells. The reader will perhaps know how close a link there was in the Middle Ages between the communal movement and the possession of a belfry equipped with a ring of bells. From the thirteenth to the fifteenth century many towns in Flanders, Artois, and Picardy in particular, but also in Lorraine, and Normandy, benefited from such a privilege, which they sometimes lost. In the nineteenth century, to give only one instance, the inhabitants of Metz were deeply proud of the famous "Mutte." The same could be said of the municipal bells of Douai, Arras, Abbeville, Cambrai, Amiens, or Péronne. As the mayor of Bar-le-Duc proudly wrote on 3 July 1907, "we have never had recourse to the church peals" to ring for "public holidays, reveille, curfew, the opening and closing of the electoral rolls," and to warn of "routine dangers."[78]

Conversely, it was rare in the nineteenth century to find municipal bells in rural communes. At most one might discern a limited spread of such instruments that was associated with the rise in municipal consciousness evident from 1831 onward. Generally it was school classes that led to communal bells being introduced into the countryside. At first they served to divide up the school day, but were then put to a range of other secular uses. Needless to say, there was nothing especially prestigious about such bells. The municipal council of Choiseul (Haute-Marne) resolved in 1862 that the bell hanging in the school would also be used to announce its meetings.[79] In the Bray under the Second Empire, a number of municipalities had a bell for ringing the "retreat." The tolling bell from Deville, a suppressed parish, had been placed around 1840 on the belvedere of the school in Grandcourt, and rang for both classes and the curfew.[80] In 1874 the municipal council of Humbécourt (Haute-Marne), faced with the parish priest's opposition to classes being rung, "had a small bell placed on top of the schoolhouse." The assumption was that in winter it would also be used to ring for adult classes. The mayor informed the prefect, who had his doubts about this plan, that if the administration refused to pay for it, the "heads of families" would chip in.[81]

At the end of the century municipal bells tended to be introduced where republican town halls were under construction. In the canton of Rethel (Ardennes), wrote H. Jadart in 1897, "several recently built town halls have been provided with campaniles and bells."[82] Given that since 14 July the parish priest had stopped ringing the Angelus, the municipal council of Vaubexy (Vosges) resolved in 1894 to "install a bell in the town hall." A subscription was launched and the council expressed the hope that the municipality would pay for "the little bell turret."[83] Conversely, it would be stretching a point to claim that the wish of freethinkers to see the town hall ring for marriages and secular burials led to an increase in municipal bells—this practice had been banned in 1911. It is worth noting that the municipality of Rivesaltes (Pyrénées-Orientales) had attempted to win concessions of this kind, but had failed.[84]

Where there was no municipal bell, the great majority of rural mayors hoped to gain free access to the bell tower and pass on their instructions to the individual responsible for secular peals. When this individual was not bell ringer to the parish priest he would often be the schoolmaster, the secretary at the town hall, the cantor, or one of the firemen, as was the case in Domèvre-sur-Avière (Vosges).[85] When the commune possessed a clock, the municipal bell ringer was also responsible for rewinding it. He would often be the gravedigger as well. It was up to the mayor to make such an appointment. Nevertheless, he was supposed to offer the post to the presbytery bell ringer. If he were to refuse, another individual might be appointed, subject to the parish priest's approval.

The lay bell ringer did not have the same level of expertise as his rival, and it would have been of little use to him anyway, at least prior to 1880. Up until this date he would normally just toll one of the bells in the set. He was forbidden to ring a peal, and it was precisely this that caused difficulties after 1880. From that date on the municipal bell ringer had to celebrate 14 July with all due solemnity, or in other words, in peal. On this occasion his incompetence was such that he very nearly shattered the bells. The risk was all the greater since he had to rely on "impromptu assistance." At least this was how certain members of the clergy recounted such episodes.[86] Generally speaking, parish priests and priests in charge were given to describing all those who "intruded" on bell towers as individuals up to no good, even when mayor and deputy mayor were involved. In 1880 the parish priest of Brillon (Meuse) denounced the commune's lay bell ringer as a drunkard who had slept it off beneath the vaults of the church. He was a violent character who had once been imprisoned for having "wounded" his father-in-law, and who possessed a "veritable mania for bells and the bell tower."[87] According to the priest in charge of Relanges (Vosges), the schoolmaster, who was also the rewinder of the clock, was a drunkard and a thief. More particularly, he had made off with some chandeliers from the church.[88] In 1901 the parish priest of Mazères (Hautes-Pyrénées) accused the lay bell ringer, who was reputed to be a skillful poacher, of having raided the collection boxes in his church and of having "illegally caught birds or nocturnal quadrupeds that had taken up residence in the bell tower."[89]

Conflicts over a bell ringer's personality were of two different types. When the same individual did all the bell ringing the discussion focused on his appointment, his remuneration, or the level of authority that should oversee him and decide what work he should do. These conflicts often led to a separation of secular and religious peals, and to the appointment by the mayor of a municipal bell ringer.

Another type of conflict might ensue involving a clash between two people in the same bell tower. Only some kind of "arrangement" could resolve an antagonism of this kind. In 1859 the schoolmaster of Illoud (Haute-Marne), having become the mayor's adviser, clashed with the parish priest. He was, however, both the priest's cantor and bell ringer. Noting that this schoolmaster had decided to stop singing in church, the parish priest withdrew the bells from him and entrusted them to his faithful churchwarden instead. The mayor and councillors rejected this new bell ringer who had not deigned *to present his respects* to them. They continued to entrust the secular peals to the schoolmaster. The parish priest, who had no intention of letting the now retired cantor continue to toll the Angelus, denied him access to the bell tower. The dispute ended in an "arrangement."[90]

Where no agreement was reached there might be open war between the two bell ringers. These feuds reflected the struggle for local power between mayor and parish priest. Given the resulting duplication of auditory messages, news of the breach could well spread across the whole region. Such incidents were especially commonplace in two periods, namely, the beginning of the July Monarchy and the end of the century. This is not at all surprising.

In 1833 the mayor of Lézignan (Hautes-Pyrénées) decided to appoint an "*administrative bell ringer*." He had of course chosen an individual previously dismissed by his adversary, the parish priest. The priest regarded the mayor's man as "*an intruder*." In order to deny the religious bell ringer access to the bell tower, the municipality had had an extra door built. The lay bell ringer, on the other hand, had removed the clapper from the great bell so that his rival, although appointed by the parish priest, could no longer use it from beneath by means of one of the two ropes that hung down into the nave of the church. The mayor construed his action as a response to a provocation. As he explained to the prefect, "the [municipal] clock has been covered with a vast quantity of urine, which has harmed its working and at the same time spread infection in the bell tower."[91] At the same time the mayor and deputy mayor had introduced a system of double peals so that the lay bell ringer repeated the Angelus morning, noon, and night. At the prefect's request the justice of the peace from Lourdes came in May to try for a reconciliation. He admitted, however, that he could do nothing since the population of the commune had "divided into two [warring] parties." Three months later the subprefect of Argèles came to see whether he might heal the rift. He decided to have a single bell ringer elected by *an assembly of notables*, consisting of the town councillors and ten other individuals who would meet at the town hall. The parish priest's party[92] contested the composition of this electoral body, which it did not regard as competent to decide such matters and which, as it turned out, elected an "intruder." Then, adding insult to injury, the mayor's men, "according to six of the notables, who were supporters of the parish priest, paraded around the whole village beating the national guard's drum and chanting disgraceful things."[93]

Other conflicts of this type erupted during this same period, yet far away from the Pyrénées. As the bishop of Langres wrote in 1838: "There is a parish where, *for five years now*, a regular routine has been established for so-called secular bell ringing. The two bell ringers, one being responsible for religious ringing and the other for secular ringing, take turns ringing, one for the prayer for the Angelus, morning, midday, and evening, and the other for what by general consent is termed the summons to work, the midday, and the cessation of work. The first comer endeavors each morning to cause difficulties for his antagonist, sometimes by unhooking the clapper of the bell, sometimes by hitching up the ropes, sometimes by changing the locks, etc.; as you can well imagine, the mischief is not restricted to the consecrated edifice. Tempers flare up, and others are drawn in to the dispute and *take sides*. Soon order and peace give way to disturbance and division."[94]

Disturbances of this kind were still more frequent toward the end of the century. In January 1895, the parish priest of Marseillan (Hautes-Pyrénées), being opposed to the auctioning of bell ringing , decided to appoint his own bell ringer. He suspected the "communal carillonneur" of being the individual responsible at the start of the year for covering the portals of the presbytery with excrement, and for placing two straw scarecrows draped in tricolors on top of them. I should add that this communal bell ringer "took the liberty, after he had rung the matins [this may mean the peal for daybreak], of ringing the three bells in peal for twenty-four minutes."[95] The commune had been divided by such conflicts over sound for three months. On 27 January the lay bell ringer had "carillonned" from half past two in the morning until quarter to three.[96]

The mayor had the locks to the bell tower changed, and as a result the parish priest could no longer get access to the ring of bells. Furthermore, the priest was the victim of a charivari lasting ten or more days. The mayor stuck by his explanation: if the municipal "carillonneur" had rung for so long it was because he had been insulted, and even shut up in the bell tower by the parish priest, who did not wish to abide by the bidding system any longer. From then on this commune had no choice but to have its peals repeated.

The parish priest of Souyeaux (Hautes-Pyrénées) was likewise hostile to the principle of auctioning. In 1889 he entrusted the religious peals to an individual of his own choosing. The ousted bell ringer, "supported and egged on by the mayor" and remunerated by the inhabitants, at first refused to return the keys to the tower. Subsequently, the one considered by the parish priest to be the sole holder of the post "often found excrement inside the bell tower. One Sunday morning the seats, the stalls reserved for particular families, and the childrens' pews were found to be coated with fecal matter."[97] Everyone knew who the guilty party was. A few months later, after having acquiesced for a time to the previous custom, the parish priest decided once again to appoint his own bell ringer. His choice was ratified by the mayor and the local inhabitants. A person who had been previously elected, however, sorely offended at being passed over, took the liberty of repeating the peals. On Sundays, "at the precise moment of the *Sanctus* and the consecration, while the official bell ringer was announcing this solemn part of the Mass with the grave peal customarily used, the former bell ringer seized hold of a second bell's rope and set it ringing in peal, thus creating only too painful a scene for the congregation." If we turn to the East, we find that between 1883 and 1889 the commune of Marac (Haute-Marne) was periodically split by a drawn out dispute between the two bell ringers.[98] In 1889 the priest in charge of Tollaincourt (Vosges), who had had the peals on 5 May stopped after two minutes, complained about the lay bell ringer. Apparently the ringer had walked through the church wearing his hat, and had waited for the priest *to salute him first* when they encountered one another in the bell tower.[99]

There are many other instances of such conflicts, especially in the Pyrénées. In Pouyastruc in 1885, the peals were repeated. "*We seem ridiculous in the eyes of all our neighbors*," the president of the parochial church council wrote to the prefect on the evening of one of his visits. "This very morning," he went on, "you may well have noticed that the church was almost full after the second stroke [of the bell] for Mass because our parish, being very far-flung, had mistaken the municipal peal for the first stroke for Mass."[100] In Betpouy in 1893, the bell ringer, though dismissed by the parish priest, continued to ring the Angelus at the mayor's behest. To avoid such a repetition the priest instructed his sexton to back down. Conversely, in Bazus-Neste the following year, the peals were repeated by the two bell ringers.

The belated incidents that erupted in Claracq, in the Basses-Pyrénées, were of a more banal nature. On 25 February 1908, the mayor decided to have Master Larroudi—who had been elected by the local residents and was paid in kind—ring at noon or the time for the midday meal, and in the evening when work stopped. Needless to say, the priest in charge's bell ringer likewise intended to use the bells. "While the [two] men, being somewhat more calm, merely argued," the *Gazette des tribunaux* record-ed, " the women, being more agitated and excitable, came to blows so that one day the church bell ringer, when he came at noon to ring the Angelus, was violently repulsed by the mother-in-law of the lay bell ringer."[101]

Keys, Doors, and Ropes

Another series of disputes, which has attracted the attention of historians,[102] concerned access to bell towers and the right to ring. Here it was keys, doors, and ropes that were at issue. To understand what was at stake we first need to consider the function of lock and key in the rural communities of this period. The use of such instruments was both limit-ed and charged with meaning. In this context, a key signified a lack of trust or a wish to keep one's distance, the latter sentiment always being tinged with contempt. Its use could readily seem offensive within the zone of shared acquaintance since it was meant to ward off threats made by individuals who had come from outside, whether migrants, vagabonds, travelers, tinkers, or gentlemen of the road. In short, the key provided protection against "strangers"—known in Normandy as *horsains*—who could not be placed, and who did not belong to the zone of recognition.

Begging constituted one of the major problems of rural society, especially in the 1840s.[103] Vigilance was called for when beggars were "gathered together"; victuals and savings had to be *placed under lock and key*.

Nevertheless, rural society had a very relaxed attitude toward locking up. Hence the ease with which the "bande à Burgout," based in the chestnut woods of the Limousin, could commit its countless robberies at the dawn of the July Monarchy.[104] One cannot really understand the discussions surrounding the ballot box, shortly after the introduction of universal suffrage, unless one takes into account the offensive nature of mistrust arising from party spirit and electoral confrontation. To demand of the mayor that the ballot box be locked overnight between the two polls was to imply that one did not trust him. The importance of verbal agreements—especially in matters of credit and when "arrangements" were involved—was such that each had to respect public confidence. Without it, relations would break down in a world where individuals were perpetually in each other's debt.[105] When in 1884 the law entitled mayors *to have made*, without the parish priest's consent, a copy of the bell tower key, great offense was taken since, as far as some country people were concerned, this was tantamount to forgery.

To place an object under lock and key indicated that it was of great value, requiring precautions in addition to that of keeping a door shut so that it did not slam, or so it designated a space barred to animals or intruders. If the church door was *shut with a key*—and it might well be the only locked one in the whole commune—it was because of the need to guard consecrated objects and, in the strict sense of the term, to protect a treasure that was a marker of a community's identity. Such precautions were intended to prevent profanation rather than theft. Their other purpose was to block access to the bells and prevent the signal of authority from being seized.

As well as being a locked place , the church was also an edifice that was spontaneously and implicitly watched. It was one of the only sites to which, at certain times, it was impossible to gain access, and *where one ran the risk of being locked in*. In Sorbets (Landes) in 1883, several individuals—the account states that they were men—had come to make confession and were inadvertently locked in by the parish priest, who had gone to purchase two plots of land. They decided to ring the bells to summon someone to release them.[106]

As far as closing up the church was concerned, the legislation was very clear. Prior to the passing of the law of 5 April 1884, the parish priest, who had custody of the sanctuary, was the sole holder of the keys. Often he kept the bell tower key at the house of either his bell ringer or his sexton while also holding a copy in the presbytery. Where there was duplication[107] he entrusted the key to the church of his outlying parish to the president of the parochial church council. When the mayor wished to ring a secular peal he had to go to the presbytery; failing this, he had to delegate this task to the rural guard or the municipal bell ringer. Such arrangements were not without their difficulties, especially in case of fire. Often prior agreement could forestall conflict, with a key being kept at the mayor's house or on the premises where the pump was stored. Yet the parish priest was not bound by such agreements, which were a matter of local custom. Moreover, in some regions the mayor would find it humiliating to go to the presbytery and ask the parish priest for the key.[108]

Article 101 of the 1884 law overturned existing customs. Henceforth the mayor could, and should, have a key to the bell tower so he might be at liberty to ring the secular peals.[109] He therefore had to borrow the parish priest or priest in charge's key to have a copy made. If the latter refused to comply he could take a cast from the lock. If this procedure did not yield a workable key he was permitted by law to have a locksmith force the door and change all the locks.

This legislative measure proved truly traumatic for the clergy. When we consult the files devoted to its implementation in the departments[110] we find that the issue of the key constituted the main source of disagreement. Pope Leo XIII was opposed to Article 101. According to Monsignor Freppel, the bishop of Angers, the law entailed some risk of profanation; to him this secularization of the churches—for that was how he viewed it—seemed worse than a separation of church and state, were it ever to occur.[111] The archbishop of Avignon wrote on 26 June 1884: "We will endure everything, but never that." "We shall never suffer that someone other than the priest of the church should share with him the custody of the sanctuary, of the altar, and of the Eucharist. Therein lies our role and our exclusive mission, and we could not yield on this point, for that would be to betray the Church, and it would be suicide for us."[112] Three cardinals wrote to the president of the Republic requesting a stay of execution. The archbishop of Rouen, who persuaded the prefect of the Seine-Inférieure to permit a lenient interpretation of this article of the law in the concerted regulation concerning his diocese, drove the episcopate into open rebellion.[113] Some prelates held out for a long time, among them the bishops of Agen, Mende, and Châlons-sur-Marne. Others only yielded under duress. One of the most determined, the bishop of Tarbes, finally called upon his clergy to display a blend of meekness and resolution in accordance with the pope's instructions. Lend the mayor the key, he advised them, so he might make a copy "if there is a special door to the bell tower of your church"; "but if the same door leads to the church and to the bell tower, let the municipal magistrate obtain a key as best he can so that he alone may be responsible for an act that you cannot welcome but only submit to."[114]

We are now better placed to discern the contours of conflicts precipitated by keys. Ever since the nationalization of the church realized during the Revolution, they had broken out in one place or another. It was the mayors who, despite opposition from the clergy, were forever trying to obtain or keep a key to the bell tower so as to be able to ring the secular peals.[115] Between the Revolution and the passing of the 1884 law, the clergy, as it was building up its strength again, gradually recovered the copies of church and bell tower keys. This process tended to standardize customs throughout the national territory, yet it was not linear, as I shall now try to show.

At the beginning of the July Monarchy many mayors felt sufficiently confident to launch an offensive. For over a decade the general council for the Hautes-Pyrénées had asked each year that the duplicate key to the bell tower be kept in the town hall.[116] In 1833 Lézignan municipal council made this same demand in no uncertain terms.[117] During the same period in the Moselle, a good many mayors, without claiming guardianship, claimed the right to hold a key to the bell tower.[118] In this region they persisted with such demands, regardless of any shifts in the regime. They were still voicing such claims quite forcefully in 1835. The prefect sided with them and refused to grant the keys to the clergy alone. In 1840 the priest in charge of Mainvillers (Moselle), after having fought with the bell ringer when he refused to hand over the keys, had to have the door of the bell tower broken down to gain access to the ring.[119] In 1844 the mayor of Lengelsheim (Moselle) still held the keys to the church and entrusted them to the schoolmaster/cantor, who was of his party. The parish priest wrested them from this lay bell ringer. In the ensuing tussle the priest bit the bell ringer on the hand. The victim thereupon went to the mayor and councillors to show them "the marks of the priest in charge's teeth imprinted on his hand."[120] In April 1845 the mayor of Morfontaine (Meurthe-et-Moselle), an innkeeper, demanded that the keys remain in the possession of the schoolmaster, who had been the bell ringer until he was dismissed by the parish priest. According to the priest, the mayor, who now enjoyed free access to the church and indulged in any number of *peals of defiance*, could then steal the treasures of the parish.[121] In this same diocese of Metz there were many such disputes in 1847.

It sometimes happened in these disputes that mayors from other regions likewise received support from the prefectures. This was the case, for example, in the Seine-Inférieure in 1834, and Ille-et-Vilaine in 1835. According to the prefect of the first department, who was commenting on a dispute at Yvetot, taking back a key from mayors was tantamount to undermining municipal authority. Also in this region, some magistrates refused to yield.

Conversely, a deputy for the Moselle described *the tactics of humiliation* then deployed by priests against their adversaries. Once past the early years of the July Monarchy, the clergy counterattacked throughout the national territory. In regions where it was not the custom they gradually acquired sole use of the keys and, with the support of the minister and the prefecture, they recovered all those which had gone astray. This process reflects the general policy adopted during this period by the government, which entailed enforcing the norms laid down by the Concordat. Custom had decreed that one bell tower key from each parish in the Loiret be entrusted to the parish priest and another to the bell ringer, with a third being kept in the "town hall." During the July Monarchy, however, parish priests and priests in charge in this department managed to introduce a system whereby there was but one key, which the mayor had to seek out in the presbytery, the sacristy, or in the religious bell ringer's house.[122]

As would be the case later with the municipal magistrates, the clergy's victory sometimes led to the changing of locks. This is how it was in Courcelles (Oise) in 1845, and in Dampierre (Haute-Marne) two years later.[123] The prolonged humiliation suffered by the mayor of Metzeresche (Moselle) in 1847 reflected the new climate. After the archpriest had refused to hand over a bell tower key meant for the schoolmaster, the leading municipal magistrate "had a ladder placed" against the wall of the church. He succeeded in "getting a man in through an open window or skylight and [in] having removed the iron bar that kept one of the doors closed from the inside."[124] So proud he was of his victory that the mayor had a peal rung and draped a tricolor flag from the top of the bell tower. He had posted the rural guard at the door of the church so no one could enter and obstruct the operation. The municipal authorities seem to have enjoyed a complete triumph on that day. The bishop, however, laid the parish under an interdict and the subprefect forced the unfortunate mayor to hand the key back to the archpriest. Admittedly, the prefect had achieved an "arrangement," with the object under contention now being entrusted to the schoolmaster. Yet his difficulties were not at an end. The parish priest, far from honoring the terms of the agreement, left the key with the president of the parochial church council, forcing the mayor to fetch it from his house.

Such disputes occurred from time to time under the Second Empire and at the dawn of the Third Republic, but there were fewer of them. In 1861 the parish priest of Saint-Prest (Eure-et-Loir) refused to hand over a set of keys to the town council.[125] In 1869 the mayor of Colombey-les-deux-Églises (Haute-Marne) "had [the key to the bell tower] taken" from the presbytery and refused to return it.[126] A dispute of the same kind erupted in Giroussens (Tarn) in 1871.[127] Again in 1883, the parish priest of Cusey (Haute-Marne) changed the lock to the bell tower because the rewinder of the clock had refused to return the key he had used.[128]

From around 1884 to 1886,[129] with the sudden triumph of the municipal cause, disputes over keys took on a different shape. From then on the clergy was obliged by law to yield. Yet in many places, it bears repeating, they only surrendered under duress. Resistance was especially spirited when the same key gave access to both bell tower and church, and this was often the case in small rural parishes. By the same token, disputes

over keys tended to turn into quarrels over doors. During the first years
when the law was applied, one lost count of the number of forced locks
and portals battered down by mayors intent on exercising their rights
despite the opposition of the clergy. Conflicts of this kind are known to
have erupted in the Meuse, the Puy-de-Dôme, Finistère, and Tarn-et-
Garonne. Such disputes often took place at a relatively late date. In 1900
the mayor of Relanges (Vosges) had to drive back the parish priest by
grabbing his arm. The priest was trying to stop anyone from venturing
close to the lock of the bell tower door in order to take a cast.[130]

Such disputes were a matter of honor for the municipal councils
involved. In 1889 the municipality of Saint-Pierrevillers (Meuse) refused
to *pay* for the cutting of a key to the bell tower, which was supposed to
be kept in the town hall. The municipality considered this one of the
obligations of the parochial church council, which refused to meet this
expense. "The municipality has no intention of *being treated as if it were
of no importance*," the mayor declared, and it would not allow the parish
priest "to make the law." He refused to "bow and scrape" before his
adversary. The municipal council, faced with a choice between "yielding
or resigning,"[131] favored the second. The transposition of a vocabulary
drawn from national politics in this affair—although no more than one
or two francs were at stake—is worth noting. The prefect, as things
turned out, ruled in favor of the mayor.

Country priests were haunted on such occasions by the nightmare of
sacrilege. The mayor of Saint-Pierre-Quilbignon (Finistère) was well
aware of the fact, and feared that after he had broken the lock, the rector
of his parish would invent "imaginary profanations," "supernatural hap-
penings," or the "sudden disappearance of objects used in divine worship."[132]

I now want to consider disputes over doors. The issue was less
straightforward than it might at first seem. Sometimes it was a simple
question of access. The mayor merely wished that, in accordance with
the law, the lay bell ringer or the rewinder of the clock might have possession of a key, thereby enjoying free access to the bell tower. Some
parish priests would then try, *through threats* or *through force*, to ban the
"intruder" from the stairway to the tower. The priest in charge and the
lay bell ringer were then involved in exchanges of insults, scuffles, or

brawls—more simply termed "fights." Such incidents were commonplace in the Ariège.[133]

One solution that naturally occurred to magistrates was to cut a new,
separate door at the base of the bell tower that would give the lay bell
ringer direct access to the peal or the clock. This highly symbolic *separation of the two routes* was the solution adopted in 1885 by the municipality of Bergères-les-Vertus (Marne).[134] But it did not invariably dispel all
tensions; it sometimes happened that both of the bell ringers then considered themselves entitled to *unrestricted access*. In Velleron (Vaucluse)
there was a door enabling the rewinder to proceed directly from the public thoroughfare to the inside of the bell tower. In 1878, however, the religious bell ringer claimed the key to that door and, by the same token, the
right to take that route himself. His claim seemed sufficiently important
to come to the attention of the prefecture.[135]

It was more common, however, for conflicts to be provoked by the lay
bell ringer's wish to *enter by the main door* of the church. It was a question
of honor and recognition of the prestigious nature of his office. Again,
let me stress that it was not just access that was at stake in these affairs.
The lay bell ringer, deprived as often as not of the right to use the great
bell and ring peals, and overwhelmed by his rival on all festivals and
solemn occasions except the fourteenth of July, sometimes took offense
at having no key to the main door. Local government was faced with the
thorny problem of deciding who had the right to choose the door
through which access was gained to the church. It was precisely this
question that caused a dispute in the small commune of Biesles (Haute-
Marne).[136] Several different issues were at stake involving at once the
appointment of the bell ringer, the ringing of the secular peals, and the
choice of the door giving access to the church. The latter, however,
seems to have been the crux; it dictated the shape of this premonitory
conflict, which unfolded in the middle years of the Second Empire.

For ten years or so, the commune of Biesles was prepared to pay the
religious bell ringer 240 francs—a substantial sum that was well above
the going rate—under the condition that he assume responsibility for the
secular peals. In 1856, however, the reverend Thabourin urged the ringer
to request a raise. When the town council turned down his request, the
bell ringer decided, in August, to resign. He made this decision in the

absence of the priest, who was a personal friend. The public clock
stopped and peals were interrupted. At the end of two days the lack of
auditory markers led to "popular unrest." The mayor called upon the old
bell ringer to take the place of the one who had resigned "for the sake of
the commune." The parish priest, however, on returning from his journey, refused to accept this appointment. He made it clear to the intruder
that he had better cease what he was doing immediately. Then he showed
him to the door of the church (19 September). The conflict thereupon
assumed the classic form of a dispute over the choice of bell ringer.

The prefect resolved to settle the matter there and then, reminding the
mayor that it was not for him to rule on such questions. He did, however, acknowledge the mayor's right to appoint the rewinder of the clock,
who had been stationed in the bell tower "since time immemorial." He
also accepted the mayor's right to demand that this assistant be granted
free access to the bell tower. This is what crystallized the conflict. As luck
would have it, an independent door led directly to the tower. The parish
priest, however, refused to let the rewinder of the clock take this route,
and insisted that he go by way of the church. In order to ensure compliance with this injunction, he had a new lock fitted to the door under dispute.[137] The parish priest further wished that the rewinder proceed *by a
side door* and not the main door. The mayor could not tolerate the person
responsible for the municipal instrument entering the church other than
by the main door. He therefore ordered the clock to be stopped. This decision "greatly upset the local population, which consisted in large part of
working men who relied on the sound [of this instrument] for their work
at night." On 10 November a "sizable delegation consisting of the most
respectable inhabitants" went to the town hall and called for "the regular
working of the clock"[138] to be restored. On 13 November the mayor, his
deputy, and the members of the municipal council, who had no intention
of giving in but who feared popular unrest, decided to offer their resignation to the prefecture.

The parish priest was prepared to argue. To begin with, the mayor
had not himself asked for anything.[139] Furthermore, it was the parish
priest's practice never to open the main door except for solemn festivals. For everyday occasions the schoolmaster, the religious bell ringer,
the congregation, and the priest himself entered by the side doors. In

his opinion, the rewinder of the clock might reasonably be expected to do likewise.

Mindful of the gravity of an affair "that threatened to take on very serious proportions," the prefect decided to pay a visit in person to judge what sort of access to the church existed. The parish priest refused to welcome him, then greeted him in an insolent fashion, and finally, would only agree to hand over the key to the outside door after the prefect had signed a receipt. On 22 November the bishop of Langres came to his priest's defense but did not seek to excuse his rudeness. In the prelate's opinion, it was not for the mayor but for the priest to decide "which door should be opened and which kept shut."[140]

On 11 December the parish priest was still withholding the key to the tower door and denying access by the main door of the church. "In order to pacify a considerable number of parishioners, who had been in an agitated state the whole morning,"[141] the rewinder of the clock decided that same day to give in and enter the church by the side door, as his adversary had proposed. The mayor deplored the rewinder's decision and asked the prefect's permission to have a key made so that either the main door or the door to the bell tower might be opened, by force if need be.

On 18 December the prefect was sufficiently worried to write to the *ministre des Cultes*, observing that the Biesles affair was "at bottom fairly serious," and that "passions had been inflamed to the highest degree." The prefect found in favor of the mayor, who simply wished for "the most convenient" access. He requested further orders from Paris since in his opinion a prompt "ministerial solution" was needed.

In the Spring of 1857 the situation deteriorated. On 1 May the parish priest, out of defiance, instructed his bell ringer to stop the secular peals or rather—in order to exert a subtler influence on public opinion—to only ring the "middays" every two or three days. Now deprived of both clock and peals, the population no longer had any temporal markers. This is when the parish priest decided to interrupt the ringing of the Sunday services.

On 13 March two individuals let themselves into the bell tower and rang the "midday." On 16 March the whole commune was in an uproar. According to the justice of the peace from Nogent-le-Roi, who had come with the cantonal commissioner and a brigade of the gendarmerie, the

situation had become extremely serious. At midday the three bells were
rung in peal. The mayor and the brigadier, who had gone to the church
with the intention of suppressing this illicit action, encountered "a sizable
gathering which had [assumed] the character of a riot, and consisted of
men, women, and children in the environs of the church and in the cemetery. It [was] made up of at least five or six hundred persons."[142] Inside
the building there was in addition a gathering "of at least one hundred
and fifty persons" who had come to back the impromptu bell ringers. The
crowd announced its intention of returning to ring the evening Angelus,
by force if need be. The gendarmes dispersed the two gatherings while
the mayor read out, to the sound of the drum, a ban on forcible ringing.

The situation was still not resolved. On 22 June twelve citizens of
Biesles complained once again to the prefect: "Our bells are no longer
rung, *and this also causes an immorality to reign* in the locality when it is
time for workers to take their midday meal." In addition, they said, the
commune was deprived on the eve of Sundays and festivals of "the kind
of carillon that *used to give the working man some hope of recreation* for the
next day."[143]

It was not until 19 December 1857, a full year and a half after the start
of the affair, that the *ministre des Cultes*, in consultation with the minister
of the interior, resolved to impose a settlement. In his view the parish
priest was not overstepping his powers in choosing the door through
which "the agent responsible for operating the clock" was to pass. There
was no longer any dispute and the mayor was obliged to yield.

Access to the bell tower was no guarantee that a bell ringer could
carry out his duties. In most communes "bell ringing was not done in the
bell tower but in the church itself, by means of ropes."[144] These ropes
were a familiar sight to workers in the countryside, and were mostly
made on the spot out of hemp produced in the region. This was also true
of the ropes that worked the peal. Inside the bell tower such ropes had to
be looked after and watched over to prevent risk of inopportune ringing,
be it for alarm, honor, or derision. In a society in which hanging was the
preferred means of suicide for men, the fact that the bell tower contained
so many ropes and had a magical quality sometimes ascribed to it, gave
an atmosphere of unease to this mysterious and somber site. As a precaution some bell ringers shut the ropes up in a chest after they had been

used; others preferred to hitch them up so that they could not be used by disrespectful youth.

Hiding, hitching up or, conversely, bringing the ropes down were all tactics that might, depending on the circumstances, be used to thwart an adversary. In 1847 the parish priest of Dampierre (Haute-Marne) wished to keep the lay bell ringer out of both the bell tower and the church. He thus decided to lengthen the ropes and pierce through the vault of the porch to the church to allow them to hang there. In pursuing this plan he had ordered the parish to seek out as much hemp as it could find. The mayor rightly pointed out to him that the ropes would henceforth be within reach of the first urchin who happened to pass that way, and who might amuse himself by ringing the tocsin.[145]

The more usual procedure was to hitch up the ropes so that they were out of reach. This proved particularly effective when one's adversary had no key to the bell tower. I have already remarked on the sad fate of the mayor of Parnes, who injured himself trying to catch the end of the ropes looped up in precisely this fashion by the parish priest. There was another way of attaining this same end that involved removing the clapper from the inside of the bell or bells.[146] It would be tedious to cite too many instances of this practice, although we have encountered several in earlier chapters. More radical still was the decision by one of the bell ringers to opt for sabotage or, to be more precise, the deliberate damaging of bells.

CHAPTER EIGHT

The Principal "Clashes"

Burials Conducted in Silence

Tensions in a village crystallized around two categories of peals. First, throughout the nineteenth century there were disputes about who should have the power to decide when bells were to be rung and when they were to remain silent during rites of passage. At stake, in other words, was control of *auditory certification*. Second, the ringing of festivals of sovereignty and various national celebrations precipitated many of the campanarian conflicts that divided rural communities during this period. These disputes were situated at a different level, since they signified integration into the nation. On such occasions bell ringing played a part in the major political debates that reached beyond the local area.

The meaning of conflicts over peals for the dying, for death itself, and for burial evolved during the nineteenth century. This gradual evolution, however, was masked by the quasi-permanent shape of such disputes. On the one hand, the clergy would refuse to ring while the municipal authorities would do their utmost to breach the silence imposed on both family and community.

Up until the triumph of the Third Republic the ecclesiastical authorities' refusal to ring had formed part of a long-established tradition justified by canon law. The silence of bells was deemed an apt accompaniment to the denial of any religious ceremony or sacralizing of death. The point was further reinforced by the closing of the sanctuary. Taken together, these measures constituted a formidable weapon in the hands of the clergy.

Some parish priests refused to ring at the death of children who had not been baptized, or who had not been within the three days permitted by canon law.[1] The clergy denied the bells to suicides as well as to mortal sinners who had shown no signs of repentance or received the last sacrament. A good many parish priests or priests in charge used the silence of bells to pass judgment on the lives of parishioners whom they judged to have been dissolute, especially when they had lived in concubinage. Here we turn one of the final pages in the great history of marks of infamy and signs of exclusion in rural society—which has never been unduly respectful of the independence of private life. From this point of view I cannot stress too strongly how deafening this silence of bells for the dead must have seemed.

"The laws of the Church," the archbishop of Amiens explained in 1833, forbid *admittance to the church* and *the sound of bells* "to persons who have died refusing until the very last moment to *disavow a public scandal* against morality and justice, or who made an overt and stubborn profession of impious principles."[2] Depending on the circumstances, such penalties affected more or less large circles of individuals. At the dawn of the nineteenth century some parish priests withheld the bells from those who had rallied during the Revolution to "bad priests." During the early years of the July Monarchy priests in charge in some places banned the ringing of bells for the deaths of republicans, officers in the national guard or, more broadly, individuals guilty of having resisted or obstructed them. In 1831 the parish priest of Dingé (Ille-et-Vilaine), much to the outrage of the mayor, came out against using the bells to

announce the funeral of a municipal magistrate. The following year the
parish priest of Villeréal (Lot-et-Garonne) refused to ring the demise of
a lieutenant in the national guard of the commune. He did the same to a
plain sergeant from the same outfit who, until he breathed "his last sigh,"
had never stopped repeating "that he wished to die a true republican."[3]
Some pastors penalized parishioners in this way if they had failed to participate in the purchase or recasting of the peal. Needless to say, the
silence of the bells was also used against "miscreants." Even if we restrict
discussion to the eastern part of the country, this refusal caused conflicts
in Phalsbourg (Moselle) in 1833, in Giromagny (then in the Haut-Rhin)
in 1837, and in Weyersheim (Bas-Rhin) in 1847.[4]

One should nevertheless take care not to exaggerate. Parish priests and
priests in charge often preferred to look the other way to defuse potential
disputes. In the Orne, under the July Monarchy, custom dictated that a
parish priest refusing to attend the burial ceremony of individuals who
had died without receiving the last sacrament would nevertheless let them
be "rung."[5]

On 1 July 1837, the Chamber of Deputies considered a petition presented by Master Pichon. The latter "asks that he may be allowed to ring
the bells despite the opposition of the parish priests, in order to *announce*
deaths when the families of the deceased ask it, and that for this purpose,
the keys of the church might be kept in the town hall."[6] The chairman,
Chasles, deputy mayor of Chartres, was hostile toward the petition: "we
do not see why the bells should be made available *to suit the convenience of
individuals*, and why, for example, the families of the deceased should
have the right to celebrate the obsequies of their relatives with one of *the
elements of the religious ceremony*, when the ceremony itself has not been
held."[7] The second argument, which would come to be repeated time and
again,[8] seems powerful enough. I shall concentrate, however, on the first,
which implies a refusal to incorporate the sound of the bell into the private sphere, and a concern to keep it in the public domain.

It is clear why Master Pichon made his request. From the early years of
the July Monarchy the problem concerning the ringing of secular burials
had become pressing. In October 1830 a mayor from the Loiret, with the
backing of the prefect and the royal procurator, rejected a request made
by Master Gauthier that his son's death be rung, although the son had

been intent on being buried "in one of his properties," "without any religious ceremony, without any ecclesiastical presence,"[9] and without his body being presented at the church. In 1834 the parish priest of Viviers-le-Gras (Vosges) complained about the mayor of the commune ringing "for" a dead person whom he had refused religious burial and who in fact wished to be buried in his own garden. This had been an additional challenge as far as the priest was concerned; the mayor, who had rung in the morning, repeated the offense in the evening—after the priest had complained from the pulpit about the attitude of his adversary. The mayor left the prefect in no doubt as to the *offense* that had been given "to the dead man and his family."[10]

"To be rung" or to be buried "to the sound of a bell" was a matter of honor,[11] both for the individual and for the kin. On 13 April 1837, the mayor of Belval (Vosges) wrote to the "schoolmaster" of Saint-Jean-d'Ormont, then bell ringer at the parish church: "Master Joseph Fister entreats me to ask you to have the bells rung to *make known the death* of his father, David Fister, and in my opinion I believe that, since the dead man paid for the bells, he has the same right as the rest of us. . . . Please be assured, Sire, of my most cordial greetings. I remain yours sincerely, J.B. Pierron." Further down the page we may read: "the mayor of the commune of Le Mont undersigned hereby declares that he willingly gives his consent to David Fister *being rung*. J.B. Charpentier." As it happened, three communes (Belval, Le Saulcy, and Le Mont) were dependent parishes of Saint-Jean-d'Ormont, and all three mayors were agreed that despite the parish priest's refusal to comply, "the body should receive the honors of burial with the sound of the bell."[12] David Fister had a right *to the use of* the instrument for which he had helped pay. The priest's decision, which had been approved by the *ministre des Cultes*, "quite bewildered the assembled congregations *of the dependent communes* who accompanied . . . the mortal remains of the deceased, who was generally mourned by his fellows." This bewilderment reflected the clash of two logics. The priest's stance was at odds with that of the congregation, who saw it as a matter of honoring a moral contract. In their view such refusals jeopardized the equality of parishioners. Being deprived of bells was, moreover, a painful experience for members of communities that had been demoted to the status of dependent parishes and were therefore obliged to accept the decisions of the priest of the parish church situated in another commune.[13]

The dispute in Belval may be taken as typical in that conflicts arising from a refusal to ring for the dead almost always followed much the same scenario. Being informed of the parish priest's refusal, the family would lay the matter before the municipality. Sometimes the mayor or his deputy would then decide to ring or have the bells rung by force. This is what happened in Villeréal during the dispute I just described. In December 1832, "not content with seizing by force the keys to the bell tower to have the bells rung in mourning despite my express ban on this," the parish priest declared, "the mayor permitted a horde of bandits to present me in the evening with a charivari, which ended with the most reprehensible act, that of smearing my door with every sort of filth."[14] In 1835, upon the death of the sergeant of the national guard, "the mayor again seized control of the bell tower and, despite my ban, did as he pleased with the bells." In 1840 the death of a man who had just lost his eighteen-year-old son the day before led to an outpouring of grief in the parish of Récanoz-Lombard (Jura). Despite the parish priest's ban, the deputy mayor rang three strokes of the bell. He was rebuked , but the family had the mayor intervene, together with several of its members, who were local notables. The latter complained bitterly about the affront to the dead man and his relatives.[15] In 1838, despite a ban by the priest in charge of Fays (Haute-Marne) on "ringing the bells for a man who died falling from a tree, and who was living in concubinage,"[16] the mayor ordered that the family's wishes be respected.

Faced with the parish priest of Giromagny's refusal to ring at the death of a twenty-eight-year-old Protestant, the mayor gave free rein to the men of his own party. "On Sunday morning," the priest reported, "around seven o'clock, five individuals, among them the butcher . . . *grabbed the bells* immediately after the Angelus despite the protestations of the sexton, and rang until a quarter to eight. Consequently, it was impossible to ring for the first Mass, which should be said around half past seven. . . . As the dead woman's cortege was setting out . . . they forced the door of the church tower, grabbed the bells, and rang for as long as they pleased."[17]

Sometimes the point at issue was the duration of the peal rather than a decision to withhold the bells. "In Marcilly (Haute-Marne) they claim," the priest in charge observed in February 1848, "that ringing for the dead is the municipal council's responsibility. . . . They hold that when a person is lying on their bier, one rings five times a day for half an hour at a stretch without having the courtesy to allow me to announce the times of services on Sundays. At every death you would think it was All Souls' Day, and the holy place is turned into a kind of stable."[18] The priest avenged himself by ruling that in future "sunset" would only be rung with a single bell whereas "since time immemorial" it had been rung by two. "[The] *entire commune*, young and old," wrote the mayor, "felt *a sort of indignation at being deprived of a bell* that used to be rung every evening at Angelus."[19]

After the triumph of the Third Republic, as anticlerical policies were at first intimated and then elaborated, incidents of this type—in which local communities opposed clerical censorship that in their view overstepped the mark—gave way to disputes over the refusal to grant secular burials. Consequently, the fact of being denied bells took on new meanings. First, it had far less to do with the community than in the past. When the family or friends of the deceased demanded a peal, it was now rare for them to seek to sacralize the death with a religious ceremony. The clergy's stance was now part of a wider struggle that entailed a broader defensive strategy. The concern was now not so much to inflict a punishment as to avert a desacralizing of bells.

By the same token, ringing for the dead became a theoretical problem. The arguments advanced by atheists were situated at two different levels. First, they embodied a wish to distinguish between the death of a man and an animal. "We are not dogs," Fonsegrive has someone remark to the freethinker hero of his book who, nevertheless, still wishes for a mortuary peal.[20] This preoccupation bears comparison with the wish of dechristianized populations to have their children christened to place them once and for all outside of animality and beyond the reach of the devil.[21] This desire for a modicum of sacralizing proved that anticlericals, or rather atheists, were susceptible to the clergy's argument that secular burial was little better than the sort of depositing in the ground to which animals were subjected.

For a great many agnostics or freethinkers the debate was at another level. As far as they were concerned, the death peal was an integral part of

the death itself. It was regarded as a right deriving from the simple prin-
ciple of "municipal equality." A motion to this effect was passed at the
Congress of the National Association of Freethinkers of France in
November 1908. The ban on ringing for baptisms, marriages, and secular
burials "turns freethinkers into *veritable pariahs*."[22] Two months later
Francis de Pressensé, deputy for the Rhône and president of the French
League for the Defense of the Rights of Man and the Citizen, informed
the minister of the interior of the express wish of this section of Saint-
Pierre-de-Chandieu (Rhône) that equality *"of honors as regards the ringing of the bells"* be granted.[23] That same year, 1909, *La Lanterne* noted
with approval the rulings adopted by the municipality of Rivesaltes and
conducted a campaign in support of them. This newspaper added an
argument that seemed to link up with the past, to the effect that equal
respect was due one and all—freethinkers or otherwise—at their death.
"We ring for the deceased if they are Catholic but not if they are unbe-
lievers. The result is that the deaths of the latter seem not to have, as those
of the former do, *the quality of a general mourning*." Only in the case of
Catholics is "the community of inhabitants notified."[24] The attitude of
Rivesaltes council, which sought to incorporate the municipal peal into a
new secular ritual of death, seems exemplary yet, let me repeat, it was
condemned by the ministry as being contrary to the law of 15 November
1887. The law stipulated that the municipalities should remain neutral.
The introduction of a municipal peal for burials implied a lack of any
"distinction based upon the beliefs of the deceased."[25] The mayor of
Rivesaltes planned, however, to reserve the municipal bell for secular
burials.

The clergy's arguments were based on the need to sacralize death. The
bell was an object that had been blessed, and the clerical press waxed ironical about freethinkers who wanted their demise to be rung. On 6
December 1907, *Le Journal de Chartres* poked fun at atheist mayors
demanding funeral peals. The author of the article in question wondered
whether they might not next be calling for the aspergillum and holy water
to give "lay and secular absolution."[26] Catholics invoked the history of
bells and recalled that the parish priest was the sole regulator of religious
peals. A reading of the regulations signed after the 1884 law revealed that
marriages and secular burials did not appear on the list of peals for which

the mayor was responsible.[27] Regardless of the wishes of freethinkers, the legislation was not modified.

The clergy anyway had an apt riposte at their disposal—they could lay the parish under interdict and cancel all religious peals. In July 1884 the bishop of Annecy imposed precisely this punishment on the commune of Ville-en-Sallaz (Haute-Savoie), where the mayor had had the bells rung for the funeral of a suicide. Two years later the same prelate laid the parish of Bonne under interdict[28] because a secular burial had been rung there.

When we read the documents in the archives, conflicts of this kind strike us as both innumerable and monotonous. Nevertheless, the problems intrinsic to the process of preservation of primary sources mean that they do not by themselves give us a balanced picture. The status of disputes over bells changed at the end of the nineteenth century. They ceased to be a strictly local matter and became closely linked to the great debates over national policy. Administrators no longer displayed the ironical condescension with which they had once regarded these manifestations of trifling passions. For the first time some organs of the national press devoted a column to "disputes over bells." By the same token, historians were liable to treat as a sudden ascent what was in fact merely an increase in visibility.

Be this as it may, the mass of documentation accumulated on a national scale defies any attempt at summary.[29] Such incidents were frequent during the last two decades of the century, and became still more commonplace subsequently, especially between 1908 and 1911. This is borne out by the Eure-et-Loir, which I shall use as an example here. On 28 June 1891, the mayor of Nogent-sur-Eure had the rural guard ring a secular burial. On 6 August 1891, his colleague in Saint-Arnoult did the same.[30] In the early years of the twentieth century a harsher note was sounded. In 1908 the mayor of Châtillon declared that regardless of the ban imposed by the prefecture, he would continue to ring secular marriages and burials.[31] The mayor of Marboué, who was according to the subprefect of Châteaudun, "avowedly republican," adopted the same stance. According to him, the majority of his commune's population was either indifferent or anticlerical. All year round they had to tolerate the sound of unauthorized bells imposed upon them by the clergy. This made them wish all the more deeply that the passing bell might be tolled at every death. Such, anyway, had been the local custom. Besides, the commune was very big, so that if the bell remained silent, the majority of those living in Marboué would not be aware that a fellow citizen had died. In the Eure-et-Loir, the desire to ring at secular burials did not stem from a handful of freethinkers but, if we follow the mayor's account, rather it reflected the deepest convictions of the village communities.[32]

In order to preempt any resort to force by the municipality, the parish priest of Marboué removed the clapper from the great bell. That proved no obstacle, however. The mayor simply rang the secular burials with the small bell and then, growing weary of the fight, had the lock of the bell tower changed (12 May 1907). The parish priest prepared his response and carried the day. "As I can no longer get to the bells," he wrote, "I am trying to remain master of the ropes. Consequently, I am shutting and firmly barricading the doors."[33] The mayor was therefore not able to use the bells on 16 July to announce a secular burial. The magistrate's reply was not long in coming. On 21 July he ruled by decree that the door of the "communal" church should remain open from six in the morning to six in the evening in summer, and from seven to four in winter. By virtue of this decree the municipality (on 9 August) smashed the locks, latches, and bolts, thinking this would prevent the priest from shutting up the church. On 9 September, however, the parish priest had a new lock fitted, at his own expense, to the door of the sanctuary. On 13 September the municipality tore out this new system of locks. On 2 December the parish priest, proud of his own wiles, described his latest tactic: "I simply barricade the door with a few pews and an iron bar."[34] His triumph was short-lived, however, for the rural guard with the help of a workman, acting upon the municipality's orders, forced open the door.

In some cases the mayor was not content merely to have the bells rung. Remaining loyal to tradition even though secular burials were involved, he would enter the church with the funeral procession after having picked the lock.[35] Sometimes he would have the prayer for the dead recited.[36] Needless to say, parish priests and priests in charge viewed all such actions as profanations.

The parish clergy, however, extended the list of reasons for withholding the bells. In the Meuse, for example, they now refused to ring at the death of individuals who had omitted to pay the church offering—what the mayor of Bulainville called "the worship tax."[37] On 22 June 1909, the parish priest of Came (Basses-Pyrénées) denied a municipal councillor from that commune both the passing bell and a religious burial for that reason. On the day of the funeral, a cortège preceded by the mayor in his sash, the rural guard, and the schoolmaster, bore the coffin to the church. Those present recited the prayers, intoned the customary funeral chants, and rang the bell. The court of Bayonne found the mayor and the rural guard, although not the schoolmaster, guilty of exceeding their authority.[38]

Between 1908 and 1911 such disputes over bells proceeded in parallel with quarrels over the ringing of the Angelus, as I have already described. The discussion turned on the validity or otherwise of the municipal decrees defining both the duration of religious peals and the list of authorized secular peals. By virtue of these decrees, which were contested by the clergy, parish priests and priests in charge were in the wrong when they rang for too long or refused the bells for secular burials and marriages. Mayors had the rural guards or the gendarmes keep a record of such infractions; they would then take their adversaries to court. The members of the clergy tried to have the municipal regulations annulled.

Confusion ensued, which was further heightened by the press on either side. I shall try to summarize the vicissitudes of this struggle, which remained unresolved for a long time. The mayor often but not always prevailed when he took the parish priest to the departmental court for infringing municipal regulations governing bell ringing. The press commented on the court decisions in Angoulême, Narbonne, Neufchâteau, Châtillon, and Épinal in particular.[39] The clergy also lost in the supreme court of appeal. On 21 December 1907, this review body ruled that in the absence of associations for the purposes of worship laid down by the law, no one could lodge a complaint against such municipal decrees. Arguing on the basis of local custom,[40] the court further recognized the mayor's right to include secular marriages and burials on the list of peals for which he was responsible.

Conversely, members of the clergy prevailed in the Council of State. On 5 August 1908, the Council annulled Article 3 of a decree issued by the mayor of Vendeuvre-sur-Barse (Aube) stipulating that the bells should be rung three times[41] at secular burials, and that peals should be rung during ceremonies for secular marriages, which were held at the town hall. The Council of State ruled that the mayor, "when regulating the use of bells, is obliged to reconcile the need for order and keeping the peace with respect for freedom of worship."[42] It therefore refused to recognize the right to ring secular marriages and burials. The long sequence of annulments decided on by the Council of State seem gradually to have discouraged anticlerical magistrates. After 1911 this battle, on a national level at any rate, appears to have lost its intensity.

National Bells

The disputes I have described once again involve an articulation of the local with the national. There is another peal, however, that expresses still more clearly this widening of the horizon, namely, the one for celebrating festivals of sovereignty. Some parish priests sought to be the sole regulators of how bells were to be used; they assumed they could give their consent or express their opposition as they saw fit to the peals claimed by the mayor. All the concerted regulations drawn up by the prefects and the bishops, however, stipulated that festivals of sovereignty, described as national festivals from 1830 on, should be celebrated.[43] A parish priest who refused to let the bells be rung on such occasions was thus in breach of the principles established by the Concordat.

Bells were perhaps never rung so much during festivals of this type as under the Restoration. Each year on 21 January all the churches in the kingdom rang "the ends of the year" to commemorate and expiate regicide.* In Montauban, for example, all the bells "of the town and the suburbs" were set ringing on the evening of 20 January 1830. The funereal bell ringing was taken up again the following day "for hour after hour," from daybreak until noon.[44] The fête du roi, the Saint-Louis on 25 August, and the Saint-Charles on 4 November were rung equally regularly.[45] When there was conflict it did not mean that there was any opposition from the clergy, but merely that the authorities were vying for the honor of using the bells. This was the case in Dol-de-Bretagne on 25 and 26 August 1821, and in Montréal (in the Gers) on 20 January 1829.[46] The two bell

---

*the date upon which Louis XVI was executed in 1793.

ringers—the mayor's and the parish priest's—quarreled over the bells on that day, which was the eve "of the Martyr King's birthday."

Under the Bourbons, the extent and duration of the peals on festivals of sovereignty were not in dispute. In this sphere at least, the Restoration was characterized by heightened attention toward the patrimony of communities, and it was an epoch during which symbols were reclaimed, treasuries reconstituted, and emblems reassembled. There was also an intense engagement with collective memory, which found expression, as we have seen, in bitter intercommunal struggles, sometimes incorporated into cycles of claims and counterclaims rooted in the past. Campanarian history during this period was essentially concerned with the identity of rural communities, which were often indifferent or even hostile toward the patrimony of nobles and congregations. At the village level the Restoration was therefore characterized by a tension between a wish to preserve and the vandalism of the *bandes noires*.*

Campanarian history under the July Monarchy was, however, radically different.[47] During this period conflicts gradually assumed a shape dictated by the existence of national peals. This configuration would prevail up until the First World War. The positions of the antagonists may be characterized as follows. Many municipalities saw in the festival of sovereignty an opportunity to vaunt regained liberties, to celebrate the Charter and the national king, to flaunt the tricolor flag, and thereby to proclaim the primacy of secular authorities over ecclesiastical power. This accounts for the readiness of a good many mayors to multiply the number of festive occasions. The first two years of Louis-Philippe's reign marked the heyday of political banquets in villages.[48] At no other point in the nineteenth century had the national guards displayed themselves so proudly in the countryside. These years also witnessed a symbolic marking of the communal territory that involved not so much the building of monuments—rural town halls were to come later—but rather the proliferation of emblems. In rural areas the new regime was greeted with a plethora of busts of the king, liberty trees, bell tower cocks, and tricolor flags.[49] From 1831 on the ceremonial aspect of the elec-

---

*bandes noires: deals struck by individuals to win bids at the public sale of properties.

toral process, as we have seen, further enhanced the rise and increased
ostentation of the municipal. The campanarian sphere was likewise
marked by these changes. The "promenades with the flag" and the
"impromptu festivals" characteristic of this short but crucial moment in
the history of public opinion in France were accompanied by secular and
political peals, which the prefect of Ille-et-Vilaine judged retrospectively
to have been incessant and unauthorized.[50]

The high point of this ebullient phase was marked by the national festivals. There were three in all,[51] namely, the funeral festivals of 27–29
July, the *fête du roi* on the first of May, and the anniversary of the swear-
ing of the Charter on 9 August, which was soon dropped.

Given their bitter memories of the revolutionary period, their sense of
living through a recrudescence of the spirit that had originally characterized it, their distress at the absence of church representatives at the ceremony staged on 9 August, and finally, their avowed loyalty to the
Bourbons—which led them to brand the king of the French a monstrous
usurper—many country priests were left feeling hostile.[52] The intensity
of the anticlerical demonstrations staged at regular intervals during the
first year of Louis-Philippe's reign, the increasingly heated nature of
political discussion at village level, the proliferation of challenges issued
by the municipalities, the involvement of youth in festive demonstrations
treated as excuses for excess, the inordinate use of secular peals and the
demands made by magistrates for the keys to bell towers disturbed a good
many priests in charge and strengthened their will to resist.[53]

Generally speaking, the July Monarchy, at least at the level of the
locality, was characterized by frequent conflicts over the respective
spheres of competence of secular and religious authorities. There was
massive reliance on a taxonomy of local custom that allowed the administration to pose as the spokesman of the village community. In this milieu
reference to locality toppled over, and so, therefore, did the elements constituting local identity. The latter had once been based on an evocation of
symbolic objects; now it rested on the immemorial character of customs.
The system of evaluation developed by scholarly elites within the
Académie Celtique[54] now assumed a popular form, took   hold of and
penetrated local antiquarian societies—which were wide-ranging in their
interests—and, crucially, municipal councils in rural areas, which suc-

cessfully used the recording of customs as a sort of weapon. This was especially evident in the campanarian sphere.

The disputes caused by national peals were legion. On 8 March 1831, for example, the captain of the guard in Meyras (Ardèche) convened a picket to attend the raising of a new flag on the bell tower of the church. The previous one had apparently been removed "out of spite." The justice of the peace for the canton, the mayor, and the deputy mayor of the commune presided over the secular ceremony. "Some young people," we read in the report from the gendarmerie, "rang the bell in peal as a sign of rejoicing." The priest in charge, "upon hearing the bell, climbed the bell tower and tried to stop it ringing." The mayor, "being informed of this opposition," sent several national guardsmen "with orders to continue regardless of any resistance on the part of His Reverence the priest, who was showing such determination to prevent the orders of His Honor the mayor from being carried out that one of the guardsmen was obliged to brandish a bayonet against them. The priest, once he had come down again, dressed in his priestly vestments and approached the mayor, with whom he had had an altercation, saying that his office as mayor did not give him the right to have the bells rung nor to place a flag on the bell tower without authorization."[55] In the evening a charivari was staged to punish the priest in charge. "A group of armed persons having formed up before the door to the presbytery, a few rifle shots were fired. . . . "

From among the many incidents that occurred I shall comment briefly on those in the Calvados. "In a large number of communes in the department," the prefect wrote on 16 August 1832, "in order to vest the July festivals with more solemnity, the mayors had the bells rung; in the towns, this caused no difficulties. Such was not the case, however, in the rural communes. Some parish priests and some priests in charge were formally opposed to it."[56] This kind of dispute, he further observed, was new to the Calvados. In 1832 there was unrest in Aulnay[57] during the July festivals. On the twenty-sixth of that month "the mayor ordered the *custos* to *ring in the morning* on the twenty-seventh *from six in the morning until the 'retreat,'* "[58] meaning *for fifteen hours in a row*. By paying tribute in this fashion to the victims of Paris he meant to glorify "our immortal revolution" and "the triumph of liberty."[59] The parish priest was opposed to the

plan. On the morning of 27 July, however, the mayor had the door of the
tower forced open by two locksmiths. His men rang the whole day long,
"with a discordant sound, sometimes in mourning and sometimes by
striking the bells in such a way that they were, according to the parish
priest, chipped in several places."[60] The municipal council felt this
mourning peal to be very harmonious; "if the sound seemed discordant
to some ears," we read in the minutes book, "it was because they belonged
to Legitimists."

The same document stated that the rural guard had spent the whole day
at the bell ringers' side, observing their conduct to ensure that they were
on their best behavior. The following day the mayor again had the bells
rung at four o'clock in the morning; on this occasion the three bells were
rung "in peals," a circumstance that, according to the parish priest, greatly
distressed "all the people in the *bourg*."[61] He emphasized, as far as thresholds of tolerance were concerned, a division that, even as late as 1958, was
the root cause of the incidents in Lonlay-l'Abbaye. At dawn on 29 July,
the municipal bell ringers resumed activity. The mayor, in a conciliatory
mood, nevertheless asked them to stop at six o'clock in the morning. He
instructed them to carillon again uninterruptedly from six o'clock "in the
afternoon" "until nine o'clock in the evening," while he had a tricolor flag
draped over the top of the bell tower. Throughout these days the mayor
took care that the announcement of religious services was not interrupted; secular peals and religious peals might thus succeed one another
for three whole days. If on 29 July it had proved impossible to ring the
Angelus—thereby causing a serious incident—this was quite simply
because, according to the municipal councillors, a rope had become
detached.

In truth, the parish priest and the mayor of this commune had long
been at odds. To judge by the minute book it was the priest who had commenced hostilities by "removing from the church the pew of honor,
which from time immemorial had been reserved for members of the
council."[62] It would nevertheless be a reasonable estimate that the bells of
Aulnay had carilloned for around *thirty-six hours between the morning of
27 July and the evening of 29 July.*

In the Loir-et-Cher campanarian episodes were likewise commonplace
during the first years of the regime. According to the bishop of Blois, the

mayor of Nourray had taken to "having a flag put in the gallery of the church on particular days as stipulated by himself, and having it removed subsequently and reintroduced on some other occasion . . . and each time this flag was introduced and taken away the mayor never failed to have the bells rung and carillonned, having at hand some young people willing to carry out his orders."[63] The subprefect of Vendôme emphasized that "this *highly serious* issue is one that has very often to be faced."[64]

The bishop of Châlons-sur-Marne objected to these funeral peals for the July festivals while the bishop of Périgueux protested against those rung on 1 May 1833.[65] In the Dordogne some "clashes" occurred on this same occasion involving mayors and parish priests. The municipal authorities insisted that without the use of bells it was impossible to "enable [the inhabitants] to take part in the public celebrations" and to "impart a greater degree of solemnity to these extraordinary days."

On 5 June 1833, the count of Argout, *ministre de l'Intérieur et des Cultes*, attempted to defuse the situation. He laid down a number of unambiguous principles. The clergy, he ruled, had no right to refuse to ring for the *fête du roi* since they had been prepared to do so "during previous reigns." The mayors should abide by what was current practice at the time. They should refrain "from tiring out an entire commune to take revenge on the ill will of the parish priest by ringing a prolonged peal, as had happened in many places." Conversely, the minister could not "accept that it was right and proper to lay claim to bell ringing to celebrate the anniversary of the *journées* of July 1830," since it was a question "as things now stood" of a "strictly secular festival in which the clergy is not called upon to play any part whatsoever."[66] Beginning in 1833, therefore, it was only the *fête du roi* that one could celebrate with peals. This occasion was thus far more solemn than any of its rivals.[67]

Despite ministerial injunctions a good many mayors continued to ring out of *bravado*. The case of Aulnay was no exception. Peals lasting twelve hours were by no means rare on the day of a national festival. On 23 June 1835, Persil, the *ministre des Cultes*, wrote that in the course of disputes over bells it was generally the mayors who took the initiative. That year "some of them were so unreasonable that they were prepared to deafen a whole population with ten to twelve hours of bell ringing on the *fête du roi*, simply to defy"[68] the clergy.

In Pontacq (in the Basses-Pyrénées) the conflict assumed a somewhat different form. The mayor, who was a retired colonel, councillor-general, the recipient of a July 1830 decoration, and a member of the Légion d'honneur, decreed in 1835 that the celebration of the *fête du roi* should be brought back to Sunday the third of May. He hoped that field hands might stand a better chance of taking part in the celebrations. The text of this ruling was read out "to the sound of trumpet and drum" in all the streets of Pontacq, and affixed to the walls of the town hall. The parish priest, who had had 30 April and 1 May carillonned, refused to repeat the peals on this occasion. The magistrate, with two municipal guards in attendance, had the door to the bell tower broken down on the evening of 2 May. Then he had some of his own men carillon in the presence of the parish priest and his two curates.[69] In the opinion of the royal prosecutor, this affair should be regarded as being "of the greatest significance." As an educated man he saw it as a local transposition of the dispute "between the priesthood and the Empire."[70] He feared that any proceedings instituted against the mayor of Pontacq "would stir up trouble." He therefore advised dismissing the said official in as discreet a fashion as possible.

This type of dispute did not entirely die out after 1835, when the regime underwent a change in direction and a stabilization. The following year the mayor of Pleine-Fougères (Ille-et-Vilaine), not content with seeing the parish priest ring on the evening of 30 April and on the morning of 1 May, which was the *fête du roi*, planned peals for midday and evening. The priest refused, hitched up the ropes on the first floor of the tower, and locked up the bell tower. The mayor, having donned his sash, ordered a locksmith to force the door and rang for an hour.[71] We have already seen how as late as 1845 the *fête du roi* gave rise to a dispute over bells in Wahl-lès-Faulquemont.[72] Nevertheless, at the end of the reign the situation proved less favorable to mayors than it had once been. In 1847 the *ministre des Cultes* forcefully reiterated the judgment formulated by Argout in 1833. He rebuked the mayor of Givry (Saône-et-Loire), who planned to ring for the July festivals, reminding him that he had no right to "demand the sound of bells"[73] on a strictly secular festival. The prefect professed astonishment. "Since 1830," he wrote, "the sound of bells had announced the celebration of the July festivals in this little town."[74] That year the mayor overruled the priest. In the presence of a sizable gathering he himself rang to mark the eve of the festival. The following day, by way of retaliation, the parish priest *refused to open the main door* of the church to the municipal authorities. The priest had arrived in a procession to attend the funeral service held in honor of the glorious victims of July. This affair, if we follow the prefect's account, "caused considerable turmoil in the area" and, in his view, had political ramifications. He extracted a promise from the mayor not to ring the first of May . . . 1848.

Once the "June Days" had passed, the leaders of the Second Republic showed some timidity in their handling of national and secular peals. It was as if they feared to clash with the clergy and foster revolutionary sentiments. In the Spring of 1848, a departmental "commissioner"[75] addressed an alarmed communication to the *ministre de l'Instruction publique et des Cultes*. In virtually all the communes of the Vosges, he wrote, the Revolution has been celebrated and *rung*.

Some parish priests had nevertheless refused to carillon while "others acceded reluctantly" to the mayors' demands. "In festivals that should in the future mark the era of our young republic, it would be tiresome if the whim of a priest were to shatter its patriotic harmony." The minister's reply, which was cutting in tone, arrived on 21 July. In such matters one should abide by the judgment formulated by the legislative committee of the Council of State in 1840, namely, that "the purpose of bells consecrated for worship is essentially religious, and the pastor of each parish is in sole charge of bell ringing."[76]

The following year the law of 15 February 1849 instituted national festivals on 24 February and 4 May, the anniversary of the proclamation of the Republic. Instructions were given to sing a Te Deum on such days in every church, and to *ring in celebration of the festivities*. Soundings made in the Meuse suggest that during these three years (1849–1851) the law was implemented without incident, and with the approval of the diocesan authorities.[77] In the majority of communes, or so it seems, these two national festivals were carillonned and celebrated. The same was not the case, however, in every department. In 1849 the prefect ruled in favor of several parish priests from the Vosges who refused to ring in celebration of the *journée* of 24 February. In 1850 the mayor and the parish priest of Tréguier were at loggerheads. The former wanted the national festival of 4 May rung, whereas the parish priest was opposed to the idea. The mayor called for "some individuals to set the bells ringing, the usual bell ringers having refused."[78] He was roundly rebuked. The prefect and then Parieu, *ministre de l'Intérieur et des Cultes*, judged that a mayor could only insist that the peal of bells accompany the artillery salvo and the fireworks "on the day of a national festival."[79]

We are thus the better able to understand the success of the Second Empire in such matters. There is no trace of anyone refusing to ring on 15 August. Some eight years after the fall of the regime, in 1878, the parish priest of Vaucouleurs (Meuse) refused to ring for the republican festival of 30 June. The mayor protested. "During the Empire," he wrote, "*that was done quite naturally* without your being informed of the fact and without anyone dreaming of opposing it."[80] I should add that, in an epoch characterized by the rise of the Marian cult and the promulgation of the dogma of the Immaculate Conception, it is hard to see how one could ever have banned the bells on the eve or the day itself of the Assumption of the Virgin, which was one of four retained festivals.

The sheer volume of sound produced on 15 August prompts me to emphasize, by way of contrast, the interruption suffered by the festivals of sovereignty and the national peals between 15 August 1870, the republican ceremonies of 30 June 1878[81] and, above all, of 14 July 1880. There is perhaps no more telling sign of the prolonged vacillation of the regime than this interruption. This symbolic void, which was unprecedented since the Revolution, must have been strongly resented, given the importance of the sound of bells to the culture of the senses shared by country dwellers.[82] By the same token, we may gauge how important the return of civic and national bells must have seemed in a great number of French communes on 14 July 1880.[83]

The associations linking that particular day to campanarian history were not without a certain nobility. In July 1776 the Liberty Bell had rung to mark the Declaration of Independence of the American colonists. On 14 July 1790, all the peals of France, which were then at their peak, had carillonned the *fête de la Fédération*. In 1880, however, such unanimity was far from prevailing. Before considering how things stood on the ground, it seems worth looking more closely at the theoretical debate.

The novelty of the situation, as far as the clergy were concerned, did not lie in ringing a national or a republican festival, but in celebrating with a peal of bells a date which was felt by many of its members to be odious. This anniversary of the Revolution "that has overturned the altars" served in their eyes to exalt "a revolt, an act of treason, an orgy, and bloodshed." In a word, the celebration was designed to commemorate "a terrible *journée*."[84] In contrast with the fifteenth of August or the *fêtes des souverains*—which were also the festivals of their respective patron saints—the date of 14 July referred to nothing whatsoever in the religious calendar. Furthermore, unlike the program of festivities for the national celebration of 24 February, 4 May or, 15 August, the festival of the four-teenth of July did not imply any religious ceremony.[85] It required peals of bells simply because such a display of rejoicing was an immemorial cus-tom. Where the clergy was opposed the mayor could, on this occasion at least, have the bells rung by force.

For many parish priests and priests in charge, the fourteenth of July was not a day of collective rejoicing but a strictly partisan celebration. Withholding the bells on such an occasion amounted to banning the "political carillon" and preventing the peal from being secularized and the ring itself desacralized. The conflicts unleashed on that day hinged on the politicization of auditory markers, and thus entailed a reversal in the meaning of campanarian rejoicing. Furthermore, the members of the episcopate thought it best to be prudent since this national festival, which was without any religious significance and referred only to the political calendar, might easily be shifted to another date. "Who knows what the future holds," the bishop of Mende wrote to the prefect of the Lozère, "[these festivals] may later have as their object the glorification of the Paris Commune or some other event that has proved pernicious both for the Church and for society."[86]

The specter of profanation and sacrilege was at large; the strictly sec-ular bell ringing of 14 July might see hordes of intruders bursting into the churches, or so many priests in charge supposed. The bells would then not be treated with the respect due objects that had been blessed. As the parish priest of Fouesnant (in Finistère) wrote to the mayor of his commune, on the eve of 14 July 1891: "I cannot allow the first drunk or urchin who hap-pens along to enter the church and wreak havoc under the pretext of ring-ing the bells."[87] He asked his correspondent to give him the name of his authorized bell ringer.

The presence of the municipality's men in the bell tower on the eve and the day itself of the national festival was often viewed as a victory for the mayor and as a sign of the dispossession of "the community as signified" beyond that of the divine signifier. "*This evening, the bells are mine!*," exclaimed the mayor of Brénod (Ain) on 13 July 1891 in the parish priest's hearing. "And without letting me speak," the priest recalled, " he noisily entered the church, shouted to his men to follow, and led them to the bell tower committing who knows what improprieties as they went."[88]

This is very much how the bells rung on the fourteenth of July were regarded by the other party, as is evident enough from an article devoted to the topic in *La République française* on 29 July 1884. National bell ringing is presented there as a victory for the town hall, as a sign of the secularization of bells and, above all, as proof that the community had captured the bell tower from the clerical authorities. The *républicains opportunistes** called upon militants to capture the emotional power and symbolic attributes of the bells and to deploy them in the service of the republic. Evidently the stakes were high.

What did mayors in the provinces feel about such things? We have recovered some pointers from the survey set up in 1884, which was designed to find out what the wishes or prevailing customs of the municipalities were in this regard. These documents lead one to suppose that the attraction of the peals on the fourteenth of July varied from region to region. In the Côtes-du-Nord it was not much of an issue. The subprefect of the arrondissement of Dinan wanted the bells to be rung on the fourteenth of July but recognized that "this type of bell ringing has not yet become part of local tradition in Brittany." The subprefect of Guingamp declared that it was a "recent custom" that was restricted to a small number of communes." The subprefect of Lannion had consulted the mayors of the canton capitals and of the most important localities. He concluded that "the republican mayors, and they alone, judge that

*The Opportunists were republicans, foremost among them Gambetta, who sought accommodation with the moderate right, and postponement of the separation of church and state. Their stance, maintained by the majority of republican deputies in the 1880s, should be contrasted with that of the more intransigent radicals, for example, Clemenceau and Rochefort.

the secular authorities should have the right to have the bells rung" on the day of the national festival. Conversely, in the arrondissement of Saint-Brieuc the mayors seem to have been in favor of the practice.[89] Out of twenty-six mayors from the Ille-et-Vilaine whose answers are extant, only seven wished to be able to ring on 14 July.[90] In the Eure-et-Loir, on the other hand, eighty municipalities used the bells on that day,[91] still only a tiny minority.

In any event, there were many disputes on the ground. On the actual day of 14 July it was the bells that precipitated the greatest number of disputes. Out of 482 writs issued concerning the national festival in 41 departments, 110, or 23 percent, concerned the use of bell ringing.[92] Over half of these campanarian conflicts took place in 1881 and 1882 or, in other words, before the passing of the law of 1884 and, in particular, of its Article 101. Between 1883 and 1888 the number of disputes over bells precipitated by the fourteenth of July dwindled. There was a fresh burst between 1889 and 1892, but the *Ralliement* meant that such conflicts tended to disappear afterward.* Needless to say, the situation varied from region to region, with disputes occurring with greater frequency in the Maine-et-Loire, which was then under the crozier of Monsignor Freppe.[93]

It was the mayors, their deputies, and the municipal councillors who took the offensive in such affairs, as had been the case in 1830 and 1831. Their "intense desire to annex the bell tower for republican rites"[94] was consistent with their wish to achieve, through the building of town halls and other monuments, a symbolic reconquest of the communal territory. While attempting to capture as far as possible the constitutive elements of the sacralizing of space achieved by the clergy, a good many republican magistrates sought to develop new festive itineraries, to establish new "approaches to walking," to modify "the topography of mistrust,"[95] and to restore the attraction of objects or sites that the priest had taught his parishioners to scorn. They plainly welcomed a symbolic confrontation,

*In 1889 the Third Republic, having surmounted the Boulangist crisis and celebrated the centenary of the Great Revolution of 1789, began to adopt a more conciliatory attitude toward conservatives and Catholics who, at Pope Leo XIII's recommendation, were in turn increasingly prepared to "rally" to the regime.

hence the great importance of emblems in the unfolding of such contests. On the fourteenth of July itself, disputes over bells were often linked to quarrels over flags. The municipal authorities were supposed to respect the presbyteries but, as in 1830, they were granted the right to deck the bell tower with bunting, even when the parish priest refused permission. Nevertheless, such marking of religious edifices was not supposed to be permanent. The members of the parochial church council in Moissac (Tarn-et-Garonne) protested at the mayor's intending *to impose "fixed decoration* on their bell towers and the facades of their churches," when the prefectorial circular on this topic had stipulated that bunting be used only on the fourteenth of July.[96]

That same day the use of bells either harmonized with or was substituted for the republican sonorities that some mayors sought to promote through the composition of fanfares.[97] The subprefect of Louviers noted in 1902 that in Surtauville (Eure) they had rung for the previous twenty years on the afternoon of 14 July, both before and after prize giving at the public school. The bells carillonned "so that in the absence of any musical society the festival would have more solemnity."[98]

When we consider these rural fourteenths of July, we are struck by the discipline, size, and decorum of the municipal delegations that came to ring or drape the flags, as well as by the solemnity of their gestures and the ostentatious nature of their insignia and uniforms.[99] It was also an occasion for a great deal of triumphalism. Having for so long been deprived of bells and having suffered so many humiliations, the mayors were sorely tempted to indulge themselves. The mayor of Blosville (Manche) gave his authorization for the bells to be rung *the whole day of the fourteenth of July 1882*.[100] In Tauriac (Lot) that same year the mayor had the bells carillonned for a whole hour on the day of the national festival.[101] On the fourteenth of July 1885 the mayor of Mézières (Ille-et-Vilaine) had done wrong, according to the prefect, and had also had the bells rung for too long, calling upon some hardened drinkers for the purpose.[102] If we go by the bishop of Nevers' account, all the campanarian disputes associated with the national festival in the department of the Nièvre had turned on the length of the peals. For this same reason in 1888 the prelate laid the commune of Fourchambault under interdict for eight days.[103] The prefect of Tarn-et-Garonne advised the mayors not to indulge in any excesses.[104] The parish priest of Montbazin (Hérault) had carillonned at five o'clock in the morning, at midday, and at seven o'clock in the evening on the fourteenth of July 1893. The mayor deemed that insufficient and five times asked the parish priest for the keys to the bell tower so he could ring some more.[105] The mayor of Ménarmont (Vosges), on 13 and 14 July 1903, instructed "some young people who are not bell ringers"[106] to repeat all the peals that the sexton had rung under the orders of the priest in charge. If we are to believe the priest, their clumsiness was such that they broke the bell ropes. The *ministre des Cultes* thus took care in 1884 to specify the length of authorized peals.[107]

The peal rung on the evening of the festival was especially controversial. The clergy, prepared to carillon on the eve and morning of 14 July, rejected this new nocturnal peal, which was liable to become a celebration of the disorder and immorality of evenings given over to public rejoicing.[108] On such occasions the mayor would sometimes, simply out of defiance, decide to let a veritable "charivari of bells" be inflicted upon his adversary. "On 13 July [1905]," wrote the president of the parochial church council in Saint-Sulpice (Tarn), " at noon and in the evening on 14 July at ten in the morning, and on 15 July at noon and at nine fifteen in the evening, twenty or so persons who were strangers to the church were let into the bell tower to ring all the bells of the church in full peal and in a *crazed fashion.*"[109] "The persons who had invaded the bell tower broke the ropes and chains that set the clappers in motion, unhooked these same clappers, and used them to strike with redoubled force on the outside of the bells," which they thus chipped.[110]

Such an incident forms part of an anticlerical masquerade, modeled after those performed during the Revolution and the mocking procession held at the time of the sack of the archbishop's palace in Paris in 1831. After the "reactionary" candidate had been defeated in the legislative elections of 1893, the bells of the church of Phalempin (Nord) were set ringing with the permission of the mayor, who was newly elected. A cortège formed as if in mimicry of a procession. "Men were dressed in women's shirts in the guise of surplices; children carried crosses and banners and processed to the beating of a drum along the streets of the *bourg*. The crowd kneeled down in mockery before a chapel crying 'Down with the cloth! Down with the host!'; it then paused in front of the presbytery and inflicted a terrible charivari on the parish priest and the nuns from the Catholic school."[111]

Some magistrates plainly took delight in forcing or solemnly breaking down—with the help of the rural guard, the brigadier of the gendarmerie, and the municipal councillors—the doors of bell towers that the clergy refused to open. On 13 July 1881, the mayor of Saint-Marcel (Saône-et-Loire), realizing the impossibility of breaking down the door of the bell tower, which the parish priest had barricaded with a pew nailed in place, used axes and crowbars to make an opening at the base of the door. This task took the rural guard a full three-quarters of an hour and he broke two axe handles in the process. A crowd of onlookers had gathered. Once the wood of the door had splintered, the rural guard slipped in through the opening. He then opened the door for the mayor and his men, who set all five bells ringing at once.[112]

The overall shape of such contests gradually altered through the increasing frequency and *stylistic formality of the epistolary exchanges* between the two authorities. They reflect the rise in the use of the written word between people whose lives touched, and who knew each other well. Some mayors, as we have seen, deemed it humiliating to have to fetch the bell tower key from the presbytery; the risk of meeting with a refusal was too great. Others in the past had been treated with discourtesy or, worse, shown the door. Such men would not even contemplate crossing the parish priest's garden. They preferred to write. In 1900 the mayor of Aunay-les-Bois (Orne) declared to the prefect that from now on he would not deign to "stoop so low as to ask" the priest in charge to ring the peals for the national festival.[113]

The clergy, now on the defensive, had recourse to a wide range of different tactics. Some parish priests simply refused to ring and then were absent on the day of the festival. They were gambling on the timidity of the municipal authorities. Other priests in charge decided to lock the bell tower door; they made off with the key, went to ground in their presbyteries,[114] and did not ring any Angelus that day.[115] Others, being less confident, decided to barricade the tower door.[116] The priest in charge of Sublaines (Indre-et-Loire) removed the mechanism that opened the door, thus rendering all access to the bell tower impossible. Finally, still others, with the help of their bell ringers, removed or hitched up the ropes,[117] loosened the knots, or unhooked the clappers from the bells. When the mayor asked the parish priest of Saint-Père (Ille-et Vilaine) how it was that the rope had fallen when they wanted to ring the bell on 14 July 1889, the priest feigned surprise. "This knot was tied," he declared, "twenty-two years ago."[118] In October 1891 the bell ringer from Harnes (Pas-de-Calais) was convicted by the court of Béthune for having deliberately damaged the bells of the church to prevent the peal of the fourteenth of July being rung.[119]

Yet clerical resistance went still further. When obliged to ring some priests in charge did it insolently. On 14 July 1882, the parish priest of Saint-Vincent (Lot-et-Garonne) had the service for the dead tolled. The following year the priest in charge of Bethincourt (Meuse) rang "ding-dong" so as to make fun of the mayor.[120] In 1886 the parish priest of Murvaux likewise decided to toll the passing bell, but in a ridiculous way.[121] Olivier Ihl is right to emphasize this use of grotesque, outrageous, and mocking sounds. As he has observed, "clerical insolence" was a response on that particular day to the excesses perpetrated by the secular authorities.[122]

The anticlerical policies pursued by various governments led some particularly daring priests to redefine the meaning and the uses of bells. The priests, in the thick of the battle, struck them as valuable allies. In 1902, when anticlerical policies were at their height, Father Léon called for these powerful sonorities to be deployed as boldly as possible. He regarded the bronze bells as "God's sentries" hung in bell towers that were the "headquarters" of guardian angels. He recommended that at every opportunity they set ringing "these accusatory voices," which were drawn up "for battle"[123] and which, more effectively than any other instrument proclaimed the rights of God—all the more so because their real fatherland, as everyone knew, was Rome, where the pope was held prisoner.

Aside from national festivals and civic peals, some members of the clergy therefore issued ever more auditory challenges and "peals rung in protest."[124] Such was the case with the parish priest of Le Vigan (Gard) in 1883,[125] and the parish priest of Salon-la-Tour (Corrèze),[126] who like others refused to ring on the fourteenth of July but carillonned on the fifteenth, which was Saint Henry's day.

In 1892 the parish priest of Arbois (Jura) had the church bells rung to announce prize giving at a school run by the Brothers of the Christian Doctrine.[127] In 1901 the parish priest of Garennes (Eure) tried to disrupt the prize giving at the lay school "by having the bells rung at the very moment that the ceremony was about to begin for a woman whose demise had not even been declared yet at the town hall. They had to break off, the mayor recorded, and wait until the peal had ended before continuing with the ceremony."[128] On 13 July 1901, the parish priest shut the church, thereby forcing the mayor to go to the presbytery as a petitioner. For the previous two years on the festival of Corpus Christi he had had a *temporary altar* built opposite the town hall to taunt the majority of the municipal council.

Some priests deployed irony, humor, or an arrogant tone in attempts to humiliate their adversaries. When the mayor's representatives came to ask for the key to the bell tower to ring on 14 July 1886, the parish priest of Laville-aux-Bois (Haute-Marne) asked if there was a fire.[129] In 1881 the parish priest of Curtil-sous-Burnand (Saône-et-Loire) answered the mayor of the commune by saying "that he would only surrender that key to a man in whom he had full trust." "The defiant tone [of this answer]," the offended magistrate wrote, "constituted a grave insult."[130] On 13 July 1888, the parish priest of Le Faou (Finistère), ensconced in the bell tower, spent over an hour[131] railing against the mayor, who was having the bells rung to mark the eve of the national festival.

Sometimes ecclesiastics did not restrict themselves to verbal violence. The peals on the fourteenth of July, for example, might lead to a physical confrontation. Sometimes the archetypal situation would arise whereby the two men officially entitled to ring a peal would clash; at other times the two teams of bell ringers would be involved. In Beauvin (Orne) in 1903 the "sexton" took it upon himself to ring for the national festival to "humiliate" the ringer chosen by the town council.[132] On 14 July 1891, the verger of Pleyben (Finistère) threw himself on the town hall secretary, who had been appointed bell ringer by the municipality and who had come "with his men" to ring for the national festival at half past five in the morning. He grabbed him "by the waistcoat and the shoulder" and forced him to withdraw. In addition, he "beveled off the pins of the great bell,"[133] to render it unusable. A year later this dispute, described by the mayor as a "wretched business,"[134] was still not settled.

It was not uncommon for the priest and the representatives of the municipality to actually come to blows. In Germainvilliers (Haute-Marne) in 1880, during the first celebration of the fourteenth of July, matters took a very serious turn. On the previous day Mr. Clémentin Jacquot, an innkeeper and a municipal councillor, went "of his own accord" "to ring at noon to announce the holiday."[135] The parish priest resorted to force to halt what he regarded as an act of provocation. The following day the mayor, accompanied by his son and two assistants, decided to go and ring the bells himself. Having used a forged key to open the door of the church that the parish priest had locked, he found that his adversary had "hitched up the ropes in the bell tower." He asked the blacksmith to pick the lock to the tower. But the parish priest "leaned against the door of the bell tower so that it could not be opened." Faced with such determined opposition, the secular authorities decided to withdraw.

When the priest returned to his presbytery shortly afterward, the mayor once again gave orders for the bell tower door to be opened and for the bells to be rung. The first peals brought the priest in charge running. He tried to stop the ringing by grabbing hold of the ropes. Then he launched himself at the mayor's bell ringer, one Henri Molard, and proceeded "to give him a good drubbing." He "tripped him to make him fall, but to no avail. Then Molard grabbed His Reverence by the back of the head with both hands, without hitting him, and then released him. His Reverence next sought to punch him in the neck to fell him, but this he failed to do. Henri Molard then grabbed him by the cassock and held him around the chest for several seconds against the frame of the bell tower." The parish priest came down from the tower and locked the ringers in; then he "barred" the door of the church despite the opposition of the mayor, who was plainly endowed with less physical strength. The conflict, as the brigadier of the gendarmerie noted in his report, "has already caused much talk in the canton." The details of the dispute give us some insight into the way in which the lay bell ringer succeeded in reconciling his desire to resist the priest physically with his respect for the sacred character of his person.

On the fourteenth of July 1888, the prefect of Finistère received a telegram from the mayor of Plougastel-Saint-Germain, the text of which requires no comment: "Impossible to ring the bells [,] priest seizes revolver."[136]

Some priests, being of a less violent nature, preferred to exorcize what they construed as the interference of demons, or to expiate what they regarded as a sacrilege. The parish priest of La Châtagneraie (Vendée) withdrew the Holy Sacrament from the tabernacle on the fourteenth of July, 1883.[137] The following year the parish priest of Magnac-Bourg (Haute-Vienne) dispensed with the bell that had rung the national festival; for several days he announced Mass with a rattle.[138] As we have seen, a commune might be placed under interdict. The bells therefore fell silent immediately after the fourteenth of July. In 1884 the bishop of Verdun placed an interdict for a whole month on the bells of the church of Aulnois-sous-Vertuzey (Meuse) because the mayor had rung to mark the opening of the ball held on the national festival.[139] The parish priest of Queyssac (Dordogne), who had been unable to ban the peals, cast an *anathema upon the municipality*, which to his mind consisted of a "pack of *incendiaries*."[140] Other pastors simply refused the sacraments to those who rang the national festival. Retaliation could sometimes be still more petty. On the fourteenth of July 1885, the parish priest of Nestier (Hautes-Pyrénées) forbad the "carillonneur" to ring. A crowd then gathered in the square outside the church. Finally, the mayor's authority prevailed and the peals were greeted, according to his own account of this episode, with cries of "Long live the republic!" The parish priest took his revenge by barring the carillonneur's daughter from catechism classes.[141]

The intensity of such contests shows how important they were. When disputes over bell ringing on the fourteenth of July erupted an absorbingly interesting debate ensued, although on a markedly smaller scale than the political conflict unfolding at the national level. The stakes were power in the village or, to be more precise, the right to speak for the community, the control over the signs of its identity, and, needless to say, the defense of its sacred patrimony and its auditory rhetoric. Study of the characteristic shape assumed by these turn-of-the-century struggles confirms the collapse of meaning we have discerned. It shows a secularizing and a partial and temporary desacralizing of the bells until, subsequently, their religious function was consolidated at the expense of their deeper meaning for the community. Once this withdrawal had been effected after the separation of church and state, bell ringing would cease to have the same symbolic range or perform the same function of identification; from then on the municipalities would no longer be unduly concerned with it. The conflicts that we have just described are characteristic of the period that runs from the fourteenth of July 1880 to the eve of the First World War.

In the preceding chapters, for the sake of clarity I have omitted any analysis of thresholds of tolerance for the loudness of sound. Likewise I have not yet considered the evocative power of rural bells. Yet one should be wary of supposing that the criteria governing the evaluation of such things were in any sense static. The history of the battles I have described is indissociable from that of the culture of the senses, as I shall now endeavor to show.

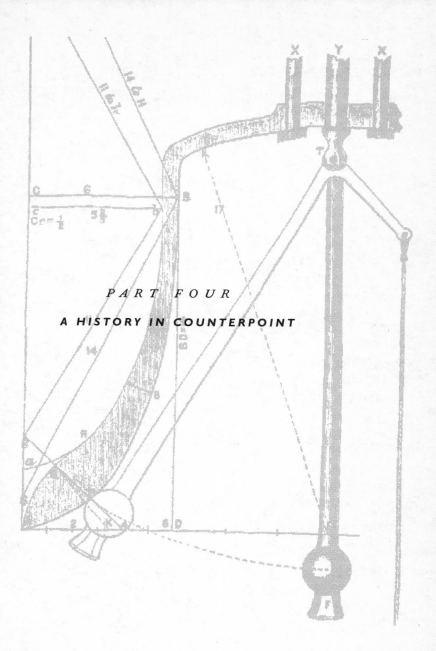

PART FOUR

A HISTORY IN COUNTERPOINT

CHAPTER NINE

From a Deduced to a Proclaimed Sensibility

M indful of the fact that we lack direct testimonies allowing us to identify the changing criteria governing the evaluation of village bells, I have attempted to deduce these criteria from the study of social practices, the management of the symbolic, the overall shape of conflicts, and signs of collective emotion. My inquiry has shown how strong the attachment was to the bell, which was a consecrated object as well as a symbol of the identity and cohesion of the community. The bell tower and the ring of bells were regarded as crucial elements in a patrimonial landscape. Like the cemetery, which was just then undergoing a transformation, they made perceptible the chain binding the living and the dead. Without a detailed study of peals, we would not be able to grasp with any precision the rhythms of village life, the experienced shape of territories, the acquiescence in and resistance to the expression of hierarchies and, above all, the subtleties of a rhetoric that structured, to the same extent as rumor, the procedures involved in communication.

My archival research has confirmed the intense indignation felt by villagers at being deprived of their bells. A refusal to ring wounded individuals and cast a slur on family honor. The silence of a hamlet's bell was experienced as a slur on the very existence of the group. When diocesan, parochial, or municipal authorities banned peals or made them less frequent, there would be confusion, mutterings, and hostile gatherings.

Finally, we have come to realize just what emotional power bells possessed. Peals solemnized an occasion and gave rise to or expressed rejoicing. They were far more effective in this regard than were "rough music" or the charivari. Any collective emotion that ran deep involved use of a bell, be it the threat of fire or bloodshed announced by an alarm or the terror aroused by the passing bell tolled during epidemics. By the same token, controlling the uses of bell ringing, holding the key to the bell tower, or having access to the ropes constituted major factors in the unfolding of the power struggles that shook these microcosms. Sometimes these contests also reflected a reluctance or a readiness to be integrated into overarching structures.

In parallel to the history of sensibilities deduced thus from collective acts and modes of behavior, there is another history that could be written on the basis of documents produced by outside observers who have given attention to village bells. Needless to say, such sources tell us mainly about the system of representations and aesthetic values of the speakers themselves. The picture painted of the sensibility of the other is constrained by logics that structure the social imagination. It is nevertheless rewarding to analyze in broad outline the vertical gaze of travelers, tourists, antiquarians, publicists and, subsequently, folklorists, not to mention the campanarian sensibility discernible in poetic discourse, since it was very often poetry that dictated the way in which the aesthetic quality of pealing bells would be evaluated.

Romantic Bells

My intention is by no means to contrast elite culture and popular culture. In the preceding chapters it has not been possible to avoid a degree of mediation. Indeed, the gaze of administrators, magistrates, priests, and gendarmes has served as a filter and, as such, has contributed much to the history of sensibilities attempted here. Furthermore, study of the ringing of bells clearly shows that cultural history consists of an endless series of exchanges. My principal aim in the present chapter is to demonstrate that the Romantics explicitly advocated such a social circulation of emotions. The glorifying of village bells enabled them to celebrate an agreement and an encounter between the people and the poets, who were united in mutual admiration and in their convergent attempts to aestheticize this auditory rhetoric. By way of conclusion I shall try to identify the logical link that, after 1860, bound to the subsiding of this Romantic trope to a growing intolerance toward sonorities that for many had come to seem both meaningless and irksome.

The cluster of sentiments involved were Germanic in origin. At the end of the eighteenth century, or more particularly in 1797, the year in which Camille Jordan delivered his celebrated apology for the bells, a great text by Schiller established stereotypes of campanarian literature that were to remain in place for over half a century. Together with Goethe's poem, which is slightly later in date, this text radically revised a system of evaluation that had once been under the sway of religious symbolism and had been based on the glorifying of "ringing towns"[1] since the Renaissance.

The depiction of the Romantic bell entails a counterpoint and tension between several major themes. The German Romantics' fascination with the depths of the mine is well-known.[2] Schiller exalted *the bond between bell and earth*. He celebrated the chthonic character of the consecrated bronze, which was born of a subterranean fire and was imbued with the telluric forces that had presided over its birth.

The motif of the bell also allowed the poet to recapitulate the stages of individual destiny and interweave his text with evocations of rites of passage. Schiller's poem is punctuated by descriptions of the bell in its subterranean womb; of the fusion of the alloy, a symbol here of the wedding; of the tocsin that proclaims the horrors encountered in life's drama; and of the passing bell announcing the loss of the other and his return to the earth. This was consistent with the renewed importance of the theme of the "ages of man" at the end of the eighteenth century.

When we read this text it is as if the powerful ringing of the bell represented a victory over chaos and, for a community, a symbol of cohesion regained; it was an instrument whose sound enabled people to assemble, and it was the sign of a social order founded on the harmony of collective rhythms. As a voice from on high it guaranteed the triumph of civilization over revolution. Goethe, in a more ambiguous text, treats the bell as an instrument by means of which disciplines are interiorized. His heavy bronze is in danger of crushing the child who imagines in his nightmare that he is being pursued by this monstrous mass that reminds him of parental injunctions.[3]

French authors preferred to emphasize the evocative power of bell ringing, which caused the heart to beat a little faster and tears to flow. The memory of the characteristic sounds of one's birthplace merged with the sense of simply existing and the earliest memories of selfhood. The sound of the bell was itself an expression of rootedness, and of being reconquered by the earth.[4] Like the scent of a flower[5] it was a matter of instant recall. It seemed to abridge existence and gather in memories. It showed that forgetting was impossible. It combined the presence of the past with foreboding.[6] In short, it anchored the gnawing sense of *nevermore*[7].

The Romantic bell, which was listened to from afar, was first and foremost that of one's native village; it called to mind inaugural femininity, that of mother or sister. The moaning of the passing bell, which brought sadness to the valley, "lent souls to the stones" [and] "a melody to the tombs."[8] It described a poetic space and compounded the harmony of the Lamartinian meditation, which was a spiritual exercise and a melancholy prayer as well as an inner song.

Chateaubriand, in *Le Génie du Christianisme*—closer to English Romanticism than to the German poets as it happens—makes palpable the newly cosmic implications of the messages emitted by the consecrated bronze. The sound waves of the bell evoke a shoreless sea; its loud and sublime vibrations, borne by air and cloud, turn into a voice of nature.[9] This sonority, which is both an "inner voice" and the enchantment of the world, sometimes mingles with the sound of the winds, the thunder, waterfalls, or crowds. The imperative force of the bell is thereby enhanced. Its nocturnal voice inspires remorse. It reiterates the threat of death in the ears of the atheist; it disturbs the tyrant; it reminds the adulterous woman of the voice of duty.

Napoleon became the tutelary hero of this campanarian sensibility. Two texts in particular were constantly invoked, one being an extract from Bourrienne's memoirs and the other a passage from the *Mémorial*. "The sound of bells produced an extraordinary effect on Bonaparte, and one that I was never able to explain, for he listened to them with the utmost delight. When we were at the Malmaison and we used to walk along the alley that led to the plain of Rueil, I lost count of the number of occasions when our conversations were interrupted by the sound of the bell from that village. He would stop so that the sound of our steps did not in any way detract from the loveliness of the reverberations. He seemed almost annoyed that I was not as deeply moved as he was. The impression made on his senses was so great that his voice faltered as he said to me then: 'That reminds me of the first years I spent at Brienne. I was happy in those days!' "[10]

"I cannot hear the Angelus on Saint Helena," the prisoner on the island declared much later, "and I cannot get used to no longer hearing it. The sound of bells has never struck my ear without taking my thought back to the sensations of my childhood. When I used to hear it below the woods of Saint-Cloud, and this was often, people used to suppose that I was dreaming of a campaign or a law for the Empire when in fact I was simply resting my thoughts and allowing myself to return to the earliest impressions of my life."[11]

In 1831 Victor Hugo added to the coherent network of stereotypes defining the figure of the Romantic bell by bringing out the historical function of its sonorities or, in other words, their propensity to tell of a multiplicity of historical periods. Without bells Notre-Dame would have been dumb; its presiding genius, Quasimodo, would not have been able to express himself. Without ever quitting the present, the act of listening to the tenor bell enabled one to plunge back into the fifteenth century. It brought about a scrambling of temporalities, and to this the novel owed its particular savor.

The bell now made one aware of the proximity of the people, or at least it fostered the hope that they might be discovered and perhaps encountered. It was no longer acceptable to entertain the mistrust once displayed by Jean-Baptiste Thiers, for whom "the crudest people are those who love the bells and the sound of the bells the most." The proof of this, in his opinion, was supplied by the love for them of the Germans and the Flemish, as well as by "the paisants [sic] and the people of lowly circumstance, children, the mad, the deaf, and the dumb."[12] The din of the bells was to his ears no more than a disagreeable racket and the polar opposite of refinement. After Camille Jordan had made known the people's attachment to bells before the members of the Council of the Five Hundred in Prairial Year V (June 1797), it was forever being noted, discussed, and exalted. The instrument was used by composers such as Rossini, Meyerbeer, and Verdi when they wished to evoke the changing moods of the crowd.[13]

As one of the commissioners of the Republic for the department of the Vosges wrote in 1848, "the inhabitants of the countryside in general love the sound of bells; when the belfry resounds their minds withdraw into themselves and grow exalted; on solemn occasions they love to *let their cries of enthusiasm mingle* with the clamorous sound of the bronze."[14]

The bell was regarded as a *support for collective memory*, and with good reason. The people long preserved the imprint of its sonority. It is worth noting that older men remembered not only sounds that had long since disappeared,[15] but also castings and bell casters, blessings, godparent-hoods and, where they had occurred, abductions. One cannot help but be struck, as we have seen, by the existence of a long memory that is particularly attentive to the silence of the bells, a phenomenon associated with defeat, humiliation, sacrilege, plague, or interdict.

It is not hard to explain why feelings about this auditory "void" in the soul[16] should have been so intense, or why memories of it should have endured. The countryside knew nothing then of "the profane din" in which so many elements could be heard at once, and that constituted the background noise familiar to city dwellers. The auditory landscape, intercut with broad swathes of silence,[17] here consisted of tollings or percussion that could be easily located. The hearing of sounds of metal against metal, wood on wood, or of human voices served to demarcate family or vicinity. In an auditory landscape of this kind the brilliancy of the bell and the roll of the drum stood out. Bell ringing defined the event it signaled as extraordinary, so being deprived of it was all the more deeply resented.

Being so firmly anchored in popular memory the bell gave rise to many legends, as did fountains, ponds, and pits. Hidden bells, buried bells, and submerged bells that continued to toll or carillon under the earth or under water were themes consistent with the wish to make sound waves cosmic, and delighted observers engaged in the quest for popular poetry.[18]

The bell did not merely evoke one's early years. According to some witnesses it fascinated children, who would spontaneously invent songs and rhymes to accompany its rhythms.[19] In the countryside words were heard in the peals and one imagined the various instruments chatting with each other. Campanarian percussion formed part of the popular and primordial language that the Romantics were perpetually seeking. The many references to bells in nursery rhymes, proverbs, riddles, and sayings, as well as their presence on banners[20] and the people's desire to give them a name enhances the sense of a spontaneous harmony.

We know that attachment to bells was closely linked to the worship of saints. In some places, moreover, it was rendered still more intense by a belief in their magical properties. As far as the people were concerned, bell ringing had premonitory attributes. This is borne out by the fact that some would anxiously listen for "coincidences of bells."[21]

Taken together, these data collected in the last century inform us about the modes of attention and the intensity of emotion produced by the sound of the bell. In addition they point to the existence, where observers are concerned, of a broad *spectrum of curiosities and expectations*. They reflect a quest for languages, beliefs, and emotions linking bells to the primordial. From this point of view, despite the chronological discrepancies, there was for a period a close link between the Romantic poets' conception of the bell and the procedures involved in campanarian "exploration" and, subsequently, "inquiry." I now wish to consider this latter practice, which was spurred on by nostalgia and was contemporary with the dismantling of a poetic figure under whose influence it remained.

Campanarian Exploration and the Symbolism of Bells

Campanarian exploration may be regarded as a continuation of the endeavor undertaken at an earlier date and on a broader scale, and which at the dawn of the July Monarchy in particular, involved the recording of existing usages.[22] Because the authorities accorded particular importance to immemorial peals, information about them was collected with great care. Campanarian exploration arose in the middle of the century out of several needs. There was a growing awareness that vandalism at many levels posed a serious threat to the patrimony. Arcisse de Caumont, to mention only the most important of the "antiquarians," regarded recasting as equally destructive as the catastrophe—or the "deluge," to use Dr. Billon's term—brought about by the governments of the Revolution. At a time when itinerant bell makers and the manufacture of bells in the village itself were fast disappearing, the intrusion of new and powerful sounds, no longer produced by the bronze, inspired the antiquarians with a fresh curiosity for the sonorities of former times. The "explorers" endeavored from then on to preserve the old bells and, above all, to reconstitute in their imagination the richness of the sonorities of yesteryear. Dr. Billon strove to recreate peals that had disappeared, in much the same way as the hero of Huysmans' novel, des Esseintes, attempted to recreate the perfumes of former times.[23] These scholars shared the conviction of Jules Corblet, for whom an ancient bell gave a truer account of the history of the past than a mutilated stone.

As early as 1844 Arcisse de Caumont had devoted an article in the *Bulletin monumental* to the ancient bells. Yet it was another Norman, Dr. Billon, who would be hailed as the inventor of the campanarian inquiry. "One fine day in the month of April [1853] . . . [that is to say, at a time when the history of bells was already teetering]," one of his friends recorded, "we set out at M. Billon's prompting to explore a part of the lovely valley of Pont-l'Évêque. . . . We were on foot, straying to the right or to the left of the road in order to pick a flower, to peer at a pitched roof or a chimney that seemed to us to mark the site where some old manor might have stood." During this day of exploration Dr. Billon climbed the bell tower of the church of Coquainvilliers (Calvados), where he found an old bell. "It was a revelation. . . . No one before him had considered the value of this kind of monument. . . . Dr. Billon's mind was in need of some unbeaten tracks. He devoted himself to the study of bells."[24] Until his death in 1866 the learned doctor explored the former bishopric of Lisieux. "When during his archaeological excursions," Arcisse de Caumont wrote, "their sound waves, reflected by the hillsides, reached him he would pause and withdraw into himself so as to grasp the tone and harmony of the bell. He always wanted to see close up these instruments from which he received melancholy and religious impressions, and he had the inspired idea of recording the inscriptions. . . . He thus inaugurated, under the title of campanarian epigraphy, *a new path* in historical research. . . ."[25]

In his nostalgic quest Dr. Billon undertook both to "save from oblivion" and to "reconstitute" ancient sonorities. As he himself wrote, "we have drawn upon the memories of old men. When we have come across ancient belfries it has been a simple matter to deduce the number of bells by counting the cases they had occupied. We have carefully measured the diameter of the circular openings by which they were brought up."[26] I am not concerned here with analyzing the methods and contributions of this aerial mode of excavation, which was rendered at once heroic and perilous by the ever-present threat of vertigo.[27] The crucial aspect for us concerns the history of emotions. In 1877 J.D. Blavignac drafted the first campanarian synthesis; he evoked the pleasure of listening to the "creaking of the timbers" when in the evening mists the inquirer, ensconced within the mystery of the bell towers, felt himself to be hearing "the church itself breathing."[28]

The practice of campanarian exploration spread during the 1860s. Dieudonné Dergny roamed the Bray. The Count of Toulouse-Lautrec described in 1863 his exploration of the Haut-Comminges, with its stresses and exalted emotions. "I wanted to see close up," he wrote, "these bells to which I have often owed a religious and melancholy impression."[29]

After France's defeat by Prussia, while historical science was being subjected to new criteria, campanarian exploration yielded to systematic inquiry. The model was no longer the good Dr. Billon but the archivist Joseph Berthelé, who with the assistance of Canon Brugière set out to make a complete record of the bells of Périgord. On 1 October 1874, a double questionnaire was sent out to mayors, parish priests, schoolmasters, and "enlightened inhabitants."[30] In 1881 Michel Hardy published a set of guidelines for the aspiring campanographer that was the first of its kind. His system was meant to record systematically the dimensions and shape of the bell, the nature of the metal, the patterns used in the orna-

mentation, the text of the inscriptions and, where relevant, the certificate
of "baptism" preserved in the parish registers. By the same token, such
inquiries tended to neglect existing usages and the culture of the senses;
they were becoming strictly archaeological, paralleling contemporary
advances in epigraphy. Nevertheless, the recruitment of campanologists
was not perceptibly different from what it had been at the end of the
Second Empire. This ever-expanding group still consisted of erudite clerics, doctors enamored of antiquities, aristocrats in learned societies,
teachers, and archivists.

By the end of the century campanarian inquiries had become fashion-
able. Specialists attended conferences on the subject and contributed to
specialist journals. As Henri Jadart, a historian of the Ardennes, recalled,
"never has there been so much interest in bells as in our own period." He
even spoke of "campanomania" and himself dreamed of an inquiry covering every department in France. According to him campanography had
become a *vast work-site*,[31] a term redolent of the so-called positivist conception of history. For the time being Jadart ruled out all hopes of the
synthesis to which he ultimately aspired.[32] The latter, of course, would
never be realized. Campanarian inquiry is now a fact of history[33].

In parallel to the struggle, between 1853 and the First World War, to
preserve and reconstitute ancient peals in the imagination, some clerics
endeavored, as we have seen, to revive the symbolism of bells and integrate them into their militant vision.[34] According to Huysmans after his
conversion, the bells now had the mission to compensate for the dumb-
ness of human voices, which had lost the habit of prayer.[35]

At the same time—and it is crucially important to appreciate the syn-
chronicities involved—republican, agrarian, and nationalist ideologies
fought over a campanarian symbolism, which was imbued with nostalgia.
Françoise Cachin has shown how in the sphere of landscape painting a
"re-centering on the bell tower" occurred, with the work of Corot constituting the most characteristic example. The village landscape then
exemplified the classical schema of a "reassuring closure of vision,"[36]
which enabled each person to recover some visual and auditory memories. This exploiting of the "hereditary setting," this symbolization of the
duration, solidity, and stability of the environment was consistent with
the harmonious *picture of France* drawn in 1906 by Vidal de la Blache.[37]

This cluster of sentiments would inspire a few years later the finest pages ever devoted to the village bell towers, namely, those which open the description of Combray in the first volume of Proust's *A la recherche du temps perdu*. It was "in its steeple that the church seemed most truly to find itself, to affirm its individual and responsible existence. It was the steeple that spoke for the church." "It was the steeple of Saint-Hilaire that shaped and crowned and consecrated every occupation, every hour of the day, every view in the town."[38]

The motif of the bell tower proved important, as we have seen, for the depiction of republican France, which was regarded as a collection of rural cells. It seemed crucial to many republican magistrates to incorporate this domineering verticality into the horizontality characteristic of the various municipal symbols. At the same time the church steeple—a privileged marker for the viewpoint indicators scattered across the territory—benefited from the vogue for panoramas and "views." Glimpsed from a train or a car, the bell tower was a premonition of the village. Agrarians were apostles of the "*petite patrie*" and advocated going "back to the land." Like the regionalists they were only too ready to indulge in enraptured descriptions of the bell tower. "Hear . . . the sound of the bells," advised the campanologist Henri Jadart, "that serve to remind you of the heroic exertions of our fathers." "Let us read once more on the bronze the names of those who preceded us and the joyful echo of which resounds in our ears." The function of this auditory cemetery is to ward off "ideas of pessimism, decadence, shirking, or surrender"; it enjoins those who listen "not to desert their fatherland, nor the *quiet milieu* in which, like us, so many generations of ancestors lived and worked."[39]

The glorifying of the bell tower's solid tranquillity and of its auditory messages paved the way for the cult of the chain of the dead. The speech in praise of the village church delivered by the author of the *Roman de l'énergie nationale* before the assembled deputies on 17 January 1911, is the key text in this regard. Sar Paladan had already extolled the bell towers, calling them "France's other flag." "We are used . . . to its shadow . . . in our public squares . . . like the shadow of our trees in our orchards." This "aerial point" writes "the most vital impulses . . . on the blue page that is our firmament."[40] The sound of bells, Maurice Barrès wrote, summons *the deepest forces.* "There is in our utmost depths . . . an obscure domain which [the] scientific psychologists recognize as the layer that nourishes our clear thoughts." The village church and its sonorous bells urge on "this momentous activity within . . . this *dark consciousness*"; they help to "allay the deep anxiety" emanating from the "abysses of preconscious life." By the same token "the village church purifies the territory in the midst of which it is planted."[41] In forcing the unconscious French style, which was then flourishing under the aegis of Pierre Janet,[42] to serve as a defense against the barbarism of the soul, Maurice Barrès had come full circle. Just as Schiller and Goethe had once done, he treated the bell tower and its peal as instruments of discipline. Here, however, it was a matter of taming the "formidable depths of the soul."

I do not in any way wish to minimize the significance of these references to the emotional power of the village bell tower for the rise and spread of nationalist sentiment. It nevertheless remains the case that all the work done in the field of campanarian archaeology and symbolism could not mask the fact that the schema of the Romantic bell had disintegrated. As casting in the village became a thing of the past and campanarian production was industrialized, the meaning of the peals tended to be lost. The growing unwillingness to tolerate the sound of bells was a telling sign of such changes. To analyze this phenomenon I shall make a short detour through the urban milieu.

Intolerance of Noise and the Right to Sleep

The history of sensibilities is based on the study of variations in thresholds of tolerance. This is what I tried to show in relation to the process of the "deodorization" undertaken at the end of the eighteenth century.[43] The evolution of the system of evaluation proves to be quite different in the auditory sphere. Each of us is familiar with the tension nowadays—in a world characterized by the ubiquity of electronic signals and muffled voices on the airport intercom—between a concern to reduce sound levels and make auditory messages discrete, and the desire for a din such that "ghetto-blasters" incapable of deafening would be disqualified. In short, there is no single threshold of tolerance identifiable since thresholds vary with the context. Social divisions that were once so significant—whereby "rough music" long remained a monopoly of the people—have, in this domain at least, become inoperable.

In the nineteenth century hostility to noise, as I have stressed before, was much less discernible than the anxiety aroused by unpleasant odors. This century, let me repeat, had to put up with new kinds of din, a fact that seemed to pose no dangers; many listeners seemed to delight in the gradual increase in the volume of the Romantic orchestras up until the eve of the First World War. In no sense, then, can one posit a global increase in touchiness about sound. In fact it seems to be quite the reverse; there were ever higher thresholds for what was heard and what could be borne. Nevertheless, the evolution of systems of evaluation varied according to the nature of the noises and sounds.

Complaining of the discomfort caused by the din of bells was a venerable *urban tradition*, and one that fit with the familiar theme of the drawbacks of town life. It formed part of a struggle of the elites, who were intent on imposing their fastidious tastes and reducing noises to some sort of harmonious order, against "rough music," charivaris, and rackets, which all served to define the people. Théodore of Béza in 1560, Ménage, and Benserade in particular, contributed to this diatribe.[44] Boileau likewise, in his sixth *Satire*, laid into the bells, which, "to honor the dead, cause the living to die." In 1757 Father Carré himself described the inconvenience caused by the peals. During the Revolution this discomfort was invoked by those who wanted to see an end to the sounds of superstition and would have preferred the bronze of the bells to toll only against the defenders of tyrants. A few decades later Alfred de Musset was still voicing his loathing for these irksome bells.

Conversely, it was one of the *topoi* of nineteenth-century campanarian literature to maintain that, in a rural milieu, a bell was never any trouble. "They love the sound of bells," wrote the bishop of Blois on 25 October 1802 to the prefect of the Loir-et-Cher. "For them it is never disagreeable."[45] In 1884 the prefect of the Haute-Savoie emphasized the gulf separating the inhabitants of the countryside from the townsfolk in this regard. The former could not do without the peals; conversely, in town, there were some, he said, "who wished not to be disturbed by the sound of bells before half past four in summer and before five in winter."[46] My own investigations bear out this claim and I believe that I have shown

why. Except for in exceptional circumstances that I will describe, I have
encountered only three cases of intolerance toward the bells in a rural
milieu, the first being in Courlon[47] and the second in Raon-l'Étape
(Vosges). In 1832 the inhabitants of this latter commune "complained
daily that the bells were being rung for far too long."[48] The noise troubled
the sick and disturbed the rest of people in good health. By his own
authority the mayor ordered the peals to stop on the night of All Saints'
Day. In 1839 a municipal decree of the commune of Labresse banned this
same peal for the dead. The deputy mayor, in his efforts to ensure that the
measure was respected, invoked the plight of the sick, whose "sufferings
[were] exacerbated" by the bell, respect for "public rest," and "the dissolute conduct" of the young bell ringers, who on that night turned the
church into "a place of lewdness."[49] The bishop pointed out to the prefect, however, that this custom existed in every commune in the Vosges,
and that the inhabitants of the countryside set great store by it.

Yet there were two occasions on which reservations were expressed in
rural areas regarding the sound of bells, although the first essentially concerned the authorities. As convinced as Cabanis of the close links between
the physical and the moral aspect of man, administrators in the early nineteenth century banned funeral bells during epidemics. This prohibition
appeared in many concerted regulations.[50] As an inhabitant of the commune of Longny (Orne) wrote on 16 Frimaire Year XIV (7 December
1805) to the *ministre des Cultes*, "it had been noticed that [during a particularly devastating epidemic] the sound of the bells serving to announce
the death agonies and *the death* of those who had succumbed had produced
the most dreadful effects upon persons stricken by the illness, and that this
state of affairs was further aggravated by the funeral chants heard in the
street, and [by] the noise of the handbells preceding the funerary [sic] ceremonies. . . . When I communicated my observations on this subject to the
École de médecine in Paris, they too were of the opinion that where the
health and recovery of the sick during an epidemic was concerned, the
sound of bells and any funereal apparatus *that strikes the senses* cannot help
but inspire very dangerous fears, disturb the course of illnesses, and
sometimes render them mortal."[51] So as "to avoid fears that might prove
dangerous to the sick," the bishop of Valence instructed in 1806 that
under such circumstances "funeral prayers should be said in a lowered

voice."[52] In 1832, at the height of the Asiatic cholera epidemic, the mayor of Bettancourt (Haute-Marne) issued a decree banning the great bell, and likewise any carillon. Ringing to mark deaths and burials was prohibited. "Only the Angelus and the hours of work" could be announced, but even then "for the shortest possible time." "Mass on Sundays would be rung with two chimes, the first with the small bell and the second with the second bell, and without a full peal."[53] The prefect thought these measures excessive except in the case of peals announcing deaths, since they were liable, in his view, to "spread the epidemic by terror."[54] In short, the sound of the bells did not strike him as dangerous, nor was its loudness intrinsically irksome; it was the meaning conferred upon it that could prove harmful.

What might trouble country folk was not the morning peals, on which they were entirely reliant, but the *vesperal* peals *in summer*. In this milieu claims were made, although somewhat clumsily expressed, to an actual right to sleep. A prefectorial decree followed by a circular spelling out how it was to be implemented, dated 1851 and 1852, aroused a storm of protest in the rural communes of the Meuse. "So as to moralize the populations of the department" and standardize customs, the prefect, in agreement with the bishop, had in fact ruled that the "retreat" should henceforth be rung at ten o'clock in summer in every commune in the department. The usual custom in the countryside, however, had been to ring the bell at nine o'clock and even, in some places, at half past eight. In the summer the laborer from the Meuse would go to bed early in order to be better able to rise at four o'clock, or even at half past three in periods when the most demanding tasks had to be tackled. The ten o'clock peal disturbed and alarmed those who had just fallen asleep.

On 16 April 1852, the mayor of Ancerville protested, "for the sake of a handful of idlers and a few young people who cheat their parents, the public has to be awoken at ten o'clock in the evening."[55] In the summer, the mayor of Contrisson pointed out, "the workers generally go to bed at half past eight." They are awoken at ten o'clock; "they are [then] inclined to believe," he added, "that a fire has broken out. I myself once supposed as much."[56] The mayor of Longeville, wishing to suspend the ringing of the "retreat" in summer, invoked another argument, namely, that "the bell ringer complains about having to stay up until ten o'clock in the evening after being worn out by the labors of the day."[57] It was difficult to find a volunteer willing to ring at so late an hour, the mayor of Salmagne likewise insisted.[58] In the summer, the mayor of Velaines wrote, the inhabitants of the countryside are accustomed to ending their labors *"almost* at sunset, so as to return to their lodgings early enough to be able to do without light both in preparing their meal and in seeing to their livestock, and then to go to bed immediately around nine o'clock."[59]

Furthermore, the curfew bell seemed pointless in summer: "travelers who might benefit from the formal ringing of the "retreat" have nothing to fear from the inclemencies of the season,"[60] and the country taverns were deserted during this time of year.[61] Conversely, the same peal in the wintertime seemed altogether indispensable to mayors since it told the time long after sunset, served to guide the traveler, announced the closing of taverns when they were used quite heavily, and finally, did not disturb the working men who were assembled at the *veill*ée.[62]

In the town, on the other hand, it was in the morning that the sound of the bell seemed more and more burdensome. The system of evaluation here reflected a different nycthemeral rhythm and, more broadly, a fundamental difference in chronobiological behavior. Furthermore, city dwellers were better able to adjust to a schedule of peals that followed a yearly pattern. Country dwellers favored more flexibility. As we have seen, some even wished for a structure that was continually being adjusted to match the movements of the sun. The discrepancy of one hour that was tending to be imposed between summer and winter seemed to many in the countryside to be both insufficient and too rigid.[63]

The city dweller's diatribe against bells grew increasingly strident in the nineteenth century. In this sphere too, the 1860s marked a turning point. From this date on there was a greater determination *to lay claim to one's morning sleep*. This was because a whole series of new developments, among them advances in streetlighting, the adoption of Haussmann's approach to urban planning, the reign of the commodity, changes in the modes of display, the circulation of elites within the town, and finally, the novel presence of women in public space together produced a gradual modification in nocturnal behavior. An enhanced desire for individual liberty prompted challenges to standardized rhythms. This growing need for rest in the morning consigned to oblivion the earlier model originally inspired by monastic life and then handed down by boarding schools. According to this earlier model, one's bed, the night, and sleep were domains haunted by dangerous phantasms, while the dawn bell, by the same token, called one to give thanks to God for having successfully traversed the temptations of the night.

There were scattered indications of a more intolerant attitude even before the end of the century. In 1832 Chartres municipal council decided to make the peals less intrusive. It asked that no bells be used before six o'clock in summer and seven o'clock in winter, and it further requested that, if at all possible, peals should not last more than five minutes.[64] In 1837 the excessive use of bells gave rise to controversy in the village of Courlon. "The sick," wrote one inhabitant of that commune, "have been gravely affected by it, and people in good health have [sometimes] had to go away."[65] In 1831 and 1832 Parisians living in the rue du Bac, with the support of the prefect Gisquet, clashed with the sisters of Saint-Vincent-de-Paul, who woke them at four in the morning whereas the parish priests in Paris only began ringing between half past five and six o'clock. The mother superior regarded the involvement of the commissioner on behalf of the district as a political manoeuvre. In Babylone barracks, she pointed out, drum rolls were to be heard every morning "around four o'clock." The *ministre des Cultes* decided in her favor and observed that in many localities the Angelus was rung at that time of morning.[66]

In the 1860s the controversy grew more lively. Watering places, which were then proliferating at a great rate, were the habitual site for such confrontations. After the triumph of the Republic the debate became intertwined with the campaigns led by anticlericals.[67] In 1883 Nadar, worn out by the peals from Aix-les-Bains, sent the *ministre des Cultes* a strongly worded open letter, which soon became a text to which those involved in such controversies referred.[68] He invoked the *right to leisure* and the *right to silence*, which was "the most natural of rights." He spelled out the risks of neurosis and called for peals to be put in the category of insalubrious industries. "The question of the bells," he wrote, "is a matter of *general preservation* for all those craving peace and rest." Nadar declared war "upon a *noise* [that is] *excessive*, pointless, and incompatible with every right or with our liberty." "With my own eyes I have seen," he added, "in the town square, dogs protesting, dazed by the sudden onslaught, nervous to the point of paroxysm, and returning howl for howl." This "boiler-makers' riot," a "brutal noise, idiotic, as every noise is," constituted an "infringement upon my liberty to take my rest." The clergy had no right to "violate my free enjoyment of my sense of hearing" with this hideous voice which, in former times "gave the signal for the fire to be lit under the stakes in Seville."

On 21 October 1886, *La Lanterne*, which was famed for the efficacy of its campaigns, called for respect for the sleep of local residents, and for all bells to be banned before eight o'clock. The editorial even advocated the use of alarm clocks. The newspaper fought for the "law-abiding people [living next to churches] who have better things to do than roam the streets before sunrise in order to go and catch pneumonia in those unhygienic establishments called churches."[69] Ten years later *L'Avenir du Cantal* printed a petition signed by the women of Aurillac who, on behalf of "delicate, impressionable, and fragile people" asked to be spared the lugubrious and terrible rumbling of the tenor bell from Notre-Dame-aux-Neiges. It had the twofold disadvantage, the complainants wrote, "of battering us about the head and instilling sadness and grief in our hearts, banishing the sweet thoughts and tender feelings that we harbor toward sex."

Under the Combes ministry the controversy grew more heated. In 1902 the municipal council of Vals-les-Bains (Ardèche) was involved in a lengthy dispute with the bishop of Viviers. It culminated in the prefectorial decree of 7 March 1905, which applied to all the thermal spas in the Ardèche. From then on one could not carillon or ring a peal before six o'clock between 1 May and 1 October or, in other words, during the high season. Masses would be announced by a simple tolling lasting a minute at most. Formerly, and much to the annoyance of those taking the waters, the Angelus had been rung at half past four. The municipal council would have preferred the ban to apply the whole year round.[70] On 3 February 1903, *Le Radical* spoke out in support of the Council of State, which had just refused to quash the mayor of Limoges' decree banning ringing before six o'clock in the morning. "No torture can be compared to that of living close to a monastery," wrote the journalist in question, who also complained about the din produced by *la Savoyarde*, the loudest bell in the Sacré-Coeur.[71] The mayor of Romainville blamed the bells from his own commune for making work inside the town hall quite impossible.[72] In 1903—and this is a fact with wider implications—the French League for the Defense of the Rights of Man sent a petition signed by the inhabitants of Pantin to the prefect of the Seine protesting against bells being rung too early in the morning. Invoking the right to silence, they asked that the bells be treated as strictly as were whistles and sirens in industrial establishments.[73]

Five years later, while the battle over the Angelus was raging, Henry Nadal came to the support of the mayor of Salins (Jura) and himself denounced, in the pages of *L'Aurore*, what he termed "torture by bells." "Nothing is more intolerable, irritating, and exasperating than the ding-dang-dong of the first masses of the morning. . . . these *clapping sounds* . . . that beat at you and hammer at your eardrum . . . The bell is indeed a kind of torture, and the proof is that the Chinese, with all the refined cruelty of which a senile people is capable, classified it in the first rank of instruments imagined for such a purpose: in the garden of torments, death by bells holds the place of honor." Now that "countless people stay up until around midnight," in theaters or in cafés-concerts, it is a "rank absurdity" to ring in order to summon "a tiny number of the faithful to the early bird mass."[74]

Through this episode of anticlerical combat, which also concerned processions and all the external manifestations of the act of worship, we are able to discern demands for another order which indicate at once transformations in the culture of the senses, a novel insistence upon individual freedom from everyday rhythms, the desire for a certain standard of living and, above all, a fading in the meaning of the peals.

The model of the Romantic bell, which, the anticlericals jeered, could only be appreciated from a distance, had plainly been discredited. Zola, the author of *Le Rêve*, gave a precise description of the range of sensations and sentiments aroused by the din of bell ringing: the anticipation of the divine sacrifice, the manner in which the vibrations of the tenor bell from Bourges cathedral permeated the Huberts' house, the collective rejoicing, and Augustine's enraptured state followed by her flight in response to the heavenly call of the angel, which is also that of the wedding bell. Yet the analysis has a distant feel to it as if it were a clinical record. The emotional power of the bell, laid bare here and desacralized, is simply the agency that produces the dream; it is intrinsically linked to hallucination.[75] The religious symbolism is in some way turned inside out like a glove.

Although no systematic inquiry is possible, we can catch glimpses here and there of the gradual loss of meaning suffered by the messages borne by bells. Consider, for example, the letter that the actor Charles Fechter wrote to his mistress, Virginie Déjazet, on 18 April 1852: "The weather is terrible, it is raining, it's Sunday, the bells are tolling mournfully, and do you know what effect these melancholic carillons, which are supposed to call the faithful to prayer, have on nervous natures? Well, it is just such a *painful impression* that I am suffering from, and I cannot help but feel a kind of anxiety with regard to you."[76]

Such an admission serves as a prelude to the loss of meaning proclaimed by Baudelaire.[77] "Then suddenly the bells swing angrily / And hurl their terrible howl into the sky / Like wandering, homeless spirits / Beginning their relentless wailing." The city dweller had now lost the experience of time as a quality. The *non-meaning of the peals* referred to this absence, which paved the way in this sphere for the gradual decline of listening.[78]

The disintegration of earlier modes of evaluation and listening is discernible in various interlinked factors, namely, the nostalgia inspiring the attempts made to record and reconstitute peals in the imagination, the bid to instill new life into campanarian symbolism, the growing reluctance to tolerate the din produced by city bells, and the judgment, both formulated and expressed, that the sounds they produced were intrinsically absurd. The glorifying of the village bell tower seems to be simply a fallback position, and one that hardly compensates for the decline suffered by the schema of the Romantic bell.

In fact an entire section of the culture of the senses was impoverished in a still broader sense from the 1860s on, with a whole web of sound seemingly fading away. If we are prepared to allow that a landscape is fundamentally a thing that is read, a way of directing one's gaze, or of being prepared to listen, the slow obliteration of the landscape that had been delineated by village bells preceded the bell towers' falling into silence and into rack and ruin.

My aim here has been to write a history of this auditory landscape, to describe it in all its magnificence, and then to retrace the process by which it disintegrated. This disintegration, contrary to what one might expect, was not linked to any drop in the size of peals. Indeed, it was quite the reverse. Village bells were both louder and of superior quality in 1880 than they had been at the beginning of the July Monarchy. It was rather that their meaning seemed to fall away, modes of attention collapsed, the usages and rhetoric of the bells grew narrower so that, in short, a whole range of auditory messages were increasingly disqualified.

Many different factors may serve to account for this decline. During the second half of the nineteenth century rural communities found other symbols for their identity; the rise of the municipal, and the falling back on the religious message helped to undermine the prestige of the peals. The disenchantment of the world and the desacralizing of life and the environment somehow disqualified the act of listening to bells. Bells had gradually stopped being signs, portents, or talismans. Dechristianization caused the withdrawal within oneself enjoined by their calls to prayer to be forgotten. The intrusion of other rhetorics increasingly disqualified campanarian signals from functioning as a mode of communication. As the decades passed, authority was not so much expressed in auditory injunctions as in written texts. In the nineteenth century, posters, printed summonses, the dials of private clocks, and calendars gradually ensured the predominance of the visual. The function of the bell declined at the same time as the primacy of rumor was obliterated, and the leeway left to the interpretation of events was reduced. Campanarian history collapsed at the precise moment that illiteracy became a minority affair.

The act of listening to bells also suffered from the enrichment and renewal undergone by the panorama of sound. The steam engine and its puffing, with the internal combustion engine still to come, the electric motor, the siren in particular, and the new ways of sounding the alarm gradually deprived the bell of the seal of modernity that had initially been its own. In the twentieth century, amplifiers have wrested from the peal of bells its monopoly of solemnity. The honorific function of the bell has gradually been forgotten. The possibility of the people and the elites finding common ground in the shared evaluation of campanarian sonorities has lost its urgency and yielded to many other sorts of agreement. From this perspective it would be of interest to reflect on the way in which simple rhythms, being so much in favor nowadays, whether as the concrete rhythms of rock music or as the ponderous scansion of *country music*, are a means for bringing people together.

Discernible at present, although along new lines, is a yearning for the countryside, evident in the fashion for country cottages and holidays on the farm. This enthusiasm would be enhanced by a deeper understanding of the peasants of former times. It has seemed to me that careful analysis of the forgotten prestige of village bells might offer us something like Alice's burrow. The resurrection of a lost world is achieved by grasping whatever there is at its heart that today strikes us as most unusual.

NOTES

PREFACE. *Exploring a Vanished World*

1. This is an extract, as are the following quotations, from the delibera-
    tions of the municipal administration of the canton of Brienne.
    Archives départementales (henceforth A.D.), Aube L354. Emphases
    added both here and below.

2. Extract from the proceedings of Brienne municipal council, 6
    December 1830, A.D. Aube 2 o 774.

3. As it turned out, the remonstrations of parishioners led the council to
    alter its plans and set aside what was raised by the sale for an annuity,
    the interest from which would go to the parochial church council. This
    was designed to allow the municipal council to scrap the annual con-
    tribution that it had formerly made to the church council. The church
    council, a body composed of both clergy and laity, was responsible for
    administering funds allocated to the church and the parish.

4. Letter from the mayor of Brienne to the subprefect of Bar-sur-Aube,
    10 January 1833, A.D. Aube, v41.

310 PREFACE

5. Letter from the bishop of Troyes to the mayor of Brienne, 15 December 1832, quoted by the latter, A.D. Aube, v41.

6. Report by the subprefect of the arrondissement of Bar-sur-Aube to the prefect of the Aube, 2 February 1833, A.D. Aube, v41.

7. Ibid.

8. See p. 289.

9. I have described this episode in *Time, Desire, and Horror: Towards a History of the Senses*, translated by Jean Birrell (Cambridge: Polity Press, 1995), pp. 183–84.

10. I have tried to employ the terms that would have been used in this period by the various protagonists in the dispute.

11. See p. 171–72.

12. An observation made at the social and cultural history seminar, the University of Paris I, March 1983.

ONE. An Impossible Revolution in Sensibility

1. For discussion of the tension arising during the Revolution between the wish to protect private life by according due recognition to individual liberty and the threats or actual attacks that changes in family structure produced in the private sphere, see Lynn Hunt, in Philippe Ariès and Georges Duby, general editors, *A History of Private Life*, translated by Arthur Goldhammer, vol. 4, *From the Fires of Revolution to the Great War*, edited by Michelle Perrot, translated by Arthur Goldhammer (Cambridge, Mass.: Harvard University Press, 1990), pp. 13–45.

2. P. Ariès, *The Hour of Our Death*, translated by Helen Weaver (Harmondsworth, U.K.: Penguin, 1983).

3. Cf. A. Corbin, "A history and anthropology of the senses," in *Time, Desire, and Horror*, pp. 181–95.

4. See pp. 286–91.

5. In this regard, note the attention the young Monsignor Pie pays to the sensual aspect of bells. See, for example, Mgr. Pie, *Notice historique concernant la sonnerie ancienne et moderne de l'église cathédrale de Chartres* (Chartres, 1841).

6. Schmit, *Les Eglises gothiques*, as quoted by Mgr. Pie, *Notice historique*, p. 22.

7. Cf. J. D. Blavignac, *La Cloche: Etude sur son histoire et sur ses rapports avec la société aux différents âges* (Geneva, 1877), p. 24; Dr. Michel Brocard, *Etudes campanaires: Les cloches de la cathédrale Saint-Mammès de Langres* (Langres, 1924), p. 5; or, more recently, Antoine Trin, *Les Cloches du Cantal: Archéologie, histoire, folklore* (Aurillac:

Gerbert, 1954), p. 13. The harangue features in François Rabelais, *Vie très horrificque du grand Gargantua*, ch. 19 (Paris, 1955 [Pléiade edition]), pp. 80–81. *La Satyre Menippée* was a pamphlet written in 1594 by several hands and aimed at the Catholics. The *Gallia Christiana* is a compilation, dating from the beginning of the seventeenth century, of materials on Christian Gaul.

8. Compare pp. 290–91.

9. On the nonobservance of these norms in the Bray, see Dieudonné Dergny, *Les cloches du pays de Bray avec leurs dates, leurs noms, les inscriptions, leurs armoiries, leurs fondeurs* (Paris, 1865), 1:8.

10. Paluel-Marmont, *Cloches et carillons: Leur histoire, leur fabrication, leurs légendes* (Paris: Segep, 1953), p. 147.

11. Dr. Billon, *Campanologie: Etudes sur les cloches et les sonneries françaises et étrangères* (Caen, 1866), pp. 7–29.

12. Compare pp. 292–93.

13. Dr. Billon, *Campanologie*, pp. 12–14 and 77–89.

14. M. Brocard, *Études campanaires*, p. 5.

15. Dr. Billon, *Campanologie*, pp. 160–61. We should nonetheless bear in mind the approximate nature of such estimated weights because they often concern bells that have since disappeared.

16. In this regard, compare Trin, *Les Cloches du Cantal*, p. 13.

17. Dergny, *Les Cloches du pays de Bray*, 1:11-12 and 2:412.

18. Trin, *Les Cloches du Cantal*, p. 35. For this little region, our estimate would therefore be that parish bell towers possessed on average four bells. Studies of *biens nationaux*, though undertaken with other ends in mind, sometimes shed further light on this rich inheritance of bells.

19. This concerned the community of parishioners but, to judge by J.-P. Jessenne's observations regarding Artois, the former was often equated with the assembled inhabitants.

20. Compare the references given in my own book, *The Foul and the Fragrant: Odor and the Social Imagination* (London: Macmillan, 1996), *passim*.

21. V.E. Veuclin, *Quelques notes inédites sur les cloches de Bernay* (Bernay, 1888), pp. 9–12.

22. In the Haute-Maine such events still took place up until September 1793. The number of communes within this region where bells were blessed during the Revolution was as follows: four in 1790, one in 1791, five in 1792 and 1793. For the evidence consult Henry Roquet, *Les Vicissitudes des cloches ecclésiastiques et d'objets du culte dans le département de la Sarthe sous la Révolution et le Consulat (1790–1814)* (Le Mans: Jobidon, 1942).

23. From 1789 on, the contracts agreed upon with the caster were sup-

posed to be presented to the new administrations at both district and department level.

24. From Alphonse Aulard to Michel Vovelle, a large number of historians of the French Revolution have paid attention to bells. I draw the reader's attention to the valuable pages on this topic by Mona Ozouf, in *La Fête révolutionnaire* (Paris: Gallimard, 1988), pp. 374–387.

25. On all these points, and also regarding the following paragraph, compare the survey made by Paluel-Marmont, *Cloches et carillons*; Samuel Bour, *Études campanaires mosellanes* (Colmar: Alsatia, 1947), 1:45–46; Blavignac, *La Cloche*, pp. 46–47; Dr. Billon, *Campanologie*, p. 214; and D. Dergny, *Les Cloches*, 2:15.

26. Compare p. 195.

27. Jean Nanglard, *Les Cloches des églises du diocèse d'Angoulême* (Angoulême: Imprimerie ouvrière, 1922), p. 63. In his *Traité des cloches*, the abbot Jean-Baptiste Thiers lays great emphasis upon this form of punishment. Here is an example from the period of the French Revolution. On 4 May 1793, the General Council of the department of the Tarn gave orders that *all* the bells from communes where conscription had led to popular riots should be brought in to the *chef-lieu* of each district. See Count R. de Toulouse-Lautrec, *Les Cloches dans le Haut-Comminges* (Paris, 1863), p. 33.

28. From the plethora of studies on the earliest phase of campanarian policy during the Revolution, I would single out a highly precise, although old article by L.A. Hustin, "Le sort des cloches," in *Bulletin de la Société historique du Raincy* (October 1924). This study rests upon a very careful reading of the *Archives parlementaires*, and it brings out the tentative nature of the policies adopted in this sphere during the early months of the Revolution. It is worth noting that, in January 1791, the decision had been made to sell the bells together with the other national property "*de première origine.*" Condorcet, Fourcroy, and Tillet were among the experts consulted at this stage. Various other customs were described in these debates, notably the fabrication of mortars, pestles, taps, and pulleys. Regarding this policy, see also Bour, *Études campanaires*, ch. 3, "La Révolution française et son oeuvre," 1:15ff.

29. Owing to the mixture of metal in the bells, which were made both of yellow and red copper, pieces to the value of five *sols*, two *liards*, and one *liard* were struck in August 1792 and, subsequently, pieces to the value of one *décime*, five *centimes*, and one *centime*. The bells therefore played a by no means negligible part in the diffusion of this "people's money," as Bernard Traimond has dubbed it, in "Ethnologie historique des pratiques monétaires dans les Landes de Gascogne"

(thesis, University of Paris I, 1992), which was embraced in some
country areas by those who, up until then, had largely practiced barter
and only in exceptional circumstances used gold or silver coin,
regarding them as the attributes of property owners and merchants.

30.   Bour, *Études campanaires*, 1:17. In the district of Bernay the taking
down of bells was likewise carried out at high speed. In the month of
July alone, sixty-one bells were sent to the copper foundry of
Romilly-sur-Andelle (Eure). Such an attitude seems to have been
somewhat exceptional (see Philippe Duval, "La Révolution et la dis-
persion du mobilier des communautés religieuses de l'Eure," in *A travers la Haute-Normandie en Révolution 1789–1800*, Comité régional
d'histoire de la Révolution française, 1992, p. 239). In the district of
Amiens, all such operations were carried out between 19 September
1791 and 23 May 1792, during which sixty-one bells were taken down.
Removal was easy enough in suppressed churches since the entrances
were then under seal, and in the monasteries, which the monks had all
abandoned. Conversely, the exercise must have been postponed in the
nunneries, which were still inhabited. There, the taking down of bells
can only have occurred after the end of May 1792. (René Vaillant,
"Archives campanaires: Le sort des cloches d'Amiens pendant la
Révolution," in *Bulletin de la Société des antiquaires de Picardie*,
January-March 1985, pp. 49–64).

31.   Abbot Barraud, *Notice sur les cloches* (Caen, 1844), pp. 11-12.

32.   As far as the bell ropes were concerned, the administration made no
mention of them until 1794.

33.   Joseph Berthelé, H. Jadart, P. Gosset, *Enquêtes campanaires rémoises*
(Rheims, 1905), p. 27; Bours, *Études campanaires mosellanes*, 1:19; and
Vaillant, "Archives campanaires," p. 59.

34.   The register of secular marriages was kept at Moncé-en-Belin town
hall. Father Lelardeux gave his account of this episode as early as 6
January 1792, and it is quoted by Roquet, in *Les Vicissitudes des
cloches ecclésiastiques*, pp. 14–16.

35.   Compare Roger Caillois, *L'Homme et le sacré* (Paris: Gallimard,
1950), p. 62. If one wished to assess the extent to which people were
rallying to the new ideas, the mapping of attitudes toward the requisitioning of bells would not prove especially rewarding. Given
the essentially ambivalent nature of what was at stake, such pointers would be none too reliable. One could easily be deeply attached
to a bell while regarding it as a potential vehicle for the secularization of spatial and temporal markers and, likewise, as the voice of
municipal authority.

36.   Consider, however, the examples that I cite later, p. 19. It goes with-

out saying that in this regard there is a great difference between bells and consecrated vessels, which constituted the treasure of a church. Compare, as an example, the manner in which the inhabitants of Saint-Georges-de-Rouelley (Manche) disguised their consecrated vessels on 27 February 1791, A.N. F^{19} 246.

37. Bour, *Études campanaires mosellanes*, 1:27.

38. Compare the observations, although they are of a more general kind, made by Michel Vovelle, in *La Révolution contre l'église, de la raison à l'être suprême* (Paris: Editions Complexe, 1988), pp. 259–261.

39. Compare Vaillant, "Archives campanaires," pp. 51–53.

40. In the ensuing months there were more and more such sacrifices. The general council for the department of the Sarthe decreed on 21 July that communes should take down their bells and recast the metal as cannons (Roquet, *Les Vicissitudes des cloches* , p. 27).

41. Quoted by Dergny, *Les cloches du pays de Bray*, 1:35.

42. Vovelle, *La Révolution contre l'église*, p. 96.

43. Quoted by Vovelle, *La Révolution contre l'église*, p. 99.

44. Vovelle, *La Révolution contre l'église*, pp. 53 and 88. As early as 1922, Jean Nanglard had noted that in the Charente there was "often a readiness to sacrifice consecrated vessels and reliquiaries," but not bells (Nanglard, *Les cloches*, p.30).

45. Elizabeth Liris, *"Vandalisme et régénération dans la mission de Fouché à l'automne 93,"* in *Révolution française et vandalisme révolutionnaire* (Paris: Universitas, 1992), p. 222. Regarding Loudéac, A.D. Côtes-du-Nord, 15L14, quoted by Yves Tripier, in "Vandalisme révolutionnaire en Bretagne ou imposition par le pouvoir républicain d'une nouvelle culture? (1793–1795)," in *Révolution et vandalisme*, p. 149. In the Ardèche the taking down of the bells was carried out swiftly. Compare Jean-Louis Issartel, *"Bourg-Saint-Andéol, cité carrefour et centre révolutionnaire dans la moyenne vallée du Rhône"* (thesis, University of Paris I, 1991).

46. Bour, *Études campanaires mosellanes*, 1:27, and, regarding Échallon, Trenard, "Le vandalisme révolutionnaire dans les pays de l'Ain," in *Révolution et vandalisme*, p. 256.

47. Roquet, *Les vicissitudes des cloches*, pp. 18–20.

48. Regarding Bernay, see Veuclin, *Quelques notes inédites*, p. 18; regarding Lisieux, see Billon, *Campanologie*, pp. 84–86.

49. Once again, I do not wish to address the question here as to whether dechristianization was then authoritarian or spontaneous. Yet since my argument directly concerns village bells, I find myself in agreement with those historians who, from Albert Mathiez to Richard Cobb, have been led to conclude that in such milieus, in the vast

majority of cases, dechristianization was imposed from outside by
members of urban *sociétés populaires.*

50. Alain Corbin, *The Village of Cannibals: Rage and Murder in France
(1870),* translated by Arthur Goldhammer (Cambridge, Mass.:
Harvard University Press), 1992.

51. The quotations that follow are drawn from V.E. Veuclin, *Les Grands
événements au village sous l'Ancien Régime: La fonte des cloches*
(Bernay, 1888), pp. 41–43.

52. Nanglard, *Les Cloches, passim,* and, for the Aisne, Yves Dreux,
"Religion et révolution en Picardie et dans le district de Saint-
Quentin" (master's thesis, University of Paris I, 1985), p. 135.

53. Vaillant, *"Archives campanaires,"* p. 63.

54. Berthelé et al., *Enquêtes campanaires rémoises*, pp. 30–31.

55. Roquet, *Les Vicissitudes des cloches*, p. 28.

56. Dreux, *Religion et révolution*, and, for Bourg-Saint-Andéol, Issartel,
Bourg-Saint-Andéol, p. 474.

57. In other words, in the thick of the debate surrounding Article 101 of
the law of 1884 (compare pp. 240–43). Abbot L. Berthout, priest of
Yvrandes, *Les Cloches imprenables: Episode de la Révolution à Saint-
Cornier-des-Landes (Orne 1793–1794)* (Paris, 1887). The quotations
that follow are also drawn from Bethout, pp. 5, 9, and 25.

58. Trin, *Les Cloches du Cantal*, p. 36.

59. For all these details regarding the Moselle, consult Bour, *Études campanaires mosellanes*, 1:28. Regarding the Swiss border, see Brocard,
Études campanaires, p. 24.

60. Henri Brugière and Joseph Berthelé, *Exploration campanaire du
Périgord* (Périgueux, 1907), p. 271.

61. Veuclin, *Les Grands événements*, p. 41.

62. Trin, *Les Cloches du Cantal*, pp. 35–36.

63. Burial was also a tactic adopted when Vendéens were thought to be
approaching, and likewise out of fear that there might be an "abduction." In December 1793, on the eve of the capture of Le Mans by the
insurgents, a number of the district's bells were thrown into a well,
only to be recovered from it later and sent to Paris in casks. Roquet,
Les vicissitudes des cloches, p. 31.

64. Brocard, *Etudes campanaires*, p. 24.

65. Rodolphe Reuss, *La Constitution civile du clergé et la crise religieuse en
Alsace (1790–1795)* (Paris: Istra, 1922), 2:249.

66. Alexandre Bande, *Déchristianisation et résistance populaire en Alsace
pendant l'an II* (master's dissertation, University of Paris I, 1987), p. 61.

67. Jean-Claude Meyer, *La Vie religieuse en Haute-Garonne sous la
Révolution (1789–1801)* (Toulouse, 1982), p. 396.

68. These were the two main stores from which bells to be used subsequently in public buildings were withdrawn. Thus, the bell of Saint-
Germain-l'Auxerrois, which had rung on St. Bartholomew's Day,
was allocated, at Marie-Joseph Chénier's request, to the Théatre de la
Nation, to be used as a stage prop.

69. Between January and August 1792, one hundred and two of them
were sent to the mint in Lille; the others were conveyed to Épernay.
Vaillant, "Archives campanaires," p. 60.

70. Berthelé et al., *Enquêtes campanaires rémoises*, p. 26.

71. One hundred and forty two of them were subsequently dispatched to
Paris or Metz, and ninety-nine to Besançon. Brocard, *Études campanaires*, pp. 24–25.

72. Trin, *Les Cloches du Cantal*, pp. 34–35.

73. J. Déchelette, *Inscriptions campanaires de l'arrondissement de Roanne*
(Montbrison, 1893), p. 34.

74. The bells from the district of Amiens were melted down in the Saint-
Maurice district; those from the district of Reims were no longer dispatched toward Paris, but toward Metz. From November onward, the
bells from the district of Roanne were sent to Le Creusot.

75. Those bells still not melted down on the eve of the signing of the
Concordat were sold off to scrap iron merchants, who scattered them
far and wide. On 23 Nivôse Year VI (12 January 1798), a decree from
the Directory had ordered the sale of requisitioned bells, and the
Council of State, on 25 Brumaire Year IX (16 November 1800), had
ruled in favor of this measure. Cf. Bour, *Études campanaires mosellanes*, 1:23. Specialists in campanarian history have tried to draw up a
balance sheet, each covering their chosen region, for the requisitions.
Unfortunately, in each case the calculations follow a different
method, and it is therefore not possible to use the results to produce a
composite picture. For example, 129,675 pounds of bell metal were
ready to be melted down in the district of Chauny (Aisne) alone, by
the end of the month of Brumaire Year II (20 November 1793) (cf.
Dreux, *Religion et révolution*, p. 137). Between October 1791 and 27
January 1792—in a little over three months—the department of the
Meuse sent 60,376 pounds of bronze to the Mint in Metz. C. Aimond,
*Histoire religieuse de la Révolution dans le département de la Meuse et le
diocèse de Verdun (1789–1802)* (Paris: De Gigord, 1949), p. 204.

76. Notably by Blavignac, *La Cloche*, p. 418 and, in the following century,
by Trin, *Les Cloches du Cantal*, p. 34.

77. This is, for instance, what Jean Nanglard's calculations regarding the
bells of Charente suggest (*Les Cloches*, pp. 31ff). Thus, Angoulême had
thirty-four bells on the eve of the Revolution but in 1802 had just four.

78. Vovelle, *La Révolution contre l'église*, p. 240.

79. Louis Pérouas and Paul d'Hollander, *La Révolution française, une rupture dans le christianisme? Le cas du Limousin (1775–1822)* (Les Monédières: 1988), p. 183.

80. On Albitte, see François Burckard, "Six destins," in *A travers la Haute-Normandie*, pp. 414–17; Vovelle, *La Révolution contre l'église*, pp. 81–82. More particularly, Philippe Boutry provides an exhaustive list of studies devoted to Antoine-Louis Albitte, and especially to the "hundred days" spent by him in the department of the Ain (22 January–30 April 1794). More broadly, he offers a valuable bibliographical survey on revolutionary "vandalism." "Le clocher," in P. Nora, ed., *Les Lieux de Mémoire*, vol. 3, "Les France," pt. 2, "Traditions" (Paris: Gallimard, 1992), pp. 87–88. Let me also emphasize the intrinsic interest of a book by Serge Bianchi, *La Révolution culturelle de l'an II: élites et peuple (1789–1799)* (Paris: Aubier, 1982).

81. Once again, this is something of an oversimplification. Albitte was convinced that he had gotten rid of all the bell towers in this department. In fact, both here and in the Savoie, he very often managed to do no more than demolish the towers of deconsecrated chapels. In Spring 1794 he was compelled, moreover, to temper his policy to check the massive emigration in the direction of Piedmont. Nevertheless, according to Philippe Boutry, Albitte had some magnificent Romanesque towers razed. "Le clocher," p. 78.

82. Maurice Dommanget, *La Déchristianisation à Beauvais et dans l'Oise (1790–1801)* (Besançon: Millot, 1918), p. 41.

83. R. Reuss, *La Constitution civile du clergé*, 2:293–295.

84. Meyer, *La Vie religieuse en Haute-Garonne*, p. 294.

85. A.D. Aube, L1625.

86. See pp. 183–89.

87. See Maurice Agulhon, ed., *Les Maires du Consulat à nos jours* (Paris: Publications de la Sorbonne, 1986), pp. 70–71.

88. I have in mind here the shortcomings of the procedure whereby maps are superimposed in order to identify correlations.

89. Quoted by Mona Ozouf, in *La Fête révolutionnaire*, p. 379. With this in mind, I have myself explored series C and F^{19} of the Archives nationales as well as series V and, in part, series L of the Archives of the fourteen departments in my sample. One should note that, through her analysis of series F^1 cIII of the Archives nationales, Mona Ozouf came to the same conclusion. In particular, she observed that there were many incidents involving bells in the Doubs.

90. Olivier Planchon, *La Déchristianisation post-thermidorienne dans le*

département du Cher (1794–1799) (master's thesis, University of Paris I, 1985), p. 176.

91. Dergny, *Les Cloches du pays de Bray*, 1:36.

92. A.D. Eure, 53VI.

93. Ferdinand Saurel, *Histoire religieuse du département de l'Hérault pendant la Révolution* (Paris, 1896), 3:296, and 4:43.

94. Trin, *Les Cloches du Cantal*, p. 37.

95. On all these points, see Pérouas et al., *La Révolution française*, pp. 257–258.

96. Meyer, *La Vie religieuse en Haute-Garonne*, pp. 394–396, pp. 397–398, and p. 518. In this region a refusal to tolerate the silencing of the bells symbolized and crystallized a broader refusal—indeed a sort of dissidence that found expression, in particular, in a wave of desertions. On the notion of dissidence and the various forms it may take, see Jean-François Soulet, "Dissidence et histoire," in *Revue historique*, no. 2 (1987) pp. 429–41.

97. Bour, *Études campanaires mosellanes*, 1:25.

98. A.D. Aube, L1625, and A.D. Eure, 53VI.

99. A.N. F^{19} 458, Orne.

100. Roquet, *Les Vicissitudes des cloches*, pp. 33–34.

101. Guy Lemarchand, "La Seine-Inférieure: un département sous le Directoire au calme relatif," in *A travers la Haute-Normandie*, p. 353.

102. Planchon, *La Déchristianisation post-thermidorienne* , p. 178.

103. Ibid, 183.

104. A.N. F^{19} 462, Hautes-Pyrénées.

105. A.N. F^{19} 405, Ariège.

106. Aimond, *Histoire religieuse de la Révolution*, p. 394, and Planchon, *La Déchristianisation post-thermidorienne*, pp. 184–185.

107. Register of decrees for the department of the Maine-et-Loire, public session of 2 Pluviôse Year IV (22 January 1796), A.N. F^{19} 445. A later decree, dated 2 Germinal Year V (22 March 1797), endorsed the severity of the measure.

108. On all these points, see file A.N. F^{19} 447.

109. A.N. F^{19} 467, Saône-et-Loire.

110. A.N. F^{19} 430, Hérault.

111. This is how it was in Finistère. From what the bishop said, since here the custom of ringing was followed almost everywhere (5 Frimaire Year VI, 25 November 1797), counterrevolutionaries took a malicious pleasure in denouncing and bringing about the condemnation of patriot priests (with regard to the proceedings against five such men). A.N. F^{19} 425, Finistère.

112. A.N. F^{19} 414, Charente.

113. AN. F^{19} 451, Meurthe.

114. Camille Jordan, "Rapport sur la police des cultes," Council of the
      Five Hundred, session of 29 Prairial Year V (17 June 1797). In
      Discours de Camille Jordan (Paris, 1826), pp. 37, 39, 40 and 41. "Only
      signs speak to the people," declared Jordan (p. 43), who Gerando tells
      us was very familiar with Locke's writings before he was even twenty
      years old. Mona Ozouf, in *La Fête révolutionnaire*, p. 375, has stressed
      the importance of the notion of the sign in these debates. Ballanche,
      in the panegyric to Camille Jordan delivered on 27 August 1823,
      recalled the immense popularity the orator won himself through this
      speech.

115. A.N. F^{19} 442, Lot, and Planchon, *La Déchristianisation*, p. 180.

116. Commissioner for the Directory with the department of the Seine-et-
      Marne (7 Vendémiaire Year VI / 28 September 1797), A.N. F^{19} 473,
      Seine-et-Marne.

117. A.N. F^{19} 462, Hautes-Pyrénées.

118. Here is a late example of such firmness. On 27 Nivôse Year IX (17
      January 1801), the parish priest of Villespassans (Hérault) was sen-
      tenced to a year's imprisonment for having used the bells. The sen-
      tence was posted up "in a large format poster" in all the communes
      of a department "in which the bells were still going." There seems
      to have been a large number of infractions in the Hérault. The pre-
      fect, with the same firmness as before, issued a circular on 21 Prairial
      Year X (10 June 1802); he was encouraged in this regard by Portalis,
      who asked (on 28 June) that priests abstain from ringing until "the
      establishment of the episcopal seat." Saurel, *Histoire religieuse*, 4:41
      and 4:73.

119. A.N. F^{19} 463, Pyrénées-Orientales.

120. A.N. F^{19} 442, Lot.

121. Roquet, *Les Vicissitudes des cloches*, p. 42, and then A.D. Aube, L1625
      and L354.

122. Maurice Gobillon, *Le Blésois entre la fin de l'Ancien Régime et le second
      Empire* (thesis for the doctorat d'État, University of Paris X-
      Nanterre, 1992), 2:453; letter from the commissioner attached to the
      administration of Onzain canton (11 May 1800).

123. Minister for general police to the prefect of the Tarn (23 Floréal Year
      IX / 13 May 1801). A.D. Tarn, 1v8, and letter from the prefect of the
      Eure-et-Loir to the mayors of the same department (25 Floréal Year
      IX / 15 May 1801), A.D. Eure-et-Loir, v8. The bells were rung in La
      Chaussée, in particular, and in the neighboring communes.

124. A.D. Ille-et-Vilaine, 1v12. Complaint of 10 Floréal Year VIII (30
      April 1800).

125. A.D. Eure, 58VI.

126. Circular from the subprefect of the arrondissement of Argentan to the mayors, 4 Messidor Year VIII (23 June 1800). A.D. Orne, 9VI. And the subprefect of Domfront to the prefect, 13 Ventôse Year IX (4 March 1801), ibid.

127. Subprefect (Dinan) to the prefect, 2 Nivôse Year IX (23 December 1800). A.D. Côtes-du-Nord, v31.

128. An act that serves yet again to underline the crucial importance of having the key in one's possession. Cf. pp. 240–43.

129. A.D. Orne, 9VI.

130. In this regard there is a significant passage in Blavignac, *La Cloche*, p. 35.

131. On this text see p. 288.

132. The licit use of bells implied that a bishop had rejoined his diocese. One should nevertheless note that this solemn installation was generally carried out to the sound of bells. This was the case in, for example, Grenoble, on 30 October 1802. Jean Godel, *La Reconstruction concordataire dans le diocèse de Grenoble après la Révolution (1802–1809)* (Grenoble 1968), p. 95. This was also the case in Agen and the Lot-et-Garonne on 3 Messidor Year X (22 June 1802). Letter from the prefect to Portalis, A.N. F 5659.

133. A.N. F^{19} 5659. Portalis was then the councillor of state responsible for all matters having to do with public worship.

134. Citizen Moulinneuf, former notary, to the prefect of the Eure-et-Loir, 12 Prairial Year XI (1 June 1803). A.D. Eure-et-Loir, v8.

135. Letter from the mayor of Montchevrel to the prefect, 12 Germinal Year XI (2 April 1803), A.D. Orne, 9VI.

136. A.D. Ille-et-Vilaine, 1V2.

137. Two days later, the bishop of Saint-Brieuc, while waiting for a concerted regulation to be signed, wrote to the prefect informing him of his decision to ring on Saint Cecilia's Day at nine o'clock, nine-thirty, and ten o'clock to give pleasure to the inhabitants. I am struck here both by the evidence for a collective expression of the desire for bell ringing and by the prelate's concern to abide by administrative conventions. A.D. Côtes-du-Nord, v31. Letter from the bishop of Saint-Brieuc to the prefect, 28 Brumaire Year XI (19 November 1802).

138. The references are as follows: Côtes-du-Nord, A.N. F^{19} 4375, Sarthe, in Roquet, *Les Vicissitudes des cloches*; Manche (14 Prairial Year XI / 3 June 1803), A.N. F^{19} 4376; Eure (28 Messidor Year X / 17 July 1802), A.D. Eure, 53VI; Loir-et-Cher (3 Brumaire Year XI / 25 October 1802 and 24 Frimaire Year XI / 15 December 1802), in Gobillon, *Le Blésois*; Aube (16 Prairial Year X / 5 June 1802) and Seine-et-Oise (17 Messidor Year X / 6 July 1802), A.D. Aube, v34; Pas-de-Calais, A.N.

F^{19} 4375; Hautes-Alpes (27 Floréal Year XI / 17 May 1803), A.N. F^{19} 402; Drôme, A.N. F 4375; Hérault (27 Frimaire Year XI / 18 December 1802), in Saurel, *Histoire religieuse*, 4:122–123 (regulation that was modified without joint agreement, it seems, through the episcopal ordinance of 27 February 1806); Hautes-Pyrénées and diocese of Bayonne (27 Pluviôse Year XI / 16 February 1803), A.N. F^{19} 462; Tarn (10 and 13 Fructidor Year XII / 27–31 August 1804), A.D. Tarn, 1v8.

139. Prefect of the Eure, circular to the mayors, 18 Ventôse Year XI (9 March 1803), A.D. Eure, 53v1.

140. Ibid., together with the letter from the prefect of the Eure to the bishop of Évreux, 13 Germinal Year XII (3 April 1804).

141. A.N. F^{19} 4376, Pas-de-Calais.

142. In this regard see Thierry Gasnier, "Le local," in Nora, ed., *Les lieux de mémoire*, vol. 3, Les France, vol. 2, Traditions, pp. 463–525.

143. As an example, in the Gironde and the Landes (Armand Fourcade, *De la mise en valeur des landes de Gascogne*, quoted by Bernard Traimond, *Ethnologie historique*, pp. 294–295), the municipal expenses incurred between 1854 and 1877 through the building of churches and presbyteries (3 million francs) far outweighed those incurred by the construction of town halls and schools (1.6 million francs), and the difference would assuredly have been still more stark during the first half of the century. It is worth noting evidence of this sort, which is all too often neglected. Regarding the financial efforts made by the parishioners, the communes, and the state, see also the information furnished by Philippe Boutry in the works referred to in n. 152, and by Claude Langlois, *Le Diocèse de Vannes au XIXe siècle (1800–1830)* (Paris: Klincksieck, 1974), pp. 361–362. This latter notes "feverish rebuilding." He emphasizes the part played by the prefects, and also the direct involvement of the clergy. Michel Lagrée likewise emphasizes the financial efforts made on behalf of the churches, in *Mentalités, religion et histoire en Haute-Bretagne au XIXe siècle* (Paris: Klincksieck, 1977), pp. 277–278). The same is true of Yves-Marie Hilaire in relation to the diocese of Arras in *Une chrétienté au XIXe siècle? La vie religieuse des populations du diocèse d'Arras (1840–1914)*, pp. 66–67 and p. 374ff. The author is at particular pains to emphasize the efforts made between 1850 and 1880, a period that he regards as the "heyday of the country priests," p. 306. Nadine-Josette Chaline refers to a church-building movement on a massive scale in Normandy, from the beginning of the Second Empire to the end of the century, in *Des catholiques normands sous la Troisième République: Crises, Combats, Renouveaux* (Roanne: Horvath, 1985), p. 33.

144. In a letter dated 17 Fructidor Year XIII (4 September 1805), Portalis set out the principles informing such decisions.

145. See pp. 48–50.

146. There is a thick file concerned with this procedure in A.N. F^{19} 4373.

147. Brocard, *Études campanaires*, p. 28.

148. Cf. A.D. Finistère, 1v232.

149. Under the Second Empire this type of request was more favorably received.

150. See p. 19 and the references given on pp. 391–93.

151. Déchelette, *Inscriptions campanaires*, pp. 5–33.

152. Philippe Boutry, "Les mutations du paysage paroissial, reconstructions d'églises et translations de cimetières dans les campagnes de l'Ain au XIXe siècle," in *Ethnologie française*, t. 14 (1985), no. 1, pp. 7–35. The author identifies periods in which the rebuilding of clock towers was particularly intense. The first (1800–1820) was designed to compensate for the destruction ordered by Albitte while the second (1850–1880) reflected a wish to upgrade such edifices. See also Philippe Boutry, *Prêtres et paroisses au pays du curé d'Ars*, part 1, "Modernité paroissiale" (Paris: Editions du cerf, 1986), pp. 17–185.

153. There is a correlation in the nineteenth century between involvement in campanarian matters and levels of recruitment to the clergy. In this regard see Claude Langlois, "Permanences, renouveau et affrontements (1830–1880)," in François Lebrun, ed., *Histoire des catholiques en France*, (Toulouse: Privat, 1980), pp. 321–406.

154. Closer inspection of the diagrams reveals brief interruptions in campanarian activity in 1830 and 1831, in 1848 and 1849, and again in 1870 and 1871, which is precisely what one would expect. Within the same department the distribution of bells proves often to have been very uneven; this is the case in 1922 with, for example, the 675 bells hung in the 450 churches and chapels of the Charente (Nanglard, *Les Cloches*, *passim*). Here there is no discernible correlation between density of bells, degree of religious fervor, or wealth of communities. The contrasts are primarily explicable in terms of history, and, more precisely, in terms of the levels of destruction inflicted in the fifteenth and sixteenth centuries, and at the end of the eighteenth century. The latter account for the shortage of bells in the south of the department, which had been harder hit during such episodes.

155. Nanglard, *Les Cloches*, p. 25.

156. Bour, *Études campanaires mosellanes*, 1:31–32.

TWO. The "Abductors of Bells"

1. This was the term, with its obvious sexual connotations, used by the victims whose complaints have been preserved in the archives.

2. We should not lose sight of the fact that the process of turning something into a part of one's patrimony was governed by different logics in antiquarian milieux and in rural communities.

3. François Ploux, "Rixes intervillageoises en Quercy (1815–1880)," in *Ethnologie française* t. 21 (1991), no. 3, pp. 269–276.

4. As well as the taking down of crucifixes and the removal of the statues of saints, which were regarded as protectors of the community / communities. In the Lonlay-l'Abbaye affair, described in the preface, the conflict over the use of bells was preceded by a crisis of this type. The parish priest, intent on returning the church to its Gothic purity, had removed the statues of the twelve apostles, which were installed in the nave. Each and every one of these statues, however, had been offered at various dates to the church by one of the main hamlets in the parish. Consequently, this removal, or "abduction," was much resented, and left the "country folk" feeling more than somewhat hostile toward the priest.

5. On the extreme importance of this approach to the resolution of conflicts in the nineteenth-century countryside, see François Ploux, "L'arrangement dans les campagnes du Haut-Quercy (1815–1850)," in *Histoire de la Justice*, no. 5 (1992), pp. 95–117.

6. An interlocking of senses of belonging that reflected, often enough, the multifariousness of the social uses of time.

7. Henri Brugière and Joseph Berthelé identified twenty-one "transferred" bells in the department of the Dordogne alone, but they were not able to take into account all those that had been recast between the Revolution and the date of their inquiry. To arrive at an accurate estimate of the extent of such transfers, one should also take the sale and purchase of secondhand bells into account. We will thus never be in a position to make a tally of the transfers carried out across the entire territory. Existing studies do nevertheless show that their number exceeds that of the conflicts they caused, which leads one to suppose that in a great many cases the feeling of being deprived was surmounted, no matter what residue of bitterness was left.

8. Report addressed to the First Consul, 27 Ventôse Year XI (18 March 1803), A.N. F[19] 4373.

9. Nanglard, *Les Cloches*, p. 91.

10. Dergny, *Les Cloches du pays de Bray*, 1:271.

11. For a bibliography with particular reference to the works of Colin

Lucas, cf. A. Corbin, *The Village of Cannibals* (Cambridge: Polity Press, 1992), p. 82, p. 143:n48.

12. Prefect of the Deux-Sèvres to the minister of the interior (30 September 1819), A.N. F^{19} 4373.

13. Subprefect of the arrondissement of Mauriac to the prefect of the Cantal (13 January 1815), A.D. Cantal, IV126.

14. A.N. F^{19} 4373.

15. Ibid.

16. Ibid.

17. *Ministre des Cultes* to the prefect of the Indre (16 May 1825), A.N. F^{19} 4373.

18. A.D. Ille-et-Vilaine, IV684.

19. A.N. F^{19} 4373.

20. This was exceptional, however, for restitutions were quite common in this department. A.D. Gers, V841.

21. The file on this affair may be found in A.N. F^{19} 4373.

22. There was no longer a mayor or a parish priest in Herbilly.

23. Letter of the bishop of Blois to the *ministre des Cultes*, 20 August 1851. A.N. F^{19} 4373.

24. Parochial church council to the *ministre des Cultes*, 21 March 1852, ibid.

25. According to Marcel Launay, in *Le Bon Prêtre: Le clergé rural au XIXe siècle* (Paris: Aubier, 1986), pp. 114ff, there were 34,868 cures at the end of the Old Regime. Around 27,000 (cures in the *chef-lieu* of a canton and succursals in the majority of other communes) were reestablished at the time of the Concordat. At the end of the First Empire there were 2,855 cures and 26,000 succursals (giving a total of 28,855). Subsequently, several thousand additional parishes were created. In 1848 there existed 3,350 cures and around 29,000 succursals (giving a total of 32,350). At the end of the Second Empire, the number of parishes was 34,031. Many communes during this period thus did not have the status of parishes. Pierre Pierrard presents virtually identical data, save that he calculates there were 40,000 parishes in 1793, in *La Vie quotidienne du prêtre français au XIXe siècle (1801–1905)* (Paris: Hachette, 1986), p. 66. As for Philippe Boutry ("Le clocher," p. 65), he posits 36,000 parishes and 5,500 dependencies in 1789, with 29,000 parishes in 1814. I would further note that an ordinance of 28 March 1820 authorized the vestries of succursals established since the general circumscription of parishes of 28 August 1808, or that would be at some future date, to set about reclaiming property that formerly belonged to their church. An ordinance of 8 August 1842 recognized bells as property liable to be handed back. These measures likewise engendered conflicts.

26. It is also worth consulting Maurice Halbwachs, *Les Cadres sociaux de la mémoire*, (Paris: Alcan, 1925).

27. This manner of abandoning a cemetery differed markedly from the practice, followed during this period in many rural communes, of merely moving it.

28. A.N. F^{19} 4373, together with the letter from the mayor of Monclar to the subprefect of the arrondissement of Condom.

29. Compare the detailed observations made by Jean Godel on this subject, in *La Reconstruction concordataire dans le diocèse de Grenoble après la Révolution (1802–1809)* (Grenoble, 1968), pp.133 and 135. Philippe Boutry ("Le clocher," p. 68) has also analyzed "the complaints of orphaned communities." I refer the reader to this text, which was published after the present chapter had been drafted. In Boutry's view, it was the urgency of death that made the want of a priest in residence particularly tragic. Michel Lagrée finds that a *conscience collective* of this order was most often met with in small communes, and that the bitterness was particularly pronounced among dispossessed members of parochial church councils, in *Mentalités, religion et histoire en Haute-Bretagne au XIXe siècle* (Paris: Klincksieck, 1977), p. 262. Charles Ledré and Philippe Papet have likewise remarked on the suffering of communities that lost "their liturgical independence" and often found that they did not even have any prospect of a future "parochial existence." Ledré, *Le Cardinal Cambacérès: La réorganisation d'un diocèse français, au lendemain de la Révolution* (Paris: Plon, 1943), pp. 243ff, p. 277; Papet, *Cléricaux et anticléricaux dans l'arrondissement de Senlis (1870–1914)* (thesis for the University of Paris iv, 1992), pp. 51ff.

30. Letter from the mayor of Saint-Christophe to the prefect (19 May 1819), A.D. Ille-et-Vilaine, iv15.

31. Prefect of the Seine-Inférieure to the *ministre des Cultes* (1 April 1819), A.N. F^{19} 4373.

32. Report by the prefect of the Eure-et-Loir (8 October 1821), A.N. F^{19} 4373.

33. Letter from the former mayor of Cuigny to the minister of the interior (22 January 1822), A.N. F^{19} 4373.

34. Letter of the prefect of the Eure to the *ministre de l'Intérieur et des Cultes* (14 March 1831), A.N. F^{19} 4373.

35. Subprefect of the arrondissement of Louviers to the prefect of the Eure (28 March 1831), ibid.

36. Petition of the inhabitants of Neuville to the *ministre des Cultes* (31 January 1831), A.N. F^{19} 4373.

37. Letter of the prefect of the Eure to the *ministre des Cultes* (29 March 1831), ibid.

38.   There are numerous documents concerning this conflict in the *Archives départementales* of the Gers (v841) and in the *Archives nationales.*

39.   Report of the subprefect of the arrondissement of Condom (11 March 1831), A.N. F[19] 4373.

40.   A.D. Gers, v841.

41.   There seems to have been a particularly large number of conflicts in the Limousin between suppressed parishes and those to which they had been linked. Louis Perouas and Paul d'Hollander, while insisting that they represented no more than a sample, mention nine such conflicts that involved some eighteen communities, in *La Révolution française, une rupture dans le christianisme? Le cas du Limousin (1775–1822)* (Les Monédières, 1988), p. 336.

42.   Deliberations of the parochial church council of Lavignac (2 March 1849), A.N. F[19] 4373.

43.   Ibid.

44.   Letter of the bishop of Limoges to the prefect of the Haute-Vienne (12 January 1849), ibid.

45.   *Letter of the ministre des Cultes* to the prefect of the Haute-Vienne (19 May 1849), ibid.

46.   A.D. Eure-et-Loir, v8.

47.   *Ministre de l'Instruction publique et des Cultes*, Note on the Goupillières affair (28 September 1858), A.N. F[19] 4373.

48.   Deliberations of Aize municipal council (27 May 1868), ibid, although in fact the deed was done in 1809.

49.   It is worth noting that the precise season had left a trace in people's memories.

50.   Report of the bishop of Châteauroux (27 May 1872), ibid. On the policies adopted in this sphere in the department of the Indre during the First Empire, see A.N. F[19] 432.

51.   This type of inquiry bears out this observation, which I had made before during an oral history project carried out in 1967, in Alain Corbin, *Prélude au Front populaire: Contribution à l'histoire de l'opinion publique dans le département de la Haute-Vienne* (thèse de troisième cycle, Poitiers 1968), p. 6.

52.   Opinion of the Minister for Trade and Public Works, M. d'Argout (30 May 1831), A.N. F[19] 4373.

53.   *Ministre de l'Instruction publique et des Cultes,* ibid.

54.   Letter quoted in n52. After the failure of the plan for a rural code in 1807, the time came, at the dawn of the July Monarchy, for recording all the customary usages that shaped everyday life and socioeconomic relations in rural communities. For those seeking to understand the

nineteenth-century countryside, the attention paid, no matter how condescendingly, to another level of analysis to that upon which the members of the government were situated, constitutes a historical fact of some significance. It remains the case , paradoxically enough, that the recording of what up until then had been universally agreed upon—of what in some sense went without saying—gave rise to a classification, written and arbitrary, into the licit and the illicit, and thereby led to the dismantling over the longer term of systems of custom. As far as bell ringing was concerned, such a process did occur, as we shall see. The surveying and recording of local usages finally enabled regulations to be drafted and, under cover of apparent concessions to the locality, uniformity of practices to be imposed.

55. Prefect of the Drôme to the *ministre de l'Instruction publique et des Cultes* (3 November 1849), A.N. F^{19} 4373. The quotations that follow are drawn from this file preserved in the Archives nationales.

56. Mirmande's parish priest to the *directeur général des Cultes* (31 July 1849).

57. Deliberations of the parochial church council, 14 July 1849.

58. Report of the prefect of the Drôme to the *ministre des Cultes* (17 July 1849).

59. Report of the prefect of the Drôme to the *ministre de l'Instruction publique et des Cultes* (3 November 1849).

60. Ibid.

61. Ibid.

62. Manuscript letter from the prefect of the Drôme to Bérenger (de la Drôme), president of the Court of Cassation, 27 March 1850.

63. Ibid.

64. The expression "abductors of bells" was used, in particular, by the president of Mirmande parochial church council in a letter to the *ministre des Cultes* (30 May 1850).

65. Deliberations of Mirmande parochial church council (7 July 1850), (likewise the quotations that follow).

66. Bishop of Valence to the *ministre des Cultes* (10 June 1850).

67. Philippe Vigier, *La Seconde République dans la région alpine: Etude politique et sociale* (Paris: PUF, 1963), t. 2, "Les paysans," especially pp. 288–89.

68. Letter of the members of the parochial church council to the *ministre de l'Instruction publique et des Cultes* (6 October 1850).

69. *Ministre de l'Instruction publique et des Cultes* (17 September 1850).

70. Report of the brigadier of Loriol gendarmerie (3 November 1850).

71. Prefect of the Drôme to the *ministre de l'Instruction publique et des Cultes* (20 November 1850).

72. I have borrowed this term from Alphonse Dupront, in *Du sacré: Croisades et pèlerinages, Images et langages* (Paris: Gallimard, 1987 *passim*.

THREE. Communities and Their Bells

1. This is how it was in the Ardennes, the Artois, the Yonne, and in Touraine. Cf. H. Jadart and P. Laurent, *Épigraphie campanaire ardennaise: Les cloches du canton d'Asfeld* (Sedan, 1896), p. 9. Jean-Pierre Jessenne, *Pouvoir au village et Révolution: Artois (1760–1848)* (Lille: PUL, 1987), pp. 39–40. Charles Porée, *Cloches et fondeurs de cloches: Enquête campanaire dans l'Yonne* (Paris, 1911), p. 5. In Crain in 1787, the inhabitants decided to pay 25 *sols* per hearth to buy a bell. Brigitte Maillard, *Les Campagnes de Touraine au XVIIIe siècle* (thesis, Rennes II, 1992).

2. H. Jadart, F. Baudemant, J. Carlier, *Épigraphie campanaire ardennaise: Les cloches du canton de Château-Porcien* (Rethel, 1899), p. 36.

3. Evaluation was in accordance with the strict hierarchy of urban peals laid down in the sixteenth century by Carlo Borromeo (cf. p. 98), and endlessly reiterated subsequently.

4. The terms "ring" or "peal" refer to the set of bronze instruments enclosed in a bell tower.

5. The parish priest of Lencloître's petition, in 1809, to the cardinal-bishop of Poitiers, A.N. F[19] 4373.

6. D. Dergny, *Les Cloches du pays de Bray avec leurs dates, leurs noms, leurs inscriptions, leurs armoiries, leurs fondeurs* (Paris, 1865), 2:299.

7. Dergny, *Les Cloches*, 2:53.

8. Mayor of Gahard to the prefect, 24 April 1821, A.D. Ille-et-Vilaine, 1V684.

9. Cf. Bour, *Études campanaires mosellanes* 1:p. 43. This observation concerns the Moselle. Gérard Bouchard likewise emphasizes, in relation to the previous century, what a contemporary termed "the honor of having large bells," in *Le Village immobile: Sennely-en-Sologne au XVIIIe siècle* (Paris: Plon, 1972), p. 319.

10. For examples of such grievances, see abbot Jules Corblet, *De la liturgie des cloches à propos d'une bénédiction de cloches à Saint-Germain d'Amiens* (Amiens, 1854), p. 62; Arcisse de Caumont, *Annuaire des cinq départements de la Normandie*, 27th year (1861), pp. 448–449; quoted by H. Brugière and J. Berthelé, *Exploration campanaire du Périgord* (Périgueux, 1907), p. 50.

11. Dean for the council at the prefecture of the Gard to the minister of the interior and religion, 29 March 1845, A.N. F[19] 4373.

12. A.D. Tarn, 1V8. In 1881 the Protestants of Nègrepelisse complained

about the Catholics ringing their new bells while they were holding
their services. The rift lasted for several years. A.D. Tarn-et-
Garonne, 30v2.

13.   Roger Devos, Charles Joisten, *Moeurs et coutumes de la Savoie du Nord
au XIXe siècle: L'enquête de Mgr Rendu* (Annecy: Académie salesiene,
1978), p. 329. One should, however, note that Savoie at this date was
not French since it only again became so in 1860. Dergny, *Les Cloches*,
2:183.

14.   Jadart et al., *Épigraphie campanaire*, p. 28.

15.   See pp. 43ff.

16.   A.D. Ille-et-vilaine, 1v12.

17.   Ibid.

18.   A.D. Finistère, 1v276.

19.   Dergny, *Les Cloches*, 2:202.

20.   A.N. F^{19} 4373 and, for Neuville-au-Pont, A.N. F^{19} 4374.

21.   On 17 Fructidor Year XIII, when the peals were once again beginning
to weave each day a web of sound across the whole of France, we
read in a report from the *ministère des Cultes* that many communes
already wanted to recast their bells in order to increase their number.
There was then, however, a risk of reducing their range and rendering them less useful for secular usages, formerly the only ones that
were officially recognized. An attitude of this sort, the author of the
text observes, meant that the administration had to keep a careful
watch on recasting operations. Report of 17 Fructidor Year XIII,
ministère des Cultes, A.N. F^{19} 4373.

22.   The file on this affair is in A.N. F^{19} 4373. The quotations are taken
from this file.

23.   This was the case in Scrignac (Finistère) in 1885. Cf. A.D. Finistère,
1v276.

24.   Corblet, *De la liturgie des cloches*, p. 51.

25.   Cf. J.D. Blavignac, *La Cloche. Etude sur son histoire et sur ses rapports
avec la société aux différents âges* (Geneva, 1877), p. 262.

26.   Complaint of the mayor of La Croix-aux-Mines to the subprefect of
Saint-Dié, 7 October 1884, A.D. Vosges, 14v5.

27.   A. Trin, *Les Cloches du Cantal. Archéologie, histoire, folklore* (Aurillac,
1954), p. 41.

28.   Quotations drawn from the complaint of the mayor and the municipal council, A.N. F^{19} 4376, Pas-de-Calais.

29.   Both operations had to be authorized by the prefecture.

30.   A point made by Bour, *Études campanaires mosellanes*, 1:108.

31.   It would likewise be worth pondering the fact that it was deemed
desirable to place particular bells next to each other, with given

sequences implying permanence and a political connotation. Consider, as an example, the petition addressed to the Emperor Napoleon III by the parish priest and churchwardens of Saint-Quentin on 28 November 1866. This document reflects a desire to inscribe the Bonaparte dynasty in the chain of those preceding it, and to reinforce its perenniality by means of the supposed everlastingness of the metal in the bell:

The great sovereigns, who were Your Majesty's predecessors, have in turn granted this basilica the marks of their benevolent protection. As Clovis, Charlemagne, Saint Louis, and Napoleon I had done, Your Majesty has likewise visited the tomb of the apostle of Belgian Gaul. . . . When, after the fire that in 1669 devoured the roof timbers and bell towers of this vast monument, the chapter of the church of Saint-Quentin had the old bells recast, King Louis XIV and the Queen his wife gave to the largest of the tenor bells the name that it still bears today, "*Nomen mihi impositum a Ludovico Magno et Maris Theresia ejus sponsa.*" The vestry had just voted to purchase a new, and larger tenor bell, which, "having featured in the Universal Exhibition of 1867, will take its place in our belfry alongside 'Maria Theresa.' " Following the example set by the chapter of our collegiate church, we shall, Sire, very humbly entreat Your Majesty to deign to designate the names for this new bell. . . . The sacred bronze that shall perpetuate the testimony respecting this fact in the centuries to come will thus bear, engraved together, the blessed names of Napoleon and of Eugénie, just as their love is forever engraved in our hearts.

32.   Bour, *Études campanaires mosellanes*, 1:56.

33.   J. Nanglard, *Les Cloches des églises*, p. 19.

34.   Joseph Berthelé, *Enquêtes campanaires: Notes, études et documents sur les cloches, du VIIIe au XXe siècle* (Montpellier, 1903), pp. 13–14.

35.   On this question, and on the ancient techniques of on-site casting, cf. Joseph Berthelé, *Une fonte de cloches au temps jadis* (Poitiers, 1890), which is an extract from *Bulletins de la Société des Antiquaires de l'Ouest*, 4th quarter (1889).

36.   Cf. Joseph Berthelé, *Notes et études campanaires: Cloches diverses de l'arrondissement de Château-Thierry* (Château-Thierry, 1900), pp. 69ff.

37.   Cf. Jean Salmon, *Au pays des cloches: De Choiseul à La Mothe, du XIe au XXe siècle* (Langres, 1978), p. 35.

38.   Cf. Nanglard, *Les Cloches*, pp. 19–20.

39. Through the efforts of Mersenne, in particular.
40. The Archives départementales for the Gers (v841) contain a fine collection of agreements signed with the bell casters. That said, on-site casting seems to have been less common in that department than in northern France. Many casters there were based in towns, in Auch in particular, from the dawn of the July Monarchy.
41. Cf. H. Brugière, J. Berthelé, *Exploration campanaire du Périgord* (Périgueux, 1907), p. 323. When compared with certain eighteenth-century contracts, the clauses here seem to be simplified but nevertheless not radically different.
42. The nineteenth-century campanarian inquiries furnish some astonishingly precise information.
43. Dergny, *Les Cloches*, 2:270.
44. Bour, *Études campanaires mosellanes*, 1:55.
45. Nanglard, *Les Cloches*, p. 99. In 1819 and 1820, the two men from Lorraine, Prosper Mutel and François Peigney, who had come to refashion the peal of Notre-Dame-la-Grande in Poitiers, set up alongside the Jaubert bridge. In 1830 the same François Peigney and his brother Nicolas recast the bells of Notre-Dame-de-Niort, in a corner of the Place de la Brèche. Some bell casters, as we have seen, were creatures of habit, and would return each year to cast in the same spot. Between 1830 and 1840, the Petit-fours, father and son, following in the footsteps of their uncle Cornevin, regularly returned to cast in Nevers, at the town's Hôtel du Poids, and in Bourges, at widow Mousse's, who kept the Hôtel du Cheval Blanc. On all these points, see Berthelé, *Enquêtes campanaires*, pp. 16ff, and Berthelé, *Une fonte de cloches*, pp. 6ff.
46. Letter of January 1870, A.N. F^{19} 4373.
47. Bour, *Études campanaires mosellanes*, 1:84.
48. A.D. Gers, v841.
49. Sentiments expressed by the mayor of Durban, 15 November 1843, A.D. Gers, v841.
50. Bour, *Études campanaires mosellanes*, 1:83, and the next example is taken from the same source.
51. Trin, *Les Cloches du Cantal*, p. 40 and, for what follows, pp. 41–43.
52. In 1857 the "employees and workers of Stiring" (Moselle) rounded off a sum given by the Emperor for the purchase of the great bell. In 1892 the miners of Algrange (Moselle) collected the sum required for the purchase of a bell in honor of Saint-Barbe, in Bour, *Études campanaires mosellanes*, 1:82.
53. Bour, *Études campanaires mosellanes*, 1:83.
54. Brugière et al., *Exploration campanaire du Périgord*, p. 303.

55. See p. 60.

56. Bour, *Études campanaires mosellanes*, 1:54.

57. Berthelé, *Cloches diverses de l'arrondissement de Château-Thierry*, pp. 77–78.

58. Nanglard, *Les Cloches*, p. 22.

59. Berthelé, *Enquêtes campanaires*, p. 39. The same custom existed in the Cantal, cf. Trin, *Les Cloches du Cantal*, p. 40.

60. This was not so much the case in towns, where it was paid workers who generally assisted the bell caster. The Archives départementales of the Gers (v841) contains a letter from a landowner-farmer claiming, in 1816, 44 "pounds," [sic] sixteen for having worked in 1813 for thirty-two days "in helping the caster make the preparations for casting the bell" in Averon. This missive gives us some idea of how long the operation took.

61. Jadart et al., *Epigraphie campanaire ardennaise*, p. 25; Dergny, *Les Cloches*, 2:270. On 17 August 1826, the ring of bells in Rethel was recast in the Place des Capucins around midnight before a very large crowd. Jadart, P. Laurent, *Épigraphie campanaire ardennaise*, p. 21.

62. Berthelé, *Fonte de cloches*, p. 10.

63. This is how it was in Nolléval, in the Bray. Dergny, *Les Cloches*, 2:49.

64. Brugière et al., *Exploration campanaire du Périgord*, p. 293.

65. L. Breton, *Les Cloches de la cathédrale de Bourges* (Bourges: Tardy, 1934), pp. 46ff.

66. A.D. Gers, v841.

67. Brugière et al., *Exploration campanaire du Périgord*, p. 290.

68. Quoted by Jadart et al., *Épigraphie campanaire ardennaise*, p. 19.

69. I use this term to refer both to the parochial church council and the municipal council, in spite of the by no means negligeable number of disputes between them over bells (see Part 3).

70. Report of the prefect of the Sarthe to the *ministre de la Justice et des Cultes* (18 December 1868), A.N.F[19] 4373. The blessing of the bell came under the bishop's ministry, but was often delegated. As an example, out of seventy-four blessings of bells celebrated in nineteenth-century Dordogne and remarked upon by H. Brugière and J. Berthelé (*Exploration campanaire du Périgord*, p. 78), nine were celebrated by the bishop, nine by a vicar-general, six by a titular canon, five by the archpriest of the arrondissement, fourteen by the dean of the canton, nineteen by the parish priest, and twelve by other clerics of various ranks.

71. As an example, the inscription on the bell cast in 1836 in Hodeng-en-Bray (Seine-Inférieure) bears out this practice. Dergny, *Les Cloches*, 2:342.

72. Consider the case of the Périgord. Henri Brugière and Joseph
     Berthelé note only three invocations of God, three of the Holy
     Trinity, two of Christ—if we discount the eight dedications to the
     Sacred-Heart, all after 1870—and the four references to the Holy
     Family, which are likewise belated. The phrase "*Jesus Maria*," once
     very common, had totally disappeared in this context since the
     Revolution. Conversely, there were countless dedications to, and
     invocations of, the Virgin, and their number rose through the cen-
     tury. Contrary to what one might expect, given the importance of the
     Angelus in campanarian customs, angelic greetings only appeared
     rarely. The Virgin was invoked by the phrase "*Ave Maria, Sancta
     Maria ora pro nobis*," or in terms of the Immaculate Conception (13
     instances), the latter usage being very common in the last forty years
     of the century, after the Dogma had been promulgated.
        Yet the above pale into significance when compared with the plethora
     of references to the saints. Reliance on saints had clearly spread far and
     wide. Forty saints were mentioned on the bells of the Périgord in the
     nineteenth century, but no single one of them is encountered very
     often. The most commonly invoked, Saint Peter, only appears eight
     times. Saint John the Baptist is invoked five times, Saint Front, Saint
     Roch, and Saint Martin three times. The thirty-five other names in the
     catalogue appear only once or twice on the bells of this region. The list
     of saints inscribed on the Perigordian peals had grown much longer
     since the eighteenth century. Intensified reliance on saints, and on inter-
     cession, served to spread the names still further. Campanarian epigra-
     phy here reflects larger-scale shifts in the history of Christian names,
     and of their spread across the social order as a whole. Thus, we may
     read on the bells of the Moselle cast in the nineteenth century (cf. Bour,
     Études campanaires mosellanes) forty-seven Christian names that did
     not appear on the bronze in earlier centuries. The intensification of
     reliance on saints in campanarian epigraphy is again evident here—
     twenty-eight saints were invoked, although they had never been previ-
     ously, on the Mosellane bells cast in the nineteenth century. The evolu-
     tion I have in mind seems to tally with the conclusions reached by
     Marie-Hélène Froeschlé-Chopard, in *Recherches sur les mutations de l'e-
     space sacré, l'iconographie paroissiale et les confréries en Provence et en
     France du XVIe au XIXe siècle* (thesis, University of Paris I, 1993). She
     identifies, through her analysis of inventories of statues, a division of
     sacred space between post-Tridentine devotions and cults of reliance,
     between the top and bottom of the nave. Given this perspective, my
     own observations seem to reinforce the equation between the bell
     tower and the bottom of the nave.

73. I am tempted to mention Metz's "Mademoiselle Turmel" and the "merchant's bell," which hangs in the tower of the church of Argentan.

74. Dergny, *Les Cloches*, 2:140.

75. *Bulletin religieux . . . de la ville et du diocèse de Versailles*, 2nd year, 26 September 1864. In 1897 the blessing of the bells of Bergerac (Brugière et al., *Exploration campanaire du Périgord*, p. 251) prompted articles in at least nine newspapers, two of them national.

76. We do not really know in what period this practice became current. Sometimes these delicacies weighed a considerable amount. In 1922 in Lixheim (Moselle), 248 kilos of sugared almonds were distributed in this fashion. Bour, *Études campanaires mosellanes*, 1:p. 139.

77. Dom Remi Carré, *Recueil curieux et édifiant sur les cloches de l'église avec les cérémonies de leur bénédiction à l'occasion de celle qui fut faite à Paris le jeudi 3 juin 1756 . . .* (Cologne, 1757), pp. 76–77.

78. The consecrated nature of bells meant that their use had to be subject to regulation.

79. As late as 1881, the bell of La Feuillade (Dordogne) had not been "christened"; "on account of the irreligion of the leading municipal dignitary," the parish priest had not wished it. Brugière et al., *Exploration campanaire du Périgord*, p. 77. There is good reason, however, to suppose that by this date a weapon of this sort was already somewhat blunted.

80. Well before this date in some regions, as we have seen.

81. See pp. 8–32.

82. Pierre Laurence, "Cloches, grelots et sonnailles," in *Terrain*, no. 16 (March, 1991), "Savoirs faire," p. 29.

FOUR. The Auditory Markers of the Village

1. This is the constant refrain of those who deplore the loss of territorial frameworks through which the memory of individuals or groups was built up, and the representations of society delineated. Cf. the already fairly old study by Maurice Halbwachs, *Les Cadres sociaux de la mémoire* (Paris: Alcan, 1925). On the perceptual structuration of space, "the territorial sentiment," and the distinction between territoriality and rootedness, see Marcel Roncayolo, in *Territoires*, ENS, no. 1 (Paris, 1983), pp. 4–21, and in particular, his observations on Marcel Mauss's contribution to the debate.

2. Cf. the works of Jacques Rancière.

3. Marcel Maget, "Remarques sur le village comme cadre de recherches anthropologiques," in *Bulletin de psychologie*, t. 8, special issue no.

7–8 (April, 1955), pp. 376–382. On the marking of territories and the indicating of boundaries, see also Jacques Boutier's observations in *Territoires*, pp. 42ff.

4. Marcel Maget also studies the ways in which each group was emblazoned, a process in which the bell was plainly involved.

5. See Christophe Studeny, *Le Vertige de la vitesse: L'accélération de la France (1830–1940)* (thesis in 5 vols., EHESS, 1990). Likewise, Jacques Léonard, *Archives du corps: La santé au XIXe siècle* (Rennes: University of Rennes II, 1986), especially pp. 18–20.

6. In this regard, Olivier Ihl, "Du politique au sacré: Les fêtes républicaines dans les campagnes de la Creuse (1870–1914)," in *Mémoires de la Société des sciences naturelles et archéologiques de la Creuse* (forthcoming), and, above all, Ihl, *La Citoyenneté en fête: Célébrations nationales et intégration politique dans la France républicaine (1870–1914)* (thesis, EHESS, 1992, supervised by Mona Ozouf).

7. "In towns with several parishes," we read in the regulation for peals agreed upon between the archbishop of Rennes and the prefect of the Ille-et-Vilaine in 1885, "the bells shall be rung when the procession passes across the territory of one of the parishes, and in the church of that parish" (A.N. F^{19} 4375, Ille-et-Vilaine).

8. On the meaning of localism and on the existence of particular discourses and territories, local memory, and the culture of local space, cf. Thierry Gasnier, "Le local: Une et indivisible," in Nora, ed., *Les Lieux de mémoire*, vol. 3, pt. 2, "Traditions" Paris 1992, pp. 463–525.

9. As is borne out by reading the volumes of the *Bibliographie annuelle de l'Histoire de France*.

10. Which is why it was something of a gamble even to embark upon the writing of the present study, since it aspires to impose some order on this proliferating history of the miniscule.

11. For an inventory of such sounds, see the pioneering article by Guy Thuillier, "Les bruits," in *Pour une histoire du quotidien au XIXe siècle en Nivernais* (Paris and The Hague: EHESS-Mouton, 1977), pp. 230–244.

12. Dupront, *Du sacré*, p. 447.

13. Cf. pp. 206–207.

14. Cf. J.D. Blavignac, *La Cloche: Etude sur son histoire et sur ses rapports avec la société aux différents âges* (Geneva, 1877), pp. 22ff.

15. A ruling confirmed by the Congregation of Rites on 21 March 1606 and 9 February 1608.

16. Before 1240 the Franciscans were not permitted bells. Subsequently, as a token of humility, their monasteries very often only possessed one of them.

17. Cf. p. 292.
18. Conversely, according to ancient law (cf. Blavignac, *La Cloche*, p. 256), the extent of a given jurisdiction was sometimes defined in terms of the range of its bell.
19. Carré, *Recueil curieux et édifiant*, p. 7.
20. A.N. F^{19} 4373 and A.N. F^{19} 4377, Haute-Savoie.
21. A.D. Finistère, 1v9.
22. Ibid., 1v276.
23. Ibid., 1v276. For another example of this type of complaint, in the Dordogne, in 1863, A.N.F^{19} 4373.
24. A.D. Haute-Marne, 48v2.
25. A.N. F^{19} 4377, Tarn. The shape of this affair is reminiscent of the conflict in Lonlay-l'Abbaye in 1958.
26. Dergny, *Les Cloches*, 2:18.
27. Dergny, *Les Cloches*, and Trin, *Les Cloches du Cantal*, p. 13.
28. Dergny, *Les Cloches*, 2:18–21 for the examples that follow.
29. Cf. p. 299. A.D. Meuse, 37v1.
30. In Normandy, it is claimed that William the Conqueror was saved in 1044, while in the neighborhood of Bayeux, by the peal from an evening bell. He thereafter gave the order for the curfew to be rung in every town and village in the Duchy to put lost travelers back on the right road.
31. For all these examples, cf. Dergny, *Les Cloches*, 2:21.
32. A.D. Finistère, 1v276.
33. Thiers, *Traité des cloches*. On the aims of Thiers, see Jean-Marie Goulemot, Introduction to Thiers, *Traité des superstitions: Croyances populaires et rationalité à l'âge classique* (Paris: Le Sycomore, 1984). Regarding the virtue of bells acknowledged at the dawn of modern times, Thiers refers in particular to the provincial council of Milan of 1565, to the Roman pontificates of Clement VIII and Urban VIII, to the Roman ritual of Paul V, and to many diocesan rituals.
34. Thiers, *Traité des cloches*, p. 136.
35. Cf. Dupront, *Du Sacré*, p. 72.
36. *Essai sur le symbolisme de la cloche dans ses rapports et ses harmonies avec la religion* (Poitiers, 1859), an anonymous work usually attributed to the abbot Sauveterre, p. 89. The author, whoever it was, was fully convinced by the argument that the bell was a "salutary preservative" (p. 90).
37. Thiers, *Traité des cloches*, pp. 136 and 142.
38. Trin, *Les Cloches du Cantal*, p.51.
39. Fernand Pottier, *La Voix du Seigneur dans nos cloches* (Montauban, 1895), p. 5.

40. The examples from the Dordogne are in Brugière et al., *Exploration campanaire du Périgord*, pp. 70ff.

41. Brocard, *Études campanaires*, pp. 38–40.

42. Quoted by Blavignac, *La Cloche*, pp. 164–65.

43. Trin, *Les Cloches du Cantal*, p. 49; Bouchard, *Le Village immobile*, p. 318.

44. Bour, *Études campanaires mosellanes*, 1:262.

45. Berthelé et al., *Enquêtes campanaires rémoises*, p. 21.

46. Bour, *Études campanaires mosellanes*, 1:262.

47. Maillard, *Les Campagnes de Touraine* (thesis, University of Rennes II, 1992).

48. Cf. p. 29.

49. Dupront, *Du Sacré*, p. 431.

50. Cf. Goulemot, *Traité des superstitions*, p. 18.

51. Pluche, *Le Spectacle de la nature*, p. 324.

52. Quoted by Blavignac, *La Cloche*, p. 157.

53. Corbin, *The Foul and the Fragrant*.

54. Pluche, *Le Spectacle de la nature*, p. 325.

55. Cf. Blavignac, *La Cloche*, p. 257.

56. On all these details, cf. Blavignac, *La Cloche*, pp. 155ff; Bour, *Études campanaires mosellanes*, 1:261.

57. A.N. F^{19} 4373.

58. *Essai sur le symbolisme de la cloche*, p. 95.

59. "Notion scientifique de la foudre," quoted by Dom Jules Baudot, *Les Cloches* (Paris, 1913), p. 53. Conversely, Charles Le Maout, a chemist, published in 1861 in Saint-Brieuc a work entitled *Météorologie, effets du canon et du son des cloches sur l'atmosphère*, in which he emphasized the disastrous nature of such effects. Bells and cannon, in his view, posed a grave threat to climatic equilibrium. Le Maout called for draconian regulation of the use of bells, observing, in particular, that rung festivals were followed by formidable storms. Conversely, "as soon as one stops . . . ringing the bells, when the sky is cloudy or overcast, the weather clears up, the blue of the sky reappears, the sun shines and the clouds contract or fill out" (p. 13).

60. This is yet another instance of the discrepancy between systems of beliefs and the prevailing scientific tenets of the period.

61. Blavignac, *La Cloche*, p. 157.

62. Dergny, *Les Cloches*, 2:18.

63. A.N. F^{19} 4374.

64. Trin, *Les Cloches du Cantal*, pp. 49–50.

65. Letter of M. du Miral to the *ministre de la Justice et des Cultes* (20 June 1846), A.N. F^{19} 4374.

66.   A.D. Gers, v841. Circular from the prefect to the mayors of the department (1839).

67.   Parish priest of Lavardens to the prefect (25 June 1839), A.D. Gers, v841.

68.   Response of rector Birraux (31 May 1845), quoted by Devos et al., *Moeurs et coutumes de la Savoie,* p. 248. On the incorporation of the relics of Saint Theodulus, see pp. 44 and 261 (testimony of the rector of Saint-Nicolas-la-Chapelle). Regarding La Chapelle-d'Abondance, note the rector's response (16 May 1845), quoted on p. 291.

69.   Christiane Marcilhacy, *Le Diocèse d'Orléans au milieu du XIXe siècle* (Paris: Sirey, 1964), pp. 264 and 390.

70.   Cf. the file in A.N. F^{19} 4374.

71.   Rather than meaning to insult the king, the parish priest seemed chiefly to be trying to vex the mayor, who would have liked to force him to "accept the schoolmaster as cantor."

72.   A.D. Haute-Marne, 48v2.

73.   After the Franco-Prussian War, the region became German.

74.   On what follows, Bour, *Études campanaires mosellanes,* 1:265.

75.   Nanglard, *Les Cloches d'Angoulême,* p. 223.

76.   Bour, *Études campanaires mosellanes,* 1:263–64.

77.   The role of the bell here forms part of a system of beliefs that attributes to consecrated objects the capacity to disrupt a maleficent logic.

78.   See the crucial study by Krzysztof Pomian, *L'Ordre du temps* (Paris: Gallimard, 1984). I have myself already tackled "The daily arithmetic of the nineteenth century," in *Time, Desire and Horror,* pp. 1–12.

79.   In 1869 the subprefect of Neufchâteau (Vosges) wrote that there were, in his arrondissement, "over a hundred communal clocks." A.D. Vosges, 14v3. That said, the parish priest of Autrécourt (Meuse) observed in 1866 that the public clock "cannot usually be heard outside the villages, beyond the orchards." A.D. Meuse, 174M1.

80.   Cf. pp. 240–51ff.

81.   A.D. Meuse, 37v1.

82.   A.D. Drôme, 48v2. Quoted by Olivier Ihl, *La Citoyenneté en fête,* p. 379.

83.   Mayor of Les Bottereaux (25 August 1907), A.D. Eure, 53v1.

84.   Letter from the parish priest of Autrécourt to the prefect (1 August 1866), A.D. Meuse, 174M1.

85.   With respect to all these points in relation to the Nivernais, see the fine article by Guy Thuillier, "Le temps," in *Pour une histoire du quotidien au XIX siècle,* pp. 205–229 and 407–420.

86.   A.N. F^{19} 4377, Tarn.

87. A.N. F^{19} 4376, Basses-Pyrénées.

88. Saurel, *Histoire religieuse du département de l'Hérault*, 4:260.

89. A.D. Haute-Marne, letter from the Mayor of Breuvannes to the prefect (28 December 1844).

90. A.D. Eure, 53VI.

91. See Corbin, "The daily arithmetic of the nineteenth century," in *Time, Desire and Horror*, p. 4; and Stephen Kern, *The Culture of Time and Space (1880–1918)* (Cambridge, Mass.: Harvard University Press, 1983).

92. C. Demay, "La sonnerie pour les vignerons et les laboureurs à Auxerre," in *Bulletin de la Société des sciences historiques et naturelles de l'Yonne*, vol. 41 (1887), pp. 129–147.

93. A.D. Ille-et-Vilaine, IV12.

94. Nowadays the practice of ringing the evening Angelus at seven o'clock or half past seven, legal time (that is, five o'clock or half past five, solar time) no longer bears any relation to the cosmic order. Nineteenth-century regulations, in summer, held back the evening peal so that it corresponded more closely to the movement of the sun. It was the invention of leisure that led to a redefinition of the notion of the vesperal and the customs of the night, especially in the high season. The discrepancy introduced between the cosmic order and legally imposed rhythms commits us to the absurd contortions involved in permanently recalculating solar time before, for example, determining the heat of the sun's rays or the foreseeable duration of the day.

95. An almost complete collection, in A.N. F^{19} 4375, 4376 and 4377.

96. I have in fact been able to find only sixteen regulations drawn up during this period. Two of them (Basses-Pyrénées and Marne) fixed the times of the morning peals at five o'clock in summer and six in winter.

97. When the prefect and the bishop were unable to reach an agreement, the ministry imposed a standardized regulation based on a model of its own devising.

98. A.N. F^{19} 4375. It is worth noting that today the island of Molène (Finistère) holds to solar time, so there is a two hour discrepancy between the commune and the mainland, which is only a few kilometers away.

99. A.N. F^{19} 4376.

100. A.D. Eure, 85VI, and A.D. Eure-et-Loir, VIO. The Archives départementales for the Meuse (174MI) also house a fine collection of municipal decrees dating from this period, but the majority of mayors had here chosen to adopt a prefectorial model.

101. Cf. pp. 136–39.

102. I have italicized the most common duration of the period of rest, according to this mode of calculation.

103. This was the case in Limousin. See Alain Corbin, *Archaïsme et modernité en Limousin au XIXe siècle* (Paris: Marcel Rivière, 1975), 1:299–301.

104. A.N. F[19] 4374. It is worth noting that seasonal variation was very significant here in the mornings.

105. Dupront, *Du Sacré*, p. 530.

106. Ibid., pp. 422 and 531.

107. This policy is very clearly expounded in A.N. F[19] 4376, file for the Meurthe-et-Moselle.

108. This, anyway, was the list of "devotional festivals" drawn up by the bishop of Saint-Dié for the attention of the prefect of the Vosges, on 6 February 1832. A.D. Vosges, 14VI. The bishop did not refer to the Nativity of the Virgin.

109. Portalis, letter to the bishop of Le Mans (16 January 1806), A.N. F[19] 4377. The emperor set great store by the work done on "suppressed festivals." On 1 June 1811 he attacked the bishop of Séez, and with unprecedented violence berated him for being too tolerant in this regard. The unfortunate prelate from then on suffered "complete disgrace." Ledré, *Le Cardinal Cambacérès*, p. 296.

110. Prefect of the Haut-Rhin to the minister for general police (19 June 1812), A.N. F[19] 4374. Emphases added.

111. And endlessly repeated.

112. A.N. F[19] 4374.

113. A.D. Finistère, 1V29.

114. A.N. F[19] 4374. Letter from the mayor of Saint-Chinian to the subprefect (7 July 1806).

115. A.D. Tarn, 1V8.

116. A.N. F[19] 4377.

117. A.D. Eure, 53VI.

118. Ibid.

119. Letter from the mayor of Rugles to the prefect (19 September 1834), and letter from the parish priest of Rugles to the prefect (7 October 1834), A.D. Eure, 53VI. On the "factories" at Rugles, see Jean Vidalenc, *Le Département de l'Eure sous la monarchie constitutionelle* (Paris: Marcel Rivière, 1952), p. 452.

120. On the Norman confraternities, see Michel Bée, *La Croix et la bannière. Confréries, église et société en Normandie du XVIIe siècle au début du XXe siècle* (thèse d'État, University of Paris IV, 1991). Unfortunately for us, the author does not address the question of bell ringing.

121. The file on this dispute is in A.D. Finistère, 1V29.

122. A.D. Vosges, 14V1.

123. Ruling concerning Finistère (1831) (A.D. Finistère, 1V29), Seine-et-Marne (1832) (A.N. F^{19} 4374), Sarthe and Mayenne (1836) (A.N. F^{19} 4377, Sarthe), Orne (1840) (A.D. Orne, 9V1).

124. A.D. Orne, 9V1.

125. Arnold Van Gennep, *Manuel du folklore français contemporain* (Paris: Picard, 1958), t. 1, vol. 6, pp. 2841 and 2842.

126. Trin, *Les Cloches du Cantal*, p. 48.

127. Letter from the bishop of Aurillac to the prefect of the Cantal (1 June 1842), A.D. Cantal, 1V76.

128. Pierrard, *La Vie quotidienne du prêtre*, p. 230.

129. Blavignac, *La Cloche*, p. 67.

130. Dergny, *Les Cloches*, 2:12.

131. On the preceding observations, see Dergny, *Les Cloches*, 2:12–13.

132. A.D. Oise, 1V15, quoted by Barnett Singer, *Village Notables in 19th Century France: Priests, Mayors, Schoolmasters* (Albany: State University of New York Press, 1983), p. 81.

133. On this subject, cf. Robert Sauzet, *Les Visites pastorales dans le diocèse de Chartres pendant la première moitié du XVIIe siècle: Essai de sociologie religieuse* (Rome, 1975), p. 263, "Les cloches de la Toussaint." The author also mentions the "insolences, the drinking sessions, and the dances held on All Souls' Day in the diocese of Meaux," in R. Lecotté, *Recherches sur les cultes populaires dans l'actuel diocèse de Meaux* (1954), pp. 27, 72, and 182. On the hostility shown by the clergy of this period toward the bells of All Saints' Day, see also Didier Pasquer, *La Réforme catholique et la mentalité populaire dans le diocèse de Tours au XVIIe siècle* (master's thesis, Tours 1984), pp. 103ff. I would add that in 1670 the bishop of Angers had banned these peals after nine o'clock in the evening. Cf. François Lebrun, *Le Diocèse d'Angers* (Paris: Beauchesne, 1981), p. 488.

134. According to Dominique Julia, these peals were designed to calm the souls of the deceased. Cf. "Discipline ecclésiastique et culture paysanne aux XVIIe et XVIIIe siècles," in *La Religion populaire* (Paris: CNRS, 1979), p. 208. The author—like Jean-Baptiste Thiers and like twentieth-century folklorists—also emphasizes the use of bells during Midsummer Night. This practice was meant to "ward off" the evildoings of witches for the rest of the year. However, in the numerous documents I have consulted concerning the nineteenth century, I have found no mention of this custom.

135. A.N. F^{19} 4374.

136.   For all the details that follow, cf. Bour, *Études campanaires mosellanes*, 1:237.

137.   Letter from the bishop of Évreux to the prefect, A.D. Eure, 53V2.

138.   Regulation agreed upon between the prefect of Corsica and the bishop of Ajaccio (2 May 1886), A.N. F^{19} 4375.

139.   File on this conflict is in A.N. F^{19} 4374. In particular, report of the subprefect of Gourdon to the prefect of the Lot (2 November 1808), and memoir drafted by the members of the parochial church council.

140.   A.N. F^{19} 4377, Somme.

141.   Ibid.

142.   Letter from the treasurer of the vestry of Commana to the bishop of Quimper (November 1842), and letter from the mayor to the subprefect of Morlaix (1 December 1842), A.D. Finistère, 1V29.

143.   Letter from the bishop of Quimper to the prefect (16 December 1842), A.D. Finistère, 1V29.

144.   Prefect of the Ardennes to the *ministre de l'Instruction publique et des Cultes* (24 August 1886), A.N. F^{19} 4374.

145.   Dupront, *Du Sacré*, p. 530.

146.   According to Breton, *Les Cloches de la cathédrale de Bourges*, pp. 27–28.

147.   In 1909 the mayor of Les Arcs (Var) imposed the same time limit. A.N. F^7 12389.

148.   A.N. F^{19} 4374.

149.   Eugen Weber, *France fin de siècle* (Cambridge, Mass.: Harvard University Press, 1986), pp 69–70.

150.   Demay, "La sonnerie pour les vignerons et les laboureurs à Auxerre."

151.   Pierrard, *La Vie quotidienne du prêtre français*, p. 250.

152.   With the exception of Saturday evening and Sunday. These indulgences date from the pontificate of Benedict XIII.

153.   On this question, cf. Baudot, *Les Cloches*, p. 56.

154.   Dupront, *Du Sacré*, p. 529.

155.   A.N. F^{19} 4375 and 4376.

156.   Complaint by the members of the parochial church council of Pin-la-Garenne (5 November 1832), A.D. Orne, 9V1. Certain communes are proud of the thanksgiving peals or funereal peals that are exclusive to them. In Courlon (A.N. F^{19} 4374), they have rung for several centuries past on 23 November from six o'clock to eight o'clock in the evening, and on 24 November from five o'clock to nine o'clock in the morning, to announce the funeral service commemorating the massacre of the town's inhabitants by the Huguenots. A similar ceremony is held the following day in Pont-sur-Yonne, and it too is announced by the ringing of bells.

157.   Letter from the parish priest of La Baussaine to the bishop of Rennes (15 April 1842), A.D. Ille-et-Vilaine, 1V12.

158.   Dergny, *Les Cloches*, 2:12.

159.   Dupront, *Du Sacré*, p. 433.

160.   See Sauveterre, *Essai sur le symbolisme de la cloche, passim.*

161.   Dupront, *Du Sacré*, p. 431.

162.   We would do well to bear in mind the continuing significance of eschatology in the nineteenth century.

163.   Prefect of the Seine-Inférieure to the *ministre de l'Instruction publique et des Cultes* (25 April 1857), and letter from the priest in charge of Cottévrard (24 February 1857), A.N. F^{19} 4374.

164.   Regulation of 5 July 1833, A.N. F^{19} 4376, Lot.

165.   A.D. Haute-Marne, 48v3.

166.   Cf. Baudot, *Les Cloches*, p. 48.

167.   Dergny, *Les Cloches*, 2:20.

168.   Cf. pp. 133–34.

169.   Cf. pp. 299–303.

170.   The reader will notice that leisure is simply not mentioned on these occasions.

171.   Complaint to the subprefect of Mirecourt (8 April 1891), A.D. Vosges, 14V5.

172.   The file on this affair is in A.N. F^{19} 4374.

173.   A.N. F^{19} 4376, Nord; and A.D. Aube, v34.

174.   Letter from the mayor of Autrécourt (2 August 1866), and letter from the parish priest to the prefect (1 August 1866), A.D. Meuse, 174M1.

175.   Letter from the subprefect of Mirecourt to the prefect of the Vosges (8 July 1884), A.D. Vosges, 14V4.

176.   The quotations that follow are drawn from: A.D. Haute-Marne, 48v3, Humberville. Letter from the prefect of the Haute-Marne to the bishop of Langres, 16 December 1843.

177.   On this series of affairs, consult the file in A.N. F^{19} 4375, Côte-d'or.

178.   Prefect of the Eure to the *ministre de la Justice et des Cultes* (9 August 1884), A.D. Eure, 53V2.

179.   A.D. Eure-et-Loir, VII.

180.   And thus a very late date, so this was something of a rearguard action on his part.

181.   File on this dispute, A.D. Eure-et-Loir, VII.

182.   As an example, consider the attitude of the prefect of the Eure as reflected in comments made to mayors between 1909 and 1912. A.D. Eure, 85V1.

183.   On 24 November 1911, the Council of State for this reason quashed the municipal decrees respecting these secular peals for the "*points du*

jour." Cf. the affair in which the priest in charge in Cursan (Gironde) was involved; and cf. A.D. Meuse, 174MI. What was in fact a local custom in many regions was thereby condemned.

184. This opposition also appears, cf. p. 261, in debates over secular burials.

185. Boxfile A.N. F^{19} 5650 contains a miscellaneous collection of numerous press cuttings from 1908 to 1912 concerning this type of affair, notably from *L'Univers, Le Matin, La Croix, Le Figaro, La Libre Parole, La Lanterne, Le Siècle, Le Rappel, L'Éclair, Le Gaulois, Le Temps, L'Aurore,* and *La Gazette du Palais,* to mention only the national press. Boxfile A.N. F^{19} 12389 contains a plentiful collection of petitions concerning such disputes. I shall refrain from giving a detailed analysis of these repetitive debates, and I shall limit myself to accounting for them in broad outline.

186. Thus, in Cirfontaines-en-Azois (Haute-Marne), on 9 February 1883, the municipal council asked the prefect if they might have "the reveille," "the midday," "the recall," and "the retreat" rung. A.D. Haute-Marne, 48V2.

187. Petition of the retailers of Arches (29 December 1859), A.D. Vosges, 14V6.

188. And even between municipal dials. The mayor of Suriauville (Vosges) wrote to the subprefect on 31 December 1859, that the police, knowing that the clocks of the canton were not synchronized, so arranged things that by moving "from village to village" they would "always have a good average of the time." A.D. Vosges, 14V6. The prefect of the Haute-Saône wrote in 1884: "In many communes there is no communal clock, and often retailers themselves have no timekeepers. (A.N. F^{19} 4377, Haute-Saône). Hence the indecision of those in authority, and *the discussions as to what the time might really be.*" He would have liked an official signal "against which none would be prepared to protest." This desire to *overcome the uncertainty of the hour* is entirely characteristic of this period, which predates the introduction of legally defined time.

189. A.D. Meuse, 174MI.

190. Letter from the mayor of La Martyre to the subprefect of Brest (22 June 1862), A.D. Finistère, 1V29.

191. Blavignac, *La Cloche,* p. 59.

192. Carré, *Receuil curieux et édifiant,* p. 79.

193. Billon, *Campanologie,* p. 155.

194. Brugière, J. Berthelé, *Exploration campanaire,* p. 75.

195. Prefect of the Drôme to the *ministre de l'Instruction et des Cultes* (2 February 1844), A.N. F^{19} 4374. The mayors rang the "retreat" in some communes, with the agreement of the priests in charge,

although this practice does not appear in the regulation governing bell ringing of 1 April 1839.

196. Mayor of Mont-Saint-Jean (Aisne) to the prince-president (15 November 1852). He complained that the parish priest—"and yet I get on fairly well with him"—forbade him to ring "the retreat," although it was the practice in neighboring communes. A.N. F^{19} 4374.

197. A.D. Haute-Marne, 48v2, petition of 5 November 1848.

198. A.D. Finistère, 1V29.

199. A.D. Vosges, 14V5.

200. Letter from the mayor of Saint-Caradec to the prefect (7 December 1896). The curfew was rung at nine o'clock on Sundays and holidays. The parish priest refused to put this peal back an hour so as to have it coincide with the official closing time of the taverns, as was the practice in neighboring communes. A.D. Côtes-du-Nord, v2941.

201. On 21 February 1895, the mayor of Plounérin obtained permission to ring the "retreat" on Sundays and holidays, A.D. Côtes-du-Nord, V2557.

202. Dergny, *La Cloche*, 2:21. In the Haute-Saône, on the other hand, this peal fell into abeyance after 1870. Prefect to the *ministre des Cultes* (15 November 1884), A.N. F^{19} 4377, Haute-Saône.

203. Mayor of Senon (3 December 1849), and letter of the parish priest of Senon (20 January 1850), A.N. F^{19} 4373.

204. A.D. Haute-Marne, 48v3.

205. Cf. p. 99.

206. A.D. Haute-Marne, 48v2.

207. File on this dispute over bells in Chatonrupt, in A.D. Haute-Marne, 48v2. Including letter from the mayor to the prefect (12 November 1867), report of the commissioner of police for the canton of Joinville to the prefect (9 January 1868), and letter from the prefect to the subprefect (17 January 1868).

208. This interpretation seems all the more convincing for the fact that, at least in northern France, "the old use of legends and mottos that had the bell in some sense speaking and praying" had been abandoned, and the patron saint of the church had even been forgotten. The names of godfathers and godmothers stood out all the more prominently as a consequence. Cf. Jadart et al., *Épigraphie campanaire ardennaise*, p. 66. In the South it was still the practice to characterize the mission of bells by means of texts borrowed from holy books or composed in *Latin* and French by poets and epigraphists. Cf. p. 102, and, for an especially characteristic example, see the inventory undertaken by Gustave Vallier, *Inscriptions campanaires du département de l'Isère* (Montbéliard, 1886).

209. Especially prior to the advent of the Third Republic.

210. The order implied by my definition of these pairs should not be taken to imply any value judgments one way or the other.

211. As we shall see, it was in the *bocage* of the Orne, perhaps the most devout region in the country—once the epicenter of the Norman *chouannerie*—that communities were least prepared to tolerate the attack mounted by the clergy on certain secular peals (notably those for elections and for the public reading of official texts), in the middle of the July Monarchy. This gives us cause to mistrust the excessively simple notion, formerly advanced by André Siegfried, of "clerical democracy."

212. Cf. the works already mentioned by Jadart, Bour, Dergny, Vallier, Trin, Nanglard, Brugière, and Berthelé. Éric Sutter, in the context of the Société française de campanologie, is at present engaged in compiling an exhaustive inventory. "He has established a bank of information on bells, and almost six thousand appear in it, out of an estimated total of a hundred thousand." Cf. Jean-Baptiste de Montvalon, "Les cloches," in *Trouvailles*, no. 98 (July–August 1992).

213. Billon, *Campanologie*, and Toulouse-Lautrec, *Les Cloches dans le Haut-Comminges*.

214. For what follows, cf. Brugière et al., *Exploration campanaire du Périgord*, p. 81.

215. During this same period there appear a few rare mentions of "honorary godfathers," which seems to be a cut-rate way of extending the list of personages to whom one wished to pay homage.

216. Dergny, *La Cloche*, t. 2, *passim*.

217. Bour, as we have seen, lays stress upon the continuities in campanarian epigraphy, *Études campanaires mosellanes*, 1:108.

218. Michel Denis, *Les Royalistes de la Mayenne et le monde moderne (XIXe-XXe siècle)* (Paris: Klincksieck, 1977); Claude-Isabelle Brelot, *La Noblesse réinventé: Notables de Franche-Comté de 1814 à 1870* (Besançon: Annales littéraires de l'université de Besançon, 1992, pp. 617ff. During the Restoration the princes of the royal family were inundated with flattering but self-interested requests that they be godfather to bells. Subsequently, going to the count of Chambord in some places was evidence of legitimist loyalties.

219. "I am owing to the generosity of all the inhabitants of Saint-Paul-Laroche, but above all to that of the Mlles Moreau de la Peyzie, of Baron Maurice Dubut de Saint-Paul, de Lavallade. . . . of Mme de Quainsac, du Pairier . . . ," we read on a bell from Saint-Paul-Laroche (Dordogne) christened in 1894, its bronze becoming a veritable regional Gotha. Cf. Brugière et al., *Exploration campanaire du*

Périgord, p. 316. Sometimes the bell lists the names of hamlets, then of individuals dwelling in the village. It is worth noting the practice, both widespread and significant, followed by people from the same hamlet of grouping their gifts together and merging their identity with that of the community, whereas offerings made by people from the village were individualized.

220. Dergny, *La Cloche*, 2:51–52.

221. To become the godfather of a bell committed these notables to lavish displays of generosity, even if it were only to meet the expense of the "christening," and in particular that of the banquet laid for such an occasion. The new bell of Sepvret (Deux-Sèvres), which was blessed on 23 July 1866, had M. Gaborit de Montjou as its godfather and Mme d'Herveault as its godmother. The ceremony was rounded out with a banquet of sixty-eight places, held "beneath a thatched cabin decorated with greenery, flowers, and oriflammes, given after a shower of sugared almonds." It followed on from "a fine bonfire . . . lit by the godfather and godmother to the sound of the fanfare of Saint-Sauvant." Berthelé, *Enquêtes campanaires: Notes, études et documents sur les cloches, du VIIIe au XXe siècle* (Montpellier, 1903), pp. 200–201.

222. Petition signed by the inhabitants of Marignié (January 1870), A.N. F^{19} 4373.

223. One hundred and three signatures appear on the text, including those of the women.

224. A.D. Gers, v841. Extract from the minutes of Lombez municipal council.

225. Trin, *Les Cloches du Cantal*, p. 41.

226. Berthelé, *Enquêtes campanaires*, pp. 179 and 198.

227. Admittedly, this term was then highly ambiguous.

228. That is, Saint-Louis' Day, the fête du roi.

229. Dergny, *La Cloche*, 2:155.

230. Jadart et al., *Épigraphie campanaire ardennaise* (Sedan, 1896), p. 7.

231. Jadart et al., *Épigraphie campanaire ardennaise* (Rethel, 1899), p. 29.

232. Ibid., p. 64.

233. Bour, *Études campanaires mosellanes*, 1:110.

234. Brugière et al., *Exploration campanaire du Périgord*, p. 376.

235. Ibid., p. 93.

236. Ibid.

237. Bour, *Études campanaires mosellanes*, 1:110.

238. Jadart et al., p. 47.

239. Bour, *Études campanaires mosellanes*, 1:110.

240. Jadart et al., *Épigraphie campanaire ardennaise*, p. 42.

241. Dergny, *La Cloche*, 2:167.

242. Jadart et al., *Épigraphie campanaire ardennaise*, p. 24.

243. Ibid., p. 14.

244. Bour, *Études campanaires mosellanes*, 1:110.

245. Dergny, *La Cloche*, 2:204.

246. Jadart et al., *Épigraphie campanaire ardennaise*, p. 32.

247. Ibid., p. 35.

248. Jadart et al., *Les Cloches du canton de Rethel*, pp. 21–22.

249. Dergny, *La Cloche*, 2:69.

250. A.N. F^{19} 4373. Report from the subprefect of the arrondissement of Mantes to the prefect (16 November 1864).

251. Complaint from the mayor of Libaros to the *ministre des Cultes* (30 March 1872); discussions at Libaros parochial church council (14 January 1872); letter from the minister of religion to the prefect (28 April 1872), A.N. F^{19} 4373.

252. Dergny, *La Cloche*, 2:7; and Jadart et al., *Épigraphie campanaire ardennaise*, p. 34.

253. Cf. pp. 209–12.

254. Trin, *Les Cloches du Cantal*, p. 40.

255. A.D. Finistère, IV9.

256. Billon, *Campanologie*, p. 57.

257. Cf. p. 289.

258. A.N. F^{19} 4377, Somme.

259. In 1884, on the eve of signing the regulations governing the peals, the prefect of the Côtes-du-Nord set up an inquiry to discover the wishes of the town halls with respect to use of bells. Only the mayor of Lamballe explicitly wished the bells to be rung for the passage of the president of the Republic (A.D. Côtes-du-Nord, v32, v33). In the Eure-et-Loir (A.D., v9), the documents concerning an inquiry, likewise implemented in 1884, into the use of bells have been very well preserved. The question put to the municipalities read as follows: "Indicate under what circumstances, following existing local customs, the municipal authorities make use of the bells." Twenty-two memoranda from the arrondissement of Chartres mentioned the official passage of the head of state, although it should be borne in mind that this questionnaire about customs was used in areas on the presidential itinerary.

260. Cf. Juliette Didierjean, *Les Voyages de Poincaré dans les départements français: 1913–1914* (master's dissertation, University of Paris I, 1993). The decree of 16 June 1907, in *Journal officiel* (20 June 1907), pp. 4274–4279, was designed to overhaul that of 24 Messidor Year XII.

261. Dergny, *La Cloche*, 2:129.

262. Lysiane Lafond, *Le Voyage de Charles X dans les départements de l'Est* (master's dissertation, University of Paris I, 1991).
263. A.N. F^{19} 4374 contains the file on this affair and, in particular, the letter I have quoted from the bishop of Poitiers to the *ministre des Cultes* (13 July 1835). The minister refers to the "great question of bell ringing."
264. Bour, *Études campanaires mosellanes*, 1:265.
265. Letter from the mayor of Saint-Dié to the subprefect, A.D. Vosges, 14v6.
266. Letter from the archbishop of Rennes to the *ministre de l'Instruction publique et des Cultes* (23 August 1859); letter from Minister Rouland to the prefect (27 August 1859), A.N. F^{19} 4374.
267. A.D. Eure, 53v1.
268. Singer, *Village Notables in 19th Century France*, p. 86.
269. A.N. F^{19} 4376, Manche. Concerted regulation governing peals (11 June 1885).
270. Letter from the mayor of Point-Croix to the prefect of Finistère (31 October 1831), A.D. Finistère, 1v29.
271. Letter from the mayor of Créancey to the prefect of the Haute-Marne, A.D. Haute-Marne, 48v2.
272. Letter from the mayor of Lannilis to the sub-prefect (7 September 1860), A.D. Finistère, 1v29.
273. Cf. p. 16.
274. Prefect of the Orne to the *ministre de l'Intérieur et des Cultes* (15 January 1833), A.N. F^{19} 4374.
275. A.N. F^{19} 4376, Manche. Debate on this subject between the prefect and the bishop.
276. Letter from the subprefect for the arrondissement of Châteaulin to the prefect of Finistère, A.D. Finistère, 1v29.
277. Letter from the mayor of Milizac to the subprefect (12 January 1875); and letter from the subprefect to the prefect (14 January 1875), A.D. Finistère, 1v46.
278. Letter from the mayor of Kernével to the subprefect of the arrondissement of Quimperlé (17 January 1881); ibid.
279. Letter from the mayor of Esquibien to the prefect of Finistère (25 January 1881); ibid.
280. Complaint made by the parish priest for Saint-Uniac (30 June 1881), A.D. Ille-et-Vilaine, 1v12.
281. Letter from the deputy mayor of Landudal to the prefect of Finistère (21 May 1896), A.D. Finistère, 1v46.
282. Complaint made by the priest in charge of Moyemont to the prefect of the Vosges, A.D. Vosges, 14v5.

283. Cf. pp. 173–74.
284. Letter from the prefect of the Haut-Rhin to the minister for general police (19 June 1812), A.N. F[19] 4374. On the use of bells in Baroque funerals, Vovelle, *Piété baroque et déchristianisation en Provence*, pp. 87–98 and 399; and François Lebrun, *Les Hommes et la mort en Anjou* (Paris, EHESS, 1971), pp. 467–469. In the previous century (1629), the archdeacon of Vendôme asked that the bell ringers be instructed "to ring more and better than had been done for our recently deceased colleagues." Quoted by Robert Sauzet, "Autour d'une pompe funèbre à Chartres au début du XVIIe siècle," in *Mémoires de la Société archéologique d'Eure-et-Loir* (1969), p. 8.
285. Letter from the mayor of La Roche to the *ministre de l'Instruction publique et des Cultes* (1872), A.N. F[19] 437. As we shall see (p. 167), in some communes in Seine-Inférieure, the "toll of regret" was rung at the death of the parish priest.
286. They should not be confused with those that were ordered simply in terms of their cost, as specified on the tariff of oblations.
287. Letter of 26 August 1886, A.D. Hautes-Pyrénées, v90.
288. I shall return to this question later in the context of a discussion of rites of passage (cf. pp. 164–65).
289. A.N. F[19] 4375, Ille-et-Vilaine.
290. Cf. pp.79–80, especially in relation to Réty.
291. The file on this conflict is in A.D. Meuse, 37v1.
292. A.D. Lot, 3U2953 (Figeac *tribunal de première instance*).

FIVE. The Density of Truth

1. As Rémi Carré wrote in 1757 in *Recueil curieux et édifiant sur les cloches de l'église*, p. 83, "the time, the hours, and the ways of ringing should be regulated in each church and known by all the faithful." In Paris, in the parish of Saint-Gervais, to mention but one example, "the five o'clock mass was announced by fifty strokes of the bell, that of half past five by forty strokes and that of six o'clock by thirty strokes." The Angelus, depending upon the parish, was rung with the small, the middle, or the great bell, or sometimes, with a special instrument. Cf. Blavignac, *La Cloche*, p. 139.
2. That is to say, to one who is not from the "locality" or "country."
3. A.N. F[19] 4375, Dordogne.
4. Cf. the affair described on p. 139.
5. Letter from the prefect of the Loir-et-Cher to the *ministre des Cultes* (4 July 1889); and the minister to the prefect (12 July 1889), A.N. F[19] 4376, Loir-et-Cher.
6. Secretary general of the prefecture of the Orne to the subprefect of

Domfront (3 July 1840), A.D. Orne, 9v1. During the Revolution campanarian policy was defined in terms of this distinction.

7.   A.N. F^{19} 4376, Haute-Marne.

8.   Bishop of Langres to the prefect of the Haute-Marne (30 March 1846); ibid.

9.   Cf. Bour, *Études campanaires mosellanes*, 1:307ff.

10.   Dergny, *Les Cloches du pays de Bray*, 2:13.

11.   Cf. Ferdinand Farnier, *Notice historique sur les cloches suivie des prières et cérémonies pour la bénédiction des cloches* (Robécourt, 1882), p. 74. "When one senses that the bell is about to stop, or when it stops ringing its continuous strokes, you bring it gently to a halt by letting the weight of your body go with the movement of the bell as it rises or falls, while taking good care not to lose contact with the pavement or to let yourself be hung."

12.   Dergny, *Les Cloches*, 2:13–14.

13.   In this regard, cf. Billon, *Campanologie*, p. 146.

14.   Cf. pp. 225ff.

15.   That is to say, in this context, to ring in peal. One needs to pay close attention to the polysemic nature of the term "carillon."

16.   File on the Appenay affair in A.N. F^{19} 4374, and in particular the report quoted from the prefect of the Orne to the *ministre des Cultes* (2 Messidor Year XIII / 21 June 1805).

17.   Some time later the priest in charge, upon receiving the victim's son at his house, assured him "that it was because his father had used some stones from the church in his building" that "the fire had caught there." The confusion introduced into the language of the bells had thus brought on divine punishment. Report of the imperial prosecutor to the minister of justice (2 Thermidor Year XIII / 21 July 1805).

18.   A.D. Ille-et-Vilaine, 1v12.

19.   Letter from the mayor of Clinchamp to the prefect of the Haute-Marne (15 January 1893), A.D. Haute-Marne, 48v2.

20.   Which was anyway against the law.

21.   In interviews conducted in the Haute-Vienne countryside in 1968, when country people were asked how they set about reading the newspaper, the majority confided to us that they began by consulting the pages on which births, marriages, and deaths appeared. This way of reading fits with what we are saying here about ways of listening to bells. Corbin, *Prélude au Front populaire* (troisième cycle thesis, Poitiers 1968), p. 48.

22.   A.N. F^{19} 4376, Manche.

23.   It is worth noting that in the nineteenth century the custom of ringing the bell to announce to the community that a woman was in "dan-

gerous labor" was abandoned, although Rémi Carré had referred to the practice in 1757, in *Receuil curieux et édifiant sur les cloches*, p. 28.

24. Petition submitted by eighty inhabitants of Longny-au-Perche (12 November 1840), A.D. Orne, 9VI. On the attribution of this meaning to baptism in the life of the small child, cf. François Loux, *Le Jeune Enfant et son corps dans la médecine traditionelle* (Paris: Flammarion, 1978).

25. Van Gennep, *Manuel du folklore*, t. 1, vol. 1, pp. 135ff.

26. Devos et al., *Moeurs et coutumes de la Savoie du Nord*, pp. 108–109, 150 and 321.

27. Blavignac, *La Cloche*, p. 115.

28. Cf. regulation for peals, Oise (29 May 1840), A.N. F^{19} 4376. The prayer books from different dioceses contained prayers to be recited on such occasions.

29. Petition quoted of the inhabitants of Longny-au-Perche.

30. Cf. Vovelle, *Piété baroque*.

31. Cf. pp. 257–58.

32. For all the detailed information that follows regarding the Moselle, cf. Bour, *Études campanaires mosellanes*, 1:228–229.

33. Dergny, *La Cloche*, 2:8.

34. Ibid. pp. 8–9.

35. Ibid., p. 9. There is no need to emphasize how interesting such details are for the historian of gender.

36. Dergny, *La Cloche*, p. 10.

37. Inhabitants of Longny-au-Perche, petition quoted in n24.

38. Dergny, *La Cloche*, 2:11.

39. Regulation of 20 May 1886, A.N. F^{19} 4374 and debate on this custom.

40. Van Gennep *Manuel du folklore*, t. 1, vol. 2, pp. 689–698 contains numerous detailed accounts of the ways the death agony, the death, and the burial were rung. "For several thousand communes," the author concludes (p. 694), the death was rung as follows: three strokes for men and boys, two strokes from women and girls, one stroke for children. Sometimes, regardless of distinctions of sex, one rings one stroke for each year the dead person had lived. In some communes the boys ring the death of one of their own, and the girls that of one of their fellows. Finally, it could happen that at the end of the ceremony "the return from the graveside" and "the last farewell" were rung. All of this analysis lends credence to my own argument. Given Van Gennep's relaxed approach to matters of chronology, I have preferred to limit myself to precisely dated regional studies.

41. Decree issued by the mayor of Beaubray (12 June 1908), A.D. Eure, 85VI.

42.   Cf. the retrospective treatment of this question in *L'Ami du clergé* (18
      June 1885). On the history of norms governing the use of posters in
      the parish, cf. Jean Kerlévéo, *L'église catholique en régime français de
      Séparation* (Paris: Desclée, 1956) 2:259–264.

43.   Cf. Kerlévéo, *L'église catholique*, 2:261, which the author in fact disputes.

44.   M. de Parieu, circular of 25 June 1850, quoted in *L'Ami du clergé*, issue
      quoted in note 42; and J. Kerlévéo, *L'église catholique*, 2:262.

45.   Cf. pp. 240–45.

46.   For those interested in the history of procedures used for transmitting
      information and for communication, a fine-grained study of the prac-
      tices of billposting would usefully complement my own investigation
      of bells.

47.   Letter from the mayor of Coësmes to the subprefect (21 May 1812),
      A.D. Ille-et-Vilaine, 1V12.

48.   Circular from the prefect of the Ille-et-Vilaine to the mayors of the
      department (January 1851), A.D. Ille-et-Vilaine, 1V12.

49.   Letter from the mayor of Lannilis to the subprefect of the arrondisse-
      ment of Brest (7 September 1860 and 11 June 1861), A.D. Finistère,
      1V29.

50.   A.D. Orne, 9V1. "Pulling the bell" meant in the local idiom ringing
      the bell, i.e., pulling the rope to ring the bell.

51.   Letter from the mayor of Les Monceaux to the prefect of the Orne
      (24 September 1840), A.D. Orne, 9V1.

52.   Letter from the mayor of Lonlay-le-Tesson to the subprefect (15
      November 1840); and letter from the deputy mayor of Le Grais (7
      August 1840), A.D. Orne, 9V1. My own emphasis.

53.   Mayor of Verrières (22 July 1840), and mayor of Origny-le-Butin (4
      August 1840), A.D. Orne, 9V1.

54.   In many cases it could as well be a peal of rejoicing or sorrow as one
      serving to announce.

55.   Saurel, *Histoire religieuse du département de l'Hérault*, 4:83.

56.   Bour, *Études campanaires mosellanes*, 1:196–198.

57.   Ibid., 1:235. It is worth noting that at the death of Louis XV the bells
      of every church in Périgueux and its vicinity were rung "in mourn-
      ing" for forty days and forty nights, in Brugière et al., *Exploration
      campanaire du Périgord*, p. 76.

58.   This is how it was in the Côtes-du-Nord.

59.   Godel, *La Reconstruction concordataire*, p. 314.

60.   Brigitte Ferri-Dufour, *Le Rendez-vous manqué: Biographie politique de
      Louis-Antoine de Bourbon, duc d'Angoulême (1775–1844)* (master's dis-
      sertation, University of Paris I, 1992).

61.   Bour, *Études campanaires mosellanes*, 1:198–199.

62.   We have already tackled this type of peal above with regard to the bell of the "town hall sermon," which was both a signal to assemble and an announcement.

63.   Letter from the prefect of the Basses-Pyrénées to the *ministre des Cultes* (20 December 1834), A.N. F^{19} 4376, Basses-Pyrénées.

64.   Mayor of Poullaouen (16 March 1853), A.D. Finistère, 1v29.

65.   Subprefect of Lannion to the prefect of the Côtes-du-Nord (5 September 1884), A.D. Côtes-du-Nord, v33.

66.   Cf. A.D. Orne, 9v1.

67.   In the department of the Orne under the July Monarchy, it was proposed that the use of the bell be kept for all civic proceedings including elections, the turning out of the guard, and the reading of official documents. Cf., as an example, letters from the mayors of Sainte-Honorine-la-Chardonne (4 August 1840), Guêprei (8 August 1840), Les Préaux (12 August 1840), and Saint-Pierre-la-Bruyère (28 July 1840), A.D. Orne 9v1.

68.   Letter from the prefect of the Charente to the *ministre de l'Instruction publique et des Cultes* (10 January 1832), A.N. F^{19} 4374.

69.   Letter from the bishop of Séez to the prefect of the Orne (20 June 1840), A.D. Orne, 9v1.

70.   Persil based his position on the writings of Portalis and Bigot de Préameneu, as well on numerous texts quoted by the *Journal des conseils de fabrique*. Letter to the minister of the interior (23 June 1835), A.N. F^{19} 4374).

71.   I shall return to these "excessive" peals, pp. 265ff.

72.   Circular from the prefect of the Ille-et-Vilaine to the mayors of his department (January 1851), A.D. Ille-et-Vilaine, 1v12.

73.   Prefect of the Jura to the *ministre de la Justice et des Cultes* (14 March 1840), A.N. F^{19} 4375, Jura.

74.   This commune was the object of an in-depth ethnological inquiry under the name of Chardonneret.

75.   For all these documents, cf. A.D. Orne, 9v1.

76.   Letter from the mayor of Alençon to the prefect of the Orne (13 December 1839); and from the mayor of Bellême (27 July 1840); ibid. Emphases added.

77.   Prefect of the Sarthe to the *ministre des Cultes* (20 December 1831), A.N. F^{19} 4374. In 1846 the mayor of Caudan (Morbihan) attempted to introduce the election bell into his commune, an act that brought protests from the bishop of Vannes. Cf. bishop of Vannes to the *ministre des Cultes* (7 July 1846), A.N. F^{19} 4374.

78.   References to this affair may be found in a letter from the mayor of Ségrie-Fontaine to the subprefect of Domfront (4 August 1840),

A.D. Orne, 9V1. As the mayor noted, "now, in certain localities in the arrondissement of Saint-Lô we are weary of hearing the sound of bells, because Messieurs the priests in charge wished in many cases to refuse them."

79.   Letter from the mayor of Gaillon to the prefect of the Eure (21 November 1831), A.D. Eure, 53V1.

80.   Letter from the mayor of Bellou-en-Houlme to the subprefect of Domfront (9 June 1840), A.D. Orne, 9V1.

81.   Letter from the bishop of Séez to the municipal council of Argentan (9 January 1849); ibid.

82.   In a letter addressed to the prefect of the Orne (10 February 1849); ibid.

83.   Cf. Patrick Lagoueyte, *Candidature officielle et pratiques électorales sous le Second Empire* (thesis, University of Paris I, 1990).

84.   Mayor of Lannilis to the subprefect of Brest (22 June 1861), A.D. Finistère, 1V29.

85.   A.N. F^{19} 4376, Manche. Vicar general to the prefect of the Manche (12 December 1884).

86.   Mayor of Trévérec, response to the prefectoral inquiry of 1884 on uses of bells, A.D. Côtes-du-Nord, V32.

87.   Letter from the subprefect of the arrondissement of Briey (31 March 1844), A.N. F^{19} 4377. File regarding the diocese of Metz.

88.   Report from the Gendarmerie, Tulle (8 July 1831), A.N. F^7 6779. The reader will note that an election was often referred to as a "nomination" at this period.

89.   P. Lagoueyte, *Candidature officielle*.

90.   Letter from the mayor of Celles to the subprefect (13 October 1885), A.D. Vosges, 14V4.

91.   Letter from the prefect of Le Loiret to the *ministre des Cultes* (16 March 1836); and from the bishop of Orléans to the minister (10 March 1836), A.N. F^{19} 4374.

92.   Letter from the prefect to the mayor of La Chapelle-Réanville (12 June 1861), A.D. Eure, 53V1.

93.   Protest of the receiver general (18 July 1835), A.N. F^{19} 4376, Basses-Pyrénées.

94.   Prefect of the Landes to the *ministre de l'Instruction publique et des Cultes* (10 July 1832), A.N. F^{19} 4374.

95.   Letter from the mayor of Lascazères to the prefect of the Hautes-Pyrénées (2 June 1828), A.D. Hautes-Pyrénées V108.

96.   Protest of Urgons municipal council (2 November 1837), A.N. F^{19} 4373.

97.   Letter from the mayor of Montgaudry (12 December 1839), A.D. Orne, 9V1.

98. A.D. Aube, v34; and A.N. F^{19} 4376, Pyrénées-Orientales. The regulation specified the use of the bell for the tax collector on "a round of collecting and conveyancing."

99. Mayor of Montcharvot to the prefect of the Haute-Marne (18 December 1903), A.D. Haute-Marne, 48v3. The "worries" of the mayor and the parish priest constitute a historical source of the highest significance for research into nineteenth-century rural society in France.

100. Regulation of peals. Department of the Doubs, diocese of Besançon (15 June 1885), A.N. F^{19} 4375. Doubs and regulation of Bouilly parochial church council (1828), A.D. Aube, v275.

101. Letter from the prefect of the Moselle to the *ministre des Cultes* (27 March 1846), A.N. F^{19} 4377, Metz affair.

102. File on this conflict in A.D. Hautes-Pyrénées, v108.

103. Minister of the interior to the *ministre de l'Intérieur et des Cultes* (23 April 1844), A.N. F^{19} 4374. The minister ruled in favor of the bishop of Strasbourg protesting against this usage.

104. Letter from the bishop of Coutances to the mayor of the town (10 September 1839), A.N. F^{19} 4374.

105. Letter from the bishop of Coutances to the mayor (11 October 1839); ibid.

106. The legislative committee ruled in the bishop's favor.

107. Regulation of peals (5 March 1885), A.N. F^{19} 4377, Savoie.

108. Cf. note from Baron Rendu (8 February 1841), regarding the regulation for the Seine-et-Oise (1840), A.N. F^{19} 4374.

109. Petition of the mayor and municipal councillors of Lesboeufs (12 October 1872), A.N. F^{19} 4374.

110. Regulation of peals (27 October 1884), A.N. F^{19} 4376, Oise.

111. Letter from the prefect of the Somme to the *ministre de l'Instruction publique, des Beaux Arts, et des Cultes* (27 March 1896), A.N. F^{19} 4377, Somme.

112. Letter from the bishop of Bayonne to the *ministre des Cultes* (20 December 1834), A.N. F^{19} 4376, Basses-Pyrénées. It is true that it seems to be as much a question of a claim as of a custom, and of an innovation rather than a vestige.

113. Prefect of the Haute-Saône to the *ministre des Cultes* (15 November 1884), A.N. F^{19} 4377, Haute-Saône.

114. Plan for a concerted regulation drafted by the bishop of Langres (April 1838), A.N. F^{19} 4376, Haute-Marne.

115. Since the parish priest had had the church shut at times when one was supposed to ring for school, the mayor of Cuves (Haute-Marne) complained, "it has become difficult for children to arrive for classes

at *exactly* the right time." Letter from the mayor of Cuves to the prefect of the Haute-Marne (16 May 1882), A.D. Haute-Marne, 48v2.

116. Letter from the mayor of Gourzon to the subprefect of Wassy (17 March 1845), A.D. Haute-Marne, 48v3.

117. Letter from the mayor of Bouzancourt to the subprefect (12 December 1847; and deliberations of the municipal council of Bouzancourt (21 December 1847), A.D. Haute-Marne, 48v2.

118. Prefect of the Marne to the *ministre des Cultes* (31 December 1884), A.N. F^{19} 4376, Marne.

119. Testimony of the subprefect of Brest, quoted by the mayor of Lannilis (22 January 1861), A.D. Finistère, 1v29.

120. In a letter addressed to the *ministre des Cultes* on 20 December 1831, A.N. F^{19} 4374.

121. See Roger Chartier, ed., *La Correspondance: Les usages de la lettre au XIXe siècle* (Paris: Fayard, 1991).

122. Which reflects the rise of the notion of time as a thing that is consumed.

123. This is an evocation, and one that was very frequent, of a category of perceived time, namely, that of immobile time. Letter from the prefect of the Hautes-Alpes to the *ministre de l'Intérieur et des Cultes* (28 May 1840), A.N. F^{19} 4373.

124. Letter from the bishop to the prefect of the Hautes-Alpes (23 May 1840); ibid.

125. Commandant of the Gendarmerie to the prefect (28 May 1840); ibid.

126. I have studied the "abduction" of bells in greater detail earlier, pp. 45–70.

127. As a bulging file of grievances from local administrations demonstrates, A.N. F^{19} 4376, Basses-Pyrénées.

128. On the defense of local liberties in the Pyrénées, cf. Jean-François Soulet, *Les Pyrénées au XIXe siècle* (Toulouse: Eché, 1987), *passim*.

129. Collective complaint by the mayors of the canton of Sauveterre, A.N. F^{19} 4376, Basses-Pyrénées.

130. Complaint quoted from Urgons council. In Saint-Aubin the conflict erupted in the summer of 1832.

131. Complaint from the mayors in the cantons of Maubeuge and Solre-le-Château (March 1844), A.N. F^{19} 4376, Nord.

132. Letter of protest from the mayor of Saint-Dié to the prefect of the Vosges (3 May 1840), A.D. Vosges, 14v4.

133. Mayor of Rambervilliers to the prefect of the Vosges (21 July 1840), A.D. Vosges, 14v5.

134. Letter from the bishop of Metz to the *ministre des Cultes* (5 April 1845), A.N. F^{19} 4377.

135. The bishop of Metz to the *ministre des Cultes* (23 October 1845); ibid.
136. The bishop of Metz to the prefect of the Moselle (18 March 1846); ibid.
137. The bishop of Metz to the *ministre des Cultes* (8 July 1847); ibid.
138. Letter from the curate of Kuntzig (18 April 1847); ibid.
139. Subprefect of Thionville, letter of 7 January 1847; ibid.
140. Cf. p. 244.
141. One should nevertheless note that the number of such uses seems to have dwindled in Basse-Normandie and the Maine.
142. In this regard, cf. the example of the Var studied by Jocelyn George, *Les Maires dans le département du Var de 1800 à 1940* (Doctorat d'État thesis, University of Paris I, 1987).
143. On the use of the bell of infamy in Geneva, cf. Michel Porret, *Le Crime et ses "circonstances." Punir à Genève au XVIIIe siècle: institutions, discours, pratiques* (thèse de doctorat ès lettres, University of Geneva 1992), p. 324. Regarding Angers, François Lebrun, *Les Hommes et la mort en Anjou*, p. 420.
144. Regulation agreed upon between the bishop of Aire and the prefect of Les Landes (28 January 1837), A.N. F^{19} 4373.
145. Cf. Bour, *Études campanaires mosellanes*, 1:192.
146. See Marc Guillaume, "La ville: nouveaux modes d'emploi," interview conducted by, and video distributed by the RATP (1991). Mona Ozouf stresses how careful the authorities were to differentiate between a "gathering" and a "mob" during the Revolution, in *La Fête révolutionnaire*, p. 374. The tocsin gave rise to a mob aroused by an unforeseeable event.
147. Bour, *Études campanaires mosellanes*, 1:325.
148. There were thus twelve such bells in the town.
149. Bour, *Études campanaires mosellanes*, 1:193. These details arose out of an oral inquiry conducted in the Moselle across a whole lifetime.
150. On this there are two fundamental studies: John Merriman, "The Norman Fires of 1830: Incendiaries and Fear in Rural France," in *French Historical Studies* (1976), pp. 451–466; and Laurent Morin, *Les Incendies de 1830 en Basse-Normandie* (master's dissertation, University of Paris I, October 1992).
151. Thiers, *Traité des cloches*, pp. 82–84.
152. Ibid., pp. 84–85.
153. Hervé Goux, *L'Interprétation officielle du coup d'état du 2 décembre 1851* (master's thesis, University of Paris I, 1991), p. 61.
154. Janine Estèbe, *Tocsin pour un massacre: La saison des Saint-Barthélemy* (Paris: Editions d'aujourd'hui, 1968). The tocsin was supposed to give the armed burghers assembled at the Hôtel de Ville the signal to

begin the massacre. But Catherine de Medici had had the bell rung
before the appointed time. The bells roused the Huguenots and took
away the element of surprise (p. 128).

155. *Gazette des tribunaux* (16 July 1848), quoted by Emmanuel Fureix,
Représentations de l'insurrection et des insurgés de juin 1848 (master's
thesis, University of Paris I, June 1993), p. 58.

156. Cf. Karine Dulong, "Regards en contraste sur le bocage normand,"
in *A travers la Haute-Normandie en Révolution 1789–1800,* Comité
régional d'histoire de la Révolution française (1992), pp. 175–179.

157. "Limoges is on fire" or "Bellac has burned down" were the sorts of
rumors that were circulating among the bands of armed peasants
scouring the Basse-Marche on 6 December 1851. Report of the prosecutor general, A.N. BB[30] 396.

158. Corbin, *Archaïsme et modernité en Limousin,* 2:502–510. On the ringing of the tocsin during revolts against taxes, see also Soulet, *Les
Pyrénées au XIXe siècle, passim.*

159. Fureix, *Représentations de l'insurrection,* p. 43.

160. Denis Beliveau, who has indexed every one of these movements,
records that in fifteen or so such affairs, the crowd rang the tocsin.
Where there were no bells it employed "the horn used by herdsmen
with livestock" (Charette, Saône-et-Loire, 1817), the bagpipes
(Souillac, Lot, 1817), the drum (Indre, 1847) or just saucepans. Denis
Beliveau, *Les Révoltes frumentaires en France dans la première moitié du
XIXe siècle* (thesis, EHESS, 1992), p. 214.

161. For a recent synthesis on this topic, see Corbin, "Histoire de la violence dans les campagnes françaises au XIXe siècle: Esquisse d'un
bilan," in *Ethnologie française,* vol. 21, (July–September 1991), pp.
221–236.

162. Report from the subprefect of Montargis to the prefect of the Loiret
(4 June 1817), A.N. F[11] 728.

163. Postmaster general of Montargis to the prefect of the Loiret (5 June
1817); ibid.

164. Subprefect of Montargis, report quoted (4 June 1817); ibid.

165. Subprefect of Gien to the Count de Choiseul, prefect of the Loiret (6
June 1817).

166. Observations of the members of the *cour prévotale* quoted by the
councillor at the prefecture of the Loiret to the minister of general
police; ibid.

167. Subprefect of Montargis to the prefect of the Loiret (6 June 1817);
ibid.

168. Subprefect of Gien to the minister of general police (10 June 1817);
ibid.

169. Report from the prefect of the Loiret to the minister of general police (10 June 1817); ibid.

170. Lieutenant-colonel, viscount de Courteilles, head of the fourth division, to the commander of the first military division (10 June 1817); ibid.

171. Prefect of the Loiret to the subprefect of Sancerre (Cher) (5 June 1817); ibid.

172. Prefect of the Loiret to the minister of general police (16 June 1817); ibid.

173. Subprefect of Gien to the minister of general police (7 June 1817); ibid.

174. Minister of general police to the prefect of the Loiret (5 June, 7 June, and 10 June 1817); ibid.

175. Anonymous correspondent to the minister of the interior (18 July 1817); ibid.

176. Beliveau, *Les Révoltes frumentaires*, p. 425.

177. A.D. Lot, 4M14. I would like to thank François Ploux for drawing my attention to these affairs in the department of the Lot.

178. A.D. Lot, 3U3, 854.

179. A.D. Lot, 3U1, 1556, Cahors Tribunal.

180. A.D. Lot, 4M21. Gendarmerie report (week of 5 to 10 December 1836).

181. A.D. Lot, 2U168.

182. A.N. 374 F^{35} quoted by Marie-Thérèse Bouyssy, *Trente ans après: Bertrand Barère sous la Restauration ou la rhétorique du Ténare* (thesis, University of Paris I, 1993), p. 374.

183. Henry Houssaye, *1814* (Paris, 1888); and *1815* (Paris, 1893).

184. Ferri-Dufour, *Le Rendez-vous manqué*, pp. 101–104.

185. Philippe Grandjean, *La Dynamique de la Séparation de l'église et de l'état en Indre-et-Loire (1880–1908)* (master's dissertation, University of Tours, 1991), using A.D. Indre-et-Loire, v12–17 March 1906.

186. On this distinction, cf. Georges Lefebvre, *Les Foules révolutionnaires*, as republished in *La Grande Peur de 1789* (Paris: A. Colin, 1988), pp. 243–64.

187. Cf. pp. 83–85.

188. There are numerous references to bells in Corbin, Noëlle Gerome, and Danielle Tartakowsky, *L'Usage politique des fêtes* (Paris: Publications de la Sorbonne, 1994).

189. Cf. pp. 263–80.

190. A.N. F^{19} 4375, 4376, and 4377.

191. For example in the debates with the prefects of the departments of the Aube, the Ariège, the Drôme, the Loiret, and the Lozère.

192. Bishop of Mende to the prefect of the Lozère (27 September 1884), A.N. F^{19} 4376, Lozère.

193. Letter from the mayor of Tréffiagat to the prefect of Finistère (22 June 1904), A.D. Finistère, 1v46.

194. On this question, cf. H. Polge, "Le dimanche et le lundi," in *Annales du Midi* (January–March 1975), pp. 15–36.

SIX. The Stakes Involved in Local Disputes

1. See in particular Singer, *Village Notables in 19th Century France*, p. 68, and all of the works by François Ploux referred to earlier.

2. See Corbin, "Histoire de la violence," pp. 221–36.

3. Their relative importance obviously varies from region to region. They are frequent in the Haute-Marne, but fairly rare in the Lot. In this department as in those that surround it, conflicts in villages tended to crystallize around pews rather than bells.

4. I have in mind works by Gabriel Le Bras, *L'église et le village* (Paris: Flammarion, 1976), and Maurice Agulhon, "La mairie," in Nora, ed., *Les lieux de mémoire*, t. 1, "La République" (Paris: Gallimard, 1986), pp. 167–95.

5. Conversely, ways of representing the church to oneself and of conducting oneself in it would be altered by the building of a town hall and by its enhanced ascendancy. Indeed, the town hall would sometimes present itself as a rival to the ecclesiastical edifice.

6. On all these points, cf. Le Bras, *L'église et le village*, pp. 33–42.

7. It would be interesting to study the extent of references to the Middle Ages imparted thus to the faithful. Schools were not the sole agencies to promote historical awareness.

8. Le Bras, *L'église et le village*, p. 39.

9. Cf. abbot Gorse, *Au bas pays de Limosin* (Paris, 1896), pp. 58–59. More particularly, with regard to the situation of the church in the villages of this region, he writes: "Its glistening cleanliness is in stark contrast to the smells and dung that sully all the doorways in the village. . . . violent altercations are never to be heard there." See also Ihl, "Du politique au sacré."

10. In this sphere too, conduct varied from region to region.

11. Cf. pp. 240ff.

12. On these characteristics of the boundary, cf. Corbin, *The Lure of the Sea: The Discovery of the Seaside in the Western World 1750–1840*, translated by Jocelyn Phelps (Cambridge: Polity Press, 1994). The present book, being devoted to a symbol of centrality, thus follows a study of the blurred boundary, which both threatens and fascinates.

13. See Caillois, *L'Homme et le sacré*, p. 67.

14. Cf. what Yves-Marie Hilaire writes, in *Une chrétienté au XIXᵉ siècle?*, on the construction of calvaries and chapels in the diocese of Arras in the nineteenth century.

15. Dupront, *Du sacré*, p. 484. In Lonlay-l'Abbaye, after the Second World War and again at the time of the dispute over bells in 1958, the "conscripts' flagstaff" was planted close to the entrance to the church, although not at all in a spirit of defiance.

16. Cf. Boutry, *"Le clocher,"* pp. 57–89 .

17. Y. Lambert, "L'évolution des rapports entre l'espace et le sacré à Limerzel au XXᵉ siècle (1900–1982)," in *Annales de Bretagne et des pays de l'Ouest*, special issue, *L'éspace et le Sacré*, (1983), p. 90.

18. On this point, see J. Silver, "French Peasants' Demands for Popular Leadership in the Vendômois (Loir-et-Cher) (1852–1890)," in *Journal of Social History*, vol. 14, no. 2 (1980), pp. 277–93.

19. I refer here to the works of Michèle Grosjean, who is engaged in the study of public space and sound and, more particularly, of the relation of the latter to the sacred, to power, and to territorial conflicts. These studies advocate an "anthropology of sonorities" and the study of "soundscapes." Such an approach cannot help but prove stimulating to historians.

20. Cf. Marcel Roncayolo, "Réflexion sur le territoire," in *Territoire et territorialité*, no. 1, (Paris: ENS, 1983).

21. Some twenty years ago Jean-Louis Flandrin gave an instance of this function, although in this case it was visual. In 1850 the parish priest of Notre-Dame de Boisset (Loire) climbed, in the afternoon after Vespers, to the top of the church tower to survey, with the help of a spyglass, the conduct of the shepherds in his parish. Flandrin, *Amours paysannes* (Paris: Gallimard-Juillard, 1975), p. 126.

22. Letter from the bishop of Langres to the prefect of the Haute-Marne, A.D. Haute-Marne, 48v3, Is.

23. Cf. Guillaume, "La ville: nouveaux modes d'emploi."

24. Petition of four parishioners in Saint-Martin-d'Oney (May, 1834), A.N. F[19] 5709.

25. Cf. pp. 148–58.

26. Letter from the parish priest of Frenelle-la-Grande (16 March 1897), A.D. Vosges, 14v4.

27. See Perrine Gonzalès de Linarès, *Le Banc d'honneur dans les églises au XIXe siècle: Enjeu politique, révélateur social (1800–1870)* (master's thesis, University of Paris I, 1992).

28. Lucien Crouzil, *Le Droit de place dans les églises (bancs et chaises)* (doctoral thesis, University of Toulouse, 1898).

29. Perrine Gonzalès de Linarès, *Le Banc d'honneur, passim*. The two examples that follow are drawn from this same dissertation, pp. 61 and 64.

30. I have borrowed this formula from Michel Bée, *La Croix et la bannière*, p. 201.

31. There are files on these affairs in A.D. Ille-et-Vilaine, 1V16.

32. A.D. Orne, 9V1.

33. Letter from the bishop of Montauban to the mayor of Monbéqui (8 May 1847), A.D. Tarn-et-Garonne, 30v²6.

34. Mayor of L'Honor-de-Cos to the prefect of the Tarn-et-Garonne (29 February 1840), A.D. Tarn-et-Garonne, 30v¹.

35. There are files on these affairs in A.D. Tarn-et-Garonne, 30v² 6. In truth, the problems posed by the positioning of the municipal pew were linked to the question of access to the sanctuary and to the threat of municipal challenges. "There are mayors," wrote the bishop of Montauban to the prefect, on 6 May 1847 (A.D. Tarn-et-Garonne, 30v2 6), "who, upon leaving the village tavern, will sometimes get it into their heads to appear in church with the municipal sash and a sort of guard wearing some kind of emblem in the guise of consular fasces." The allocation of pews was one weapon at the parish priest's disposal, akin to that offered by control over the bells. In 1866 the priest in charge of Socourt (Vosges) withdrew from the schoolmaster the right to ring the Angelus; he was none too fond of this man, who was the mayor's ally, and hoped that he would leave. With this end in mind he switched the schoolmaster's place inside the sanctuary. He hoped that this humiliation would lead the unfortunate man to ask to be moved. (There is a thick file on this affair in A.D. Vosges, 14V6).

36. Note by Baron Rendu, *ministère des Cultes* (8 February 1841), A.N. F¹⁹ 4374.

37. Cf. pp. 233–35.

38. In 1891 the commune of Aigremont (Haute-Marne) was split by a classic conflict over the Angelus. The mayor was at loggerheads with the parish priest. The mayor wanted to have "not the Angelus but midday" rung, and this by his own bell ringer. Everything therefore would lead one to suppose that the hostility of a freethinker was involved, were it not for the fact that the parish priest wrote to the prefect unabashedly: "the mayor is also my titular cantor in the church." Letter from the parish priest (25 November 1891) A.D. Haute-Marne 48v2.

39. This law involved the application of the representative principle at communal level; in small rural communes, however, it seems fair to

assume that virtually all heads of family were electors. Cf. Rachel
Gaducheau, *Le Déroulement des élections municipales sous la
Monarchie de Juillet, en fonction de la loi du 21 mars 1831* (master's the-
sis, University of Paris I, 1992). It is also worth noting that the law of
July 1837 conferred upon communes the status of civil persons.

40. Cf. Silver, "French Peasants' Demands," p. 227. With regard to the
eighteenth century, Jessenne, *Pouvoir au village et Révolution*, p. 40,
emphasizes how, in very much the same perspective, these local disputes were already of real importance.

41. I refer here to the meaning ascribed to the use of rural bells and not
to the Romantic image of the village bell, which was then breaking
down, or at least being reshaped. Cf. pp. 294ff.

42. For a brief survey of such changes, cf. Corbin, "Regards croisés sur
la société rurale (1860–1900)," in *Bulletin de la Société d'histoire moderne*, no. 3 (1986), pp. 24ff.

43. Cf. J. George, *Les Maires dans le département du Var de 1800 à 1940*
(doctorat d'État, University of Paris I, 1987), and Agulhon, ed., *Les
Maires du Consulat à nos jours*.

44. On all these points see Adrien Dubief and Victor Gottofrey, *Traité de
l'administration des cultes, 1891–1892*, t. 1, pp. 295–308. Earlier opinions formulated by M. Gaudry, *Traité de la législation des cultes et spé-
cialement du culte catholique* (Paris, 1854), 1:221 and 265, 2:517–519
and, regarding clocks, pp. 520–521.

45. Quoted by Jadart et al., *Les Cloches du canton de Rethel*, p. vii.

46. Cf. pp. 273–80.

47. Ihl, *La Citoyenneté en fête*, p. 385.

48. Eugen Weber, *La Fin des terroirs: La modernisation de la France rurale,
1870–1914* (Paris: Fayard, 1983).

49. Speech mentioned in n45. Cf. pp. 294–95.

SEVEN. The Control of Auditory Messages

1. These conflicts of a juridical nature could only be resolved by the
authorities or the courts, and are therefore not of particular interest to
us here. The arguments advanced by the town hall or the presbytery
on such occasions were stereotyped. The former regarded the peal as
communal property; the mayor and municipal council stressed that
the bells had been bought by the commune or through a subscription
launched among its inhabitants. They claimed the right to decide
when a recasting should occur, when a purchase should be made, or
who should be godparents for a bell. Conversely, the parish priest and
members of the parochial church council regarded the peal as parish
property, pointing out if need be that payment had been by the

parochial church council or the congregation. The bell was, after all, a consecrated object, and the parish priest, being recognized as the sole regulator of bell ringing, should have the right to decide on recastings, purchases, and any tunings, even when the bells were proved to be the property of the commune.

2.   Bour, *Études campanaires mosellanes*, 1:174.

3.   Sometimes nothing more than a modification to the mode of reading was involved. Before the installation of a clock, a sundial sometimes allowed one to know what the time was. In communes of the Moselle without clocks the poorest inhabitants used to consult sundials placed on the walls of churches. Bour, *Études campanaires mosellanes*, 1:174.

4.   A.D. Gers v841, agreement for the acquisition of a clock by the commune of Auradé (18 May 1838).

5.   Cf. A.N. BB18, three boxes devoted to the opposition to the census of 1841.

6.   Extract from the minutes of the municipal council of the commune of Tillac (19 May 1839), A.D. Gers, v841.

7.   For example, opinion of the bishop of Palmiers in a letter to the prefect of the Ariège (17 March 1883), A.N. F^{19} 4374. The celebration of services was likewise affected by the growing desire for accuracy.

8.   *Bulletin officiel du ministère de l'Intérieur* (1858), p. 21, quoted by the minister of the interior on 10 November 1881, A.N. F^{19} 4374. Four years previously, the jurist Gaudry (*Traité de la législation des cultes*, 2:520) had expressed a more nuanced judgment. "The clock," he acknowledged, "does not belong to the vestry; it does not even belong to the church except in cases where its installation, or the installation of its dial, have required modifications to the structure of the edifice such that its removal would cause damage. Although the clock belongs to the commune, it is judged to have attached it to the premises in perpetuity; it could therefore never have it removed." Furthermore, the mayor could not install a clock in the bell tower without the express permission of the parochial church council.

9.   Letter from the subprefect of Vitré to the prefect of the Ille-et-Vilaine (25 October 1851), A.N. F^{19} 4374. All the documents that follow are drawn from this file.

10.   Letter from the parish priest of Rhétiers to the bishop of Rennes (25 November 1851).

11.   Ibid.

12.   Protestations of the parochial church council (9 February 1848).

13.   Letter from the bishop of Langres to the prefect of the Haute-Marne (6 December 1853), A.D. Haute-Marne, 48v2, Chancenay. The prelate shared the parish priest's sense of grievance.

14.   Mayor of Chaumont to the prefect of the Haute-Marne (3 March 1868), ibid.

15.   Letter from the mayor of Humbécourt to the prefect (11 January 1877), ibid.

16.   Deliberations of Andelot parochial church council (1 August 1880), ibid.

17.   File on this affair in A.D. Vosges, 14v3.

18.   A.N. F^{19} 4373.

19.   A.N. F^{19} 4374.

20.   A.N. F^{19} 4373.

21.   Letter from the mayor of Salmagne to the prefect (11 December 1865), A.D. Meuse, 174M1. The parish priest's answer betrays the uncertain nature of timekeeping in the countryside, when there was no legal time. In order to attain any sort of accuracy one had to refer to whatever clocks were in the locality. The parish priest of Salmagne retorted, in a letter to the bishop on 19 December that the municipal clock "is virtually never right." "For some time now it has been from *twenty to twenty-five minutes ahead* of Bar, Ligny, and the surrounding localities."

22.   A.N. F^{19} 4373.

23.   It goes without saying that the term "bell ringer," or *sonneur*, does not refer here to the *sonneurs*, or players of musical instruments, described in, for example, George Sand's *Les Maîtres sonneurs*.

24.   On the listing of the bell ringer's duties, cf. Nanglard, *Les Cloches des églises du diocèse d'Angoulême*, pp. 23–24.

25.   On the cantor, a figure whom historians of the ethnomusicology of the French countryside judge to have been of crucial importance, see Jacques Cheyronnaud, "Musique et institutions au village," in *Ethnologie française*, t. 14, no. 3 (July–September 1984), pp. 265–280. This article contains some fascinating details on the apprenticeship of the sexton-cantor. The author writes (p. 270) that, until the triumph of the Third Republic, "a good many parish lecterns served—alongside the bells and the Domine Salvum fac—as local stages upon which the great dramas of national political life were played out in miniature." As for the "schoolmaster at the lectern," he seems to Jacques Cheyronnaud to have been one of the last vestiges of a model "integrated into a post-Tridentine conception of pastoral care."

26.   A point emphasized by an inhabitant of Serviès (Tarn) in a letter to the prefect dated 13 May 1841. A.D. Tarn, 1v8. He deduces this from the list of a rural bell ringer's duties.

27.   According to Article 33 of the decree of 30 December 1809, the appointment or dismissal of bell ringers was the responsibility of the

churchwardens, with names being put forward by the parish priest or priest in charge; Article 37 stipulated that payment of these salaried persons was up to the vestry. The royal statute of 12 January 1825 stipulated that, in rural parishes, the choice was that of the parish priest alone, whatever the origin of the bells. M. Gaudry, *Traité de la legislation*, 2:518.

28.   Prior to the triumph of the Third Republic, needless to say.

29.   A practice already emphasized by Dergny in *Les Cloches du pays de Bray*, 2:20, and confirmed by soundings I have taken in the departmental archives.

30.   A.D. Hautes-Pyrénées, v90.

31.   Ibid.

32.   Report from the parish priest of Andelot (1 December 1848) sent to Consigny on a good will mission, A.D. Haute-Marne, 48v2. As a general rule in this department, this priest adds, the peal was paid for "in part by the vestry, in part by the inhabitants." The mayor of Consigny had, in addition, "held a club" (note the term used to denote a traditional assembly of the inhabitants) to win support for his claims, namely, the right to choose the ringer of the curfew, to hold the keys to the bell tower, and to reject the tariff of peals drawn up by the parish priest.

33.   Regarding Braux, A.D. Haute-Marne, 48v2. It is worth noting the use of bids in Neuville-sur-Ornain and Rumont in 1852. A.D. Meuse, 37v1. In 1907 the prefect turned down the request made by Hattonchatel municipal council to put the bell ringing up for auction.

34.   In 1873 the bishop was obliged to point out that auctioning of bell ringing was contrary to the texts. He does not seem to have been heeded. In the arrondissement of Neufchâteau, to judge by the subprefect's account, auctioning of bell ringing was "generally" in use. Letter to the prefect (15 May 1889), A.D. Vosges, 14v6. This was still the case in Isches in 1892. A.D. Vosges, 14v5.

35.   Deliberations of the municipal council (14 February 1875), over terms governing the *"relaissée"* of the church peal. A.D. Haute-Marne, 48v3, Damrémont. In that year (1875), the lucky beneficiary of the *"relaissée"* was a cutler residing in the commune.

36.   A.D. Haute-Marne, 48v2, Buchey. The same procedure was followed in Recurt (in the Hautes-Pyrénées) in 1889. A.D. Hautes-Pyrénées, v90.

37.   A file on this affair is in A.D. Hautes-Pyrénées, v109.

38.   A conflict of this type erupted in Puylaroque in January 1851. A.D. Tarn-et-Garonne, 30v2. According to Article 7 of the ordinance of 12 January 1825 and the ministerial decision of 28 July 1839, however,

only the parish priest (or the priest in charge) could dismiss the bell ringer.

39.   According to Article 69 of the organic Articles; the storerooms of the departmental archives, I repeat, contain whole bundles of such documents, which are extremely detailed. In 1876 the bishop of Aire explained at length just how these tariffs were applied. A.N. F^{19} 4376.

40.   Which enabled Bour to discern a rise in income for the bell ringers of the Moselle in the nineteenth century and, above all, a great disparity in levels of remuneration from commune to commune (Bour, *Études campanaires mosellanes*, 1:292).

41.   A.D. Gers, v841. Account given by the mayor and the subprefect of Lombez.

42.   See Traimond, *Ethnologie historique des pratiques monétaires*.

43.   Complaint by the mayor of Arthès (10 February 1894), A.D. Tarn, 1v8.

44.   Cf. pp. 80 and 110.

45.   Attested to by an inhabitant of Serviès (Tarn) on 13 May 1841, A.D. Tarn, 1v8.
      With regard to the Cantal, cf. Trin, *Les Cloches du Cantal*, p. 56. In 1889 the mayor of Clavières banned this practice, which was still extant in his commune. A.D. Cantal, v32.

46.   Collections policy (21 November 1889), A.D. Ille-et-Vilaine, 1v12.

47.   Testimony of the archbishop of Albi (15 November 1893), A.D. Tarn, 1v8.

48.   Letter from the mayor to the prefect of the Tarn (22 September 1893), A.D. Tarn, 1v8.

49.   Letter from the mayor of Souyeaux (18 February 1896) and request from Burg municipal council (December 1898), A.D. Hautes-Pyrénées, v90.

50.   Deliberations of Layrisse municipal council (29 May 1895), ibid.

51.   Deliberations of Calavanté municipal council (26 May 1892). Here the "acceptable quantity of wheat" was twelve and a half liters. And letter from the mayor of Siarrouy to the prefect (10 February 1899).

52.   A particularly telling example is that of the tariff fixed in the commune of Manoir in 1858. The mayor had decided to lay down a fixed tariff to make it impossible for any bell ringer in future to "change the fixed rates of remuneration and *to quit the bells*, whenever he so pleases." He demanded that henceforth the auction should also involve a desposit. A.D. Haute-Marne, 48v3, Manoir.

53.   Deliberations of the municipal council (14 February 1875), A.D. Haute-Marne, 48v2, Damrémont.

54. Series of documents concerning this prefectorial policy in A.D. Hautes-Pyrénées, v90.
55. Cf. p.163.
56. A.N. F[19] 4373.
57. A.D. Hautes-Pyrénées, v90.
58. Reported by Brugière et al., *Exploration campanaire du Périgord*, p. 238.
59. Letter from the priest in charge of Serviès to the prefect of the Tarn (13 May 1841), A.D. Tarn, 1v8.
60. Which, needless to say, provoked conflict, A.D. Tarn, 1v8.
61. One should note that here only communal peals were involved. Letter from the mayor of Chambroncourt to the prefect (23 June 1896), A.D. Haute-Marne, 48v2, Chambroncourt.
62. The file on this complicated affair is in A.D. Haute-Marne, 48v2, Colombey-lès-Choiseul.
63. Paluel-Marmont, *Cloches et carillons*, pp. 158ff.
64. Frédéric Henriet, *Les Campagnes d'un paysagiste* (Paris, 1891), pp. 163–69, quoted by Berthelé, *Enquêtes campanaires*, p. 304.
65. Letter from the prefect of the Ille-et-Vilaine to the archbishop of Rennes (July 1885. A.D), Ille-et-Vilaine, 1v12.
66. Jadart et al., *Épigraphie campanaire ardennaise*, p. 34.
67. The reader will note the wish to leave a trace of two different histories, one having to do with bells and the other with grain, which here happen to be linked.
68. The parish priest of Salmagne (Meuse) gave assurances (letter to the bishop, 19 December 1865) that the bell ringer belonged "to one of the good families of Salmagne." Furthermore, he was "one of its most prominent members." A.D. Meuse, 174MI.
69. As the religious bell ringer for La Chapelle-aux-Bois (Vosges) emphasized in 1886, one had to take into account "the difficulty of ringing the right time" when one could not consult a clock. The bell ringers in small communes often took their cue, when possible, from the bells of the more substantial agglomerations. A.D. Vosges, 14v5.
70. Complaint from the mayor of Arthès to the prefect of the Tarn (10 February 1894), A.D. Tarn, 1v8.
71. Article by Arthur Loth, *"L'Univers"* (5 July 1892).
72. Cf. p. 171.
73. Complaint from the parish priest referred to by the *ministre des Cultes* in a letter to the prefect of the Eure (18 September 1832), A.N. F[19] 4375, Eure.
74. Complaint from the bishop of Cahors to the *ministre des Cultes* (28 April 1810), A.N. F[19] 4374.

75. On 30 Pluviôse Year II (18 February 1794), the administration of the district of Trévoux (Ain) wrote: "that each commune is equipped with a fife and drum . . . the republicans are all soldiers; they cannot do without a drum." Quoted by Boutry, "Le clocher," p. 79.

76. Letter from the subprefect of Thionville to the prefect (7 January 1847), A.N. F[19] 4377. Regarding the Orne, cf. p. 000.

77. File in A.D. Ille-et-Vilaine, 1V12. Quotations drawn from a letter from the mayor of Saint-Aubin-du-Pavail to the prefect (22 August 1816).

78. In a letter to the prefect, A.D. Meuse, 174M1. Municipal bells were a constant source of fascination to nineteenth-century historians and served to stimulate campanarian inquiry.

79. Letter from the mayor of Choiseul to the prefect of the Haute-Marne, A.D. Haute-Marne, 48v2, Choiseul.

80. Dergny, *Les Cloches du pays,* p. 408.

81. A.D. Haute-Marne, 48v3, Humbécourt.

82. Jadart et al., *Les Cloches de Rethel,* p. vii.

83. Deliberations of Vaubexy municipal council (18 April 1894), A.D. Vosges, 14v4.

84. In 1909 the municipality of Rivesaltes decided that some bells and a clock should be installed in a tower that was independent of the church. When this decision was made, a new auditory code was also formulated. It was decided that where secular funerals were concerned, "the bell ringing would take place on the eve of the funeral at eight o'clock in the evening, and on the day itself a half an hour before the ceremony and when the body was raised. For adults over seven years old the great bell of the clock would be rung; for children, the small bell reserved for the purpose would be used. . . . the peal would consist of five *double* strokes of the bell for men and five *triple* strokes of the bell for women and girls." It is interesting to note what importance these freethinkers attached to the deaths of those of the female gender. Two years later (cf. p. 258), this decision was annulled. *Le Gaulois* (12 December 1909) and *Le Radical* (12 December 1909). According to the journalist from *Le Radical,* several municipal councils in the region then put forward plans for the construction on the town hall of "a clock tower containing bells . . . for strictly secular ceremonies." This calls to mind Louis Perouas' study of the Limousin, *Refus d'une religion, religion d'un refus en Limousin rural, 1880–1940* (Paris; EHESS, 1985). The bundle F[19] 5650 in the Archives nationales contains press clippings covering such affairs.

85. It had formerly been the tradition in this commune to entrust secular peals to the firemen. Cf. letter from the mayor to the prefect (22 July 1897), A.D. Vosges, 14v4.

86.   For example, the parish priest of Gournay-sur-Marne (Seine-et-Oise) in 1886, A.N. F^{19} 4377. Or the bishop of Nancy in 1884, A.N. F^{19} 4376, Meurthe-et-Moselle.

87.   Complaint from the parish priest of Brillon (6 July 1880), A.D. Meuse, 37V1.

88.   Conflict in Relanges in 1881, A.D. Vosges, 14v3.

89.   Letter from the parish priest of Mazères (4 February 1901), A.D. Hautes-Pyrénées, v90. In order to grasp what this accusation really means, one has to bear in mind that in some regions the bell towers were used as dovecotes. This was the case in, for example, Arras. Cf. Hilaire, *Une chrétienté au XIXe siècle?*, p. 67. The author expresses surprise that the bishop should have tolerated such a practice.

90.   There is a file on this affair in A.D. Haute-Marne, 48v3, Illoud.

91.   Letters from the mayor of Lézignan to the prefect of the Hautes-Pyrénées (3 March 1833) for the first quotation, and 10 May 1833 for the second, A.D. Hautes-Pyrénées, v108.

92.   Which included several municipal councillors.

93.   Petition of six notables from Lézignan (14 July 1833), A.D. Hautes-Pyrénées, v108. It is worth noting how the fourteenth of July was celebrated in this village in 1833.

94.   Remarks attached to a draft regulation of peals sent by the bishop of Langres to the prefect of the Haute-Marne (April 1838), A.N. F^{19} 4376, Haute-Marne. This text places the emphasis on the processes through which intracommunal conflict was unleashed.

95.   Gendarmerie minutes (17 March 1895), A.D. Hautes-Pyrénées, v90.

96.   Letter from the priest in charge of Marseillan to the prefect of the Hautes-Pyrénées (3 March 1895), ibid.

97.   Letter from the priest in charge of Souyeaux to the prefect (12 January 1895), ibid.

98.   A.D. Haute-Marne, 48v3, Marac. In 1884 the municipality entrusted "the bell ringing of concern to the commune as a whole" to one of the bell ringers dismissed by the parish priest for having agreed to ring on the fourteenth of July. On the other hand, the mayor withdrew the duty of rewinding the clock from the other sexton-bell ringer who had refused to ring the national holiday. From then on there was unremitting hostility between the two men, despite the attempts made by the subprefect of Langres and the prefect of the Haute-Marne to agree on an "arrangement."

99.   There is a file on this dispute in A.D. Vosges, 14v6. The festival of 5 May 1889 celebrated the centenary of the meeting of the Estates-General.

100.   Letter from the president of Pouyastruc parochial church council to

the prefect of the Hautes-Pyrénées (6 January 1885), A.D. Hautes-Pyrénées, v90. The files on Betpouy and Bazus-Neste, ibid.

101. *Gazette des tribunaux* (19 February 1910). Exposition of the *avocat général* Feuilloley, A.N. F[7] 12389. Note, in passing, the way women are represented here.

102. Generally, however, they have treated these local conflicts in terms of their own overriding preoccupations, which concern events at the national level.

103. It also prompted a national inquiry, a good many aspects of which, appearing in the departmental archives, merit closer study.

104. Cf. Philippe Grandcoing, *La Bande à Burgout* (Limoges, 1991).

105. Cf. Frédéric Chauvaud, *Tensions et conflits: Aspects de la vie rurale au XIX siècle d'après les archives judiciaires. L'exemple de l'arrondissement de Rambouillet (1811–1871)* (thesis, University of Paris X-Nanterre, 1989).

106. Petition from the municipality of Sorbets against the priest in charge (28 April 1883), A.N. F[19] 5769.

107. That is, of the care of two parishes.

108. Cf. p. 276.

109. Cf. Dubief and Gottofrey, *Traité de l'administration des cultes, 1891–1892,* 1:307.

110. A.N. F[19] 4375–4377.

111. An important document that reflects the doctrine of intransigence in such matters. Letter from Monsignor Freppel (23 March 1885), A.N. F[19] 4376, Maine-et-Loire.

112. Monsignor Hasley, archbishop of Avignon, in an interview with the prefect reported to the *ministre des Cultes* (26 June 1884), A.N. F[19] 4377, Vaucluse.

113. The history of this show of resistance was recapitulated by Goblet, *ministre des Cultes,* in a letter to the minister of foreign affairs (29 April 1885), A.N. F[19] 4374.

114. Letter from the bishop of Tarbes (Prosper-Marie Billère) to parish priests and priests in charge (15 April 1886), A.D. Hautes-Pyrénées, v105.

115. This was the case, in 1808, in several communes in the Deux-Sèvres. Letter from the prefect to the *ministre des Cultes* (17 October 1808), A.N. F[19] 4374.

116. The prefect confirmed the regular nature of this grievance, which occasioned "such anxiety in so moderate an assembly." Letter to the *ministre des Cultes* (9 November 1839), A.N. F[19] 4374.

117. A.D. Hautes-Pyrénées, v108. The mayor refused outright to give the key of the bell tower to the parish priest. He wrote to the prefect on 8

April 1833, despite the latter's instructions: "The mayor of Lézignan cannot yield to, and never shall yield to, this demand from the priest."

118. Note on these difficulties arising in the diocese of Metz, *ministère de la Justice et des Cultes* (19 September 1845), A.N. F^{19} 4374.

119. Ibid.

120. Report from the prefect of the Moselle to the *ministre de la Justice et des Cultes* (5 June 1844), A.N. F^{19} 4374.

121. Ibid.

122. Letter from the prefect of the Loiret to the minister of justice (15 June 1836), A.N. F^{19} 4374.

123. A.D. Haute-Marne, 48v2, Dampierre; and Singer, *Village Notables in 19th Century France,* p. 72, using A.D. Oise, 1v15.

124. Report of the subprefect of Thionville to the prefect of the Moselle (27 April 1847), A.N. F^{19} 4374. Here the conflict was grafted onto a linguistic dispute. The parish priest was accused of trying to frustrate the schoolmaster's attempts to spread the use of the French language.

125. File on this affair, ibid.

126. A.D. Haute-Marne, 48v2, Colombey-les-Deux-Églises.

127. A.D. Tarn, 1v87.

128. A.D. Haute-Marne, 48v2.

129. In fact, the drafting of the new regulations governing peals had been debated for two years.

130. A.D. Vosges, 14v4.

131. Letters from the mayor of Saint-Pierrevillers to the prefect of the Meuse (15 July and 16 September 1889), A.D. Meuse, 37v1.

132. Mayor to the prefect of Finistère (3 September 1884), A.D. Finistère, 1v46.

133. A.D. Ariège, Series v.

134. A.N. F^{19} 4376, Marne.

135. A.N. F^{19} 4374.

136. There is a file on this protracted affair in A.D. Haute-Marne, 48v2, Biesles.

137. At the same time, the parish priest, who claimed the right to go wherever he pleased in the building, decided to force the lock of the municipal "clock chamber."

138. Letter from the mayor of Biesles to the prefect of the Haute-Marne (10 November 1856), A.D. Haute-Marne, 48v2, Biesles.

139. Here we recognize an attitude altogether characteristic of these kinds of conflicts, whereby the municipality would not deign to solicit any favors, deeming it too humiliating to do so.

140. Letter from the bishop of Langres to the prefect of the Haute-Marne (22 November 1856), A.D. Haute-Marne, 48v2, Biesles.

141. Letter from the mayor to the prefect (11 December 1856), ibid.
142. Minutes of the Brigadier at the Gendarmerie (16 March 1857), ibid.
143. Petition of twelve inhabitants of Biesles to the prefect, ibid.
144. Letter from the prefect of the Marne to the *ministre des Cultes* (15 December 1885), A.N. F^{19} 4376, Marne.
145. A.D. Haute-Marne, 48v3, Dampierre.
146. Procedure employed by the parish priest of Baleix (Basses-Pyrénées).

EIGHT. The Principal "Clashes"

1. In 1907 the parish priest of Bure (Meuse) still refused, for this reason, to ring at the death of a child, which caused the mayor to protest. A.D. Meuse, 174M1.
2. Manuscript note by the prelate to a letter sent by the prefect of the Somme (28 January 1833), A.N. F^{19} 4377, Somme.
3. M. Lagrée, *Mentalités, religion et histoire en Haute-Bretagne au XIXe siècle* (Paris 1977), p. 447; and letter from the parish priest of Villeréal to the *ministre des Cultes* (15 January 1836), (allusions to the two deaths occurring in 1832 and 1835), A.N. F^{19} 4374.
4. Files on these affairs are in A.N. F^{19} 4373. Cf. p. 255.
5. Usage attested to in Glos-la-Ferrière (27 July 1840), A.D. Orne, 9v1.
6. "Secular usages, public celebrations . . . " A.N. F^{19} 4374.
7. Ibid.
8. There is a lengthy discussion of this theme in Dubief and Gottofrey, *Traité de l'administration des cultes*, 1:296.
9. Letter from the prefect of the Loiret to the *ministre des Cultes* (27 October 1830), A.N. F^{19} 4374.
10. Letter from the *ministre de la Justice et des Cultes* to the prefect of the Vosges (6 February 1835). The incident dates from December 1834, A.D. Vosges, 14v6. Document from this affair in A.N. F^{19} 4377.
11. Cf. pp. 148ff.
12. Letter from the son of the dead man to the *ministre des Cultes* (18 May 1837), A.N. F^{19} 4377, Vosges.
13. Cf. pp. 53–62.
14. Letter quoted from the parish priest of Villeréal (15 January 1836).
15. Letter from the prefect of the Jura to the *ministre des Cultes* (4 May 1840), A.N. F^{19} 4374.
16. Such incidents, according to the bishop of Langres, were frequent in the diocese. Exchange of correspondence with the prefect of the Haute-Marne, with a view to drafting regulations for peals (December 1838), A.N. F^{19} 4376, Haute-Marne.

17. Letter from the parish priest of Giromagny to the bishop of Strasbourg (30 January 1837), A.N. F^{19} 4373. In November 1847 the mayor of Weyersheim had the death of a Protestant miller rung by force.

18. Letter from the priest in charge of Marcilly to the prefect (6 February 1848), A.D. Haute-Marne, 48v3, Marcilly.

19. Letter from the mayor of Marcilly to the prefect (10 February 1848), ibid.

20. Jacqueline Lalouette, "Les enterrements civils dans les premières décennies de la IIIe République," in *Ethnologie française* (1983), 2:122–123. Quotation drawn from a work by Fonsegrive, *Lettres d'un curé de canton* (Paris, 1895).

21. See Loux, *Le Jeune Enfant et son corps, passim;* and in relation to the Limousin, Corbin, *Prélude au Front populaire*, p. 54.

22. Motion proposed by M. N. Simon (publicist in Bar-sur-Seine), carried at the Congress of the National Association of Freethinkers of France, session of 2 November 1908. The motion was followed by a letter, on 16 February 1909, to Clemenceau, the minister of the interior, claiming the right to use the bells. The congress had in fact instructed Simon to give the motion as much publicity as possible. Simon waxed ironical; he wrote to Clemenceau: "I am sending you my latest pamphlet. You will read it when you are no longer in power . . . ." A.N. F^{19} 12389.

23. Ibid.

24. *La Lanterne* (13 December 1909), A.N. F^{19} 5650.

25. Clarification offered by the prefecture of the Meuse regarding this affair in Rivesaltes, and sent to the mayors of the department, A.D. Meuse, 174M1.

26. A.D. Eure-et-Loir, VII.

27. After the passing of the law of separation, the argument of the anti-clericals, based on the nonexistence of church associations, was not applicable. The law of 1907 overlooked the problem, and a circular concerned with its application sent out on 21 January 1907 by the *ministre des Cultes* is very clear in this regard: peals for baptisms, marriages, or secular burials did not come under any of the headings anticipated by the legislator. Cf. file in A.N. F^{19} 12389. Indeed, they do not appear on the list given in Article 51 of the decree of 16 March 1906.

28. A.N. F^{19} 4377, Haute-Savoie. It is worth noting that in Bonne the inhabitants rang the Angelus despite the interdict cast by the bishop.

29. As an example, box files F^{7} 12389 and F^{19} 5650 in the Archives nationales consist of bulky collections of press clippings and decrees concerning these affairs.

30. Letter from the bishop of Chartres to the prefect (28 June for Nogent-sur-Eure, and 6 August 1891 for Saint-Arnoult, A.D. Eure-et-Loir, VII.

31. Ibid. The mayor of Châtillon, after the separation of church and state, had all burials and secular marriages rung. The ordinance of the prefect of the Eure-et-Loir banning these peals is dated 24 January 1907, A.D. Eure-et-Loir, VII.

32. Letter from the mayor of Marboué to the prefect of the Eure-et-Loir (28 February 1907), A.D. Eure-et-Loir, VII.

33. Report from the parish priest to the subprefect of Châteaudun (21 December 1907), ibid.

34. Ibid.

35. Such as the mayor of Touvérac (Charente). Cf. *La Libre Parole* (6 September 1908), A.N. F[19] 5650.

36. Mayor of Bédeilhac (Ariège) in 1895. Brigitte Basdevant-Gaudemet, *Le Jeu concordataire dans la France du XIXe siècle* (Paris: PUF, 1988), p. 251.

37. Parish priest of Bulainville, letter to the prefect (18 January 1906). Nonpayment of collection had become, in this department, the most common cause for peals being withheld. (See affairs described in A.D. Meuse, 174M1). The parish priest of Bussy even went so far as to withhold the bells from those whose families had not paid in advance, according to the mayor in a letter to the prefect (9 May 1907).

38. *Le Rappel* (24 June 1909), A.N. F[19] 5650. It goes without saying that narratives of such affairs, when based on press clippings, are less reliable than those we learn about through administrative correspondence.

39. It is worth noting that this list reflects the geography of campanarian sensibility, and that the lion's share goes to the central eastern area of France.

40. Evoked by Article 51 of the decree of 16 March 1906.

41. The eve, the morning of the burial, and immediately after the lowering of the body into the trench.

42. *Le Droit: Journal des tribunaux* (28 March 1909), Cf. A.N. F[7] 12389.

43. Except from 1870 to 1880 (cf. p. 270). On these festivals of sovereignty, see the first part of Corbin et al., *L'Usage politique des fêtes*. More specifically, given the subject under discussion here, see the chapters by Corbin, Rosemonde Sanson and Olivier Ihl devoted to the July Monarchy, the Second Empire, and the Third Republic. I would stress that in this sphere the alteration in the scale of the debates does not date from the triumph of the Third Republic and the

celebration of the fourteenth of July, as the detailed studies devoted to this moment of campanarian study might lead one to suppose.

44.   Program of this festival is contained in A.D. Tarn-et-Garonne, 30VI.

45.   In Montauban the program for the festival of 4 November 1829, as communicated to the prefecture on 30 October, stipulated the ringing of *all* the bells on the eve and the day itself of the festival, ibid.

46.   The parish priest of Dol and the mayor were then at odds over the precise times when the bells should be rung. A.D. Ille-et-Vilaine, 1V12. Complaint by the parish priest of Montréal (22 January 1829), A.D. Gers, v841. The parish priest had "the anniversary of the Martyr King and his august spouse" rung, in a "solemn and particular manner," he wrote, "as I have always done." An individual then turned up and demanded to ring in the mayor's name.

47.   I would nevertheless repeat (cf. p. 43) that attempts to reconstitute the campanarian patrimony continued under this regime.

48.   These banquets, which were attended by national guardsmen and notables and which were meant to celebrate the new regime, were different in nature to the later, oppositional banquets. On these latter, see Jacques Osinski, *Les Banquets d'opposition sous la monarchie de Juillet* (master's dissertation, University of Paris I, 1991).

49.   Frédéric Martin, *La Révolution de 1830 et son écho dans les campagnes: Août 1830–juillet 1831* (master's dissertation, University of Paris I, 1990). As an example, the decking of the bell tower with flags provoked several conflicts in the Ille-et-Vilaine. A.D., 1V15. In 1831 the dean of Saint-Germain-du-Pinel made some seditious observations about the national flag draped on top of the bell tower. The prefect demanded its removal. The municipality of Sens-de-Bretagne wished, in July 1832, to remove the cross that dominated the church tower and to replace it with "a large and imposing flag," despite the protestations of the parish priest. Furthermore, the national guard had replaced a flag on the other tower of the building, "the one that had been put there in 1830 being now worn out." This was but a temporary measure, "until such time as one could put a metal one on top of this same tower." On 29 July, during the national festival, the inhabitants ran up a new flag despite the prefecture having advised against it. That evening a charivari was unleashed against the parish priest. A.D. Ille-et-Vilaine, 1V15.

50.   Circular sent to the mayors of the department by the prefect of the Ille-et-Vilaine (January 1851), ibid. Sometimes, he wrote, the mayors had even had the bells rung at night.

51.   Cf. Corbin, "L'impossible présence du roi," in *L'Usage politique des fêtes.*

52.   Cf. Fabrice Lascar, *Cris et chuchotements: Démonstrations séditieuses et injures au roi ou à la famille royale sous la monarchie de Juillet* (master's dissertation, University of Paris I, 1990).

53.   Not all parish priests and priests in charge shared these feelings of hostility. In the aftermath of the July Days, the parish priest of Saugnac (Landes) stole a march on the mayor and had a tricolor flag draped over the top of the bell tower; then he hurried to the subprefecture to have the mayor dismissed as a bad citizen. Everything suggests that in this case he used the national debate to rid himself of his adversary. Complaint from the inhabitants of Saugnac (August 1833), A.N. F[19] 5709.

54.   Cf. Mona Ozouf, "L'invention de l'ethnographie française: le questionnaire de l'Académie Celtique," in *Annales. Économies, Sociétés, Civilisations*, 36th year, no. 2 (March–April 1981), pp. 210–30.

55.   Minutes of the sergeant from the Largentière gendarmerie (8 March 1831), A.N. F[7] 6779.

56.   Letter from the prefect of the Calvados to the *ministre de l'Instruction publique et des Cultes* (16 August 1832) A.N. F[19] 4374.

57.   The present-day Aunay-sur-Odon, rendered sadly famous on account of Pierre Rivière. See *Moi, Pierre Rivière, ayant egorgé ma mère, ma soeur et mon frère ... Un cas de parricide au XIXe siècle*, presented by Michel Foucault (Paris: Gallimard-Juillard, 1973).

58.   Deliberations of Aulnay parochial church council, the parish priest's statement (10 August 1832), A.N. F[19] 4374.

59.   Deliberations of Aulnay municipal council (14 August and 19 August 1832), ibid.

60.   Ibid.

61.   Statement quoted in n58.

62.   Deliberations quoted, from 19 August 1832, ibid.

63.   Letter from the bishop of Blois to the subprefect of the arrondissement of Vendôme (25 August 1834), A.N. F[19] 4374.

64.   Letter from the subprefect of the arrondissement of Vendôme to the prefect of the Loir-et-Cher (3 October 1834). The subprefect nevertheless contested the bishop's interpretation of the mayor of Nourray's attitude. In his view, the latter had merely sought to "save the flag."

65.   Letter from the *ministre de l'Instruction publique et des Cultes* to the prefect of the Marne (28 August 1832); and letter from the prefect of the Dordogne to the *ministre de l'Intérieur et des Cultes* (22 May 1833), A.N. F[19] 4374.

66.   Response of the count of Argout, *ministre de l'Intérieur et des Cultes* to the prefect of the Dordogne (5 June 1833), A.N. F[19] 4374.

67. This shift in the regime's symbolic sphere, as manifested in campanarian history, tallies with Michel Marrinan's observations regarding the development of official portraiture in this period. *Painting Politics for Louis-Philippe* (New Haven: Yale University Press, 1988).

68. Letter in response to a question formulated by Adolphe Thiers, minister of the interior, A.N. F^{19} 4374.

69. There is a file on this affair in A.N. F^{19} 4376, Basses-Pyrénées.

70. Royal prosecutor to the general prosecutor (15 and 21 May 1835), ibid. The mayor of Pontacq had also banned the ringing of the approach of the new bishop on the occasion of his pastoral visit.

71. A.D. Ille-et-Vilaine, 1V12.

72. Cf. pp.107–108.

73. Telegram from the *ministre des Cultes* to the prefect of the Haute-Saône (28 July 1847), A.N. F^{19} 4374.

74. Letter from the prefect of the Saône-et-Loire to the *ministre des Cultes* (29 September 1847), ibid.

75. Since the signature is illegible it is impossible to identify either the author or the post he held. A.N. F^{19} 4377, Vosges.

76. Ibid.

77. The box file A.D. Meuse, 73M5 contains almost a hundred reports on these festivities. The celebration was all the more relaxed since 24 February 1850 and 4 May 1851 fell on a Sunday.

78. Letter from the prefect of the Côtes-du-Nord to the *ministre des Cultes* (4 June 1850), A.N. F^{19} 4374.

79. *Ministre de l'Instruction publique et des Cultes* to the prefect of the Côtes-du-Nord (15 June 1850), ibid.

80. Letter from the mayor of Vaucouleurs to the parish priest (3 July 1878), A.D. Meuse, 37V1.

81. I have been able to uncover relatively little information on the festival of 30 June 1878 in the provinces. I would note, however, that it was celebrated in a magnificent fashion in Vaucouleurs, once the mayor had at last decided to ring by force the evening before.

82. The mayor of Bolazec (Finistère) emphasized the extent of the interruption. Letter to the subprefect (26 July 1881), A.D. Finistère, 1V46.

83. On the festivals for 14 July see Rosemonde Sanson, *Les 14 juillet, 1789–1975* (Paris: Flammarion, 1976). Christian Amalvi, "Le 14 juillet. Du *Dies irae* à *Jour de fête*," in Nora, *Les lieux de mémoire*, t. 1; and, more recently, Ihl, *La Citoyenneté en fête*.

84. Phrases taken from the article devoted to the subject in *Le Monde* (Thursday 23 August 1883).

85. Flourens, *directeur général des Cultes*, clearly indicated as much in a

circular that features in a file concerning the commune of Lannes, A.D. Haute-Marne, 48v3.

86. Letter from the bishop of Mende to the prefect of the Lozère (20 March 1885), A.N. F^{19} 4376, Lozère.

87. A.D. Finistère, 1v46.

88. Parish priest of Brénod (Ain) to the bishop of Belley (28 July 1891), A.D. Ain, 2v34. To breach the silence of the church and to make a din there represented a crucial symbolic attack.

89. A.D. Côtes-du-Nord, v32 (arrondissement of Saint-Brieuc), v33 (arrondissements of Loudéac, Guingamp, Lannion, and Dinan).

90. A.D. Ille-et-Vilaine, 1v12. Results of inquiry launched on 22 July 1884.

91. A.D. Eure-et-Loir, v9. The question put by the prefect, on 12 July 1884, was designed to elicit usages and not opinions.

92. Ihl, *La Citoyenneté en fête*, p. 683 *bis*. The author includes in this total the rare conflicts over the use of the church facade.

93. It would be appropriate to include in the list of these affairs those provoked by the refusal of some priests in charge to ring for centenary festivals in 1889 (4 and 5 May) and in 1892 (21–22 September). As an example, the parish priest of Remiremont (Vosges) disrupted ceremonies for the centenary of the Republic. He rang at the times he saw fit, and not at those listed on the program drawn up by the mayor and distributed among the population at large. A.D. Vosges, 14v4.

94. Ihl, "Du politique au sacré," p. 15 of the manuscript.

95. Ihl, *La Citoyenneté en fête*, p. 591.

96. Letter from the bishop of Montauban to the prefect of the Tarn-et-Garonne (19 September 1881), A.D. Tarn-et-Garonne, 30v2.

97. On these political contests, see the example of the Maine-et-Loire, studied by Olivier Bellier, *Les Sociétés de musique en Maine-et-Loire au XIXe siècle* (master's thesis, University of Tours, 1986).

98. Letter from the subprefect of the arrondissement of Louviers to the prefect of the Eure (5 August 1902), A.D. Eure, 53v1.

99. Ihl, *La Citoyenneté en fête*, p. 385.

100. Ibid., p. 380.

101. Letter from the mayor of Tauriac to the prefect of the Lot (23 July 1882), A.D. Lot, 1M228.

102. Letter from the prefect of the Ille-et-Vilaine to the archbishop of Rennes (July 1885), A.D. Ille-et-Vilaine, 1v12.

103. Letter from the bishop of Nevers to the prefect of the Nièvre (7 April 1885), A.N. F^{19} 4376, Nièvre; and episcopal ordinance concerning Fourchambault (20 July 1888), ibid.

104. Letter from the prefect (10 July 1884), A.D. Tarn-et-Garonne, 30v2.

105. According to *La Vérité* (26 July 1893), A.N. F^{19} 4375, Hérault.

106. Complaint from the parish priest of Ménarmont (21 July 1903), A.D. Vosges, 14v4.

107. Circular from the *ministre de la Justice et des Cultes* to the prefects (8 July 1884).

108. Letter from the bishop of Nancy to the prefect of the Meurthe-et-Moselle (1 February 1885), A.N. F^{19} 4376, Meurthe-et-Moselle.

109. Complaint to the prefect of the Tarn (16 July 1905), A.D. Tarn, 1v8.

110. Ibid. We are of course concerned here with a belated expression of the set of gestures used in a charivari. It is worth noting the scandal caused by the *non-sense* of this use of bells.

111. According to *La Vérité* (26 August 1893), A.N. F^{19} 4376, Nord. On this anticlerical "parodic tradition," see Jean Faury, *Cléricalisme et anticléricalisme dans le Tarn (1848–1900)* (Toulouse: Université de Toulouse le Mirail, 1980), pp. 436ff. (Note, in particular, the masquerade at Albi, on Ash Wednesday in 1851, and the secular procession staged in the town of Cordes in 1880).

112. Report by the brigadier at Chalon-sur-Saône gendarmerie (16 July 1881), A.D. Saône-et-Loire, M319.

113. Letter from the mayor of Aunay-les-Bois to the prefect of the Orne (15 July 1900), A.D. Orne, 9v1. The parish priest in fact refused to ring because the mayor did not ask him to.

114. This was the attitude adopted by the parish priest of Bolazec (Finistère) on 14 July 1881. Letter from the mayor to the subprefect (18 July 1881), A.D. Finistère, 1v46. The mayor, desiring to blot out this humiliation, asked permission from the subprefect to use the bells with a few days' delay, announcing that this peal would be "the sequel to the fourteenth of July." He added: "the municipal council and the inhabitants of the commune expect it," which leads one to suppose that the parish priest's refusal caused something of a stir in Bolazec.

115. This is what the parish priest of Allons (Lot-et-Garonne) proceeded to do in 1882. Letter from the mayor of Allons to the subprefect of Nérac (15 July 1882), A.D. Lot-et-Garonne, 30M9.

116. Cf. (p. 276) the tactic employed by the mayor of Saint-Marcel.

117. This is what occurred in Vigneul (Meuse), in 1904. The *femme* Merch, responsible for bell ringing, had been deprived of the forty francs until then allocated by the town hall for ringing the Angelus. On 13 July—perhaps with the parish priest's agreement—she detached the ropes from the ring of bells and took them home. Gendarmerie report (17 July 1904), A.D. Meuse, 37v1. Regarding the attitude of Sublaine's parish priest, cf. A.D. Indre-et-Loire, 3v2, quoted by Philippe Grandjean, *La Dynamique de la Séparation de l'église et de*

l'état en Indre-et-Loire (1880–1908) (master's thesis, University of
Tours, 1991), p. 52.

118. Report by the mayor of Saint-Père (3 August 1889), A.D. Ille-et-
Vilaine, 1V12.

119. Ihl, La Citoyenneté en fête, p. 391.

120. Case mentioned by Ihl, La Citoyenneté en fête, p. 389. Bethincourt,
A.D. Meuse, 7v2bis; Saint-Vincent, A.D. Lot-et-Garonne, 1M.

121. Ihl, La Citoyenneté en fête, p. 389 (using A.D. Meuse, 17v3bis).

122. Ibid.

123. P. Léon (capucin), L'Ame des cloches (Paris, 1902). Speech delivered
on 18 June 1902 at the blessing of the bells of the basilica of Saint-
Donatien in Nantes, pp. 16 and 23–24.

124. Ibid., p. 14.

125. Basdevant-Gaudemet, Le Jeu concordataire, p. 252.

126. Ihl, La Citoyenneté en fête, p. 408 (using A.D. Corrèze, 1M107).

127. Basdevant-Gaudemet, Le Jeu concordataire, p. 251 (using A.N. F^{19}
6112).

128. Letter from the mayor of Garennes to the prefect of the Eure (4
August 1901), A.D. Eure, 53V1.

129. Complaint by the mayor of Laville-aux-Bois lodged with the prefect
(15 July 1886), A.D. Haute-Marne, 48v3.

130. Letter from the mayor of Curtil-sous-Burnand to the ministre des
Cultes (22 July 1881), A.D. Saône-et-Loire, M319.

131. According to the victim. Letter from the mayor of La Faou to the
sub-prefect (15 July 1888), A.D. Finistère, 1v46.

132. A.D. Orne, 9V1.

133. Report by the deputy mayor of Pleyben (24 July 1891), A.D.
Finistère, 1v46. As is the case with the majority of affairs discussed
here, the document quoted is drawn from a file enabling us to analyze
the conflict.

134. Complaint lodged by the deputy mayor (28 June 1892), ibid.

135. Report by the brigadier of the Bourmont gendarmerie, based on that
written by the mayor of Germainvilliers (20 July 1880), A.D. Haute-
Marne, 48v3, Germainvilliers. The quotations that follow are drawn
from this document.

136. Telegram, A.D. Finistère, 1v46.

137. Ihl, La Citoyenneté en fête, p. 380. The file on this affair, which also
contains an article from La République française (15 July 1883), is in
A.D. Vendée, 1M533.

138. Ihl, La Citoyenneté en fête, p. 391 (using A.N. F^{19} 6059).

139. The interdict was read from the pulpit by the parish priest on 20 July
1884. The municipal council disputed the notion that the mayor had

meant, by ringing the evening bell on the fourteenth of July, to mark the opening of the ball. In its judgment, it was "the music" that, "only after the drum and the bell ringing," had caused the young people to gather and make the rounds of the village. Complaint of the bishop of Verdun to the prefect (19 July 1884); and letter from the municipal councillors (31 July), A.D. Meuse, 37VI. As for the mayor (letter of 26 July), he admitted to having rung for the start of the games, but not for that of the ball.

140.   Ihl, *La Citoyenneté en fête*, p. 386 (using A.D. Dordogne, 1M102).
141.   Letter from the mayor of Nestier to the subprefect of Bagnères (14 July 1885), A.D. Hautes-Pyrénées, v90. According to the parish priest (15 July), the mayor and the innkeeper, during this incident, were "blind drunk."

NINE. From a Deduced to a Proclaimed Sensibility

1.   Friedrich von Schiller, "Das Lied von der Glocke" (1797). Johann Wolfgang von Goethe, "Die Wandelnde Glocke" (1813), in *Balladen*.
2.   Particularly by Novalis, in a period that witnessed the birth of geology and the elaboration of its stratigraphic language. Cf. Corbin, *The Lure of the Sea*, pp. 169, 178.
3.   For precisely this reason, Goethe's ballad haunted Malcolm Lowry's hero in *Under the Volcano*.
4.   This was the meaning of the bell that rang in Faust's ears during his damnation.
5.   For example, for Ramond de Carbonnières at the end of the eighteenth century, or for George Sand at the dawn of the following century. Cf. Corbin, *The Foul and the Fragrant*, pp. 78–82 and 202.
6.   It took on this meaning in Faust's ears also.
7.   "In the enchanted rêveries into which we are plunged by the sound of the bell of our birthplace everything may be recovered: religion, family, fatherland, both the cradle and the grave, both the past and the future." François-René de Chateaubriand, *René*, in *Oeuvres Complètes* (Paris 1826), 16:44.
8.   Alphonse de Lamartine, *Oeuvres poétiques complètes* (Paris 1963, [Pléiade edition]), edited by Marius-François Guyard; "La cloche" (drafted in 1835), p. 799; and "La cloche du village" (drafted in August 1838), in *Recueillements poétiques*, ibid., pp. 1160–63. Lamartine drew inspiration here from "L'angélus du matin à Saint-Point" by Henri de Lacretelle. Lamartine's text was published in its turn by Lacretelle, in *Les Cloches, poésies* (Paris, 1841).
9.   François-René de Chateaubriand, "Des cloches," *Le Génie du christianisme*, Pt. 4, Bk. 1, Ch. 1.

10. Bourrienne, *Mémoires* (Paris, 1829), t. 3, ch. 43, p. 222. It has been said time and again that Bonaparte had decided to pursue a Concordat with Rome "because he dreamed while listening to the bell of Rueil." Albert Mathiez convincingly refuted this altogether too simple explanation. Nevertheless, this rumor underlines the part played by Bonaparte in the history of bells and of the ways in which their sound has been evaluated. Cf. Mathiez, *La Révolution et l'église*, p. 283.

11. Quoted by Farnier, *Notice historique sur les cloches*, p. 9. "I have always loved the sound of country bells," Napoleon declared once again on 11 August 1816. Las Cases, *Mémorial de Sainte-Hélène* (Paris: Garnier, 1961), 2:125.

12. Thiers, *Traité des superstitions*, quoted by Blavignac, *La Cloche*, p. 443.

13. The bell is used in this fashion by Rossini in the chorus to the second act of *William Tell*, by Meyerbeer in the fourth act of *The Huguenots* to give the signal for the massacre of the Protestants, and in the *Miserere* scene from Verdi's *Il Trovatore*. Cf. Blavignac, *La Cloche*, p. 453.

14. Text from 1848. A.N. F^{19} 4377 (Vosges).

15. In Vendémiaire Year XII, the churchwarden for the commune of Castelsarrasin (Tarn-et-Garonne) had put back into the church tower what he believed to be one of the old bells of the parish, captured some ten years previously. However, wrote the mayor, on 18 Vendémiaire / 11 October 1803), "the perceptible difference in sound made it clear that it was not one of the old bells." A.N. F^{19} 4373. This capacity to recognize the sound of a bell may be compared with what specialists tell us of the sensory evaluation of cowbells by shepherds. Cf. Paluel-Marmont, *Cloches et carillons*, pp. 98ff. The shepherd would come and choose his instrument at an open air market. He would identify the desired sound, which "would blend in with the harmony of the herd's music" (p. 101). Likewise, Pierre Laurence, "Cloches, grelots et sonnailles," p. 28. This attention to "the sounds produced" by these objects was to change beginning around 1910, as sheep bells and sleigh bells were increasingly made of cast iron.

16. Sauveterre, *Essai sur le symbolisme de la cloche*, p. 34.

17. Cf. G. Thuillier, "Les bruits," pp. 230–44.

18. Cf. Bour, *Études campanaires mosellanes*, 1:266ff. Brugière and Berthelé, *Exploration campanaire du Périgord*, p. 310.

19. In the Moselle, each commune has its own. Bour, *Études campanaires mosellanes*, 1:200ff. A highly precise inquiry in this regard.

20. Cf. Blavignac, *La Cloche*, pp. 291–300.

21. "At Gomelange (Moselle)," notes Samuel Bour (*Études campanaires mosellanes*, 1:266), "if the ringing of the Angelus coincided with that of Bettange, or simply the ringing of the hour with the angelic salu-

tation, that was once a sure sign that a death would soon occur in the locality." This was also the case in Bacourt. "For other places (in Morville and Xocourt), the final stroke of the clapper indicated the direction from which the next burial would come." "People still used to say when the bells of a church rang 'clearly' or 'funnily' or 'sadly,' that one had to expect a death in the locality in the none too distant future." Elsewhere, when "the clock bell rang the time during the two elevations of the mass or during the blessing of the Holy Sacrament," it was the signal for an imminent death.

22.   For a particularly good example of this need to record campanarian usages, see the inquiry set up by the archbishop of Bordeaux in 1838. Circular to the priests of his diocese, A.N. F^{19} 4375, Gironde. The questionnaire was designed to ensure the recording of customs, etymology, antiquities, history, and "popular traditions."

23.   Chapter 10 of the novel *Against Nature* (A Rebours).

24.   Billon, *Campanologie*, biography of the author by Charles Vasseur, his friend, pp. xi–xii. This is a good example of the way in which learned societies used excursions to render their members more sensitive toward the environment.

25.   Arcisse de Caumont, in Billon, *Campanologie*, p. xvi. Note how the author disregards the fact that rural communities themselves set great store in the bells.

26.   Arcisse de Caumont, in Billon, *Campanologie*, p. 4.

27.   Emphasized by Baron de Rivières, *Études campanaires*, new series, 1 (Caen, 1891), p. 3. In particular, the "risk of vertigo incurred when making a sketch of the bells as they plunge into the void." There is a similar observation in Jadart et al., *Les Cloches de Rethel*, p. 1.

28.   Blavignac, *La Cloche*, p. 287.

29.   Toulouse-Lautrec, *Les Cloches dans le Haut-Comminges*, p. 2.

30.   Berthelé and Brugière, *Exploration campanaire*, pp. 10–12. The text by Michel Hardy appears on p. 12.

31.   Jadart et al., *Les Cloches*, p. 1; and Berthelé et al., *Enquêtes campanaires rémoises*, p. 1. The same opinion is shared by Léon Germain, in *Les Anciennes Cloches de Saugues (Haute-Loire) refondues en Lorraine* (Nancy, 1890). "Never have campanarian researches been so highly esteemed," he wrote, "as in our own day" (p. 4). He called for a systematic inventory. Aside from inquiries conducted by specialists, monographs on particular cantons or parishes furnished an infinite quantity of "campanarian notes." Léon Germain emphasizes the link between the history of bells and the efforts of local antiquaries, whose works during this period attest to a burgeoning curiosity regarding local history.

NINE. FROM A DEDUCED TO A PROCLAIMED SENSIBILITY

32. Berthelé et al., *Enquêtes campanaires rémoises*, p. 2.

33. As also its renaissance today, for example in Burgundy.

34. At the end of the nineteenth century, the symbolism of the bells was further enhanced, in line with one of the currents then dominant in literature and the plastic arts. Father Léon, as we have seen (*L'Ame des cloches*, pp. 16–17), dreamed that these "mighty daughters of the air," these "doughty apostles," who were capable of deafening, of silencing an adversary, and of "spurring on the pack of remorse," might be a useful weapon in the hands of Catholic militants.

35. Joris-Karl Huysmans, *La Cathédrale* (Paris: Le Livre de Poche, 1964), p. 121. The abbot Plomb, one of the heroes of the novel, also notes that the bells have a function of "aerial preaching" (p. 121).

36. Quotations and lines of argument drawn from the article by Françoise Cachin, "Le paysage du peintre," in Nora, ed., *Les lieux de mémoire*, vol. 2, "La Nation," pt. 1, p. 465.

37. Cf. Jean-Yves Guiomar, "Le tableau géographique de la France de Vidal de la Blache," in Nora, ed., *Les lieux de mémoire,* vol. 2., pt. 1, pp. 569–99.

38. Marcel Proust, *In Search of Lost Time; vol. 1, Swann's Way*, translated by C.K. Scott-Moncrieff and Terence Kilmartin, revised by D.J. Enright (London: Chatto and Windus, 1992), p. 35.

39. Jadart et al., *Épigraphie campanaire ardennaise*, p. 1. On the ascendancy of regionalism in the France of this period, cf. Anne-Marie Thiesse, *Écrire la France* (Paris: PUF, 1991).

40. C. Quiévreux, *La Vie à l'ombre du clocher* (Paris, 1911), pp. 23–25. The speech by Maurice Barrès is reprinted in the appendix, pp. 156–63.

41. Maurice Barrès, speech mentioned earlier, pp. 158–61. There should be no need to point out that this glorification of the bell tower might on occasion bolster anti-semitism. As an example, Paul Seynard (a former magistrate), *La Voix des cloches* (Auxerre, 1904).

42. Cf. Élisabeth Roudinesco, *La Bataille de cent ans: Histoire de la psychanalyse en France*, vol. 1, 1885–1939 (Paris: Ramsay, 1982), especially pp. 181–257.

43. Corbin, *The Foul and the Fragrant.*

44. Blavignac, *La Cloche*, pp. 441–442. Among the many epigrams by Ménage against the bells we find the following:

> You persecutors of humankind
> Who ring without pity
> Would that you had around your neck
> The rope you now hold in your hand.

And Benserade penned the following epitaph:

> He who lies here lived a gentle life
> Causing trouble to no one, and
> At his death expressly
> Forbad that anyone should ring.

45. Quoted by Gobillon, *Le Blésois*, 2:453.

46. Letter from the prefect of the Haute-Savoie to the *ministre des Cultes* (6 December 1884), A.N. F¹⁹ 4377.

47. Cf. p. 105.

48. Letter from the mayor of Raon-l'Étape to the prefect of the Vosges (1 December 1832), A.D. Vosges, 14V4. It remains the case, however, that in Courlon, as here, a split is evident in this regard between bourg and countryside.

49. Letters from the deputy mayor, the parish priest (8 November 1839) and the bishop of Saint-Dié (10 November), in a file on this affair, A.D. Vosges, 14V5.

50. For example, in those for the diocese of Besançon (1806), the Rhône (1808), and the Haut-Rhin (1812), A.N. F¹⁹ 4374.

51. Letter to the *ministre de l'Intérieur et des Cultes* (16 Frimaire Year XIV / 7 December 1805), A.N. F¹⁹ 4374.

52. Statute of the bishop of Valence (9 February 1806), A.N. F¹⁹ 4375, Drôme.

53. Decree of 24 June 1832, A.D. Haute-Marne, 48V2.

54. Letter from the prefect of the Haute-Marne to the mayor of Bettancourt (25 June 1832), ibid.

55. Letter from the mayor of Ancerville to the prefect of the Meuse (16 April 1852), A.D. Meuse, 37V1.

56. Letter from the mayor of Contrisson to the prefect of the Meuse (30 March 1853), ibid.

57. Letter from the mayor of Longeville to the prefect of the Meuse, 1 April 1853, ibid.

58. Letter to the prefect of the Meuse (10 July 1852), ibid.

59. Letter from the mayor of Velaines to the prefect of the Meuse (28 March 1852), ibid.

60. Letter quoted above from the mayor of Longeville.

61. "All the more so," added the mayor of Saint-Laurent, " given that it is a vine growing country, so that everyone has wine at home." Letter to the prefect of the Meuse (24 May 1853), ibid.

62. The mayors of the Meuse were by no means alone in reacting in this fashion. In 1838 the mayor of Saint-Sauvy (Gers) complained that on 12 July the parish priest had the bells rung in peal at nine forty-five in the evening, while people were sleeping. The bells had "awakened

[them] with a start." Letter from the mayor of Saint-Sauvy to the prefect (16 July 1838), A.D. Gers, v841.

63.   In February 1858 Brizeaux municipal council (Meuse) "wishing and desiring that the secular peal would in some way serve as a clock," asked for the bells to be rung from 1 March to 1 May at five o'clock in the morning, from 1 May to 1 September at four o'clock, and from 1 September to 1 November at five o'clock. The council also wanted the bells to be rung at eleven o'clock in the morning and at six o'clock in the evening, from 1 March to 1 November. The bishop payed no heed, rejecting out of hand such a desacralizing of the schedule of the morning peals. Deliberations of Brizeaux municipal council (7 February 1858), and letter from the bishop, A.D. Meuse, 174M1. The decision of the councillors of Brizeaux also reflected a new concern with accuracy in a commune that lacked a clock. In 1885 Domptail municipal council, in the Vosges, altered by decree the times of the morning peals. It ruled that "during the months of June and July the great bell would be rung at three o'clock in the morning, then at four o'clock during the months of May to August; at five o'clock for the months of March, April, and September; and at six o'clock during the five other months of the year, all as before." Deliberations of Domptail municipal council (June 1885), A.D. Vosges, 14v5.

64.   Deliberations of Chartres municipal council (19 September 1832), A.D. Eure-et-Loir, v8.

65.   Letter quoted, p. 123.

66.   File on this affair, A.N. F^{19} 4374.

67.   Cf. pp. 267ff. In 1881 the mayor of Douarnenez (Finistère) prohibited, by decree, any carillonning before the hour of the Angelus. Letter from the mayor to the prefect (23 January 1881), A.D. Finistère, 1v46. The parish priest in fact carillonned at half past four every morning to celebrate the mission preached in the parish. The mayor asked that, before half past five (the hour of the Angelus), the parish priest should limit himself to ringing with just the one bell. The priest refused to yield. The mayor claimed that his adversary "carillons deliberately in order to wake up his parishioners." Here the *right to wake up* really was at issue. The *ministre des Cultes* ruled in favor of the mayor (12 April 1881).

68.   *Le Cas des cloches soumis par Nadar à M. le ministre des Cultes—puisqu'il y en a encore un [sic]—à tous maires, conseillers municipaux, députés et même sénateurs* (Chambéry, 1883), pp. iii, 6, 15, 18, and 21.

69.   A.D. F^{19} 4375 (Finistère), the issue of *La Lanterne* from which I have quoted.

70.   The initiative came from the republican committee, which prompted

the municipal council to meet on 23 November 1902 (a session that also involved discussion of the banning of processions and of the salaries of curates). The prefectorial decree of 7 March 1905 was finally appended to the regulations of peals that had been officially imposed on the bishop of Viviers on 6 July 1885. A.N. F^{19} 4375.

71.   Article appearing in A.N. F^{19} 4377, Haute-Vienne. The debate was occasioned by *La Savoyarde*, a nineteen-ton bell placed provisionally in the Montmartre basilica on 5 October 1895, and definitively in 1907. The characters in Zola's novel, *Paris*, found it utterly intolerable. Conversely, abbot Lemire declared, in the chamber of deputies, that it was the symbol of a new society. Furthermore, the weight of the largest bell in Europe that rang true satisfied national pride. On this debate, cf. Jacques Benoist, *Le Sacré-Coeur de Montmartre de 1870 à nos jours* (Paris: Editions ouvrières, 1992), pp. 615–16.

72.   Grievances of the mayor of Romainville (23 May 1904), A.N. F^{19} 4377, Seine. Conversely, the mayor (27 May 1903) complained about the suppression " of peals rung when the recruiting board was to meet."

73.   Complaint transmitted by the league on 8 July 1903, ibid.

74.   Henry Nadal, "Le supplice des cloches," *L'Aurore* (21 August 1908), A.N. F^{19} 5650. Note that *Le Jardin des supplices,* by Octave Mirbeau, dates from 1899.

75.   The grip of the bell on the habitual forms of hallucination in the nineteenth century seems to confirm the importance then accorded to this instrument. Investigation in this area is, however, no easy matter. "The sick person who has been etherized is the plaything . . . of acoustic hallucinations, sometimes precipitated by dreams, and particularly by metallic tollings, by the sound of bells. . . ." E.F. Bouisson, *Traité théorique et pratique de la méthode anesthésique appliquée à la chirurgie* (Paris, 1850), pp. 223–34. Quoted by Marie-Jeanne Lavillatte-Couteau, *Une douleur supprimée, oubliée, occultée? (1846–1896)* (DEA dissertation , University of Paris I, 1991).

76.   Quoted by Simone Delattre, *Un amour en coulisses* (master's dissertation, University of Paris I, 1991), p. 207.

77.   Walter Benjamin stresses the importance of the theme of bells in Baudelaire's poetry.

78.   Charles Baudelaire, "Spleen," in *Les Fleurs du mal*, in *Baudelaire; Selected Verse*, translated by Francis Scarfe (Harmondsworth: Penguin, 1961), p. 178 [translation amended]. Note nevertheless that in "La cloche fêlée," also in *Les Fleurs du mal*, the poet deplores this loss of meaning that prevents his soul, itself cracked, from relishing "the distant memories" that the sound of the bell evokes. In

"Paysage" (*Tableaux parisiens*, LXXXVI), Baudelaire seems to confer a new meaning upon the contemplation of bell towers, "these masts of the city" that teach us how to look at factory chimneys. (I would like to thank Claude Pichois for having alerted me to the importance of this theme in the author of *Les Fleurs du Mal*). Among the masterpieces of European literature from the final quarter of the nineteenth century, it is perhaps *La Régente*, by Clarin (Leopoldo Alas), that grants the most space to a campanarian sensibility.

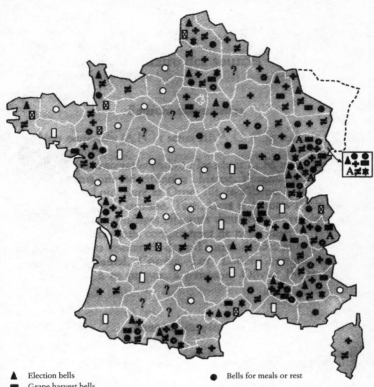

CIVIL BELLS IN USE FROM 1884–1886
(other than for natural disasters)

▲ Election bells
▬ Grape harvest bells
✚ School bells
● Curfew bells
≠ Retreat bells

A   Bells for firewood collections,
public auctions, recruitment,
animal herding, services, and
legal pronouncements.

● Bells for meals or rest

✹ Bells announcing the arrival of the

▨ collector

Municipal council meeting bells

○
▯ No bells in use
? Regulations automatically imposed
Without bells (?)

THE RECONSTITUTION OF PEALS*

	Moselle S. Bour (1)	Isère G. Vallier (2)	Seine-infre D. Dergny (3)	Ardennes H Jarart (1)	TOTAL
Consulat and Empire (1800–1814)					
Restoration (1815–1830)					
July Monarch (1831–1848)					
Second Republic (1849–1852)					
Second Empire (1853–1879)					

Number of bells cast   503
150
40
5

*The number of bells cast during the year in which each regime fell

LIST OF SOURCES

MANUSCRIPT SOURCES

Archives nationales (A.N.): series BB^{18}, C, F^7 and above all F^{19}. The box files in question are mentioned in the notes.

Archives départementales (A.D.): series L, M, and above all V, from fourteen departments have been explored: Meuse, Vosges, Aube, and Haute-Marne, Eure-et-Loir, Eure, and Orne. Ille-et-Vilaine, Côtes-du-Nord, and Finistère. Tarn-et-Garonne, Tarn, Gers, and Hautes-Pyrénées.

Conversely, the soundings taken in episcopal archives have proved disappointing, given the nature of my topic.

I was also able to draw upon information from documents stored elsewhere (cf. Cantal, Corrèze, Lot, Lot-et-Garonne, Saône-et-Loire). For this I owe thanks to Olivier Ihl and François Ploux.

Printed Sources

The main campanarian inquiries conducted in other departments constitute valuable sources:

AISNE

Berthelé, Joseph. *Notes et Études campanaires: Cloches diverses de l'arrondissement de Château-Thierry.* Château-Thierry, 1900.

ARDENNES

Jadart, H. and Laurent, P. *Épigraphie campanaire ardennaise: Les cloches du canton d'Asfeld.* Sedan, 1896.

Jadart, H., Baudemant, F., Carlier, J. *Epigraphie campanaire ardennais:. Les cloches de canton de Château-Porcien.* Rethel, 1899.

Jadart, H., Laurent, P., Baudon, A. *Les Cloches du canton de Rethel.* Rethel, 1897.

CALVADOS

Dr. Billon. *Campanologie: Étude sur les cloches et les sonneries françaises et étrangères.* Caen, 1866.

CANTAL

Trin, Antoin. *Les Cloches du Cantal: Archéologie, histoire, folklore.* Aurillac: Gerbert, 1954.

CHARENTE

Nanglard, Jean. *Les Cloches des églises du diocèse d'Angoulême.* Angoulême: Imprimerie ouvrière, 1922.

DORDOGNE

Brugière, Henri and Berthelé, Joseph. *Exploration campanaire du Périgord.* Périgueux, 1907.

ISÈRE

Vallier, Gustave. *Inscriptions campanaires du département de l'Isère.* Montbéliard, 1886.

MOSELLE

Bour, Samuel. *Études campanaires mosellanes*. Colmar: Alsatia, 1947.

SEINE-INFÉRIEURE

Dergny, Dieudonné. *Les Cloches du pays de Bray avec leurs dates, leurs noms, leurs inscriptions, leurs armoiries, leurs fondeurs*. In two volumes. Paris, 1865.

The other works used here are mentioned in the notes.

INDEX

Index 401

EUROPEAN PERSPECTIVES

A Series in Social Thought and Cultural Criticism
Lawrence D. Kritzman, Editor